Abduction is inference to the best explanation, a pattern of reasoning that occurs in such diverse places as medical diagnosis, scientific theory formation, accident investigation, language understanding, and jury deliberation. This book breaks new ground in the scientific, philosophical, and technological study of abduction. It presents new ideas about the inferential and information-processing foundations of knowledge and certainty. It argues that knowledge arises from experience by processes of abductive inference, in contrast with the view that knowledge arises noninferentially, or that deduction and inductive generalization are sufficient to account for knowledge.

This book reports key discoveries about abduction that were made as a result of designing, building, testing, and analyzing knowledge-based systems for medical diagnosis and other abductive tasks. These systems demonstrate that abductive inference can be described precisely enough to achieve good performance, even though this description lies largely outside the classical formal frameworks of mathematical logic and probability theory.

The book tells the story of six generations of increasingly sophisticated generic abduction machines and the discovery of reasoning strategies that make it computationally feasible to form well-justified composite explanatory hypotheses despite the threat of combinatorial explosion. Finally, the book argues that perception is logically abductive and presents a layered-abduction computational model of perceptual information processing.

Abductive inference

Computation, philosophy, technology

Edited by
JOHN R. JOSEPHSON
The Ohio State University

SUSAN G. JOSEPHSON
The Ohio State University
and
Columbus College of Art & Design

CAMBRIDGE
UNIVERSITY PRESS

Published by the Press Syndicate of the University of Cambridge
The Pitt Building, Trumpington Street, Cambridge CB2 1RP
40 West 20th Street, New York, NY 10011-4211, USA
10 Stamford Road, Oakleigh, Melbourne 3166, Australia

First Published 1994

Printed in the United States of America

Library of Congress Cataloging-in-Publication Data
Josephson, John R.
    Abductive inference : computation, philosophy, technology / John
R. Josephson, Susan G. Josephson.
        p.   cm.
    ISBN 0-521-43461-0
    1. Abduction (Logic) 2. Inference. 3. Knowledge, Theory of.
I. Josephson, Susan G. II. Title
BC199.A26J67 1994   93-16027
160 – dc20   CIP

A catalog record for this book is available from the British Library

ISBN 0-521-43461-0 hardback

Contents

Contributors

Note: LAIR is Laboratory for Artificial Intelligence Research, Department of Computer and Information Science, The Ohio State University, Columbus, Ohio 43210 USA

Dean Allemang, PhD
Istituto Dalle Molle di Studi
  sull'Intelligenza Artificiale
Lugano, Switzerland

Tom Bylander, PhD
LAIR

B. Chandrasekaran, PhD
LAIR

Donna Erickson, PhD
Division of Speech and Hearing Science
The Ohio State University
Columbus, Ohio

Charles Evans, MD
Southern Pathology Associates, Inc.
Chattanooga, Tennessee

Olivier Fischer
LAIR

Richard Fox, PhD
University of Texas, Pan American
Edinburg, Texas

Osamu Fujimura, DSc
Division of Speech and Hearing Science
The Ohio State University
Columbus, Ohio, USA

Ashok K. Goel, PhD
College of Computing
Georga Institute of Technology
Atlanta, Georgia

Todd R. Johnson, PhD
Division of Medical
  Informatics
Department of Pathology
The Ohio State University
Columbus, Ohio

John R. Josephson, PhD
LAIR

Susan G. Josephson, PhD
LAIR and
Columbus College of Art and
  Design
Columbus, Ohio

Susan T. Korda, MS
LAIR

Kevin Lenzo
LAIR

Terry Patten, PhD
LAIR

William F. Punch III, PhD
Computer Science Department
Michigan State University
East Lansing, Michigan

P. Sadayappan, PhD
The Ohio State University
Department of Computer
  and Information Science
Columbus, Ohio

vii

Sheldon R. Simon, MD
Division of Orthopedics
Department of Surgery
The Ohio State University
Columbus, Ohio

Jack W. Smith, MD, PhD
LAIR and
Division of Medical Informatics
Department of Pathology
The Ohio State University
Columbus, Ohio

Jon Sticklen, PhD
Computer Science Department
Michigan State University
East Lansing, Michigan, USA

Patricia L. Strohm, MT (ASCP), SBB
Western Reserve Care System
Southside Hospital Laboratory
Youngstown, Ohio

John Svirbely, MD
McCullough-Hyde Memorial Hospital
Oxford, Ohio

Michael C. Tanner, PhD
Department of Computer Science
George Mason University
Fairfax, Virginia

Michael Weintraub, PhD
GTE Laboratories
Waltham, Massachusetts

Introduction

I see abductive inferences everywhere in science and ordinary life. I believe abductions to be reasonable and knowledge-producing inferences. If this view is correct, there appear to be significant philosophical implications: It leads to a form of Realism about the objects of theory and perception; it leads to the view that Truth is attainable but extremely high certainty is not; it extends the detailed conception of Reason to better accommodate fallibility and uncertainty; it loosens the bounds on what can be known; it finds the logic of science to be very akin to reasoning in ordinary life and to the learning of children; and it moves toward restoring confidence in objectivity and progress where it has been most deeply threatened.

I have been thinking about abduction since the mid-1970s, when my doctoral philosophy of science dissertation project on Causality transmuted itself into a sustained attempt to reconstruct the logical foundations of science based on Gilbert Harman's idea of inference to the best explanation. I argued that abductive foundations are stronger than those based on induction, and that there are conceptual advantages to this view for a number of traditional philosophical puzzles, including the problem of induction.

My dissertation found abductive inferences in ordinary life as well as at the foundations of science and argued that they are epistemically warranted. It developed a process view of inference, rather than a static, evidential-relationship view, but it did not yet take a computational view. Although I discussed a research program based on trying to build robot scientists, I had not yet begun this kind of work.

I finished the dissertation in 1982 and promptly began learning Artificial Intelligence (AI) with B. Chandrasekaran (Chandra) at The Ohio State University. From Chandra I learned to take a computational, or better, an "information-processing," view of knowledge and intelligence. His research program, which I embraced, was engaged in a search for fundamental building blocks of intelligence that were expected to take the form of "generic information-processing tasks."

My dissertation proposed investigating the inferential practices of science by trying to design robot scientists, and seeing what it would take to

✓ By John R. Josephson.

1

make them work. Still, at the time it was written, I wasn't sensitive to the implications of taking an information-processing view of inference and intelligence. Since then Chandra's tutelage in AI and my experiences in designing and building knowledge-based systems have significantly enriched my view. They have especially sensitized me to the need to provide for feasible computation in the face of bounded computational resources. To provide for feasible computation, a model of intelligence must provide for the control of reasoning processes, and for the organization and representation of knowledge.

When I joined the AI group at Ohio State (which later became the Laboratory for Artificial Intelligence Research, or LAIR), it was intensely studying diagnosis and looking for the generic tasks hypothesized by Chandra to be the computational building blocks of intelligence. Besides Chandra and me, the AI group at the time consisted of Jack Smith, Dave Brown, Tom Bylander, Jon Sticklen, Mike Tanner, and a few others. Working primarily with medical domains, the group had identified "hierarchical classification" as a central task of diagnosis, had distinguished this sort of reasoning from "data abstraction" and other types of reasoning that enter into diagnostic problem solving, and was trying to push the limits of this view by attempting new knowledge domains.

My first major project with the AI group in 1983 was a collaboration with Jack Smith, MD, and others, on the design and construction of a knowledge-based system (called RED) for an antibody-identification task performed repeatedly by humans in hospital blood banks. The task requires the formation of a composite mini-theory for each particular case that describes the red-cell antibodies present in a patient's blood. Our goal was to study the problem-solving activity of an expert and to capture in a computer program enough of the expert's knowledge and reasoning strategy to achieve good performance on test cases. Preenumerating all possible antibody combinations would have been possible (barely) but this was forbidden because such a solution would not scale up.

The reasoning processes that we were trying to capture turned out to include a form of best-explanation reasoning. Before long it became clear that classification was not enough to do justice to the problem, that some way of controlling the formation of multipart hypotheses was needed. This led me to design what we now call the RED-1 hypothesis-assembly algorithm. We then built RED-1, a successful working system with a novel architecture for hypothesis formation and criticism. RED-1's successor, RED-2, was widely demonstrated and was described in a number of papers. Jack Smith (already an MD) wrote his doctoral dissertation in computer science on the RED work.

The RED systems show that abduction can indeed be made precise enough to be a usable notion and, in fact, precise enough to be programmed. These systems work well and give objectively good answers, even in complicated cases where the evidence is ambiguous. They do not manipulate numerical probabilities, follow deductive inference rules, or generalize from experience. This strongly reinforces the argument that abduction is a distinct form of inference, interesting in its own right.

RED-1 was the first, and RED-2 the second, of six generations of abductive-assembly mechanisms that we designed and with which we experimented. In the following chapters the evolution of these machines is traced as they grew in power and sophistication. They were all intended as domain-independent abductive problem solvers, embodying inference-control strategies with some pretensions of generality. One design for parallel hypothesis assembly was never implemented, but each of the other five mechanisms was implemented, at least partially, and a fair amount of experience was built up in our lab with abductive problem solving.

In the PEIRCE project (named after Charles Sanders Peirce) we made generalizations and improvements to RED-2's hypothesis-assembly mechanism. PEIRCE is a domain-independent software tool for building knowledge-based systems that form composite explanatory hypotheses as part of the problem-solving process. PEIRCE has various hypothesis-improvement tactics built in and allows the knowledge-system builder to specify strategies for mixing these tactics. Members of our group also designed and built other abductive systems, including MDX2 by Jon Sticklen, TIPS (Task Integrated Problem Solver) by Bill Punch, and QUAWDS (Qualitative Analysis of Walking Disorders) by Tom Bylander and Mike Weintraub. Other discoveries were made in collaboration with Mike Tanner, Dean Allemang, Ashok Goel, Todd Johnson, Olivier Fischer, Matt DeJongh, Richard Fox, Susan Korda, and Irene Ku. Most of the abduction work has been for diagnosis in medical and mechanical domains, but more recently, in collaboration with several speech scientists and linguists here at Ohio State, we have begun to work on layered-abduction models of speech recognition and understanding.

Susan Josephson has been my mate and a stimulating intellectual companion throughout my adult life. When the project of editing this book bogged down in the summer of 1990, Susan agreed to take the lead and set aside for a time her project of writing a book on the philosophy of AI. The present book is a result of our collaboration and consists of a deeply edited collection of LAIR writings on abduction by various authors. I take responsibility for the major editorial decisions, especially the controversial ones. Susan is responsible for transforming a scattered set of material into a unified narrative and sustained argument, and she produced the first draft. Many voices blend in the text that follows, although mine is the most common. Authors whose work is included here should not be presumed to agree with all conclusions.

In chapter 1 we set the stage with a careful discussion of abduction and

some of its relationships with other traditionally recognized forms of inference. This is followed in chapter 2 by an orientation to our view of AI as a
science and to our approach to building knowledge systems. The remainder
of the book traces the development of six generations of abduction machines
and describes some of the discoveries that we made about the dynamic logic
of abduction.

1 Conceptual analysis of abduction

What is abduction?

Abduction, or *inference to the best explanation*, is a form of inference that goes from data describing something to a hypothesis that best explains or accounts for the data. Thus abduction is a kind of theory-forming or interpretive inference. The philosopher and logician Charles Sanders Peirce (1839–1914) contended that there occurs in science and in everyday life a distinctive pattern of reasoning wherein explanatory hypotheses are formed and accepted. He called this kind of reasoning "abduction."

In their popular textbook on artificial intelligence (AI), Charniak and McDermott (1985) characterize abduction variously as modus ponens turned backward, inferring the cause of something, generation of explanations for what we see around us, and inference to the best explanation. They write that medical diagnosis, story understanding, vision, and understanding natural language are all abductive processes. Philosophers have written of "inference to the best explanation" (Harman, 1965) and "the explanatory inference" (Lycan, 1988). Psychologists have found "explanation-based" evidence evaluation in the decision-making processes of juries in law courts (Pennington & Hastie, 1988).

We take abduction to be a distinctive kind of inference that follows this pattern pretty nearly:[1]

> *D* is a collection of data (facts, observations, givens).
> *H* explains *D* (would, if true, explain *D*).
> No other hypothesis can explain *D* as well as *H* does.
>
> Therefore, *H* is probably true.

The core idea is that a body of data provides evidence for a hypothesis that satisfactorily explains or accounts for that data (or at least it provides evidence if the hypothesis is better than explanatory alternatives).

Abductions appear everywhere in the un-self-conscious reasonings, inter-

---

✓ This chapter was written by John R. Josephson, except the second section on diagnosis, which was written by Michael C. Tanner and John R. Josephson.

pretations, and perceivings of ordinary life and in the more critically self-aware reasonings upon which scientific theories are based. Sometimes abductions are deliberate, such as when the physician, or the mechanic, or the scientist, or the detective forms hypotheses explicitly and evaluates them to find the best explanation. Sometimes abductions are more perceptual, such as when we separate foreground from background planes in a scene, thereby making sense of the disparities between the images formed from the two eyes, or when we understand the meaning of a sentence and thereby explain the presence and order of the words.

Abduction in ordinary life

Abductive reasoning is quite ordinary and commonsensical. For example, as Harman (1965) pointed out, when we infer from a person's behavior to some fact about her mental state, we are inferring that the fact explains the behavior better than some other competing explanation does. Consider this specimen of ordinary reasoning:

JOE: Why are you pulling into the filling station?
TIDMARSH: Because the gas tank is nearly empty.
JOE: What makes you think so?
TIDMARSH: Because the gas gauge indicates nearly empty. Also, I have no reason to think that the gauge is broken, and it has been a long time since I filled the tank.

Under the circumstances, the nearly empty gas tank is the best available explanation for the gauge indication. Tidmarsh's other remarks can be understood as being directed to ruling out a possible competing explanation (broken gauge) and supporting the plausibility of the preferred explanation.

Consider another example of abductive reasoning: Imagine that one day you are driving your car, and you notice the car behind you because of its peculiar shade of bright yellow. You make two turns along your accustomed path homeward and then notice that the yellow car is still behind you, but now it is a little farther away. Suddenly, you remember something that you left at the office and decide to turn around and go back for it. You execute several complicated maneuvers to reverse your direction and return to the office. A few minutes later you notice the same yellow car behind you. You conceive the hypothesis that you are being followed, but you cannot imagine any reason why this should be so that seems to have any significant degree of likelihood. So, you again reverse direction, and observe that the yellow car is still behind you. You conclude that you are indeed being followed (reasons unknown) by the person in the dark glasses in the yellow car. There is no other plausible way to explain why the car remains continually behind you. The results of your experiment of reversing direction a second time served to rule out alternative explanations, such as that the other driver's first reversal of direction was a coincidence of changing plans at the same time.

Harman (1965) gave a strikingly insightful analysis of law court testimony, which argues that when we infer that a witness is telling the truth, we are using best-explanation reasoning. According to Harman our inference goes as follows:

(i) We infer that he says what he does because he believes it.
(ii) We infer that he believes what he does because he actually did witness the situation which he describes.

Our confidence in the testimony is based on our conclusions about the most plausible explanation for that testimony. Our confidence fails if we come to think that there is some other plausible explanation for his testimony – for example, that he stands to gain from our believing him. Here, too, we see the same pattern of reasoning from observations to a hypothesis that explains those observations – not simply to a possible explanation, but to the best explanation for the observations in contrast with alternatives.

In *Winnie-the-Pooh* (Milne, 1926) Pooh says:

It had HUNNY written on it, but, just to make sure, he took off the paper cover and looked at it, and it *looked* just like honey. "But you never can tell," said Pooh. "I remember my uncle saying once that he had seen cheese just this colour." So he put his tongue in, and took a large lick. (pp. 61–62)

Pooh's hypothesis is that the substance in the jar is honey, and he has two pieces of evidence to substantiate his hypothesis: It looks like honey, and "hunny" is written on the jar. How can this be explained except by supposing that the substance is honey? He considers an alternative hypothesis: It might be cheese. Cheese has been observed to have this color, so the cheese hypothesis offers another explanation for the color of the substance in the jar. So, Pooh (conveniently dismissing the evidence of the label) actively seeks evidence that would distinguish between the hypotheses. He performs a test, a crucial experiment. He takes a sample.

The characteristic reasoning processes of fictional detectives have also been characterized as abduction (Sebeok & Umiker-Sebeok, 1983). To use another example from Harman (1965), when a detective puts the evidence together and decides that the culprit *must* have been the butler, the detective is reasoning that no other explanation that accounts for all the facts is plausible enough or simple enough to be accepted. Truzzi (1983) alleges that at least 217 abductions can be found in the Sherlock Holmes canon.

"There is no great mystery in this matter," he said, taking the cup of tea which I had poured out for him; "the facts appear to admit of only one explanation."
– Sherlock Holmes (Doyle, 1890, p. 620)

Abduction in science

Abductions are common in scientific reasoning on large and small scales.[2] The persuasiveness of Newton's theory of gravitation was enhanced by its ability to explain not only the motion of the planets, but also the occurrence of the tides. In *On the Origin of Species by Means of Natural Selection* Darwin presented what amounts to an extended argument for natural selection as the best hypothesis for explaining the biological and fossil evidence at hand. Harman (1965) again: when a scientist infers the existence of atoms and subatomic particles, she is inferring the truth of an explanation for her various data. *Science News* (Peterson, 1990) reported the attempts of astronomers to explain a spectacular burst of X rays from the globular cluster M15 on the edge of the Milky Way. In this case the inability of the scientists to come up with a satisfactory explanation cast doubt on how well astronomers understand what happens when a neutron star accretes matter from an orbiting companion star. *Science News* (Monastersky, 1990) reported attempts to explain certain irregular blocks of black rock containing fossilized plant matter. The best explanation appears to be that they are dinosaur feces.

Abduction and history

Knowledge of the historical past also rests on abductions. Peirce (quoted in Fann, 1970) cites one example:

Numberless documents refer to a conqueror called Napoleon Bonaparte. Though we have not seen the man, yet we cannot explain what we have seen, namely, all those documents and monuments without supposing that he really existed. (p. 21)

Abduction and language

Language understanding is another process of forming and accepting explanatory hypotheses. Consider the written sentence, "The man sew the rat eating the corn." The conclusion seems inescapable that there has been some sort of mistake in the third word "sew" and that somehow the "e" has improperly replaced an "a." If we are poor at spelling, or if we read the sentence rapidly, we may leap to the "saw" reading without even noticing that we have not dealt with the fact of the "e." Taking the "saw" reading demands our acceptance so strongly that it can cause us to overturn the direct evidence of the letters on the page, and to append a hypothesis of a mistake, rather than accept the hypothesis of a nonsense sentence.

The process of abduction

Sometimes a distinction has been made between an initial process of coming up with explanatorily useful hypothesis alternatives and a subsequent process of critical evaluation wherein a decision is made as to which explanation is best. Sometimes the term "abduction" has been restricted to the hypothesis-generation phase. In this book, we use the term for the whole process of generation, criticism, and acceptance of explanatory hypotheses.

One reason is that although the explanatory hypotheses in abduction can be simple, more typically they are composite, multipart hypotheses. A scientific theory is typically a composite with many separate parts holding together in various ways,[3] and so is our understanding of a sentence and our judgment of a law case. However, no feasible information-processing strategy can afford to explicitly consider all possible combinations of potentially usable theory parts, since the number of combinations grows exponentially with the number of parts available (see chapter 7). Reasonably sized problems would take cosmological amounts of time. So, one must typically adopt a strategy that avoids generating all possible explainers. Prescreening theory fragments to remove those that are implausible under the circumstances makes it possible to radically restrict the potential combinations that can be generated, and thus goes a long way towards taming the combinatorial explosion. However, because such a strategy mixes critical evaluation into the hypothesis-generation process, this strategy does not allow a clear separation between the process of coming up with explanatory hypotheses and the process of acceptance. Thus, computationally, it seems best not to neatly separate generation and acceptance. We take *abduction* to include the whole process of generation, criticism, and possible acceptance of explanatory hypotheses.

Diagnosis and abductive justification

In this section we show by example how the abductive inference pattern can be used simply and directly to describe diagnostic reasoning and its justifications.

In AI, diagnosis is often described as an abduction problem (e.g., Peng & Reggia, 1990). Diagnosis can be viewed as producing an explanation that best accounts for the patient's (or device's) symptoms. The idea is that the task of a diagnostic reasoner is to come up with a best explanation for the symptoms, which are typically those findings for the case that show abnormal values. The explanatory hypotheses appropriate for diagnosis are malfunction hypotheses: typically disease hypotheses for plants and animals and broken-part hypotheses for mechanical systems.

The diagnostic task is to find a malfunction, or set of malfunctions, that best explains the symptoms. More specifically, a diagnostic conclusion should explain the symptoms, it should be plausible, and it should be significantly better than alternative explanations. (The terms "explain," "plausible," and "better" remain undefined for now.)

Taking diagnosis as abduction determines the classes of questions that are fair to ask of a diagnostician. It also suggests that computer-based diagnostic systems should be designed to make answering such questions straightforward.

Consider the example of liver disease diagnosis given by Harvey and Bordley (1972, pp. 299–302). In this case the physician organized the differential (the set of alternative hypotheses) around hepatomegaly (enlarged liver), giving five categories of possible causes of hepatomegaly: venous congestion of the liver, obstruction of the common duct, infection of the liver, diffuse hepatomegaly without infection, and neoplasm (tumor) of the liver. He then proceeded to describe the evidence for and against each hypothesis. Venous congestion of the liver was ruled out because none of its important symptoms were present. Obstruction of the common duct was judged to be unlikely because it would not explain certain important findings, and many expected symptoms were not present. Various liver infections were judged to be explanatorily irrelevant because certain important findings could not be explained this way. Other liver infections were ruled out because expected consequences failed to appear, although one type of infection seemed somewhat plausible. Diffuse hepatomegaly without infection was considered explanatorily irrelevant because, by itself, it would not be sufficient to explain the degree of liver enlargement. Neoplasm was considered to be plausible and would adequately explain all the important findings. Finally, the physician concluded the following:

The real choice here seems to lie between an infection of the liver and neoplasm of the liver. It seems to me that the course of the illness is compatible with a massive hepatoma [neoplasm of the liver] and that the hepatomegaly, coupled with the biochemical findings, including the moderate degree of jaundice, are best explained by this diagnosis.

Notice the form of the argument:

1. There is a finding that must be explained (hepatomegaly).
2. The finding might be explained in a number of ways (venous congestion of the liver, obstruction of the common duct, infection of the liver, diffuse hepatomegaly without infection, and neoplasm of the liver).
3. Some of these ways are judged to be implausible because expected consequences do not appear (venous congestion of the liver).
4. Some ways are judged to be irrelevant or implausible because they do not explain important findings (obstruction of the common duct, diffuse hepatomegaly without infection).
5. Of the plausible explanations that remain (infection of the liver, neoplasm of the liver), the best (neoplasm of the liver) is the diagnostic conclusion.

The argument is an abductive justification for the diagnostic conclusion.

Suppose the conclusion turned out to be wrong. What could have happened to the true answer? That is, why was the true, or correct, answer not the best explanation? This could only have happened for one or more of the following reasons:

1. There was something wrong with the data such that it really did not need to be explained. In this case, hepatomegaly might not have actually been present.
2. The differential was not broad enough. There might be causes of hepatomegaly that were unknown to the physician, or that were overlooked by him.

3. Hypotheses were incorrectly judged to be implausible. Perhaps venous congestion should have been considered more plausible than it was, due to faulty knowledge or missing evidence.

4a. Hypotheses were incorrectly thought not to explain important findings. For example, obstruction might explain findings that the physician thought it could not, possibly because the physician had faulty knowledge.

4b. The diagnostic conclusion was incorrectly thought to explain the findings. Neoplasm might not explain the findings, due to faulty knowledge or to overlooking important findings.

5a. The diagnostic conclusion was incorrectly thought to be better than it was. Neoplasm might have been overrated, due to faulty knowledge or missing evidence.

5b. The true answer was underrated, due to faulty knowledge or missing evidence.

Many questions to the diagnostician can be seen as indicating ways in which the answer may be wrong, each question suggesting an error of a particular type. An answer to such a question should convince the questioner that the diagnosis is not mistaken in that way.

Returning to the example, if the physician were asked, "What makes venous congestion implausible?" he might answer:

This patient exhibited no evidence of circulatory congestion or obstruction of the hepatic veins or vena cava. . . .

thus trying to convince the questioner that venous congestion was correctly ruled out. If asked, "Why not consider some toxic hepatic injury?" the physician could reply:

[It would not] seem to compete with a large hepatoma in explaining the massive hepatomegaly, the hypoglycemia, and the manifestations suggestive of infection.

thus trying to convince the questioner that the differential is broad enough.

Interestingly, in this case Bordley's diagnosis *was* wrong. Autopsy revealed that the patient actually had cancer of the pancreas. (To be fair, the autopsy also found tumors in the liver, but pancreatic cancer was considered the primary illness.) One significant finding in the case was elevated amylase, which is not explained by neoplasm of the liver. So, if we asked the physician, "How do you account for the sharply elevated amylase?" his only possible reply would be:

Oops.

The diagnosis was inadequate because it failed to account for all the important findings (item 4b in the previous numbered list).

This analysis tells us that if we build an expert system and claim that it does diagnosis, we can expect it to be asked certain questions. These are the only questions that are fair to ask simply because it is a diagnostic system. Other questions would not be about diagnosis per se. These other questions might include requests for definitions of terms, exam-like questions that check the system's knowledge about some important fact, and questions about the implications of the diagnostic conclusion for treatment. Thus, the idea of abductive justification gives rise to a model of dialogue between the diagnostician and the client. It defines a set of questions that any person, or machine, claiming to do diagnosis should be prepared to answer.

One power of this analysis lies in controlling for error, in making explicit the ways in which the conclusion can be wrong. A challenging question implies that the questioner thinks that the answer might be wrong and that the questioner needs to be convinced that it is not. A proper answer will reassure the questioner that the suspected error has not occurred.

Doubt and certainty

Inference and logic

Inferences are movements of thought within the sphere of belief.[4] The function of inference is the acceptance (or sometimes rejection) of propositions on the basis of purported evidence. Yet, inferences are not wholly or merely psychological; there may be objective relationships of evidential support (or its absence) between propositions that have nothing much to do with whether anyone thinks of them. Thus a science of evidential relationships is possible that has very little to do with empirical psychology. This science is *logic* in the broad sense.

Deduction and abduction

Deductions support their conclusions in such a way that the conclusions must be true, given true premises; they convey conclusive evidence. Other forms of evidential support are not so strong, and though significant support for a conclusion may be given, a possibility of error remains. Abductions are of this kind; they are fallible inferences.

Consider the following logical form, commonly called *disjunctive syllogism*.

P or Q or R or S or . . .
But not-Q, not-R, not-S, . . .

Therefore, P.

This form is deductively valid. Moreover, the support for an abductive conclusion fits this form if we assert that we have exhaustively enumerated all possible explanations for the data and that all but one of the alternative explanations has been decisively ruled out. Typically, however, we will have reasons to believe that we have considered all plausible explanations (i.e., those that have a significant chance of being true), but these reasons stop short of being conclusive. We may have struggled to formulate a wide variety of possible explanations but cannot be sure that we have covered all plausibles. Under these circumstances we can assert a proposition of the form of the first premise of the syllogism, but assert it only with a kind of qualified confidence. Typically, too, alternative explanations can be discounted for one reason or another but not decisively ruled out. Thus abductive inferences, in a way, rely on this particular deductively valid inference form, but abductions are conclusive only in the limit.

Of course disjunctive syllogism fits any decision by enumeration of alternatives and exclusion, not just abductions (where *explanatory* alternatives are considered). From this it can be seen that abduction cannot be identified with disjunctive syllogism.

Ampliative inference

Like inductive generalizations, abductions are *ampliative inferences;* that is, at the end of an abductive process, having accepted a best explanation, we may have more information than we had before. The abduction transcends the information of its premises and generates new information that was not previously encoded there at all. This can be contrasted with deductions, which can be thought of as extracting, explicitly in their conclusions, information that was already implicitly contained in the premises. Deductions are *truth preserving*, whereas successful abductions may be said to be *truth producing*.

This ampliative reasoning is sometimes done by introducing new vocabulary in the conclusion. For example, when we abduce that the patient has hepatitis because hepatitis is the only plausible way to explain the jaundice, we have introduced into the conclusion a new term, "hepatitis," which is from the vocabulary of diseases and not part of the vocabulary of symptoms. By introducing this term, we make conceptual connections with the typical progress of the disease, and ways to treat it, that were unavailable before. Whereas valid deductive inferences cannot contain terms in their conclusions that do not occur in their premises, abductions can "interpret" the given data in a new vocabulary. Abductions can thus make the leap from "observation language" to "theory language."

Doubt and hesitation

An abductive process aims at a satisfactory explanation, one that can be confidently accepted. However it may be accompanied in the end with some explicit qualification, for example, some explicit degree of assurance or some doubt. One main form of doubt is just hesitation from being aware of the possibility of alternative explanations. Classically, this is just how Descartes generates doubts about knowledge from the senses: Alternative explanations to the usual interpretations of sensory information are that we are dreaming or that we are being deceived by a very powerful and evil demon (Descartes,

1641). Since low-plausibility alternative explanations can be generated indefinitely, doubt cannot be completely eliminated.

On the way to a satisfactory explanation, an abductive process might seek further information beyond that given in the data initially to be explained. For example, there may be a need to distinguish between explanatory alternatives; for help in forming hypotheses; or for help in evaluating them. Often abductive processes are not immediately concluded, but are suspended to wait for answers from information-seeking processes. Such suspensions of processing can last a very long time. Years later, someone may say, "So that's why she never told me. I was always puzzled about that." Centuries later we may say, "So that's the secret of inheritance. It's based on making copies of long molecules that encode hereditary information."

Abductive conclusions: likelihood and acceptance

As we said earlier, abductions follow approximately this pattern:

D is a collection of data.
H explains D.
No other hypothesis can explain D as well as H does.
_____

Therefore, H is probably true.

The judgment of likelihood associated with an abductive conclusion should depend on the following considerations (as it typically does in the inferences we actually make):

1. how decisively H surpasses the alternatives[5]
2. how good H is by itself, independently of considering the alternatives (we should be cautious about accepting a hypothesis, even if it is clearly the best one we have, if it is not sufficiently plausible in itself)
3. judgments of the reliability of the data
4. how much confidence there is that all plausible explanations have been considered (how thorough was the search for alternative explanations).[6]

Beyond the judgment of its likelihood, willingness to accept the conclusion should (and typically does) depend on:

1. pragmatic considerations, including the costs of being wrong and the benefits of being right
2. how strong the need is to come to a conclusion at all, especially considering the possibility of seeking further evidence before deciding.

This theory of abduction is an evaluative theory, offering standards for judging reasoning patterns. It is also a descriptive and explanatory theory for human and computer reasoning processes that provides a way of analyzing these processes in functional terms, of showing what they accomplish, of showing how they manifest good reasoning (i.e., intelligence).

Best explanation: Compared with what?

There is some ambiguity in the abductive inference pattern as we have described it. What is the set of explanatory hypotheses of which *H* is the best? Perhaps this premise should say, "No other *available* hypothesis can explain *D* as well as *H* does."[7] The set of alternatives might be thought of so narrowly as to include just those hypotheses that one thinks of immediately, or so broadly as to include all the hypotheses that can in principle be formulated. Construed broadly, it would include the true explanation, which would of course be best, but then the whole inference form would seem to be trivial.

Yet it appears that the force of the abductive inference depends on an evaluation that ranges over all possible hypotheses, or at least a set of them large enough to guarantee that it includes the true one. If we think that there is a significant chance that there is a better explanation, even one that we have not thought of, that we *cannot* think of, or that is completely unavailable to us, then we should not make the inference and normally would not. After all, an unavailable hypothesis might be the true one. It is quite unpersuasive for me to try to justify a conclusion by saying, "It is likely to be true because I couldn't think of a better explanation." That I could not think of a better explanation is some evidence that there is no better explanation, depending on how we judge my powers of imagination and my powers of evaluating hypotheses, but these are just evidential considerations in making the judgment that there is not (anywhere) a better explanation. We should (and do) make the inferential leap when we judge that "no other hypothesis can explain *D* as well as *H* does." Unqualified.

In one sense the *best* explanation is the true one. But, having no independent access to which explanatory hypothesis is true, the reasoner can only assert judgments of *best* based on considerations such as plausibility and explanatory power. The reasoner is, in effect, presuming that the best explanation based on these considerations is the one most likely to be true. If we challenge an abductive justification by asking what the grounds are for judging that a particular hypothesis is best, then we properly get an answer in terms of what is wrong with alternative explanations and what is the evidence that all plausible explanations have been considered (all those with a significant chance of being true). The inference schema as stated in this chapter is not trivial, even though it ranges over all possible relevant hypotheses, because *best* is not directly a judgment of truth but instead a summary judgment of accessible explanatory virtues.

Emergent certainty

Abductions often display *emergent certainty*; that is, the conclusion of an abduction can have, and be deserving of, more certainty than any of its premises. This is unlike a deduction, which is no stronger than the weakest of its links (although separate deductions can converge for parallel support). For example, I may be more sure of the bear's hostile intent than of any of the details of its hostile gestures; I may be more sure of the meaning of the sentence than of my initial identifications of any of the words; I may be more sure of the overall theory than of the reliability of any single experiment on which it is based. Patterns emerge from individual points where no single point is essential to recognizing the pattern. A signal extracted and reconstructed from a noisy channel may lead to a message, the wording of which, or even more, the intent of which, is more certain than any of its parts.

This can be contrasted with traditional empiricist epistemology, which does not allow for anything to be more certain than the observations (except maybe tautologies) since everything is supposedly built up from the observations by deduction and inductive generalization. But a pure generalization is always somewhat risky, and its conclusion is less certain than its premises. "All goats are smelly" is less certain than any given "This goat is smelly." With only deductive logic and generalization available, empirical knowledge appears as a pyramid whose base is particular experiments or sense perceptions, and where the farther up you go, the more general you get, and the less certain. Thus, without some form of certainty-increasing inference, such as abduction, traditional empiricist epistemology is unavoidably committed to a high degree of skepticism about all general theories of science.

Knowledge without certainty

The conclusion of an abduction is "logically justified" by the force of the abductive argument. If the abductive argument is strong, and if one is persuaded by the argument to accept the conclusion, and if, beyond that, the conclusion turns out to be correct, then one has attained *justified, true, belief*, the classical philosophical conditions of knowledge, that date back to Plato.[8] Thus abductions are knowledge producing inferences despite their fallibility. Although we can never be entirely sure of an abductive conclusion, if the conclusion is indeed true, we may be said to "know" that conclusion. Of course, without independent knowledge that the conclusion is true, we do not "know that we know," but that is the usual state of our knowledge.

Summary: Abductions are fallible, and doubt cannot be completely eliminated. Nevertheless, by the aid of abductive inferences, knowledge is possible even in the face of uncertainty.

Explanations give causes

There have been two main traditional attempts to analyze explanations as deductive proofs, neither attempt particularly successful. Aristotle maintained that an explanation is a syllogism of a certain form (Aristotle c. 350 B.C.)

that also satisfies various informal conditions, one of which is that the "middle term" of the syllogism is the cause of the thing being explained. (*B* is the middle term of "All *A* are *B* ; All *B* are *C* ; Therefore, All *A* are *C* .") More recently (considerably) Hempel (1965) modernized the logic and proposed the "covering law" or "deductive nomological" model of explanation.[9] The main difficulty with these accounts (besides Hempel's confounding the question of what makes an ideally good explanation with the question of what it is to explain at all) is that being a deductive proof is neither necessary nor sufficient for being an explanation. Consider the following:

QUESTION: Why does he have burns on his hand?
EXPLANATION: He sneezed while cooking pasta and upset the pot.

The point of this example is that an explanation is given but no deductive proof, and although it could be turned into a deductive proof by including additional propositions, this would amount to gratuitously completing what is on the face of it an incomplete explanation. Under the circumstances (incompletely specified) sneezing and upsetting the pot were presumably *causally sufficient* for the effect, but this is quite different from being *logically sufficient*.

The case that explanations are not necessarily deductive proofs becomes even stronger if we consider psychological explanations and explanations that are fundamentally statistical (e.g., where quantum phenomena are involved). In these cases it is clear that causal determinism cannot be assumed, so the antecedent conditions cannot be assumed to be even causally sufficient for the effects. Conversely, many deductive proofs fail to be explanations of anything. For example classical mechanics is deterministic and time reversible, so an earlier state of a system can be deduced from a later state, but the earlier state cannot be said to be explained thereby. Also, *q* can be deduced from "*p* and *q* " but is not thereby explained.

Thus, we conclude that explanations are not deductive proofs in any particularly interesting sense. Although they can often be presented in the form of deductive proofs, doing so does not succeed in capturing anything essential or especially useful and tends to confuse causation with logical implication.

An alternative view is that an explanation is an assignment of causal responsibility; it tells a causal story. Finding possible explanations is finding possible causes of the thing to be explained. It follows that abduction, as a process of reasoning to an explanation, is a process of reasoning from effect to cause.

Cause for abduction may be understood somewhat more broadly than its usual senses of mechanical or efficient or event-event causation.[10] To get some idea of a more expanded view of causation, consider the four kinds of causes according to Aristotle: efficient cause, material cause, final cause, and formal cause (Aristotle, *Physics* , bk. 2, chap. 3). Let us take the example of my coffee mug. The *efficient cause* is the process by which the mug was manufactured and helps explain such things as why there are ripples on the surface of the bottom. The *material cause* is the ceramic and glaze, which compose the mug and cause it to have certain gross properties such as hardness. The *final cause* is the end or purpose, in this case to serve as a container for liquids and as a means of conveyance for drinking. A final-cause explanation is needed to explain the presence and shape of the handle. *Formal cause* is somewhat more mysterious – Aristotle is hard to interpret here – but it is perhaps something like the mathematical properties of the shape, which impose constraints resulting in certain specific other properties. That the cross-section of the mug, viewed from above, is approximately a circle, explains why the length and width of the cross-section are approximately equal. The causal story told by an abductive explanation might rely on any of these four types of causation.[11]

When we conclude that a finding f is explained by hypothesis H, we say more than just that H is a cause of f in the case at hand. We conclude that among all the vast causal ancestry of f we will assign responsibility to H. Typically, our reasons for focusing on H are pragmatic and connected rather directly with goals of production or prevention. We blame the heart attack on the blood clot in the coronary artery or on the high-fat diet, depending on our interests. Perhaps we should explain the patient's death by pointing out that the patient was born, so what else can you expect but eventual death? We can blame the disease on the invading organism, on the weakened immune system that permitted the invasion, or on the wound that provided the route of entry into the body. We can blame the fire on the presence of the combustibles, on the presence of the spark, or even on the presence of the oxygen, depending on which we think is the most remarkable. I suggest that it comes down to this: The things that will satisfy us as accounting for f will depend on why we are trying to account for f; but the only things that count as candidates are parts of what we take to be the causal ancestry of f.

Induction

Peirce's view was that induction, deduction, and abduction are three distinct types of inference, although as his views developed, the boundaries shifted somewhat, and he occasionally introduced hybrid forms such as "abductive induction" (Peirce, 1903). In this section I hope to clear up the confusion about the relationship of abduction to induction. First I argue that inductive generalizations can be insightfully analyzed as special cases of abductions. I also argue that predictions are a distinctive form of inference, that they are not abductions, and that they are sometimes deductive, but typically not. The result is a new classification of basic inference types.

Harman (1965) argued that "inference to the best explanation" (i.e., abduction) is *the* basic form of nondeductive inference, subsuming "enumerative induction" and all other forms of nondeductive inferences as special cases. Harman argued quite convincingly that abduction subsumes sample-to-population inferences (i.e., inductive generalizations [this is my way of putting the matter]). The weakness of his overall argument was that other forms of nondeductive inference are not seemingly subsumed by abduction, most notably population-to-sample inferences, a kind of prediction. The main problem is that the conclusion of a prediction does not explain anything, so the inference cannot be an inference to a best explanation.

This last point, and others, were taken up by Ennis (1968). In his reply to Ennis, instead of treating predictions as deductive, or admitting them as a distinctive form of inference not reducible to abduction, Harman took the dubious path of trying to absorb predictions, along with a quite reasonable idea of abductions, into the larger, vaguer, and less reasonable notion of "maximizing explanatory coherence" (Harman, 1968). In this I think Harman made a big mistake, and it will be my job to repair and defend Harman's original arguments, which were basically sound, although they proved somewhat less than he thought.

Inductive generalization

First, I will argue that it is possible to treat every good (i.e., reasonable, valid) inductive generalization as an instance of abduction. An inductive generalization is an inference that goes from the characteristics of some observed sample of individuals to a conclusion about the distribution of those characteristics in some larger population. As Harman pointed out, it is useful to describe inductive generalizations as abductions because it helps to make clear when the inferences are warranted. Consider the following inference:

All observed A's are B's
___
Therefore All A's are B's

This inference is warranted, Harman (1965) writes, ". . . whenever the hypothesis that all A's are B's is (in the light of all the evidence) a better, simpler, more plausible (and so forth) hypothesis than is the hypothesis, say, that someone is biasing the observed sample in order to make us think that all A's are B's. On the other hand, as soon as the total evidence makes some other competing hypothesis plausible, one may not infer from the past correlation in the observed sample to a complete correlation in the total population."

If this is indeed an abductive inference, then "All A's are B's" should explain "All observed A's are B's." But, "All A's are B's" does not seem to explain why "This A is a B," or why A and B are regularly associated (as pointed out by Ennis, 1968). Furthermore, I suggested earlier that explanations give causes, but it is hard to see how a general fact could explain its instances, because it does not seem in any way to cause them.

The story becomes much clearer if we distinguish between an *event of observing some fact* and *the fact observed*. What the general statement in the conclusion explains is the events of observing, not the facts observed. For example, suppose I choose a ball at random (arbitrarily) from a large hat containing colored balls. The ball I choose is red. Does the fact that all of the balls in the hat are red explain why this particular ball is red? No. But it does explain why, when I chose a ball at random, it turned out to be a red one (because they all are). "All A's are B's" cannot explain why "This A is a B" because it does not say anything at all about how its being an A is connected with its being a B. The information that "they all are" does not tell me anything about why this one is, except it suggests that if I want to know why this one is, I would do well to figure out why they all are.

A generalization helps to explain the events of observing its instances, but it does not explain the instances themselves. That the cloudless, daytime sky is blue helps explain why, when I look up, I see the sky to be blue (but it doesn't explain why the sky is blue). The truth of "Theodore reads ethics books a lot" helps to explain why, so often when I have seen him, he has been reading an ethics book (but it doesn't explain why he was reading ethics books on those occasions). Seen this way, inductive generalization does have the form of an inference whose conclusion explains its premises.

Generally, we can say that *the frequencies in the larger population, together with the frequency-relevant characteristics of the method for drawing a sample, explain the frequencies in the observed sample*. In particular, "A's are mostly B's" together with "This sample of A's was drawn without regard to whether or not they were B's" explain why the A's that were drawn were mostly B's.

Why were 61% of the chosen balls yellow?

Because the balls were chosen more or less randomly from a population that was two thirds yellow (the difference from 2/3 in the sample being due to chance).

Alternative explanation for the same observation:

Because the balls were chosen by a selector with a bias for large balls from a population that was only one third yellow but where yellow balls tend to be larger than non yellow ones.

How do these explain? By giving a causal story.

What is explained is (always) some *aspect* of an event/being/state, not a whole event/being/state itself. In this example just the frequency of characteristics in the sample is explained, not why these particular balls are yellow or why the experiment was conducted on Tuesday. The explanation explains why the sample frequency was the way it was, rather than having some markedly different value. In general, if there is a deviation in the sample from what you would expect, given the population and the sampling method, then you have to throw some Chance into the explanation (which is more or less plausible depending on how much chance you have to suppose).[12]

The objects of explanation – what explanations explain – are facts about the world (more precisely, always an aspect of a fact, under a description). Observations are facts; that is, an observation having the characteristics that it does is a fact. When you explain observed samples, an interesting thing is to explain the frequencies. A proper explanation will give a causal story of how the frequencies came to be the way they were and will typically refer both to the population frequency and the method of drawing the samples.

Unbiased sampling processes tend to produce representative outcomes; biased sampling processes tend to produce unrepresentative outcomes. This "tending to produce" is causal and supports explanation and prediction. A peculiarity is that characterizing a sample as "representative" is characterizing the effect (sample frequency) by reference to part of its cause (population frequency). Straight inductive generalization is equivalent to concluding that a sample is representative, which is a conclusion about its cause. This inference depends partly on evidence or presumption that the sampling process is (close enough to) unbiased. The unbiased sampling process is part of the explanation of the sample frequency, and any independent evidence for or against unbiased sampling bears on its plausibility as part of the explanation.

If we do not think of inductive generalization as abduction, we are at a loss to explain why such an inference is made stronger or more warranted, if in collecting data we make a systematic search for counter-instances and cannot find any, than it would be if we just take the observations passively. Why is the generalization made stronger by making an effort to examine a wide variety of types of A's? The inference is made stronger because the failure of the active search for counter-instances tends to rule out various hypotheses about ways in which the sample might be biased.

In fact the whole notion of a "controlled experiment" is covertly based on abduction. What is being "controlled for" is always an alternative way of explaining the outcome. For example a placebo-controlled test of the efficiency of a drug is designed to make it possible to rule out purely psychological explanations for any favorable outcome.

Even the question of sample size for inductive generalization can be seen clearly from an abductive perspective. Suppose that on each of the only two occasions when Konrad ate pizza at Mario's Pizza Shop, he had a stomachache the next morning. In general, Konrad has a stomachache occasionally but not frequently. What may we conclude about the relationship between the pizza and the stomachache? What may we reasonably predict about the outcome of Konrad's next visit to Mario's? Nothing. The sample is not a large enough. Now suppose that Konrad continues patronizing Mario's and that after every one of 79 subsequent trips he has a stomach ache within 12 hours. What may we conclude about the relationship between Mario's pizza and Konrad's stomachache? That Mario's pizza makes Konrad have stomachaches. We may predict that Konrad will have a stomachache after his next visit, too.

A good way to understand what is occurring in this example is by way of abduction. After Konrad's first two visits we could not conclude anything because we did not have enough evidence to distinguish between the two competing general hypotheses:

1. The eating pizza – stomachache correlation was accidental (i.e., merely coincidental or spurious [say, for example, that on the first visit the stomach ache was caused by a virus contracted elsewhere and that on the second visit it was caused by an argument with his mother]).
2. There is some connection between eating pizza and the subsequent stomach ache (i.e., there is some causal explanation of why he gets a stomach ache after eating the pizza [e.g., Konrad is allergic to the snake oil in Mario's Special Sauce]).

By the time we note the outcome of Konrad's 79th visit, we are able to decide in favor of the second hypothesis. The best explanation of the correlation has become the hypothesis of a causal connection because explaining the correlation as accidental becomes rapidly less and less plausible the longer the association continues.

Prediction

Another inference form that has often been called "induction" is given by the following:

All observed A's are B's.
_____
Therefore, the next A will be a B.

Let us call this inference form an *inductive projection*. Such an inference can be analyzed as an inductive generalization followed by a prediction, as follows:

Observations → All A's are B's → The next A will be a B.

Predictions have traditionally been thought of as deductive inferences. However, something is wrong with this analysis. To see this, consider the alternative analysis of inductive projections, as follows:

Observations → At least generally *A*'s are *B*'s → The next *A* will be a *B*.

This inference is stronger in that it establishes its conclusion with more certainty, which it does by hedging the generalization and thus making it more plausible, more likely to be true. It could be made stronger yet by hedging the temporal extent of the generalization:

Observations → At least generally *A*'s are *B*'s, at least for the recent past and the immediate future → The next *A* will be a *B*.

The analyses of inductive projection with the hedged generalizations are better than the first analysis because they are better at making sense of the inference, which they do by being better at showing the sense in it (i.e., they are better at showing how, and when, and why the inference is justified – or "rational" or "intelligent"). Reasonable generalizations are hedged. Generally the best way to analyze "*A*'s are *B*'s" is not "All *A*'s are *B*'s," as we are taught in logic class, but as "Generally *A*'s are *B*'s," using the neutral, hedged, universal quantifier of ordinary life.[13]

We have analyzed inductive projections as inductive generalizations followed by predictions. The inductive generalizations are really abductions, as was argued before. But, what kind of inferences are predictions? One thing seems clear: *Predictions from hedged generalizations are not deductions.*

Predictions from hedged generalizations belong to the same family as *statistical syllogisms* which have forms like these:[14]

m/n of the *A*'s are *B*'s (where $m/n > 1/2$).

Therefore, the next *A* will be a *B*.

and

m/n of the *A*'s are *B*'s.

Therefore, approximately m/n of the *A*'s in the next sample will be *B*'s.

These are also related to the following forms:

Generally *A*'s are *B*'s.
S is an *A*.

Therefore, *S* is a *B*.

and

A typical, normal *X* does *Y*.

Therefore, this *X* will do *Y*.

None of these inferences appear to be deductions. One can, of course, turn them into deductions by including a missing premise like "this X is normal," but unless there is independent evidence for the assumption, this adds nothing to the analysis.

Furthermore, consider an inference of this form:

P has high probability.

Therefore, P.

Such an inference (whatever the probability is taken to mean) will have to allow for the possibility of the conclusion being false while the premise is true. This being so, such an inference cannot possibly be deductive.

Thus it seems that some of our most warranted inductive projections, those mediated by various kinds of hedged generalizations, do not rely on deduction for the final predictive step. These predictions, including statistical syllogisms, are not deductions, and they do not seem to be abductions. That is, *sometimes* the thing predicted is also explained, but note that the conclusions in abductions do the explaining, whereas for predictions, if anything, the conclusions are what is explained. Thus the predictive forms related to statistical syllogism are in general nondeductive and nonabductive as well.

If predictions are not abductions, what then is the relationship between prediction and explanation? The idea that they are closely related has a fairly elaborate history in the philosophy of science. Some authors have proposed that explanations and predictions have the same logical form. Typically this is given as the form of a proof whereby the thing to be explained or predicted is the conclusion, and causation enters in to the premises somehow, either as a causal law or in some other way.

The idea seems to be that to explain something is to be in a position to have predicted it, and to predict something puts one in a position to explain it, if it actually occurs. This bridges the apparent basic asymmetry that arises because what you explain is more or less a given (i.e., has happened or does happen), whereas what you predict is an expectation and (usually) has not already happened.

Despite its apparent plausibility, this thesis is fundamentally flawed. There is no necessary connection between explanation and prediction of this sort. Consider the following two counterexamples.

Example 1. George-did-it explanations. Why is there mud on the carpet? Explanation: George did it (presumably, but not explicitly, by tracking it into the house stuck to his shoes, or something similar). Knowing that George came into the room puts me in a position to predict mud on the carpet only if I assume many questionable auxiliary assumptions about George's path and the adhesive properties of mud, and so forth. If I had an ideally complete explanation of the mud on the carpet, some sort of complete causal story, then, perhaps, I would be in a position to predict the last line of the story, given all the rest; but this is an unrealistic representation of what normal explanation is like. George-did-it explanations can be perfectly explanatory without any pretensions of completeness. This shows that *one can explain without being in a position to predict.* Many other examples can be given where explanation is ex post facto, but where knowledge of a system is not complete enough to license prediction. Why did the dice come up double 6s? Because of throwing the dice, and chance. We are often in a position to explain a fact without being in a position to have predicted it – specifically, when our explanation is not complete, which is typical, or when the explanation does not posit a deterministic mechanism, which is also typical.

Example 2. Predictions based on trust. Suppose that a mechanic, whom I have good reason to trust, says that my car will soon lose its generator belt. On this basis I predict that the car will lose its generator belt (on a long drive home, say). Here I have made a prediction, and on perfectly good grounds, too, but I am not in a position to give an explanation (I have no idea what has weakened the belt). This example, weather predictions, and similar examples of predictions based on authority show that *one can be in a position to predict without being in a position to explain.*

I believe that explanations are causal, and that predictions are commonly founded on projecting consequences based on our causal understanding of things. Thus, commonly, an explanation of some event E refers to its causes, and a prediction of E is based on its causes, and both the explanation and the prediction suppose the causal connections. However, I believe that the symmetry between explanation and prediction goes no further.

When a prediction fails, it casts doubt on the general premises on which it is based. This is part of the logical underpinnings of scientific reasoning. The view presented here is similar to what has been called the "hypothetico-deductive" model of scientific reasoning, except in insisting that hypotheses must be explanatory, and in denying that predictions are always deductive.

Predictions, then, are neither abductions nor (typically) deductions. This is contrary, both to the view that predictions are deductions and to Harman's view that all nondeductive inferences are abductions. Rather, predictions and abductions are two distinct kinds of plausible inference. Abductions go from data to explanatory hypothesis; predictions go from hypothesis to expected data. (See Figure 1.1.)

Jerry Hobbs has suggested (verbally) that, "The mind is a big abduction machine." In contrast Eugene Charniak has suggested (verbally) that there are two fundamental operations of mind: abduction and planning. The view presented in this chapter, while close to that of Hobbs in its enthusiasm for

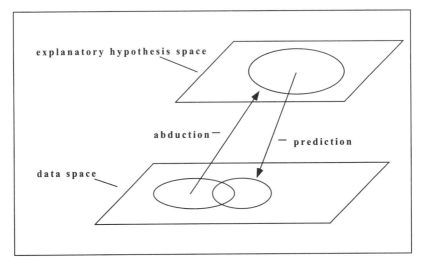

Figure 1.1. Abduction and prediction.

abduction, is actually closer to Charniak's. It elaborates that view, however, by adding that planning depends on prediction (to anticipate consequences of actions), and it is prediction that is inferentially fundamental. Planning is choosing actions based on expected outcomes. So planning is "reasoning" all right, but it is not "inference," since planning decides action rather than belief.

While asserting that abduction and prediction are inferentially distinct, we note that they are often entangled as processes. Sometimes an abduction will use prediction as a subtask (e.g., for testing a hypothesis), and sometimes a prediction will use abduction as a subtask (e.g., for assessing the situation).

Probabilities and abductions

It has been suggested that we should use mathematical probabilities to help us choose among explanatory hypotheses. (Bayes's Theorem itself can be viewed as a way of describing how simple alternative causal hypotheses can be weighed.) If suitable knowledge of probabilities is available, the mathematical theory of probabilities can, in principle, guide our abductive evaluation of explanatory hypotheses to determine which is best. However, in practice it seems that rough qualitative confidence levels on the hypotheses are enough to support abductions, which then produce rough qualitative confidence levels for their conclusions. It is certainly possible to model these confidences as numbers from a continuum, and on rare occasions one can actually get knowledge of numerical confidences (e.g., for playing blackjack). However, for the most part numerical confidence estimates are unavailable and unnecessary for reasoning. People are good abductive reasoners without close estimates of confidence. In fact it can be argued that, if confidences need to be estimated closely, then it must be that the best hypothesis is not much better than the next best, in which case no conclusion can be confidently drawn because the confidence of an abductive conclusion depends on how decisively the best explanation surpasses the alternatives. Thus it seems that confident abductions are possible only if confidences for hypotheses do not need to be estimated closely.

Moreover, it appears that accurate knowledge of probabilities is not commonly available because the probability associated with a possible event is not very well defined. There is almost always a certain arbitrariness about which reference class is chosen as a base for the probabilities; the larger the reference class, the more reliable the statistics, but the less relevant they are; whereas the more specific the reference class, the more relevant, but the less reliable. (See Salmon, 1967, p. 92.) Is the likelihood that the next patient has the flu best estimated based on the frequency in all the people in the world over the entire history of medicine? It seems better at least to control for the season and to narrow the class to include people at just this particular time of the year. (Notice that causal understanding is starting to creep into the considerations.) Furthermore, each flu season is somewhat different, so we would do better to narrow to considering people just *this* year. Then, of course, the average *patient* is not the same as the average *person*, and so forth, so the class should probably be narrowed further to something such as this: people of this particular age, race, gender, and social status who have come *lately* to doctors of this sort. Now the only way the doctor can have statistics this specific is to rely on his or her own most recent experience, which allows for only rough estimates of likelihood because the sample is so small. There is a Heisenberg-like uncertainty about the whole thing; the closer you try to measure the likelihoods, the more approximate the numbers become. In the complex natural world the long-run statistics are often overwhelmed by the short-term trends, which render the notion of a precise prior probability of an event inapplicable to most common affairs.

Taxonomy of basic inference types

Considering its apparent ubiquity, it is remarkable how overlooked and underanalyzed abduction is by almost 2,400 years of logic and philosophy. According to the analysis given here, the distinction between abduction and deduction is a distinction between different dimensions, so to speak, of inference. Along one dimension inference can be distinguished into deductive and nondeductive inference; along another dimension inferences can be distinguished as abductive and predictive (and mixed) sorts of inferences. Ab-

duction absorbs inductive generalization as a subclass and leaves the predictive aspect of induction as a separate kind of inference. Statistical syllogism is a kind of prediction. This categorization of inferences is summarized in Figure 1.2.

From wonder to understanding

Learning is the acquisition of knowledge. One main form of learning starts
with wonder and ends in understanding. To understand something is to grasp

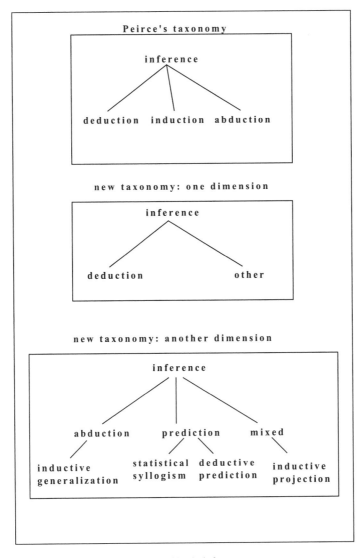

Figure 1.2. Taxonomy of basic inference types.

an explanation of it. (To explain something to somebody is to package up an understanding and communicate it.) Thus knowledge is built up of explanatory hypotheses, which are put in place in memory as a result of processes set in motion by wondering "Why?" That is, one main form of knowledge consists of answers to explanation-seeking why questions.

An explanation-seeking why question rests on a Given, a presupposition upon which the question is based. For example, "Why is the child sneezing?" presupposes that the child is indeed sneezing. This Given is not absolutely firm, even though it is accepted at the outset, for in the end we may be happy to throw it away, as in, "Oh, those weren't sneezes at all. She was trying to keep a feather in the air by blowing." Usually, perhaps always, along with the Given some contrasting possibility is held in mind, some imagined way that the Given could have been different (Bromberger, 1966). Thus, behind the *G* in a "Why *G* ?" usually there appears an ". . . as opposed to *H* " discernible in the background.

Abduction is a process of going from some Given to a best explanation for that (or related) given. Describing a computational process as abduction says *what* it accomplishes – namely, generation, criticism, and acceptance of an explanation – but superficially it says nothing about *how* it is accomplished (for example, how hypotheses are generated or how generation interacts with acceptance).

An explanation is an assignment of causal responsibility; it tells a causal story (at least this is the sense of "explanation" relevant to abduction). Thus, finding possible explanations is finding possible causes of the thing to be explained, and so abduction is essentially a process of reasoning from effect to cause.

A large part of knowledge consists of causal understanding. Abductions produce knowledge, both in science and in ordinary life.

Notes

1 This formulation is largely due to William Lycan.

2 Thagard (1988) recognizes abduction in his analysis of scientific theory formation.

3 For example, Darden (1991) describes the modularity of genetic theory.

4 The remainder of this chapter is more philosophical. It is not necessary to accept everything in order to find value in the rest of the book. The next chapter includes an orientation to our approach to AI and a discussion of representational issues. The main computational treatment of abduction begins in chapter 3. The philosophy increases again at the end of the book.

5 Thus abductions have a way of turning negative evidence against some hypotheses into positive evidence for alternative explanations.

6 This condition shows most clearly why the process of discovery is a logical matter, and why logic cannot simply be confined to matters of justification. The "logic of justification" cannot be neatly separated from the "logic of discovery" because justification depends, in part, on evaluating the quality of the discovery process.

7 Suggested by William Lycan.

8 I am ignoring here the so called "Gettier problem" with these conditions, but see Harman (1965) for an argument that successful abductions resolve the Gettier problem anyway.

9   For a brief summary of deductive and other models of explanation see Bhaskar (1981), and for a
    history of recent philosophical accounts of explanation, see Salmon (1990).

10 For a well-developed historical account of the connections between ideas of causality and expla-
    nation see Wallace (1972, 1974). Ideas of causality and explanation have been intimately linked
    for a very long time.

11 What the types of causation and causal explanation are remains unsettled, despite Aristotle's best
    efforts and those of many other thinkers. The point here is that a narrow view of causation makes
    progress harder by obscuring the degree to which all forms of causal thinking are fundamentally
    similar.

12 "It is embarrassing to invoke such a wildly unlikely event as a chance encounter between the
    entry probe and a rare and geographically confined methane plume, but so far we have elimi-
    nated all other plausible explanations" (Planetary scientist Thomas M. Donahue of the Univer-
    sity of Michigan on the analysis of chemical data from a Pioneer probe parachuted onto the
    planet Venus, reported in *Science News* for Sept. 12, 1992).

13 Note that this analysis suggests an explanation for why traditional mathematical logic has been
    so remarkably unsuccessful in accounting for reasoning outside mathematics and the highly
    mathematical sciences. The universal quantifier of logic is not the universal quantifier of ordi-
    nary life, or even of ordinary scientific thought.

14 I have not put likelihood qualifiers in the conclusions of any these forms because doing so would
    at best postpone the deductive gap.

Knowledge-based systems and the science of AI

The science of AI

The field of artificial intelligence (AI) seems scattered and disunited with several competing paradigms. One major controversy is between proponents of symbolic AI (which represents information as discrete codes) and proponents of connectionism (which represents information as weighted connections between simple processing units in a network). Even within each of these approaches there is no clear orthodoxy. Another concern is whether AI is an engineering discipline or a science. This expresses an uncertainty about the basic nature of AI as well as an uncertainty about methodology. If AI is a science like physics, then an AI program is an experiment. As experiments, perhaps AI programs should be judged by the standards of experiments. They should be clearly helpful in confirming and falsifying theories, in determining specific constants, or in uncovering new facts. However, if AI is fundamentally engineering, AI programs are artifacts, technologies to be used. In this case, there is no such reason for programs to have clear confirming or falsifying relationships to theories. A result in AI would then be something practical, a technique that could be exported to a real-world domain and used. Thus, there is confusion about how results in AI should be judged, what the role of a program is, and what counts as progress in AI.

It has often been said that the plurality of approaches and standards in AI is the result of the extreme youth of AI as an intellectual discipline. This theory implies that with time the pluralism of AI will sort itself out into a normal science under a single paradigm. I suggest, instead, that as it ages AI will continue to include diverse and opposing theories and methods. This is because the reason for the pluralism is that programs are at the heart of AI, and programs can be approached in four fundamentally different ways: (1) An AI program can be treated as a technology to be used to solve practical problems (AI as engineering); (2) it can be treated as an experiment or model (AI as traditional science); (3) an AI program can also be treated as a real intelligence, either imitative of human intelligence (AI as art) or (4) non-imitative (AI as design science). Because these four ways

√ The first section of this chapter on the science of AI is by Susan G. Josephson; the remaining sections are by B. Chandrasekaran.

31

to treat an AI program exist, the field of AI is, and will remain, diverse.

AI as engineering

When an AI program is treated as a technology to be used to solve practical problems, this is AI as engineering (of course, some programs are proof-of-principle prototypes with no immediate practicality, even though ultimate practicality is the goal). In AI as engineering, technology is used to solve real-world problems. The difference between AI programs that are only engineering and those that can be thought of as doing traditional science is whether there are any clearly distinguishable phenomena being investigated. That is, if AI is like traditional science, we expect to find theories about the nature of some phenomena being tested and confirmed; whereas, when programs are treated as engineering, the emphasis is on the accomplishment of practical tasks.

The engineering approach is important for the discipline as a whole, because it spreads AI through the culture. It applies AI technology to problems in medicine, commerce, and industry; as a result, it creates more uses for AI technology and stimulates the development of AI. When programs are treated as engineering, the emphasis is on practical technology, but it also creates a demand that supports other conceptions of AI.

AI as traditional science

When AI programs are thought of as experiments or models, this is AI as traditional science. In traditional-science AI, the theories being tested are about the phenomena of natural intelligence. Such a theory is tested by building it into a program that is run on a computer. If AI is like traditional science, running such a program is equivalent to performing an experiment and helps prove one theory to be right and inconsistent theories to be wrong. For example, Newell and Simon (1976) conceive of AI as deriving and empirically testing universal laws about intelligence. Each new machine and each new program, they explain, is an experiment. They state the physical symbol system hypothesis: "A physical symbol system has the necessary and sufficient means for general intelligent action" (Newell and Simon 1976, p. 41). This hypothesis is proven right when programs based on it work well – that is, perform "intelligently" for a range of cases in a computationally efficient manner. This hypothesis is proven wrong if general intelligent actions can be produced by a mechanism that is not a physical symbol system.

However, the standards normally used to judge AI programs (such as computational efficiency, requiring knowledge that is actually available, scaling up, working on a wide range of cases, and so on) judge programs independently of whether they provide good theories of natural intelligence. Two working programs that have radically different underlying theories might both be judged to have the same degree of adequacy by these standards. Thus, having a well-designed working program is not sufficient to confirm its underlying theory as anything but a candidate theory of some cognitive phenomena, nor is it sufficient to differentiate between competing theories.

To confirm or falsify a theory in AI as a correct theory of intelligence, we need to judge programs embodying that theory by how well they match up against the phenomena of intelligence being investigated. Given that our only sure source of data about intelligence comes from human intelligent behavior, such a program would be judged by how well it simulates human behavior. However, it is not sufficient for a program merely to simulate the input–output behavior of humans; it is quite possible for a program to simulate human behavior by using mechanisms that are nothing like those used by humans (Pylyshyn, 1979). So for a program to be judged a good model of intelligence, the underlying mechanism must have plausibility as a model of the causal mechanisms that actually produce the intelligent behavior in humans. These concerns about how humans do things lead us away from AI and toward cognitive psychology.

Cognitive psychology directly studies human cognitive behavior. From the perspective of AI as traditional science, AI and cognitive psychology study the same thing: human cognitive behavior. However, AI and cognitive psychology approach the problem of cognition in different ways. Psychology supplies the evidence that confirms or falsifies models in AI, and psychology supplies the domain that AI models are about. Cognitive psychology seeks the causal mechanisms that give rise to human cognitive behavior. Cognitive psychology can regard AI theories as possible models to be tested and refined by comparing them with observations of human behavior. Indeed, AI contributes best to cognitive psychology when a multiplicity of competing AI theories acts as a pool of hypotheses from which to choose.

AI theorists make hypotheses about the phenomena of intelligence and then work them out in computational models refined by being run on computers. Within that context, AI theorists can study these computational models as mathematics or as computer systems. The approach of AI is to understand the artifactual models themselves, whereas the approach of cognitive psychology is to see them as models of human behavior and to use them to study human behavior. Criteria such as feasibility of computation still show one AI program as better than another, but it is evidence about human beings that rules out some models as candidates for psychological theories. Practicing AI in this way means that AI models are unlike theories in physics, say, where science is conducted within a single theoretical framework. Within cognitive psychology there might be this sort of science, but not within AI. Within traditional-science AI there will continue to be a plurality of theoretical frameworks.

AI as art

When AI programs are thought of, not as models or simulations but as real intelligences that actually understand and have other humanlike cognitive states, then the standard is verisimilitude, and AI becomes art. This AI as art is often called *strong AI* (Searle, 1980).

The comparison between AI and art is not arbitrary. Both concern crafting artifacts designed to have some imitative appearance. Realistic statues, such as those of Duane Hanson, are imitations of the physical appearance of humans, whereas an AI program, such as ELIZA or PARRY, is an imitation of the appearance human thinking. Art helps us see ourselves. Machines with humanlike mentalities help us see our mental selves. Further, just as realistic sculptures give the appearance of humanness – not by using the true causal mechanism, human flesh – the AI-as-art systems give the appearance of human mentality, not by using the same causal mechanisms that humans use, but by using whatever gives the appearance of mentality.

The standards for success of AI-as-art systems, such as passing the Turing test, require that the programs imitate interesting characteristics of humans, not that they present plausible models of human mental mechanisms. An AI program passes the Turing test if it deceives someone into believing that it is a human being, not by solving difficult problems or by being useful technology. This imitation involves deception and illusion: the machines are designed to appear to have human mentalities, often even seeming to have emotions and personal lives. The goal of AI as art is to make machines that have, or appear to have, a humanlike independent intelligence. This imitative AI looks unsystematic and ad hoc from a scientific perspective.

Some theorists believe that the objective of trying to give machines humanlike intelligence is inherently misguided. They object to the claim that a machine that imitates perfectly the appearance of a humanlike mentality can be said to actually have a humanlike mentality. They say that a purely syntactic machine cannot think in the sense that humans do, cannot be given the sort of commonsense knowledge that humans have, and cannot learn in the way that humans do. Consequently, a machine can never really be intelligent in the way that humans are.

The AI that these theorists find so misguided is AI as art. Like other good art, this sort of AI is a stimulus for discussions of human nature and the human condition. AI as art serves as a focal point for criticisms of the very project of making thinking machines. That there are such criticisms shows the vitality of this sort of AI. However, these criticisms are completely inapplicable to AI as science and engineering. Whether machines can have actual humanlike cognitive states is irrelevant to modeling human intelligence in cooperation with cognitive psychology, to building information-processing systems, and to using AI technology in business and industry.

AI as design science

When an AI program is viewed as a real intelligence – not as an imitation of human intelligence but as a cognitive artifact in its own right – this is AI as design science. The information-processing-task approach of David Marr and the generic-task approach described later in this chapter view programs in this way. Design-science AI is similar to engineering in that it makes working systems that are important for what they can do, but, unlike AI as engineering, design-science AI is practiced with the intent of discovering the principles behind cognition. Although humans are our primary examples of cognitive agents, the principles sought by design-science AI are those that hold for cognition in the abstract, where humans are just one set of examples of cognitive agents and silicon-based machines are another.

Design-science AI is a synthesis of AI as art and AI as science. It is similar to AI as art in that it involves designing programs that have functions independent of modeling humans. The systems it produces are like strong AI systems in being cognitive systems in their own right rather than mere models. However, unlike AI as art, design-science AI is not interested in the mere appearance of intelligence but in the causal mechanisms that produce intelligent behavior. Design-science AI is similar to traditional science in its concern for making systems that show us new things about the phenomena of intelligence, such as reasoning and problem solving.

What is design science? Design science is a new paradigm of science. There is a Kuhnian paradigm shift (Kuhn, 1970) inherent in design-science AI. Design-science AI is a science of the artifactual or the artificial. This approach to AI was first put forth clearly by Herbert Simon in his book *The Sciences of the Artificial* (1981). Simon suggested that sciences of the artificial are close to engineering in that they are concerned with making synthetic or artificial objects with desired properties. For example, Marr (1982) analyzed the external constraints on natural vision so that he could design robot vision. Science of this sort is concerned with the organization of natural and artificial things, and characterizes such things by the functions that they perform and the goals that they achieve.

It is in this way that design science is a new paradigm. It looks at nature from the perspective of function and goal achievement in order to understand the principles that govern design. For traditional science, nature is described without teleology or design, in terms of efficient causes; for design science, nature is described in terms of final causes. From a physical-science perspective, when design science ascribes goals or purposes to nonconscious things, these are merely ascribed from the outside to tell a story about the behavior; and such talk is totally unscientific, even prescientific. Yet from a design-science perspective, there are realistic ways of looking at nature in terms of design and teleology. For example, from the perspective of design science, the heart has valves for the purpose of facilitating its task of pumping the blood. Focusing on this kind of description is essential to understanding nature from the perspective of the artifactual. If someone wants to understand why the parts are present, or why they have the forms that they have, or wants to make a heart, then that person needs to know what the parts are for. Yet if that person thinks only in terms of physical science, this sort of talk about goals and purposes appears anthropomorphic, and even false, because it talks about the heart as though it were designed for a purpose when, in fact, it was not. From the perspective of traditional science such talk seems to imply that there exists some sort of anthropomorphically conceived grand designer.

However, to design artifacts, one must look at the world in a functional way. For example, from a design perspective, artificial coffee creamer and milk are identical with respect to performing the task of whitening coffee, although they have no chemical ingredients in common. If we describe them from a traditional-science perspective, their functional similarity is invisible. The study of artifacts attends to how purposes are attained. Furthermore, one can still be talking realistically and nonanthropomorphically even though one is ascribing purposes to non-conscious things. Such purposive talk can be tested by trying it in a design and evaluating performance, or by trying to do without some component and observing the consequences. That is, functional role descriptions are empirically testable.

Another way in which design science is different from traditional physical science is that it is pluralistic. From the perspective of traditional science there ought to be one true theory, one way of modeling intelligence, or one true scheme for passing the Turing test. Thinking of AI on the model of a traditional science such as physics, all AI should use either deductive logic or connectionist networks, since only one of these orientations can be the right one. However, from the perspective of design science, such choices are matters of local pragmatic concerns for efficient computation, not abstract theoretical concerns about which is the one true theory about intelligence. Since there can be more than one good way of designing an artifact, there can be more than one "correct" theory. Design science is inherently pluralistic.

Design-science AI is concerned with discovering principles of design, computation, and information processing that generalize over more than just the human case. From this perspective intelligence can be studied directly, without the help of psychology, by studying what works and what does not work, and by designing, building, and experimenting with intelligent arti-facts. Work in cognitive psychology can add to our stock of examples of intelligent information processing, just as other examples from biology can, but so too can our experience with human-made systems.

The AI described in this book is predominantly design-science AI. Al-though human experts are interviewed in order to discover how they think through a problem, the goal is not modeling human thinking as such, but rather understanding how cognitive capacities can arise. The systems de-scribed here should be thought of as examples of complex information-pro-cessing entities about which theories can be made concerning how intelli-gence may be achieved. The core information-processing task being explored in this book is abduction. This is viewed as a task of intelligence that can be performed by both humans and machines. To learn about abduction, empiri-cal research is conducted by designing and building knowledge-based ex-pert systems that employ abductive reasoning. The resulting theory is not merely a logical theory, or a mathematical explanation of abductive infer-ence; it is a practical theory about designs and possible mechanisms of rea-soning. An abductive strategy is built into a program, and, then, when the program is run, we can see whether and how well that strategy performs. Thus the theory of abduction, which is a theory about reasoning processes discovered in humans, is generalized beyond simply a theory about humans to a design theory of abduction itself.

Unlike the thinking of people, which tends to occur in a "black box," and which we cannot directly see or control, with an artifact of our own con-struction we can see and control exactly how the reasoning process works. Potentially, an expert system might be able to reason even better than people, since the reasoning pattern, once put into a machine, can be refined, and experiments can be run to see which strategies work best. Thus, for example, since many abductive systems do diagnosis, people can study how these machines do it and then potentially learn to do diagnosis better.

Summary

AI as engineering uses discovered techniques for solving real-world prob-lems. AI as art explores the imitative possibilities of machines and the depths of the analogy between humans and machines. By doing this, AI as art acts as a focus for attacks against the very project of making artifactual intelli-gences. There are two ways to practice AI as science: One can practice tra-ditional-science AI by making models on a computer of the causal mecha-nisms that underlie human intelligent behavior, or one can practice design-science AI by making computational theories and information-processing systems that can be studied as instances of cognitive agents, thus pursuing the study of cognition and intelligence in the abstract.

To the questions of whether AI is science or engineering, what the role of a program is, and what counts as progress in AI, we have answered that there are four different orientations to AI. AI is engineering, traditional science, art, and design science. Programs play different roles for these different orientations, and progress is different for each orientation. The goal of AI as engineering is to develop technology so that we can be served by intelligent machines in the workplace and in our homes. The goal of AI as traditional science is to supply accurate models of human cognitive behavior, and thus to understand the human by way of computer-based simulations. The goal of AI as art is to make machines that are interesting imitations or caricatures of human mentality so that we can learn and benefit from encountering them. The goal of AI as design science is to discover the design principles that govern the achievement of intellectual functioning, in part by making working systems that can be studied empirically.

The reason that AI seems scattered and disunited with competing paradigms is that there are at least these four fundamentally different orientations to the discipline. Within each of these orientations many legitimate suborientations and specialties can coexist. As long as workers in AI follow the standards that are appropriate for each orientation, this plurality is not something that should be resisted or bemoaned because each approach serves a clear and important function for the whole.

Knowledge-based systems and knowledge representations

The work in our laboratory has concentrated on information-processing strategies useful for building systems for knowledge-rich problem solving, or so-called "expert systems." These systems emphasize the role of large amounts of domain knowledge compiled for specific problem-solving tasks, hence they are also called "knowledge-based systems." The word "knowledge" in "knowledge-based systems" refers to the special domain knowledge that an expert problem solver is postulated to have. The phrase "knowledge-based" in the context of AI systems arose in response to a recognition, mainly in the pioneering work of Edward Feigenbaum and his associates at Stanford in the early to mid-1970s, that much of the power of experts can be viewed as arising from a large number of rule-like pieces of knowledge. These pieces help constrain the problem-solving effort and direct it toward potentially useful intermediate states. These pieces of knowledge are domain specific in the sense that they are not general principles or heuristics that apply in many problem domains, but rather they are stated directly in the form of appropriate actions to try in various situations. An alternative to this position is that the complex problem-solving processes operate on a combination of the basic knowledge that defines the domain together with various forms of general and commonsense knowledge. In fact the underlying premise behind most work on expert systems is that once a body of expertise is built up, expert reasoning can proceed without any need to invoke general world and commonsense knowledge structures. If such a decomposition were not in principle possible, then the development of expert systems would have to wait for solutions to the more difficult problems of how to provide the machine with commonsense reasoning and general world knowledge. While the early appeal of the expert-system concept had something to do with this promise of expert-level performance without a complete, general-purpose knowledge base, later research has indicated that expert systems often behave in a "brittle" manner at the boundaries of their expertise, presumably because they lack the large body of knowledge that human experts possess, and which prevents humans from behaving in ways that go against common sense. What portion of expert problem solving in a given domain can be captured in isolation is an empirical question, but experience shows that a nontrivial portion of expert problem solving in important domains can be captured in this manner. This decoupling of commonsense and general-purpose reasoning from domain expertise is also the explanation for the seemingly paradoxical situation in AI where we have programs that display, for example, expert-like medical diagnostic capabilities, even though we are far from capturing most of the intellectual abilities of small children.

Knowledge representation has been a major concern of AI and of work on knowledge-based systems. The general assumption, and consequently the methodology, has been that there is something called domain knowledge that needs to be acquired – quite independent of the problems one might wish to solve – and that the role of a knowledge representation formalism is to help encode it. Connectionist networks, logics of various kinds, frame representations, and rule-based languages (all of which are discussed later in this chapter) have been popular proposals for families of knowledge representation formalisms. Each formalism has a natural family of inference mechanisms that can operate on it. Each knowledge representation formalism, together with the inference mechanisms that use it, defines an *architecture*. When an architecture is fixed, a "shell" has been specified for inserting knowledge. When, for example, the knowledge representation formalism has been realized in software as abstract data types, and the inference mechanisms as executable code, then the shell is realized as a tool that can be used for building knowledge-based systems.

Most of the architectures proposed in AI are computationally universal, and equivalent to Turing machines, and so they are equal with regard to what they can, in principle, compute. Thus, the important point about using them for building knowledge systems is not whether a task can be performed but whether they offer knowledge and control constructs that are natural and convenient for the task.

Connectionism

One of the major disputes in AI at the present time is between advocates of "connectionism" and advocates of traditional or "symbolic" AI. Given this controversy, it is worth spending a little time examining the differences between these two approaches.

Although connectionism as an AI theory comes in many different forms, most models represent information in the form of weights of connections between simple processing units in a network, and take information-processing activity to consist in the changing of activation levels in the processing units as a result of the activation levels of units to which they are immediately connected. The spreading of activations is modulated by the weights of connections between units. Connectionist theories especially emphasize forms of learning that use continuous functions for adjusting the weights in the network. In some connectionist theories this "pure" form is mixed with symbol manipulation processes (see Smolensky, 1988). The essential characteristic of a connectionist architecture, in contrast with a "symbolic" architecture, is that the connectionist medium has no internal labels that are interpreted, and no abstract forms that are instantiated, during processing. Furthermore, the totality of weighted connections defines the information content, rather than information being represented as a discrete code, as it is in a "symbolic" information processor.

For some information-processing tasks the symbol and non-symbol accounts differ fundamentally in their representational commitments. Consider the problem of multiplying two integers. We are all familiar with algorithms to perform this task. Some of us also still remember how to use the traditional slide rule to do this multiplication: The multiplicands are represented by their logarithms on a linear scale on a sliding bar, they are "added" by being aligned end to end, and the product is obtained by reading the antilogarithm of the sum. Although both the algorithmic and slide rule solutions are representational, in no sense can either of them be thought of as an "implementation" of the other. (Of course the slide rule solution could itself be simulated on a digital computer, but this would not change the fundamental difference in representational commitment in the two solutions.) Logarithms are represented in one case but not in the other, so the two solutions make very different commitments about what is represented. There are also striking differences between the two solutions in practical terms. As the size of the multiplicands increases, the algorithmic solution suffers in the amount of *time* needed to complete the solution, whereas the slide rule solution suffers in the amount of *precision* it can deliver. Given a blackbox multiplier, as two theories of what actually occurs in the box, the algorithmic solution and the slide rule solution make different ontological commitments. The algorithmic solution to the multiplication problem is "symbolic," whereas the slide rule solution is similar to connectionist models in being "analog" computations.

There is not enough space here for an adequate discussion of what makes a symbol in the sense used when we speak of "symbolic" theories (see Pylyshyn [1984] for a thorough and illuminating discussion of this topic). However, the following points seem useful. There is a type-token distinction: Symbols are *types* about which abstract rules of behavior are known and to which these rules can be applied. This leads to symbols being tokens that are "interpreted" during information processing; there are no such interpretations in the process of slide rule multiplication (except for input and output). The symbol system can thus represent *abstract forms*, whereas the slide rule solution performs its addition or multiplication, not by instantiating an abstract form, but by having, in some sense, all the additions and multiplications directly in its architecture. As we can see from this, the representational commitments of the symbolic and nonsymbolic paradigms are different. Thus the connectionists are correct in claiming that connectionism is not simply an implementation of symbolic theories.

However, connectionist and symbolic approaches are actually both realizations of a more abstract level of description, namely, the information-processing level. Marr (1982) originated the method of information-processing analysis as a way of conceptually separating the essential elements of a theory from its implementational commitments. He proposed that the following methodology be adopted for this purpose. First, identify an *information-processing task* with a clear specification about what kind of information is available as input and what kind of information needs to be made available as output. Then, specify a particular *information-processing theory* for achieving this task by specifying what kinds of information need to be represented at various stages in the processing. Actual algorithms and data structures can then be proposed to implement the information-processing theory on some underlying machine. These algorithms and data structures will make additional representational commitments. For example, Marr specified that one task of vision is to take, as input, image intensities in a retinal image, and to produce, as output, a three-dimensional shape description of the objects in the scene. His theory of how this task is accomplished in the visual system is that three distinct kinds of information need to be generated: (1) from the image intensities a "primal sketch" of significant intensity changes – a kind of edge description of the scene – is generated; (2) then a description of surfaces and their orientation, what he called a "21/2-d sketch," is produced from the primal sketch, and (3) finally a 3-d shape description is generated.

Information-processing (IP) level abstractions (input, output, and the kinds of information represented along the way) constitute the top-level content of much AI theory making. The difference between IP theories in the symbolic and connectionist paradigms is that the representations are treated as symbols in the former, which permit abstract rules of compositions to be invoked and instantiated, whereas in the latter, information is represented more directly and affects the processing without undergoing any symbol interpretation process. The decisions about which of the information trans-formations are best done by means of connectionist networks, and which are best done by using symbolic algorithms, can properly follow after the IP level specification of the theory has been given. The hardest work of theory making in AI will always remain at the level of proposing the right IP level abstractions, because they provide the content of the representations by speci-fying the kinds of information to be represented.

For complex tasks, the approaches of the symbolic and nonsymbolic para-digms actually converge in their representational commitments. Simple func-tions such as multiplication are so close to the architecture of the underlying machine that we saw differences between the representational commitments of the algorithmic and the slide rule solutions. In areas such as word recog-nition the problem is sufficiently removed from the architectural level that we can see macrosimilarities between symbolic and connectionist solutions; for example, both solutions may make word recognition dependent on letter recognition. The final performance will have micro-features that are charac-teristic of the architecture (such as "smoothness of response" for connectionist architectures). However, the more complex the task, the more common the representational issues between connectionism and the symbolic paradigm. There is no clear line of demarcation between the architecture-independent theory and the architecture-dependent theory. It is partly an empirical issue and partly depends on what primitive functions can be computed in a par-ticular architecture. The farther away a problem is from the architecture's primitive functions, the more architecture-independent analysis needs to be done.

Certain kinds of retrieval and matching operations, and parameter learn-ing by searching in local regions of a search space, are especially appropri-ate primitive operations for connectionist architectures. (However, although memory retrieval may have interesting connectionist components, the basic problem will still remain the principles by which episodes are indexed and stored.) On the other hand, much high-level thought has symbolic content (see Pylyshyn [1984] for arguments that make this conclusion inescapable). So one can imagine a division of responsibility between connectionist and symbolic architectures along these lines in accounting for the phenomena of intelligence.

Numerical vs. qualitative symbolic representations

When reasoning about complex systems, both human experts and expert sys-tems are necessarily compelled to use high-level, qualitative symbols, whether or not complete numerical models are available. This is because even a complete numerical model of a system will, by itself, typically not be sufficient. All of the numerical values of the various states' variables will still need to be interpreted. Identifying interesting and potentially significant states of a system requires abstraction from the low-level descriptions of variable values to higher-level, qualitative representations. To take a pedagogically effective but fanciful example, consider a household robot watching its master carelessly move his arm toward the edge of a table where a full glass of wine sits. In theory a complete numerical description of the arm and of all the objects in the room, including the volume of wine, is possible. Yet the most detailed numerical simulation will still give values only for a number of state variables. Further reasoning is necessary to interpret this series of values and to arrive at a simple commonsense statement, viz., "The arm will hit the wine glass, and wine will spill on the carpet." The reason why a complete numerical solution is not enough, i.e., why the qualitative conclusion ought to be reached by the robot, is that its own knowledge of available actions is more appropriately indexed by high-level abstractions such as "spilled wine" than by numerical values of state variables describing its environment.

Human experts (as well as expert systems) may, at specific points during their qualitative reasoning, switch to numerical methods. For example, a medical specialist may use formulas or equations to estimate the acid-base balance of a patient, or an engineer may reach for a calculator to check a design constraint, but the numerical analysis is under the overall control of a qualitative, symbolic reasoning system. It is the qualitative knowledge and problem-solving structures that are of central interest to the science and technology of AI.

Logic

In many circles some version of logic is thought to be the proper language for characterizing all computation and, by extension, intelligence. By logic is meant a variant of first-order predicate calculus, or at least a system where the notion of truth-based semantics is central and inference making is characterized by truth-preserving transformations. (Within AI, nonmonotonic logic and default logics relax the truth-preserving requirement. The thrust of the arguments here nevertheless remain valid.) The architecture of systems using logical formalism for knowledge representation generally consists of a knowledge base of logical formulas and an inference mechanism that uses the formulas to derive conclusions.

A number of theoretical advantages have been claimed for logic in AI, including precision and the existence of a well-defined semantics. In tasks where the inference chains are relatively shallow – where the discovery of the solution does not involve search in a large search space – the logic representation may be useful. Also, in logic-based systems it is possible to create a subtasking structure (when the structure of a task allows it) that can help to keep the complexity of inference low. In practical terms, however, the existence of a rigorous semantics is not typically helpful since precision is rarely the point. If one were to model, say, reasoning in arithmetic, one could represent domain knowledge in the form of axioms and use a variety of inference processes to derive new theorems. However, the computational complexity of such systems would tend to be impractical – even for relatively simple axiomatic systems – without the use of some clever (and extra-logical) "steerer" to guide the path of inference. Thus, even in domains where powerful axiom systems exist, the problem of capturing the effectiveness of human reasoning remains.

Logic as knowledge representation makes a serious commitment to knowledge as propositions and to True/False judgments as the basic *use* of knowledge. It is also closely connected to the belief that the aim of intelligence is to draw correct conclusions. In this view, what human beings often do (e.g., draw plausible, useful, but strictly speaking logically incorrect conclusions) is interesting as psychology, but shows humans only as approximations to the ideal intelligent agent, whose aim is to be correct. Since at least the late 19th century, logical reasoning has been viewed as the real test of thought. Witness the title of Boole's book, *An Investigation of the Laws of Thought on Which are Founded the Mathematical Theory of Logic and Probabilities* (1854). This has led to the almost unconscious equating of thought, with logical thought, and the attempt to seek in logic the language for representing and constructing the idealized agent. From this perspective the content of consciousness includes a series of propositions, some of them beliefs. For a certain kind of theorist, it seems entirely natural to model thought itself as basically the manipulation of propositions and the generation of new ones. From this view of thought, stream-of-consciousness imaginings, half-formed ideas, remindings, vague sensations, ideas suddenly coming to occupy consciousness from the depths of the mind, and so forth do not count as serious subjects for the study of intelligence as such.

Is "strict truth" the right kind of interpretive framework for knowledge? Or are notions of functional adequacy (i.e., knowledge that helps to get certain kinds of tasks done) or the related notions of plausibility, relevance, likelihood, close-enough, and so forth, more relevant to capturing the way agents actually use knowledge intelligently? My (Chandra's) 16-month-old daughter, when shown a pear, said, "Apple!" Surely more than parental pride makes me attribute a certain measure of intelligence to that remark, which, when viewed strictly in terms of propositions, was untrue. After all, her conclusion was more than adequate for the occasion – she could eat the pear and get nourishment – whereas an equally false proposition, "It's a chair," would not give her similar advantages. Thus, viewing propositions in terms of context-independent truth and falsity does not make all the distinctions we need, as in this case between a false useful categorization and a false useless one.

Some in the logic tradition say that before building, say, commonsense reasoners, we should get all the ontology of commonsense reasoning right. We should first analyze what words such as: "know," "cause," and so forth really mean before building a system. We should axiomatize commonsense reality. But a use-independent analysis of knowledge is likely to make distinctions that are not needed for processing and is likely to miss many that are. The logic tradition *separates knowledge from its functions*, and this leads to missing important aspects of the form and content of the knowledge that needs to be represented.

Furthermore, laws of justification are not identical to laws of thought, Boole notwithstanding. Logic gives us laws for justifying the truth of conclusions rather than laws for arriving at conclusions. For example, although we might justify our answer to a multiplication problem by using modus ponens on Peano's axioms, how many of us actually multiply numbers by using modus ponens on Peano's axioms, and how efficient would that be? While it might be useful for an intelligent agent to have the laws of logic, and to apply them appropriately, those laws alone cannot account for the power of intelligence as a process.

This is not to say that logic as a set of ideas about justification is not important for understanding intelligence. How intelligent agents generate justifications, how they integrate them with discovery processes for a final answer that is plausibly correct, and how the total computational process is controlled in complexity are indeed questions for AI as an information-processing theory of intelligence. It seems highly plausible that much of the power of intelligence arises, not from its ability to lead to correct conclusions, but from its ability to direct explorations, retrieve plausible ideas, and focus the more computationally expensive justification processes to where they are actually required.

To see biological intelligence as merely an approximate attempt to achieve logical correctness is to miss the functioning of intelligence completely. Of course there are processes that over long periods of time, and collectively over humankind, help to produce internal representations with increasingly higher fidelity; but that is just one part of being intelligent, and in any case such processes are themselves bounded by constraints of computational feasibility. Once highly plausible candidates for hypotheses about the world are put together by such processes (as abductive processes might be used in producing an explanation in science), then explicit justification processes can be used to anchor them in place.

To the extent that one believes that intelligence is at base a computational process, and to the extent that logic is a preferred language for the semantics of computer programs, logic will play a role in describing the meaning of computer programs that embody theories of intelligence. This brings logic into computational AI in a fairly basic way. Yet it is possible to be misled by this role for logic. To make an analogy, architectural ideas are realized using bricks, steel, wood, and other building materials, while classical statics and mechanics describe the behavior of these materials under forces of various kinds. Even though statics and mechanics belong to the language of civil engineering analysis, they are not the language of architecture as an intellectual discipline. Architecture uses a language of habitable spaces.

While resisting the idea of intelligence as a logic machine, I have often been impressed by the clarity that the use of logic has sometimes brought to issues in AI. Quite independently of one's theory of mind, one needs a language in which to describe the objects of thought, i.e., parts of the world. Logic has been a pretty strong contender for this job, though not without controversy. Wittgenstein is said to have changed his views radically about the use of logic for this purpose. Nevertheless, logic has played this role for many researchers in AI who are looking for a formalism in which to be precise about the knowledge of the world being attributed to an agent. For example Newell (1982) proposes a "knowledge level" where logic is used to describe what an agent knows, without any implied commitment to the use of logical representations for internal manipulation by the agent.[1]

Organizing knowledge: Frames

The knowledge representation approach in AI that first emphasized organization in the form of structured units was that of *frames*. Minsky's paper on frames (Minsky, 1975) argued against the "atomic" stance about knowledge taken by logic-based AI theories, and claimed that chunking of knowledge into larger scale frames had a number of useful properties. Three of these are described next. First, frames are especially useful in organizing a problem solver's "what" knowledge (e.g., knowledge about classes of objects) in such a way that efficiency in storage and inference can be maintained. Basically, because a frame of a concept is a structured stereotype, much of the knowledge can be stored as defaults, and only specific information corresponding to differences from the default value needs to be explicitly stored. For example, because the default value of the number of walls for a room is four, a system's knowledge about a particular room does not have to represent this explicitly, unless it is an exception.

A second useful property of organizing knowledge of objects in the form of frame structures is that one can create type-subtype hierarchies and let much of the knowledge about particular objects be "inherited" from information stored at the class and subclass levels. This again makes for great economy of storage. For instance, the *purpose* attributes of a bedroom and a living room may be different, but the parts that are common to them (e.g., typically all rooms have four walls, a ceiling, etc.) can be stored at the level of the *room* frame, and inherited as needed at the *bedroom* or *living room* level.

A third property that makes frame structures very useful in knowledge systems is the possibility of embedding procedures in the frames so that specialized inferences can be performed as appropriate for the conceptual context. This is a move away from architectures, like those typically used in the logic tradition, in which the inference mechanisms are divorced from the knowledge base.

Because of these three properties – defaults, type-subtype hierarchies, and attached procedures – frame systems are very useful for capturing one broad class of problem-solving activity, viz., where the basic task can be formulated as one of *making inferences about objects by using knowledge about more general classes to which the objects belong and by using knowledge of related objects represented elsewhere in the structure.* A whole style of programming, called "object-oriented" programming, has arisen which has a close conceptual kinship with the notion of frames.

Organizing knowledge: Scripts and plans

Roger Schank has been associated with a view in which the essence of intelligence is seen, not in normative inference (the notion that intelligence is explained by the possession of rules of correct inference applied to bodies of knowledge in a goal-directed way) but in how memory (i.e., knowledge) is organized (Schank, 1986; Schank & Abelson, 1977). The claim is that intelligence arises largely because memory holds knowledge in the form of organized chunks corresponding to scripts, goals, plans, and various other higher level packages. The theory of memory proposed by Schank is a version of the frame theory, but it proposes that there are specific types of frames that hold specific important kinds of information. Thus Schank's theory is a *content theory* of frames, making assertions about what kinds of information are held and organized by the frames. For example, Schank proposes that a generic type of frame is the *script*, a frame that holds a stereotypical representation of the temporal sequence of events in a generic episode such as visiting a restaurant. Whenever the agent is in a situation involving visiting restaurants (actually visiting a restaurant or hearing a story about someone visiting one), the restaurant script is retrieved and a number of default expectations that are encoded in the script are set up. These expectations can short-circuit the need for elaborate inferences that would otherwise be needed, and they can be used to predict what will happen and help to decide what actions to take. These expectations may be violated, in which case memory again helps with other scripts or chunks of knowledge that are indexed by the types of violations. Some of the expectations and knowledge about how to handle violations are encoded in other specialized types of chunks, such as *plans* and *themes*.

Schank's view makes explicit commitments about important issues in the study of intelligence. The role of deliberate and complex "rational" problem solving is minimized; most cognitive behavior is driven by templates such as scripts and so on. Any rationality in behavior is emergent, the result of there being knowledge of the right kinds embedded in these structures, rather than the result of explicit application of normative rules. To account for the presence and organization of knowledge of these kinds, the theory must be concerned with learning. A major concern of research in this tradition is how individual experiences are abstracted into various kinds of knowledge structures.

Our view shares some essential points with Schank's approach, but it also deviates from Schank's in some ways. We agree that organization of knowledge is important so that almost always appropriate and useful knowledge is retrieved to suit the situation and the agent's purposes. Much of the power of intelligence is a result of clever organization of the "filing system of the mind." However, because of our concern with problem solving, we have a number of differences in emphasis. First, although we agree that problem solving depends strongly on retrieval of relevant knowledge, we think that deliberative processes, and sometimes explicit application of normative concerns, are important. In particular, a certain amount of deliberative search is needed to explore options, combine them, evaluate them, and select those that are most satisfactory. Second, we think that much problem-solving knowledge is abstract (i.e., not closely tied to specific episodes) and when this kind of knowledge is available, it is typically the most efficient kind to use in solving technical problems, or even everyday problems of nontrivial complexity. Related to the second point is the belief that we need a good theory of how knowledge is indexed (both knowledge of facts and of strategies) by the kinds of tasks that we face. Thus, we claim that much of our problem-solving knowledge is task specific and method specific, and, complementary to Schank's concern with the organization of memory, we believe that we need a theory of tasks and their relationships to kinds of knowledge. (This is the subject of the final section of this chapter on Generic Tasks.)

Rule-based systems

The dominant knowledge-representation formalism in the first generation of expert systems was rules. The rule-based expert-system approach is that of collecting from the human experts a large number of rules describing activities in each domain, and constructing a knowledge base that encodes these rules. It is usually assumed as part of the rule paradigm that the rule-using (i.e., reasoning) machinery is not the main source of problem-solving power but that the power came from the knowledge.

Like the logic-based architectures, the rule-based architectures separate the knowledge base from the inference mechanisms that use the knowledge. Furthermore, logic-based and rule-based architectures are unitary architectures; that is, they have only one level. In standard rule-based systems, because the problem solver (or "inference engine," as it has come to be called) is free of knowledge, controlling the problem-solving process typically requires placing rules for control purposes in the knowledge base itself.

Such a rule-based architecture can work well when relatively little complex coupling between rules exists in solving problems, or when the rules can be implicitly separated into groups with relatively little interaction among rules in different groups. In general, however, when the global reasoning requirements of the task cannot be conceptualized as a series of local decisions, rule-based systems with this one-level architecture have significant "focus of attention" problems. That is, because the problem solver does not have a notion of reasoning goals at different levels of abstraction, maintaining coherent lines of thought is often difficult to achieve. The need for control knowledge in addition to domain knowledge is a lesson that can be applied to any unitary architecture.

Another problem that arises in unitary rule-based architectures is that, when the knowledge base is large, a large number of rules may match in a given situation, with conflicting actions proposed by each rule. The processor must choose one rule and pursue the consequences. This choice among rules is called "conflict resolution," and a family of essentially syntactic conflict resolution strategies has been proposed to accomplish it, such as "choose the rule that has more left-hand side terms matching" or ". . . has more goals on the right-hand side" or ". . . has a higher certainty factor." Conflicts of this type, I claim, are artifacts of the architecture. If the architecture were multileveled, higher organizational levels would impose constraints on knowledge-base activation so that there would be no need for syntactic conflict resolution strategies. In general, for a system to be able to focus, multiple levels of reasoning contexts, goals, and plans must be maintained.

These points apply not just to rule architectures, but to unitary architectures in general. Retrieval theories based on semantic networks (where concepts are represented as nodes and relationships between them as links) tend to explain memory retrieval by proposing that it is based on distances measured in the number of links, rather than on the types of links and the knowledge embedded in the nodes and links. These unitary architectures encourage theory making at the wrong level of abstraction. Because they are unitary architectures, they necessarily omit important higher level information-processing distinctions that are needed to give an adequate functional description of intelligence, and that may in turn require architectural support of their own. A well-known proponent of rule-based architectures once said, "Common sense is just millions and millions of rules." One might well respond, "Yes, and *War and Peace* is just thousands and thousands of sentences."

It is true that unitary architectures have been used to build impressive systems that perform tasks requiring intelligence. However, because these architectures are Turing universal (i.e., any algorithm can be implemented as a program for such an architecture), it is often hard to know if the architecture per se makes a significant contribution. It may merely provide a convenient means of implementation. The architecture, per se, does not distinguish tractable solutions from those that are intractable; it does not identify good versus bad ways of organizing knowledge.

Next we discuss how alternative architectures can be conceived that better focus and control the processes of problem solving. These architectures will begin to erase the separation of the knowledge base from the inference machinery. The intuition behind the separation of knowledge and inference is that knowledge may be used in multiple ways; however, we have contended for many years that separating knowledge from its use obscures the role of knowledge in problem solving (Gomez and Chandrasekaran, 1981). Our generic-task approach suggests an alternative point of view: that knowledge representation should closely follow knowledge use, and that different organizations of knowledge are appropriate for different types of problem-solving activity.

Generic tasks

In our work on knowledge-based reasoning, we have proposed a number of information-processing strategies, each characterized by knowledge represented using strategy-specific primitives and organized in a specific manner. Each strategy employs a characteristic inference procedure that is appropriate to the task. Let us look at the computationally complex problem of diagnosis to see how this approach contrasts with the other approaches just discussed.

Diagnostic reasoning

Formally, the diagnostic problem might be defined as a mapping from the set of all subsets of observations of a system to the set of all subsets of possible malfunctions, such that each malfunction subset is a best explanation for the corresponding observation subset. A mathematician's interest in the problem might be satisfied when it is shown that under certain assumptions this task is *computable* (i.e., an algorithm – such as the set-covering algorithm of Reggia [1983] – exists to perform this mapping). A mathematician might also want to derive the computational complexity of this task for various assumptions about the domain and the range of this mapping.

A logician in AI would consider the solution epistemically complete if he or she can provide a formalism to list the relevant domain knowledge and can formulate the decision problem as one of deducing a correct conclusion. Some diagnostic formalisms view the diagnostic problem as one more version of truth-maintenance activity (Reiter, 1987).

Now, each of these methods is computationally complex, and without extensive addition of heuristic knowledge, a problem cannot ordinarily be solved in anything resembling real time. It is clear, however, that the abstract problem of *how to go from observable states of the world to their explanations* faces intelligent agents on a regular basis. From the tribesman on a hunt who needs to construct an explanation for tracks in the mud to a scientist constructing theories, this basic problem recurs in many forms. Of course, not all versions of the problem are solved by humans, but many versions, such as medical diagnosis, are solved routinely. Chapter 1 discusses how diagnosis is fundamentally an abductive problem.

Because of our concern with the structure of intelligence, let us ask the following question: *What is an intelligence that it can perform this task?* That is, we are interested in the relationships between mental structures and the performance of the diagnostic task, not simply in the diagnostic task itself. The distinction can be clarified by considering multiplication. Multiplication viewed as a computational task has been sufficiently studied so that fast and efficient algorithms are available and are routinely used by today's computers. On the other hand, if we ask, "How does a person actually perform multiplication in the head?" the answer is different from the multiplication algorithms just mentioned. Similarly, the answer to how diagnosis is done needs to be given in terms of how the particular problem is solved by using more generic mental structures. Depending upon one's theory of what those mental structures are, the answer will differ.

We have already indicated the kinds of answers that unitary architectures would foster about how diagnosis is done. In rule-based architectures the problem solver simply needs to have enough rules about malfunctions and observations; in frame-based architectures diagnostic knowledge is represented as frames for domain concepts such as malfunctions; connectionist architectures represent diagnostic knowledge by strengths of connections that make activation pathways from nodes representing observations to nodes representing malfunctions. The inference methods that are applicable to each are fixed at the level of the architecture: some form of forward or backward chaining for rule systems, some form of inheritance mechanisms and embedded procedures for frame systems, and spreading activations for connectionist networks. The first generation of knowledge-based systems languages – those based on rules, frames, or logic – did not distinguish between different types of knowledge-based reasoning.

Intuitively, one thinks that there are types of knowledge and control that are common to diagnostic reasoning in different domains, and, similarly, that there are common structures and strategies for design as a cognitive activity, but that the structures and control strategies for diagnostic reasoning and design problem solving are somehow different. However, when one looks at the formalisms (or equivalently the languages) that are commonly used for building expert systems, the knowledge representation and control strategies usually do not capture these intuitive distinctions. For example, in diagnostic reasoning one might generically want to speak in terms of malfunction hierarchies, rule-out strategies, setting up a differential, and so forth, whereas for design problem solving the generic terms might be device – component hierarchies, design plans, functional requirements, and the like.

Ideally one would like to represent knowledge by using the vocabulary that is appropriate for the task, but the languages in which expert systems have typically been implemented have sought uniformity across tasks and thus have lost perspicuity of representation at the task level. For example, one would expect that the task of designing a car would require significantly different reasoning strategies than the task of diagnosing a malfunction in a car. However, rule-based systems apply the same reasoning strategy ("fire" the rules whose conditions match, etc.) to design and diagnosis, as well as to any other task. Unitary-architecture methodologies suppress what is distinctive about tasks such as diagnosis in favor of task-independent information-processing strategies. In addition, the control strategies that come with these methodologies do not explicitly show the real control structure of the task that a problem solver is performing. Thus these methodologies, although useful, are rather low-level with respect to modeling the needed task-level behavior. In essence, their languages resemble low-level assembly languages for writing knowledge-based systems. Although they are obviously useful, approaches that more directly address the higher level issues of knowledge-based reasoning are clearly needed.

Some elementary generic tasks for diagnosis

Intelligent agents commonly face similar computational problems, and the strategies that they adopt to solve these problems have an essential similarity. They all use plans, indexed by goals, as efficient means of synthesizing actions; they all use classification to match actions to classes of world states; and so on. The task of AI as the science of intelligence is to identify these various information-processing strategies concretely and to understand how they integrate into coherent wholes. In a sense this approach can be called "abstract psychology" because it does not discuss a particular human being or even the class of human beings. What it says is that the description of cognitive strategies provides a language in which to describe intelligent agents. Also, I think, this approach is consistent with the view of intelligence as a biological, evolvable collection of coherent kludges that work together. Intelligence is not defined as one thing—architecture or function—it is a collection of strategies. The fact that the strategies all contribute to computational feasibility is one thing that distinguishes them as a characterizable class of information processes.

The motivation in our work on diagnosis is to make a connection between diagnostic problem solving and the general properties of intelligence as a repertoire of information-processing strategies. Let us view diagnostic problem solving as a task in which the goal is to explain a set of observations of a system. The explanation is to be in terms of malfunctions that may have caused the observations. Because the malfunctions can interact in a number of ways, the problem solver has to produce a set of malfunction hypotheses that explain all the data without including unnecessary hypotheses, and it must take into account possible interactions between hypotheses.

These goals can be accomplished by decomposing the problem solving into several distinct, smaller problem-solving units, which we call *generic tasks*. At each stage in reasoning, a problem solver engages in one of these tasks, depending on the knowledge available and the state of the problem-solving activity. Each generic task is characterized by the following:

1. The kinds of information used as input for the task and the information produced as a result of performing the task. This defines the functionality of the task in terms of input and output.
2. A way to represent and organize the knowledge that is needed to perform the task. This includes a vocabulary of knowledge types, knowledge constructs that a representation language should have.
3. The process control (inference control, control of problem solving) that the task uses.

Many tasks that we intuitively think of as generic tasks are actually *complex generic tasks*. That is, they are further decomposable into components that are more elementary in the sense that each such component has a more homogeneous control regime and knowledge structure. The diagnostic task is a task of this sort. Although it may be generic in being similar across domains, diagnosis does not have a unitary task structure. Instead, it may involve classificatory reasoning at a certain point, data-abstraction reasoning at another point, and abductive assembly of multiple hypotheses at yet another point. Classificatory reasoning has a different form of knowledge and a different control behavior from those for data-abstraction reasoning, which in turn is dissimilar in these dimensions to hypothesis assembly. Similar arguments apply with even greater force to generic problem areas such as process control. Thus diagnosis, design, process control, and so forth, are compound processes, whereas the tasks that compose them are more atomic. We call these more atomic tasks, which are the building blocks of the more complex tasks, *elementary generic tasks*.

Through the years we have identified several elementary generic tasks for decomposing complex problems. By decomposing problems into collections of elementary generic tasks, the original intractable problem is converted, by the use of a series of information-processing strategies and by appropriate types of knowledge and control into a tractable problem. In the following chapters we discuss in detail the architectures of several abductive diagnostic systems that use combinations of elementary generic tasks. Note that besides the generic tasks described next for diagnosis, we have also discovered generic tasks for routine design and planning (Brown & Chandrasekaran, 1989).

In diagnosis, the elementary generic tasks into which many diagnostic problems can be decomposed are the following: hierarchical classification, hypothesis matching, knowledge-directed data retrieval, and abductive assembly of hypotheses. (See Figure 2.1.)

Hierarchical classification. A hierarchical classifier can be used to select a small set of plausible malfunctions. The task of hierarchical classification is that of mapping a set of observations into one or more tip nodes of a classification hierarchy so that each node has some plausibility or likelihood given the observations.

Each node of the classification hierarchy is identified with a "concept." The diagnostic knowledge is then distributed through the conceptual nodes of the hierarchy with more general malfunction concepts higher in the structure and more specific ones lower. (See Figure 2.2.) The problem-solving activity for hierarchical classification is performed top down, i.e., the topmost concept first gets control of the case, then control passes to an appropriate lower level successor concept, and so on downward.

Knowledge of type–subtype links and knowledge relating observations to hypotheses are needed to perform the task. The concepts in the hierarchy can be represented by active agents, not merely by static collections of knowledge. Because each such agent contains knowledge about establishing or rejecting only one particular conceptual entity, it may be termed a *specialist*, in particular, a *classification specialist*. One can view the inference machinery as being embedded directly in each specialist. That is, each classification specialist has how-to knowledge, for example, in the form of two clusters of rules: confirmatory rules and exclusionary rules. The evidence for confirmation and exclusion is suitably weighted and combined to arrive at a conclusion to establish, reject, or suspend judgment of the concept. This last situation arises if data are not sufficient to make even a tentative decision. When a concept rules itself out as being unlikely or irrelevant to a case, all its successors (subtypes) are also ruled out, so large portions of the classification structure are never exercised. On the other hand, when a concept is invoked, a small, highly relevant collection of establish-reject knowledge comes into play.

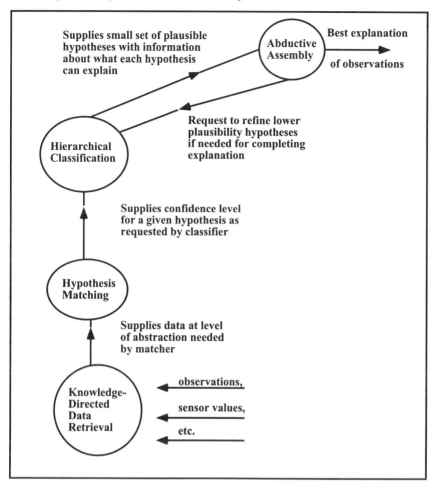

Figure 2.1. Generic-task architecture for diagnosis with compiled knowledge.

The entire collection of specialists engages in distributed problem solving. The control regime that is implicit in the structure can be characterized as an *establish-refine* type. That is, each concept specialist first tries to establish or reject itself (i.e., its concept). If it establishes itself, the refinement process consists of determining which of its successors can establish themselves. The way in which each specialist attempts to establish or reject itself will vary somewhat from domain to domain. In medicine establish-reject reasoning might be accomplished by using active knowledge, some of which look for evidence for the hypothesis, some of which look for counterevidence, and some that carry information about how to combine for a conclusion. For electrical circuits it may be more appropriate to represent the establish-reject activity in the form of functional knowledge about spe-

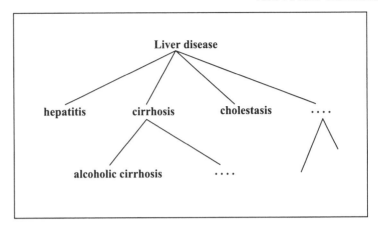

Figure 2.2. Liver disease classification hierarchy.

cific modules of a device. (That is, performance of a generic task may require the solution of some problem of a different type as a subtask.) The points to note here are that (1) the inference engine and the forms of knowledge are tuned for the classificatory task and (2) the control transfer is not necessarily centralized.

Hierarchical classification as an information-processing strategy is ubiquitous in human reasoning. How classification hierarchies are created – from examples, from other types of knowledge structures, and so forth – requires an additional set of answers. We have discussed elsewhere (Sembugamoorthy & Chandrasekaran, 1986) how knowledge of the relationships between structure and the functions of components of a device can be used to derive malfunction hierarchies.

Hypothesis matching. In the classification process, domain knowledge is required to establish or reject each of the classification concepts in the hierarchy. What is needed is a way of deciding how well a concept fits a set of situation-specific data. This function can be accomplished by using the generic strategy that we call "hypothesis matching." Each concept in the classification process is evaluated by appealing to the appropriate concept-matching structures that map from relevant data to a symbolic confidence value for that particular concept hypothesis. This matching process is independent of its application for classification and has a generic character of its own. It could be used just as readily by a planner to select from alternative plans: The features of the problem are the data, and a measure of the appropriateness of a plan is the result of the matching process.

To set up the knowledge for hypothesis matching, we can build up a hierarchy of abstractions from data to hypothesis (a hierarchy of evidence abstraction distinct from the classification hierarchy). For example, given the concept "liver disease," one way to decide the degree of fit with the data is first to see how the data match certain intermediate abstractions. Some of these might be "chemical test evidence for liver disease," "physical evidence," and "patient-history evidence." Evaluating each abstraction requires examining only a subset of the data applicable to liver disease as a whole. The applicability of each abstraction can be computed by hypothesis matching, and the value passed to the next level for further matching. Thus, overall, hypothesis matching works by mapping patterns of situation features to confidence values (or applicability values), where each situation feature may itself be computed by hypothesis matching.

Knowledge-directed data retrieval. A hypothesis matcher requires values for specific data items, and this is the function of knowledge-directed data retrieval. In the previous example, data relevant to a decision about "patient-history evidence" may be "evidence of exposure to anesthetics?" or "fever responds to drugs?" Relevant to the first question, the patient data base might contain the information that the patient underwent major surgery a few days earlier. For the latter question the data base might contain complete information about the patient's prescriptions and temperatures. In either case the information needed for hypothesis matching can be obtained by making appropriate inferences using domain knowledge (about the relationship between anesthetics and surgery for the one case and about the time course of body temperature after drug administration for the other). Thus, an inferencing data base containing case-independent domain knowledge is needed to make the necessary interpretations from raw data.

For a data concept such as anesthetics, the domain knowledge, such as default values for attributes, strategies for inferring them if they are not directly available, and so forth, can be stored with the concept, and the concepts can be organized according to their relationships. Briefly, this sets up a form of reasoning in which accessing a concept also accesses stored information about how the value of various attributes can be obtained, either directly retrieved from raw data or indirectly inferred. For example, to respond to the query "evidence of exposure to anesthetics?" a concept specialist for "anesthetics" may examine its portion of the patient data and find nothing directly recorded in it, so it will then access knowledge in the following way: (1) check if particular types of anesthetics were administered and if so answer "yes"; (2) check if any major surgery was performed and if so answer "yes"; (3) if the answer is "no" by both of the first two inferences, default to the answer "no." In a particular case the "anesthetics" specialist may find no record of various specific anesthetics and will then call on a "surgery" specialist, which will have its own knowledge in the form "check various kinds of surgeries," and eventually it will infer that major surgery was performed. The anesthetics specialist can then infer that there is evidence that the patient had been exposed to anesthetics. Mittal (1980) has worked out a partial theory of organization of such data bases and has resolved issues of temporal reasoning of certain types.

Abductive assembly. For diagnosis, the classification process generates a small number of plausible hypotheses each with a confidence value, and each explaining a specific subset of the case data. That is, certain concepts from the classification hierarchy have "established" themselves with likelihood values above some preset minimum plausibility, and additional processing determines the explanatory coverage for each of these hypotheses.

Although doing a complete abduction is a complex generic task, abductive assembly may be considered to be elementary. An abductive-assembly strategy, using knowledge about interaction among hypotheses, is used to assemble a subset of hypotheses into a composite hypothesis that best explains the data. For this to be accomplished, knowledge about the causal or logical relations among hypotheses is needed that might suggest higher or lower co-occurrence likelihoods; knowledge of general principles such as Occam's razor is also necessary. This task might use a goal-seeking control strategy, where each stage of the processing is driven by the goal of explaining the most significant unexplained datum. The control strategy specifies how hypotheses are assembled; how alternatives are evaluated; and how causal relations, hypothesis plausibilities, and degrees of explanatory power are balanced. We discuss strategies for this elementary generic task in much more detail in later chapters.

Summary. Overall problem solving for diagnosis can thus be traced as follows: The hierarchical classifier's problem-solving activity proceeds top down, and for each concept that is considered, a hypothesis matcher for that concept is invoked to determine the degree of fit with the data. The hypothesis matcher turns to the inferencing data base for information about the data items in which it is interested. The data base completes its reasoning and passes on the needed information to the hypothesis matcher. After acquiring all the needed information from the data base, the hypothesis matcher completes its matching activity for the concept and returns the value for the match to the classifier, along with the data that the concept hypothesis can explain. The classifier's activity now proceeds according to its control strategy: It either rules out the concept, or establishes it and pursues the more detailed successors (or suspends judgment, but we will not discuss that here). This process, whereby each specialist consults other specialists that can provide the information needed to perform its own task, is repeated until the classifier concludes with a number of high-plausibility hypotheses, together with information about what each can explain. At this point the abductive assembler takes control and constructs a composite explanatory hypothesis for the problem. As we shall see in following chapters, the present discussion omits many subtleties in the strategies of each of the problem solvers.

Each of these generic processes is a possible information-processing strategy in the service of a number of different tasks. Classification plays a role whenever one can make use of the computational advantages inherent in indexing actions by classes of world states. Hypothesis matching is useful whenever the appropriateness of a concept to a situation needs to be determined. Abductive assembly is useful whenever an explanation needs to be constructed and a small number of possibly competing, possibly co-occurring explanatory hypotheses are available. Each strategy can be used only if knowledge in the appropriate form is available. These elementary generic tasks can also be used in complex problem-solving situations other than diagnosis, such as designing and planning.

Under the proper conditions of knowledge availability, each of these generic strategies is computationally tractable. In hierarchical classification, entire subtrees can be pruned if a node is rejected. The mapping from data to concept can be achieved if hierarchical abstractions make hypothesis matching computationally efficient. Abductive assembly can be computationally expensive (as described in later chapters), but if another process can initially prune the candidates and generate only a few hypotheses, then this pruning can help to keep the computational demands of hypothesis assembly under control. Hierarchical classification accomplishes this pruning in the design for diagnosis just described.

The generic-task approach

The functional orientation advocated here makes possible a new approach to mental architectures that are nonunitary. We have described how intelligence can be conceived as a cooperative community of specialists, each of which specializes in a particular task, and where each has the appropriate knowledge and control strategy to do its job. The specialists occur in types (hierarchical classification specialists, hypothesis-matching specialists, etc.). Our work on problem solving has often been implemented using precisely this type of nonunitary architecture. Note that this approach does not exclude implementing the whole set of cooperative, heterogeneous problem solvers on a lower level unitary architecture, such as a rule architecture or an object-oriented programming system. We merely point out the importance of not being driven by the unitary-architecture notion at the task level, for all the reasons discussed earlier. That is, one could implement each of the previously described strategies in, say, a rule-based language or a frame-based language, but this level of implementation is completely separate from the task description. There is no mention of metarules or frame hierarchies in the strategy descriptions. To describe the strategies by using the language of rules, logic, or frames would be to describe them at the wrong level of abstraction.

Functional modularity is an important consequence of the generic-task point of view. This functional modularity makes system building and debugging easier, and the task-specific knowledge and control constructs help in knowledge acquisition and explanation. The generic-task framework proposes that, as each task and its associated forms of knowledge and control strategies are identified, languages be developed that allow easy specification of control and easy specification of knowledge of the appropriate types. Each language provides primitives to encode the knowledge needed for the particular generic strategy. In my view these primitives constitute part of the vocabulary of the language of thought. That is, the generic-task idea has strong implications for knowledge representation and suggests a view of what mentalese, the language of thought, might be.

Our group at LAIR has identified a number of generic tasks and has developed associated software tools (Chandrasekaran, 1986): For the generic task of hierarchical classification, the tool CSRL (conceptual structures representation language) was developed (Bylander & Mittal, 1986). For the task of hypothesis matching, the tool HYPER (hypothesis matcher) was developed. For the task of knowledge-directed data retrieval, IDABLE (intelligent data base language and environment) was developed. For the task of noncreative design using the integration of simple plans into an overall design, the strategy of plan selection and refinement was identified, and the tool DSPL (design specialists and plans language) was developed (Brown, 1984). For the task of abductive hypothesis assembly, the tool PEIRCE was developed (Punch, Tanner, & Josephson, 1986). (PEIRCE is described in detail in Chapter 4.)

What ultimately characterizes the generic-task approach is not the proposals for specific generic tasks, which will undoubtedly evolve empirically, but a commitment to the view that knowledge and its use need to be specified together in knowledge representation. Because how knowledge is used depends on the form in which knowledge appears, the enterprise of knowledge representation is one of developing vocabularies simultaneously for the expression and use of knowledge. The set of languages in which the generic information-processing units encode their knowledge, and communicate their information needs and solutions, collectively defines the language of thought. These languages, when implemented in a computer, facilitate knowledge-based system development by giving the knowledge engineer access to tools that work closer to the level of the problem, rather than a lower level implementation language. Complex problems are decomposed into a number of elementary generic tasks. These tasks are supported by specialized software tools that are used to construct systems that use multiple types of reasoning to solve a problem.

When we identify task-level architectures as the issue for highest leverage, a number of immediate questions arise: What is the criterion by which a task is deemed to be not only generic, but also appropriate for modularization as an architecture? What about an architecture for the generic task of "investment decision"? Diagnosis? Diagnosis or process control? Is uncertainty management a task for which it will be useful to have an architecture? Will we proliferate a chaos of architectures without any hope of reuse? What are the possible relationships among these architectures? Which architectures can be built from other architectures?

We do not propose to answer all these questions here, but they seem to be the appropriate kinds of questions to ask when one moves away from the false comfort of universal architectures and begins to work with different architectures for different kinds of problems. We can say that something is an elementary generic task if the information-processing task has a knowledge-level description (has an input–output description in epistemic, or knowledge-use, vocabulary) and has one or more feasible strategies for accomplishing it (often enough, well enough). Also, for something to be an elementary generic task, one must be able to describe the forms that the knowledge takes, and, especially, one needs to describe how processing can be controlled to make it feasible (e.g., no combinatorial explosion).

At this stage in the development of these ideas the best policy is empirical investigation of different proposals from the viewpoint of usefulness, computational tractability, and composability. Our driving goal in the development of generic-task theory has been to produce a methodology and a technology that aids in the analysis, design, construction, and debugging of practical knowledge-based systems. Consequently, we have concentrated on the generic tasks that we believed would be most useful at this stage in the development of the technology. From a practical viewpoint, any architecture that has a useful function and for which one can identify knowledge primitives and an inference method should be considered a valid candidate for experimentation. The generic tasks that are represented in our set of tools were chosen specifically to be useful as technology for building diagnostic, planning, and design systems with compiled expertise. For capturing intelligent problem-solving activity in general, we will undoubtedly require many more such elementary strategies, along with ways of integrating them. For example, the problem-solving activities in qualitative reasoning and device understanding – for example, qualitative simulation (Sticklen, 1987; Keuneke, 1989); consolidation, that is, determining the potential behavior of a system from a description of its parts (Bylander, 1986; Bylander & Chandrasekaran, 1985) (see chapter 5); and functional representation (Sembugamoorthy & Chandrasekaran, 1986) – all have well-defined information-processing functions, specific knowledge-representation primitives, and inference methods. Thus there are many candidates for generic information-processing modules in the sense that we described.

As a theory, the generic-task idea requires more work. It needs to provide a coherent story about how the tasks come together, how they are integrated, how complex tasks come about from more elementary tasks, and how learning shapes these functional modules.

The view of generic tasks presented in this chapter is the original, or classical, generic-task view with which we started our system building. Its purest implementation is in the RED systems presented in the next chapter. However this theory of generic tasks is not a static, finished thing. Our more recent view of generic tasks is described in chapters 4 and 5, in which we discuss PEIRCE and the systems built by using PEIRCE. To gain more runtime flexibility for our systems, we analyzed tasks into subtasks and methods, and we analyzed the knowledge requirements for those methods. This resulted in systems in which the method used for a task was decided at run time, instead of systems using elementary generic-task specialists with fixed strategies. In Chapter 9 we describe yet another orientation to generic tasks that is somewhat intermediate between the classical generic tasks presented in this chapter and the flexible generic tasks implemented in the PEIRCE systems. The chapter 9 version of generic tasks also uses the vocabulary of specialists and the idea that there is typically a best method for achieving a goal that is supplied to the system builder as the default. Unlike the classical generic tasks, however, in the Chapter 9 version we also allow for the possibility of more than one method for achieving each generic problem-solving goal.

Notes

1 [Some further reasons for not using classical logical formalisms in AI: (1) much of intelligence is not inference (e.g., planning) and (2) most intelligent inference is not deductive (e.g., abduction, prediction). – J. J.]

3 Two RED systems – abduction machines 1 and 2

In chapters 1 and 2, we describe abduction, design science, and the generic-task approach to building knowledge-based systems. In this chapter we examine the first two of our abductive systems, which we call here RED-1 and RED-2.[1] RED-2 extended RED-1 in several dimensions, the most important being a more sophisticated strategy for assembling composite hypotheses. RED-2 was widely demonstrated and served as a paradigm for our subsequent work on abduction. The RED systems show that abduction can be described precisely enough so that it can be programmed on a digital computer. Moreover, the RED systems do not use methods that are explicitly or recognizably deductive or probabilistic, and thus the RED systems demonstrate evidence-combining inference that apparently goes beyond those classical frameworks.

The red-cell antibody identification task

The RED systems are medical test-interpretation systems that operate in the knowledge domain of hospital blood banks. Our domain experts for these two RED systems were Patricia L. Strohm, MT (ASCP) SBB and John Svirbely, MD. The blood bank is a medical laboratory responsible for providing safe blood and blood products for transfusion. The major activities required are A-B-O and Rh blood typing, red-cell antibody screening, red-cell antibody identification, and compatibility testing. The RED systems provide decision support for red-cell antibody identification.

Blood cells have chemical structures on their surfaces called *red-cell antigens*. When a donor's cells are transfused into a patient, these antigens can be recognized as foreign by the patient's immune system. The immune sys-

✓ The Red-Cell Antibody Identification Task is by Jack W. Smith and Michael C. Tanner. The Common Architecture Underlying RED-1 and RED-2 is by John R. Josephson, Jack W. Smith, B. Chandrasekaran, Michael C. Tanner, Charles Evans, and John Svirbely. The Red-1 Overview Mechanism is by John R. Josephson, Jack W. Smith, and B. Chandrasekaran. The RED-2 Overview Mechanism is by John R. Josephson, B. Chandrasekaran, Jack W. Smith, and Michael C. Tanner, except that RED-2 performance is by Jack W. Svirbely, Patricia L. Strohm, John R. Josephson and Michael C. Tanner, and The Order of Considering the Findings is by Susan T. Korda, Michael C. Tanner, and John R. Josephson. Hypothesis Interactions is by John R. Josephson, B. Chandrasekaran, Jack W. Smith, and Michael C. Tanner.

tem builds a "memory" of antigens that it encounters, which allows it to quickly produce antibodies directed specifically against those antigens if it ever encounters them again. Antibodies directed against red-cell antigens are *red-cell antibodies.*

A patient's encounter with foreign red cells can thus produce a transfusion reaction, with possible consequences including fever, anemia, and life-threatening kidney failure. So tests must be performed to ensure that the patient does not already possess antibodies to the red cells of a potential donor, and this gives rise to the *red-cell antibody identification task.*

The first step in the overall testing process is determining the patient's A-B-O blood type. Red blood cells can have A or B structures on their surfaces, leading to possible blood types of A (the person's blood cells have A structures but not B structures), B (the other way round), AB (both), or O (neither). A person's A-B-O blood type is determined by testing for the presence or absence of A and B antigens on the person's cells, and is cross-checked by testing for the presence of A and B antibodies in the person's blood serum. (A person should not have antibodies that would react with his or her own red cells.) When we say "A antibody" or "anti-A" we mean an antibody "directed against the A antigen" (an example of final-cause naming).

People who do not have the A or B antigens on their red cells almost always have the corresponding antibody in their serum, and transfusion reactions for these antigens can be severe, so A-B-O testing is always done prior to transfusion. Rh_o (also called "D") is another structure sometimes present in the red-cell membrane. The formation of the corresponding antibody can cause major problems in both transfusions and pregnancies, so donor and patient Rh types (Rh positive or Rh negative) are routinely determined, and the same type is always used for transfusion.

In addition to A, B, and D, more than 400 red-cell antigens are known. Once blood has been tested to determine the patient's A-B-O and Rh blood types, it is necessary to test for antibodies directed toward other red-cell antigens. When this test is positive, it is necessary to determine which antibodies are present. The RED systems perform information processing for this task.

Red-cell antibodies carried by the blood serum are identified by using one or more *panels* (see Figure 3.1).[2] A panel is a set of tests performed by mixing 10 or so *cells* (red-cell suspensions, each of which is a sample of red cells from a single donor) with the patient's serum in each of 5 or so test conditions. That is, the patient's serum is mixed with red cells from perhaps 10 people, each perhaps 5 times under varying test conditions. Thus approximately 50 individual tests make up a panel. The test cells have certain known antigens on their surface and are usually provided to the testing labo-

Master Panel											
	623A	479	537A	506A	303A	209A	186A	195	164	Scr2	Scr1
AlbuminIS	0	0	0	0	0	0	0	0	0	0	0
Albumin37	0	0	0	0	0	0	0	0	0	0	0
Coombs	3 +	0	3 +	0	3 +	3 +	3 +	3 +	3 +	3 +	2 +
EnzymeIS	0	0	0	0	0	0	0	0	0	0	0
Enzyme37	0	0	1 +	0	0	1 +	0	1 +	0	1 +	0

Figure 3.1. Red-cell test panel. This panel is from case OSU 9, which will be used for illustration throughout this chapter. The various test conditions, or phases, are listed along the left side (AlbuminIS, etc.) and identifiers for donors of the red cells are given across the top (623A, etc.). Entries in the table record reactions graded from 0, for no reaction, to 4+ for the strongest agglutination reaction, or H for hemolysis. Intermediate grades of agglutination are +/- (a trace of reaction), 1+w (a grade of 1+, but with the modifier "weak"), 1+, 1+s (the modifier means "strong"), 2+w, 2+, 2+s, 3+w, 3+, 3+s, and 4+w. Thus, cell 623A has a 3+ agglutination reaction in the Coombs phase.

ratory by a supplier of medical laboratory materials. The presence or absence of approximately 30 significant antigens is known about each test cell. These known antigens may be expressed on cell surfaces with varying strengths, depending on the genetic makeup of the cell. Reliable expectations about strengths of expression can be inferred from the other antigens present and absent on the cell by using knowledge of the underlying genetic possibilities.

Antibody-antigen reactions occurring in a panel are graded by the blood-bank technologist as to strength and type of reaction. Possible reaction types are agglutination (clumping of the cells) or hemolysis (splitting of the cell walls, which allows the cells' hemoglobin to leak into the solution). The strength of agglutination reactions is expressed in blood-bankers' vocabulary, which is described briefly in Figure 3.1, and consists of thirteen possible reaction strengths.

Information about the 30 or more significant antigens on donor cells is recorded in a table called an *antigram*. Part of an antigram is shown in Figure 3.2. By reasoning about the pattern of reactions in the panel and by using the antigen information given in the antigram, the blood-bank technologist can usually, with a high degree of confidence, determine which antibodies are present in the patient's serum and are causing the observed reactions and which are absent, or at least not present in enough strength to cause reaction. The technologist sometimes takes into account other miscellaneous pieces of information (e.g., about the patient's prior transfusion history, the patient's race, or the results of previous tests). He or she looks for such things as the relative strength of reactions and whether cells with a particular antigen consistently react or fail to react. The RED systems attempt to automate this reasoning process.

Our intention in building the RED systems was to derive confident conclu-

Antigram	C	D	E	c	e	Cw	V	K	k	Kpa	Kpb	Jsa	Jsb	Fya	Fyb	Jka	Jkb
164	0	0	0	+	+	0	0	0	+	0	+	0	+	+	0	+	+
195	0	0	0	+	+	0	0	+	+	+	+	0	+	0	+	+	+
186A	0	0	0	+	+	0	0	0	+	0	+	+	+	0	+	0	+
209A	+	0	0	+	+	0	0	+	+	0	+	0	+	0	+	+	0
303A	0	0	+	+	+	0	0	0	+	0	+	0	+	+	+	+	+
506A	+	+	0	0	+	+	0	0	+	0	+	0	+	+	0	0	+
537A	+	+	0	0	+	0	0	+	+	0	+	0	+	0	+	0	+
479	0	+	0	+	+	0	+	0	+	0	+	0	+	0	+	+	0
623A	0	+	+	+	0	0	0	0	+	0	+	0	+	0	+	+	+

Figure 3.2. Partial antigram showing antigens present on donor cells. The donor cells are named along the left side (164, etc.) and the antigens along the top (C, D, etc.). In the body of the table + indicates the presence of an antigen and 0 indicates absence. For example, cell 209A is positive for C (the antigen is present on the surface of the cell) but negative for D (the antigen is absent). D is the Rh antigen, so the donor of this cell is Rh negative.

sions from test results by using principles, hypotheses, knowledge, and strategies similar to those used by human technologists. We recorded and studied many sessions of human problem solving (protocols) in this domain, and, although we do not pretend to have captured the full flexible richness of human problem-solving abilities and behavior, nevertheless the RED systems have captured enough of those abilities to get the job done quite well, as will be seen.

For any of the versions of RED, the input required to solve a case consists of at least one panel and an antigram describing the donor cells used in the panel. The output solution consists of: (1) a set of antibodies that together make up the best explanation for the reactions described in the input panel, (2) a critical markup of the antibodies in the best explanation marking which antibodies are deserving of greatest confidence, and (3) an evaluation of the presence and absence of the most clinically significant antibodies given in language such as "likely present" and "ruled out."[3]

At the completion of the antibody-identification task the patient's status is known with respect to certain specific antibodies, and the A-B-O and Rh types are known as well. Blood can be selected for transfusion on this basis. However, there may still be undetected antigen-antibody incompatibilities, or some mistake, so an additional cross-match step is performed before the blood is actually released for use. The cross-match is done by testing the patient's serum with the red cells from the actual unit of blood selected for transfusion. This procedure verifies that the patient has no antibodies to the donor cells.

The common architecture underlying RED-1 and RED-2

One way to organize a system for the abductive-assembly task exemplified by the red-cell antibody identification problem, and the organization described here for the first two RED systems, is to set up separate problem-solving modules for the distinct subtasks of hypothesis generation and hypothesis assembly:

1. The hypothesis-generation module has the function of coming up with a relatively small number of "plausible" hypotheses from a larger number of prestored hypothesis-generating patterns.
2. The hypothesis-assembly module has the function of building a "best" composite hypothesis using these plausible hypotheses as available parts, including testing and improving the quality of the composite and stimulating generation of more hypotheses as needed. (This module is sometimes referred to as *Overview*.)

The domain knowledge is primarily embedded in the hypothesis-generation mechanism, in close connection with the prestored hypothesis "concepts." Overview is a relatively knowledge-free problem solver, although it needs ready access to knowledge about how hypotheses interact. Overview and the hypothesis-generation module communicate through a shared language of the plausibility of hypotheses and of the findings that are to be explained.

These modules have as their parts generic-task problem solvers. The RED systems, RED-1, RED-2, and their successors, show the power of decomposing complex problem-solving activities into generic problem-solving tasks. The knowledge that applies to a given task is compiled into a knowledge structure that is tuned for that task. Each task is also associated with a problem-solving regime, a control strategy that coordinates the problem-solving process. Using the generic-task approach (described in chapter 2) representations and languages developed for one domain can be applied to others.

According to our analysis of the problem, antibody identification can be accomplished by a system performing four generic tasks:

1. hierarchical classification
2. hypothesis matching
3. knowledge-directed data retrieval
4. abductive assembly (and criticism) of explanatory hypotheses

The hypothesis-generation module performs hierarchical classification, hypothesis matching, and knowledge-directed data retrieval. The hypothesis-assembly module performs abductive assembly. (These generic tasks are described in chapter 2 as constituents of diagnostic reasoning.)

Hierarchical classification

In some problem situations, abduction can be accomplished by a relatively simple matching mechanism, with no particular concern taken for focusing the control of which explanatory concepts to consider, or for controlling the assembly of composite explanations. For example, if there are only a small number of potentially applicable explanatory concepts, and if time and other computational resources are sufficiently abundant, then each hypothesis can be considered explicitly. Of course it is a pretty limited intelligence that can afford to try out each of its ideas explicitly on each situation. The classification mechanism we describe here meets the need for organizing the prestored explanatory concepts and for controlling access to them. It provides a good mechanism for the job whenever knowledge of the right sort is available to make it go.

For antibody identification the classification task is that of identifying a patient's serum antibody as plausibly belonging to one or more specific nodes in a predetermined antibody classification hierarchy (see Figure 3.3).[4] CSRL (Conceptual Structures Representation Language) is a computer language that we developed at Ohio State for setting up hypothesis-matching specialists that reside in a classification hierarchy and use the establish-refine problem-solving process. CSRL is a software tool for building hierarchical classifiers. Each node in the RED antibody-classification tree is implemented as a CSRL specialist, a little software agent that has embedded in it knowledge and decision logic for evaluating the applicability of its particular class or category to the case (the hypothesis-matching task).

As described in chapter 2, the specialists are invoked using the establish-refine control strategy for classification (Gomez & Chandrasekaran, 1981) so that when a general hypothesis is ruled out, all more specific subtypes of it are also ruled out. In principle, establish-refine processing can take place in parallel, whenever sub-concepts can be matched independently. By efficiently pruning the search for plausible hypotheses, establish-refine is a significant contributor to taming the complexity of a problem. Establish-refine makes it efficient and practical to search a very large space of stored concepts for just those that plausibly apply to the case. The classification structure in RED is used to generate plausible hypotheses to be used as potential parts of a compound hypothesis to be constructed by a process of abductive assembly and criticism.

In the RED systems a separate module is devoted to the hypothesis-generation subtask, the classification structure just described. In RED-1 and RED-2 it runs first, as soon as the case is started, and produces a set of hypotheses, each the result of matching a prestored concept to the case. The hypotheses produced are all explicitly relevant for explaining features of the case, and many potential hypotheses do not appear, having been categorically ruled out. Each hypothesis arrives with a symbolic likelihood, the result primarily of case-specific quality of match but also of case-independent knowledge about frequencies of occurrence. One way in which the RED engine is distinguished from INTERNIST (Miller, Pople, & Myers, 1982), probably the best-known abductive system, and the set-covering systems (Peng & Reggia, 1990; Reggia, 1983) is that RED devotes a separate

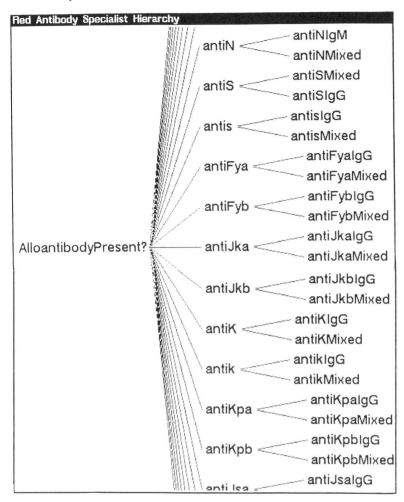

Figure 3.3. Part of the antibody-classification hierarchy used in RED-2. More refined (i.e., more specific) hypotheses are toward the right

problem solver explicitly to the hypothesis-generation subtask. The advantage of a separate problem solver is that it can be designed specifically to be
efficient for the task of hypothesis generation.

Hypothesis matching

The individual nodes in the classification hierarchy are represented by hypothesis-matching specialists, which are organized into a hierarchy with
general hypotheses near the "top" and more specific hypotheses toward the
"bottom" (in Figure 3.3, hypotheses are more general to the left and become
more specific as they proceed to the right). Each specialist performs the

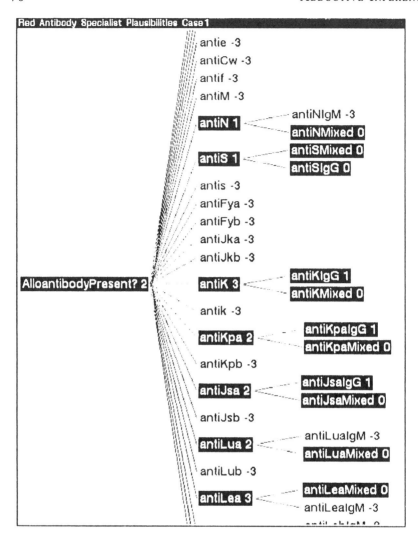

Figure 3.4. RED-2 classification hierarchy after the case data (OSU 9) have been considered. Inverted nodes are established (plausibility value at least -2). Plausibility values are shown with each node. Plausibility values should not be confused with reaction strengths (1+w, 1+, 1+s, etc.).

same abstract task, determining the plausibility of a hypothesis, though each uses different knowledge. The anti-N specialist, for example, determines the plausibility of the hypothesis that an antibody to the N antigen is present in the patient's serum. This match is accomplished in CSRL by *knowledge groups*. A knowledge group can be thought of as a cluster of rules that maps the values of a list of conditions (Boolean and arithmetic operations on data) to a conclusion on a discrete confidence scale. Typically, the knowledge in a

Anti NMixed Profile	623A	479	303A	209A	186A	195
AlbuminIS	0	0	0	0	0	0
Albumin37	0	0	0	0	0	0
Coombs	+ / -	0	2 +	+ / -	+ / -	2 +
EnzymeIS	0	0	0	0	0	0
Enzyme37	0	0	0	+ / -	0	+ / -

Figure 3.5. Reaction profile for the anti-N-Mixed antibody hypothesis for case OSU 9. The profile represents what this particular hypothesis is offering to explain for this particular case. The pattern of reactions is the most that can be explained consistently by the hypothesis. Note by comparing with figure 3.6 that the hypothesis only offers to partially explain some of the reactions.

specialist is factored into several knowledge groups, the results of which are combined by additional knowledge groups to generate the plausibility value for the hypothesis. In RED this value is an integer from −3 to +3, representing the plausibility on a symbolic scale from "ruled out" to "highly plausible." The plausibility values can be thought of as prima facie estimates of likelihood for the hypotheses, in contrast to the "all things considered" likelihood estimates that are produced later. The plausibilities can also be thought of as estimates of pursuit value – that is, the degree to which the hypotheses are worthy of further consideration. The plausibility value assigned to a hypothesis, given a certain pattern of evidence, is determined by the judgment of the domain experts.

In addition to hypothesis matching, a specialist also triggers production of a description of the test results that can be explained by its hypothesis. This description, called a *reaction profile* in the RED systems, is produced only by specialists that have not ruled out their hypotheses (plausibility value −3) (see Figures 3.4 and 3.5). Overview then uses the reaction profile in assembling the best explanation for all the reactions in the panel.

Thus each plausible hypothesis delivered by the hypothesis generator comes with:

1. a description, particularized to the case, of the findings that it offers to explain
2. a symbolic plausibility value

Each plausible hypothesis has its own consistent little story to tell and to contribute to the larger story represented by the abductive conclusion.

By filtering the primitive hypotheses, letting through only those plausible for the case, we potentially make a great computational contribution to the problem of finding the best composite. By making only moderate cuts in the number, say n, of hypothesis parts to consider, we can make deep cuts in the

2^n composites that can potentially be generated from them. For example, if 63 prestored hypothesis patterns are reduced to 8 that are plausible for the case at hand, we cut the number of composites that can potentially be generated from 2^{63} (the number of grains of rice on the last square of the chessboard in the classical story) – more than 9 quintillion – to 2^8, or 256.

How other systems screen hypotheses. The INTERNIST system for diagnosis in internal medicine (Miller, Pople, & Myers, 1982) can be viewed as doing this sort of hypothesis screening when it considers only the subset of prestored diseases that are evoked by the present findings. In this way it screens out those hypotheses that are completely irrelevant for explaining the findings. It cuts the number even further when it scores the evoked diseases for confidence and continues to consider only those above a certain threshold. This can be seen as screening out hypotheses for low likelihood of being correct, where likelihood is measured primarily by quality of match to the case data.

The DENDRAL system (for elucidating molecular structure from mass spectrogram and other data) (Buchanan, Sutherland, & Feigenbaum, 1969) performs such a hypothesis-screening subtask explicitly. During an initial phase it uses the data provided to generate a BADLIST of molecular substructures that must not appear in the hypothesized composite structures. This BADLIST is used to constrain the search space during the subsequent enumeration of all possible molecular structures consistent with the constraints. That is (in the present terms) DENDRAL first rules out certain hypotheses for matching poorly to the case data, and then generates all possible composite hypotheses not including those that were ruled out (and respecting some other constraints). Note that DENDRAL, like RED, devotes a separate problem solver with its own knowledge structures to the initial screening task.

In the Generalized Set Covering model of diagnosis and abduction (Reggia, 1983; Reggia, Perricone, Nau, & Peng, 1985) a disease is associated with a certain set of findings that it potentially covers (i.e., which it can explain if they are present). The diagnostic task is then viewed as that of generating all possible minimum coverings for a given set of findings, by sets associated with diseases (in order to use this as a basis for further question asking). In expert systems built using this model, a match score is computed for each relevant disease each time new findings are entered for consideration, and match scores are used, when appropriate, as the basis for categorically rejecting disease hypotheses from further consideration.

Knowledge-directed data retrieval

An important companion to the CSRL classification hierarchy is an "intelligent" data-base (IDB) assistant, which organizes the data from the cases and allows derivation of values by simple inferencing, inheritance, and other attached inference procedures (Mittal, 1980; Mittal & Chandrasekaran, 1980).[5] By obtaining needed information about a case through queries to the IDB assistant, the CSRL-based diagnostic structure is insulated from having to solve data-retrieval and data-abstraction problems.

The implementation of the data is based on the notion of frames (see the section in chapter 2 entitled Organizing knowledge: Frames). A frame can be viewed as a stereotypical representation for an entity, an action, or any concept. Frames allow an explicit representation of attributes and relations; procedures can be attached to frames at different places and can be executed automatically. Because procedures are attached to frames, they allow for the explicit representation of procedural knowledge in the context of its use. (Such clarity is usually not possible in more conventional data-base systems.)

The IDB assistant is loaded with three types of factual information about cases and test samples: the antigenic makeup of particular red cells, detailed medical information about individual patients, and test results from patient workups. Additionally, it has case-independent information about the characteristics of the various antigens found on red cells. This information is heavily cross-referenced in that, for example, patient information makes reference to antibody workups that have been done on the tests performed during that workup. Data about patients, red cells, and test results are organized, and have procedures attached, to answer a variety of questions analogous to those commonly asked by medical technologists during antibody identification. An important practical characteristic of this approach is the flexibility and ease of creating new data entities in an existing data structure.

The function of the IDB assistant is to provide the information needed to support the main problem-solving activity. It responds to queries by processing the information in its repositories of stored facts in accordance with the kind of question that is being asked. Thus the IDB is itself an active problem solver, able to perform tasks significantly beyond those of just information storage and retrieval. For example, antigenic information is typically entered for a particular test red cell by telling which antigens are present and which are not, but a hypothesis-matching specialist may need to know whether the cell shows a homozygous or a heterozygous expression of a given antigen (in order to infer the strength of expression on the cell surface and thus the anticipated strength of reactions). The IDB assistant can respond to this need by checking whether antigens corresponding to the given one's antithetical alleles have been reported as present. To do this, it consults its stored information about which antigens are antithetical to which.

In summary, explanatory hypotheses are generated by a process of hierarchical classification, which uses hypothesis matching to set plausibility values. Hypothesis matching relies on knowledge-directed data retrieval to derive characteristics of interest from the raw data of a case.

Abductive assembly

To this point, RED-1 and RED-2 share the same architecture. Both use classification hierarchies, although the RED-2 classification hierarchy has two levels and is more elaborate than that of RED-1, which has only one level. Both use the same hypothesis-matching and knowledge-directed data-retrieval mechanism. However, the main difference between the two systems is their abductive-assembly mechanisms.

Synthesizing a best composite can be computationally expensive: If there are n plausible hypotheses, then there are 2^n composites that can potentially be made from them. If each needs to be generated separately in order to determine which is best, the process can become impractical. Clearly, it is usually preferable to adopt strategies that allow us to avoid generating all combinations.

Sometimes an abduction problem is completely dominated by the difficulty of generating even one good composite explanation. It can be shown that the problem of generating just one consistent composite hypothesis that explains everything, under conditions where many of the hypotheses are incompatible with one another, is NP complete (see chapter 7) and thus probably has no efficient general solution.

Each of the RED engines first generates a single, tentative, best composite and then improves it by criticism followed by suitable adjustment. For the criticism to be accomplished, certain other composite hypotheses are generated, but only a relatively small number. Here again, the RED systems devote a distinct problem solver to a distinct task, in this case that of forming a best composite. The initial composite hypothesis that is formed is (under favorable conditions) one that explains all the data that needs to be explained; that is maximally plausible, or nearly so; and (in RED-2) is internally consistent.

Often, more than simply computational feasibility considerations are involved in a decision to generate the one best composite instead of generating all composites subject to some constraints. For purposes of action, an intelligent agent will typically need a single best estimate as to the nature of the situation, even if it is only a guess, and does not need an enumeration of all possible things it could be. By rapidly coming to a best estimate of the situation, the agent arrives quickly at a state where it is prepared to take action. If it had to enumerate a large number of alternatives, it would take longer, not only to generate them, but also to decide what to do next. It is difficult to figure out what to do if proposed actions must try to cover for all possibilities.

Alternatively, there may be situations in which careful and intelligent reasoning requires the generation of all plausible composites (i.e., those with a significant chance of being true), so that they can all be examined and compared. This might especially be called for when the cost of making a mistake is high, as in medicine, or when there is plenty of time to consider the alternatives. Of course generating all plausible composites is computationally infeasible if there are many plausible fragments from which to choose. Moreover, besides being a computationally expensive strategy, generating all the alternatives will not typically be required because we can compare composites *implicitly* by comparing alternative ways of putting them together. For example, in comparing hypothesis fragments H_1 and H_2, we implicitly (partially) compare all composites containing H_1 with those containing H_2.

How other systems generate composites. The authors of DENDRAL saw its job as that of generating all possible composites that are allowable given the previously established constraints on submolecules and the known case-independent chemical constraints on molecular structure. In contrast INTERNIST terminates (after cycles of questioning, which we ignore for these purposes) when it comes up with its single best composite. The set-covering model generates all possible composites of minimal cardinality but avoids having to enumerate them explicitly by factoring the combinations into disjoint sets of generators.

The RED-1 Overview mechanism

The main functions of Overview are to make strategic decisions about the progress of the problem-solving activity and to combine the judgments of the individual antibody specialists into a unified judgment about the case. Some sort of entity with this overview perspective is needed because the antibody specialists are local in their reasoning (i.e., reason only about the presence or absence of a single antibody specificity) and consequently are not capable of deciding global issues such as whether all test results are accounted for or whether the presence of a particular antibody is a superfluous hypothesis. The capacity for these global judgments is necessary if our system is to mimic the power of a human blood-bank technologist.

Overview is presented with information of several kinds: (1) the data to be explained, (2) a set of hypotheses that plausibly apply to the case, (3) information, particularized to the case, about what each hypothesis can explain, and (4) a plausibility rating, particularized to the case, for each hypothesis.

Overview's task is to use this information to assemble, if possible, a complete account of the test data. The assembly should proceed in such a way that it respects the plausibility information (i.e., prefers higher plausibility hypotheses to those with lower plausibility).

This plausibility estimate for a hypothesis is not an overall estimate of its probability or certainty of being true in the case. An estimate of this sort would need to take account of interactions between the subhypotheses and would need to be based on such considerations as whether alternative ways of explaining things are available and whether a particular subhypothesis is contrary to one already established. These considerations are more appropriate for Overview's global perspective. The plausibility estimate that Overview needs is that a subhypothesis could be true or that it is worth pursuing based (locally) only on the quality of the match between the subhypothesis and the part of the data that is specifically relevant to this plausibility estimate.

The RED-1 Overview simply starts with the most plausible hypotheses, those with the highest plausibility scores, and makes a judgment as to whether they will together account for all the test results. Reaction strengths are added appropriately if more than one antibody hypothesis offers to partially explain a reaction on a particular panel cell. *If the most plausible hypotheses taken together are not yet sufficient to account for all the test results, less and less plausible hypotheses are included, as needed, until a set sufficient to account for all the results is reached.* RED-1 cannot proceed beyond this point if a sufficient set cannot be found.

When a set of antibodies is found that is sufficient to explain all the reactions, the antibodies in this set are examined one by one to determine which are *essential*. An antibody is considered to be essential if no other plausible way is available to account for some reaction for which this antibody can account. For each antibody in the set, this is determined by combining all of the other plausible antibodies into one large composite, calculating what this composite will account for, and calculating whether there is an *unexplained remainder*; an unexplained remainder implies that the antibody in question is essential (for explaining that remainder).

Antibodies classified as essential are further classified as *confirmed* if they pass the domain-specific Rule of Three for breadth of the evidence: that there should be at least three reacting cells with the antigen and at least three nonreacting cells without the antigen. The antibodies not ruled out by their specialists and not classified as confirmed are *unresolved*. These antibodies may be further classified into guess categories of *likely present* or *likely absent* on the basis of their plausibility values and their explanatory usefulness in extending the set of essential antibodies to a complete explanation.

RED-1 performance

Following is an edited transcript of the output of RED-1 for a case in which the first panel was not conclusive and further testing was required to settle the remaining ambiguities of the case.[6] This output represents the state at the end of the first inconclusive panel. The correct answer after further testing turned out to be: ANTI-FY-A, ANTI-K, and ANTI-D (i.e., antibodies to the antigens FY-A, K, and D). As can be seen, RED anticipated the correct answer, although it was unable to confirm it.

The set of antibodies with specificities to (FY-A K E D C) appears sufficient to explain all of the test results.

Antibody towards FY-A is not essential for explaining the test results.

Antibody towards K is essential for explaining.

((PANCO-8 ENZYME-37 1)
(PANCO-8 ENZYME-IS 1)
(PANCO-8 ALBUMIN-COOMBS 2)
(PANCO-8 ALBUMIN-37 1))

[Comment: These are test results encoded as (cell, test conditions, reaction strength) triples.]

Antibody towards E is not essential for explaining the test results.

Antibody towards D is essential for explaining

((PANCO-9 ENZYME-37 1)
(PANCO-9 ALBUMIN-37 1)
(PANCO-9 ALBUMIN-IS 1))

Antibody towards C is not essential for explaining the test results.

ANTIBODY STATUS REPORT:

The following antibodies have been ruled out:

(ANTI-LU-B ANTI-SMALL-S ANTI-S ANTI-M ANTI-P1 ANTI-LE-A ANTI-JK-B ANTI-JK-A ANTI-FY-B ANTI-JS-B ANTI-KP-B ANTI-SMALL-K ANTI-V ANTI-SMALL-F ANTI-SMALL-E ANTI-SMALL-C)

The following antibodies have been confirmed to be present:

(ANTI-K ANTI-D)

[Comment: These were actually present, as was confirmed by later tests. This is a weak confirmation, as is noted next.]

PLEASE NOTE:

The presence of the confirmed antibodies is INSUFFICIENT to explain all of the test results.

The following antibody is unresolved but is likely to be present: (ANTI-FY-A).

[Comment: This is the third antibody that was actually present.]

PLEASE NOTE:

The antibodies considered to be unresolved but likely to be present, and those considered to be confirmed as present, together are SUFFICIENT to explain all of the test results.

The following antibodies are unresolved and are likely to be absent: (ANTI-LU-A ANTI-LE-B ANTI-CW ANTI-E).

[Comment: They were absent.]

The following antibodies are unresolved: (ANTI-N ANTI-C).

[Comment: Actually absent.]

Type the name of an antibody if you would like an explanation of why it was classified the way it was.

>>>>ANTI-FY-A

ANTI-FY-A was classified as Unresolved But Likely Present because it was rated at high plausibility by its antibody specialist, and its presence is a particularly useful way to explain some reactions.

Discussion

RED-1 treated the abductive process as one of classification and hypothesis assembly, proceeding through these stages:

(i) forming plausible primitive hypotheses by classification

(ii) assembling a tentative best explanation using a strategy of adding primitive hypotheses to a growing composite in order of likelihood (based on match score) until all the findings have been accounted for

(iii) removing explanatorily superfluous parts of the hypothesis

(iv) criticizing the composite hypothesis by testing for the existence of plausible alternative explanations for what various parts of the composite offer to account for

(v) assigning final confidence values to the primitive hypotheses on the bases of explanatory importance and match scores

Thus we succeeded in automating a form of best-explanation reasoning for a real-world task using a strategy that has some degree of generality.

The RED-2 Overview mechanism

RED-1 behaved reasonably on test cases, but we wanted a more sophisticated version that would handle more complicated interactions between primitive hypotheses. RED-1 could handle interactions in which the hypotheses are mutually compatible and represent explanatory alternatives where their explanatory capacities overlap. However, RED-1 could not handle incompatibilities between hypotheses or the knowledge that the truth of one hypothesis suggests the truth of another. Besides, we believed that the problem-solving process could be made more efficient in search, especially by using what needs to be explained as a way to focus on a subset of the plausible hypotheses. Consequently, we built RED-2, which incorporated a new strategy for hypothesis assembly based on a means-end control regime.

Just as with RED-1, the main functions of the Overview procedure in RED-2 are to make strategic decisions about the progress of the problem-solving activity and to combine the judgments of the individual hypothesis specialists into a unified judgment about the case. Besides the judgment as to whether its antibody is present, each specialist decides how its antibody, if present, is reacting in the current series of tests. This description of how its antibody is reacting is encoded in the reaction profile (as in Figure 3.5) and is available for Overview to use in deciding how to proceed with the case. After the hypothesis generator produces plausible hypotheses, they are treated as candidate fragments of a larger composite hypothesis, and the Overview module takes over to construct an overall best explanation for the findings of the case.

One new consideration introduced in RED-2 is hypothesis-incompatibility knowledge. This consists of pairwise relationships of exclusion: h_j is incompatible with h_k means that if h_j is true, then h_k cannot be, and vice versa. Although expert knowledge of this sort is available for certain red-cell antibodies, it was ignored in RED-1, which had no means of taking advantage of this knowledge.

Assembling a tentative composite hypothesis

In its first stage of activity, Overview uses a hypothesis assembler to form a tentative composite hypothesis. This is accomplished, in effect, by reducing the problem of explaining all the reactions on the test panel to a series of subproblems of explaining particular reactions. The hypothesis assembler focuses on one finding at a time, finds the best way of explaining that particular finding (the most plausible way, breaking ties by a procedure too complicated and unimportant to describe here), and includes that hypothesis fragment in the growing composite hypothesis. Incompatible parts of the composite hypothesis are removed as necessary to maintain the consistency of the assembly. After each new hypothesis is included in the assembly, the total explanatory power of the composite is computed and is compared with the original data that need to be explained. The *unexplained remainder* is then computed, and a new finding is chosen for focus of attention. The cycle of focusing on an unexplained finding, selecting a hypothesis that explains that finding for inclusion in the growing assembly, and computing the unexplained remainder repeats until all of the findings are explained. This process is illustrated in Figure 3.6 a–m.

If a finding is encountered whose only available maximally plausible explainers are incompatible with something already present in the growing hypothesis, then one of these newly encountered hypotheses is included in the growing hypothesis and any parts inconsistent with the new one are removing from the composite. If we remove parts from the growing hypothesis,

To Be Explained

	623A	479	537A	506A	303A	209A	186A	195	164
AlbuminIS	0	0	0	0	0	0	0	0	0
Albumin37	0	0	0	0	0	0	0	0	0
Coombs	3 +	0	3 +	0	3 +	3 +	3 +	3 +	3 +
EnzymeIS	0	0	0	0	0	0	0	0	0
Enzyme37	0	0	1 +	0	0	1 +	0	1 +	0

Figure 3.6. (a) RED-2 case OSU 9. The data to be explained. The disparity between this and Figure 3.1 is that RED-2 does not try to explain the reactions on the screening cells (Scr2 and Scr1).

To Be Explained

	623A	479	537A	506A	303A	209A	186A	195	164
AlbuminIS	0	0	0	0	0	0	0	0	0
Albumin37	0	0	0	0	0	0	0	0	0
Coombs	3 +	0	3 +	0	3 +	3 +	3 +	3 +	**3 +**
EnzymeIS	0	0	0	0	0	0	0	0	0
Enzyme37	0	0	1 +	0	0	1 +	0	1 +	0

Figure 3.6 (b) The focus of attention is on explaining a particular reaction.

Growing Hypothesis

The growing hypothesis:
antiLeaMixed

Figure 3.6 (c) The anti-Lea-Mixed antibody hypothesis is chosen to explain the reaction and becomes the first part of a growing composite hypothesis.

Anti LeaMixed Profile

	186A	195	164
AlbuminIS	0	0	0
Albumin37	0	0	0
Coombs	3 +	3 +	3 +
EnzymeIS	0	0	0
Enzyme37	0	+ /-	0

Figure 3.6 (d) What the anti-Lea-Mixed hypothesis offers to explain.

Still To Explain

	623A	479	537A	506A	303A	209A	186A	195	164
AlbuminIS	0	0	0	0	0	0	0	0	0
Albumin37	0	0	0	0	0	0	0	0	0
Coombs	3 +	0	3 +	0	3 +	**3 +**	0	0	0
EnzymeIS	0	0	0	0	0	0	0	0	0
Enzyme37	0	0	1 +	0	0	1 +	0	+ / -	0

Figure 3.6 (e) Unexplained remainder with a new focus of attention.

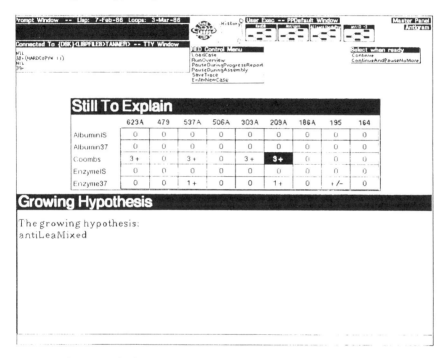

Figure 3.6 (f) The problem state as it appears on the screen of the Xerox 1109 Lisp machine in the Loops environment.

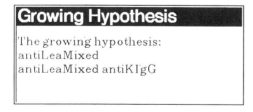

Figure 3.6 (g) Anti-K-IgG included in the composite hypothesis (the new two-part hypothesis is the bottom entry).

Still To Explain

	623A	479	537A	506A	303A	209A	186A	195	164
AlbuminlS	0	0	0	0	0	0	0	0	0
Albumin37	0	0	0	0	0	0	0	0	0
Coombs	3 +	0	0	0	3+	0	0	0	0
EnzymelS	0	0	0	0	0	0	0	0	0
Enzyme37	0	0	0	0	0	0	0	0	0

Figure 3.6 (h) Unexplained remainder with new focus of attention.

Growing Hypothesis

The growing hypothesis:
antiLeaMixed
antiLeaMixed antiKIgG
antiLeaMixed antiKIgG antiP1Mixed

Figure 3.6 (i) Anti-P1-Mixed included, which makes a three-part hypothesis.

Still To Explain

	623A	479	537A	506A	303A	209A	186A	195	164
AlbuminlS	0	0	0	0	0	0	0	0	0
Albumin37	0	0	0	0	0	0	0	0	0
Coombs	3+	0	0	0	1 +	0	0	0	0
EnzymelS	0	0	0	0	0	0	0	0	0
Enzyme37	0	0	0	0	0	0	0	0	0

Figure 3.6 (j) Unexplained remainder, new focus of attention.

Growing Hypothesis

The growing hypothesis:
antiLeaMixed
antiLeaMixed antiKIgG
antiLeaMixed antiKIgG antiP1Mixed
antiLeaMixed antiKIgG antiP1Mixed antiSIgG

Figure 3.6 (k) Anti-S-IgG included, which makes a four-part hypothesis.

Still To Explain

	623A	479	537A	506A	303A	209A	186A	195	164
AlbuminIS	O	O	O	O	O	O	O	O	O
Albumin37	O	O	O	O	O	O	O	O	O
Coombs	O	O	O	O	O	O	O	O	O
EnzymeIS	O	O	O	O	O	O	O	O	O
Enzyme37	O	O	O	O	O	O	O	O	O

Figure 3.6 (l) All Explained.

Overview progress report window

Initial hypothesis: antiLeaMixed antiKIgG antiPIMixed antiSIgG

Figure 3.6 (m) The four-part hypothesis is tentatively accepted and will be subjected to criticism.

we introduce the danger of an infinite loop, but this is dealt with fairly readily. We suitably raise the standards for reintroducing a hypothesis in precisely the same situation in which it was first introduced. The second time around we require that there be no net loss of explanatory power resulting from reintroducing the hypothesis and removing its contraries from the assembly. (There are a variety of acceptable measures of explanatory power that will serve here to guarantee progress.) The basic idea is that the finding must be explained, even if doing so forces a major revision of the growing hypothesis.

If the initial assembly process concludes successfully, the result is a composite hypothesis that is consistent, explanatorily complete, and nearly maximally plausible (at each choice point the most plausible alternative was chosen). Note that the hypothesis assembler does a good job of producing a composite hypothesis that combines the virtues of consistency, completeness, and plausibility. The relative priorities for these virtues is implicit in the algorithm. The least important virtue is plausibility: If RED can make a consistent, complete explanation only by using implausible hypotheses, it does so. Completeness is next in importance, with consistency being the highest priority. The hypothesis assembler will enforce consistency throughout the process. If it cannot find a consistent explanation for a finding, it stops and yields the best consistent explanation it has found to that point, even if the explanation is incomplete.

Criticism

The second stage of Overview's processing begins only if the assembly stage produced a complete, consistent explanation. If so, Overview enters a

```
┌────────────────────────────────────────────────────────────────────────┐
│ Overview progress report window                                          │
├────────────────────────────────────────────────────────────────────────┤
│ Initial hypothesis: antiLeaMixed antiKIgG antiPIMixed antiSIgG           │
│                                                                          │
│ Parsimonized hypothesis: antiKIgG antiSIgG                               │
│                                                                          │
└────────────────────────────────────────────────────────────────────────┘
```

Figure 3.7. OSU 9 after criticism for parsimony.

criticism stage to evaluate the quality of the explanation and, if possible, to improve it.

RED-2 uses two kinds of criticism: for parsimony and for essentialness. The strategy used in hypothesis assembly makes parsimony criticism necessary; the process of adding explanatory hypotheses one at a time can render a hypothesis already in the composite explanation explanatorily superfluous. So, if the tentative initial hypothesis is complete, it is examined by a "parsimonizer" to see if any of its constituent parts no longer have any explanatory function. Any explanatorily superfluous parts are removed (in order from lower to higher plausibility scores) and a parsimonious hypothesis results (see Figure 3.7). At this stage the composite hypothesis is explanatorily complete, maximally plausible (or nearly so), and parsimonious.

Note that this form of parsimony (a version of Occam's razor) has clear epistemic virtues. Logically, the composite hypothesis is a conjunction of little hypotheses, so, if we remove one of the conjuncts, the resulting hypothesis is distinctly more likely to be true because it makes fewer commitments. Superfluous hypothesis parts make factual commitments, expose themselves to potential falsity, with no compensating gain in explanatory power. To put it more classically: if hypothesis parts are treated as logical conjuncts, then an additional part introduces an additional truth condition to satisfy. Thus the hypothesis that is simpler (in not including an unneeded part) is more likely to be true. Thus the sense of parsimony we use here is such that *the more parsimonious hypothesis is more likely to be true.*

After parsimony criticism, a second process of criticism begins in which each hypothesis in the composite is examined to see if it is essential, that is, to see if part of what it explains can be explained in no other way. There are two ways to find essentials. The first is during the initial assembly process. If only one hypothesis offers to explain a finding on which attention is focused, that hypothesis is a *discovered essential.* The second way to find essentials is that an attempt is made for each part of the composite hypothesis, not already known to be essential, to assemble a complete alternative hypothesis not including that part. If the attempt succeeds, it shows that there are other ways of explaining the same things, even though they may not be as good as the original. But if the attempt fails, it shows that there is

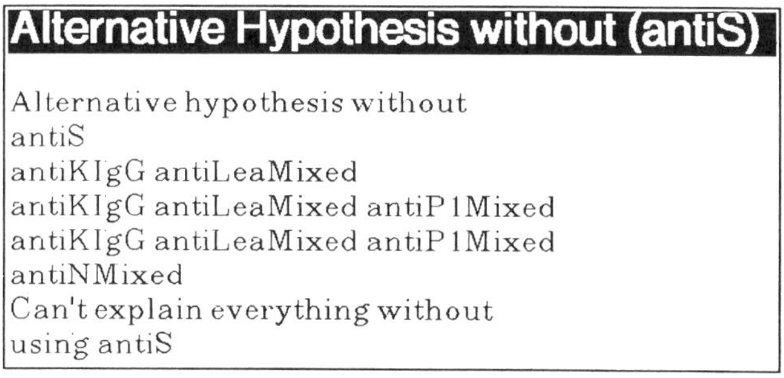

Alternative Hypothesis without (antiS)

Alternative hypothesis without
antiS
antiK IgG antiLeaMixed
antiK IgG antiLeaMixed antiP1Mixed
antiK IgG antiLeaMixed antiP1Mixed
antiNMixed
Can't explain everything without
using antiS

Figure 3.8. Anti S is essential.

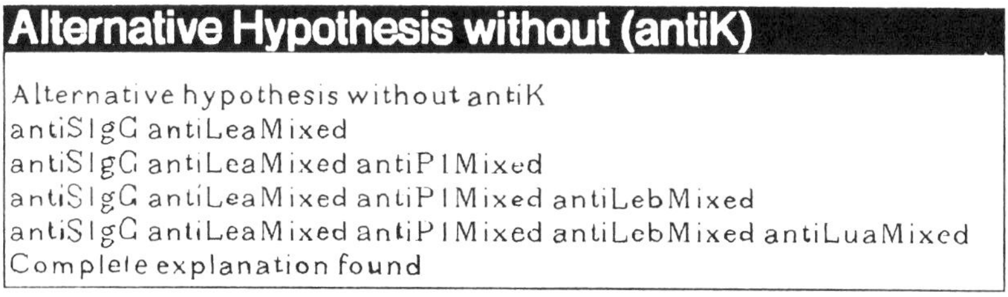

Alternative Hypothesis without (antiK)

Alternative hypothesis without antiK
antiS IgG antiLeaMixed
antiS IgG antiLeaMixed antiP1Mixed
antiS IgG antiLeaMixed antiP1Mixed antiLebMixed
antiS IgG antiLeaMixed antiP1Mixed antiLcbMixed antiLuaMixed
Complete explanation found

Figure 3.9. Anti K is not essential. The reactions can all be explained without this hypothesis.

something that has *no other plausible explanation* other than by using the hypothesis part in question (see Figures 3.8 and 3.9). Note the distinction between hypothesis parts that are nonsuperfluous relative to a particular composite, that is they cannot be removed without explanatory loss, and essentials without which no complete explanation can be found in the whole hypothesis space. An essential hypothesis is very probably correct, especially if it was rated as highly plausible by its specialist.

Essential hypotheses are collected into an *essential kernel* representing the part of the tentative composite that is most certain (Figure 3.10). This essential kernel is passed as a seed to the assembler and is expanded in the most plausible way to form a complete, consistent explanation. This second composite hypothesis is also submitted to the parsimonizer for removal of any explanatorily superfluous parts. At this stage the best explanation has been inferred, or at least *a* best explanation has been inferred, there being no a priori guarantee that a best explanation is unique (Figure 3.11). Under some circumstances the reasoning process will have virtually proved the correctness of its conclusion. If each part of the composite is essential (in the sense just described), then the system has, in effect, proved that it has found the only complete and parsimonious explanation available to it. This must be the correct explanation, assuming that the data is correct and the system's knowledge is complete and correct. When parts of the conclusion

Overview progress report window
Initial hypothesis: antiLeaMixed antiKIgG antiPIMixed antiSIgG
Parsimonized hypothesis: antiKIgG antiSIgG
Essential kernel of the hypothesis: antiSIgG

Figure 3.10. Essential Kernel.

Overview progress report window
Initial hypothesis: antiLeaMixed antiKIgG antiPIMixed antiSIgG
Parsimonized hypothesis: antiKIgG antiSIgG
Essential kernel of the hypothesis: antiSIgG
Rebuilt hypothesis: antiSIgG antiKIgG
Parsimonized rebuilt hypothesis: antiKIgG antiSIgG

Figure 3.11. Best explanation.

Antibody Classification Report
The best available explanation for the reactions in the workup is: antiSIgG antiKIgG
The following antibodies have been ruled out: antiD antiC antic antiE antie antiCw antif antiM antis antiFya antiFyb antiJka antiJkb antik antiKpb antiJsb antiLub antil
There are no antibodies that have been classified as CONFIRMED.
The following antibody is classified as WEAKLY CONFIRMED: antiS
The following antibody is classified as LIKELY PRESENT: antiK
The following antibodies are classified as LIKELY ABSENT: antiN antiLua antiLea antiLeb antiPI
The following antibodies are classified as UNRESOLVED: antiKpa antiJsa

Figure 3.12. Final report giving the status of the antibody hypotheses.

are not essential, the system will have discovered that alternative explanations are possible, so appropriate caution may be taken in using the abductive conclusion. A final report draws conclusions about what is known about the presence or absence of important antibodies (Figure 3.12). An explanation facility is also provided whereby the system may be asked for the reasons for its answers (Figure 3.13 a–d).

In general it is not sufficient just to produce a composite best explanation; it is also important to have more information about how good the explanation is, so that an agent can decide whether to act boldly or to be cautious,

---

Any Questions?

Type the name of an antibody if you would like an explanation of why it was classified the way it was.

Type A if you would like to see the antibody classification report again.

Type E to end consideration of the case.

>>>

>>>antiN

antiN was classified as LIKELY ABSENT because it is not part of the best explanation, and it was not rated as highly plausible by the antibody specialists.

>>>antiS

antiS was classified as WEAKLY CONFIRMED because it is the only plausible way to explain the indicated reactions, all of the reactions in the workup can be explained, but the Rule of Three for sufficiency of the evidence was not passed.

Can only be explained by the presence of antiS

	623A	479	537A	506A	303A	209A	186A	195	164
AlbuminIS	0	0	0	0	0	0	0	0	0
Albumin37	0	0	0	0	0	0	0	0	0
Coombs	2s	0	0	0	0	0	0	0	0
EnzymeIS	0	0	0	0	0	0	0	0	0
Enzyme37	0	0	0	0	0	0	0	0	0

Figure 3.13. (a-d) Obtaining an explanation of the system's conclusions.

for example deciding to gather more evidence before taking action. Some critical assessment is necessary because, as we said, the appropriate confidence for an abductive conclusion depends in part on how well it compares with the competition. This applies to the evaluation of composite hypotheses no less than it applies to simple ones.

How other systems criticize. For each composite hypothesis it constructs, DENDRAL generates a prediction of how the mass spectrogram should appear. Hypotheses whose predictions mismatch sufficiently are excluded, and the rest are ranked on the basis of the quality of this match. Again, DENDRAL devotes a special knowledge-based problem solver to the task, although it is tuned to predictions based on molecular fragmentation, and is not domain-independent in character. INTERNIST and the set-covering model appear not to do anything corresponding to the RED-2 sort of criticism. Indeed, INTERNIST commits itself irrevocably to each hypothesis in the growing composite before it goes on to decide on the next, and it has nothing corresponding to the RED-2 engine's tentative initial assembly. The set-covering model builds in the simplicity criterion in the form of a guarantee that the problem solver will produce composites with the minimum cardinality sufficient to account for all the findings.

RED-2 performance

RED-2 was implemented in InterLisp™ and the LOOPS™ language for object-oriented programming (from Xerox Corporation), and it was run on a Xerox Lisp machine.[7] RED-2's performance was initially evaluated by using 20 selected test cases chosen, not as a representative sample of blood-bank problems, but rather, to fully exercise the capabilities of the system. These cases are used in training blood-bank technologists, some from textbooks and some from course materials. Each case has an associated correct answer that was used as the standard of comparison. Twenty cases were chosen, 6 in which the accepted answer involved a single antibody; 6 had two antibody answers; and the remaining 8 required three or more antibodies in the conclusion. This is actually a much more trying distribution than is typical of the blood bank, where most cases involve only a single antibody. The answers generated in the blood bank are not "scientifically pure" in that the goal is to detect medically important antibodies, not simply to discover which are present; thus answer acceptance has a pragmatic component.

Of the 20 cases chosen, 3 of the complex ones had accepted answers that were very indefinite. RED-2's answers on these cases were not inconsistent with the textbook, but we were unable to evaluate its performance in detail. Remaining were 17 cases in which performance could be more closely evaluated, varying in difficulty from simple to very complex. In 12 of the 17 cases, RED-2's answers were precisely the same as the textbook answer. In 1 other case, RED-2's answer differed from the textbook answer but was still quite acceptable, according to our expert.

In 3 cases RED-2 overcommitted by including an extra antibody that was not in the textbook answer. That is, RED-2 decided that the antibodies in the textbook answer were not sufficient to explain all the reactions and included another antibody to make up the difference. According to our expert, RED-2's answers on these 3 cases were acceptable but more cautious than a typical blood-bank technologist. This discrepancy was probably a result of two factors.

First our intention in building the system was that RED-2 should simply interpret panel data and make a statement about which antibodies appear to be present. This means that certain pragmatic considerations about therapeutic significance were left out of RED-2's knowledge. For example, a technologist may be reluctant to accept an explanation of some reactions in terms of a common but clinically insignificant antibody, for fear that a too ready acceptance of such an answer may mask something clinically more dangerous.

Second, RED-2 is inflexible about how much reaction can be explained by an antibody. Once it decides how much of the panel data to attribute to a particular antibody, it never revises its estimate. From our analysis of protocols taken from blood-bank specialists, it seems that humans are willing to consider stretching the explanatory power of hypotheses. The result is that where RED-2 might assume an additional antibody to explain a small remaining reaction, the human expert might simply assign the small remainder to an antibody already assumed to be present.

RED-2's answer was unacceptable (partly) in only one case. In this case RED-2 built a five-antibody best explanation, whereas the expert answer was a three-antibody solution. RED-2 detected two of the three "correct" antibodies but missed the third, actually building a compound three-antibody alternative to using the expert's third antibody. Most troublesome was that RED-2 identified this antibody as LIKELY ABSENT because it was not part of its best explanation and was not especially plausible (according to its hypothesis specialist). Each of the three antibodies RED-2 used instead of the accepted one were rated as more plausible than the accepted one, which is why they were chosen instead. According to our expert, RED-2's plausibilities were reasonably assigned, but the blood-bank technologist would prefer the simpler explanation, even though it uses an antibody that was fairly implausible under the circumstances.

One interpretation for RED-2's behavior on this case is related to the way it judges the plausibility of compound hypotheses. RED-2 depends heavily on the individual plausibility of simple hypotheses and knows little about the plausibility of collections (although it does know about logical incompatibilities). As a result, it can produce an answer containing many individually plausible antibodies that are collectively implausible. This is most likely to arise when the case is complex. In these cases neither RED-2 nor the human expert can be very certain of an answer, so more testing is usually required.

Another measure of performance is a simple count of the number of antibodies correctly identified. In the 20 test cases RED-2 identified 31 of 33 antibodies that were asserted to be part of correct answers. In addition, RED-2 never ruled out an antibody that was part of the correct answer. This is especially important clinically because ruling out an antibody that is actually present in the patient can have disastrous consequences. Of lesser importance, but still interesting, is that RED-2 never confirmed an antibody that had been ruled out in the textbook answer.

In summary, RED-2 produced clinically acceptable answers in 16 of 17 cases and correctly identified 31 of 33 antibodies. It never ruled out an antibody that was part of the correct answer or confirmed an antibody that was not part of the correct answer. Thus the performance of the system was, overall, quite good, demonstrating that "abductive logic" had been correctly captured, at least to some degree.

RED-2 also shows the power of decomposing complex problem solving into more primitive problem-solving tasks. The performance of RED-2 on the 20 test cases lends strong credence to the idea that the task decomposition embodied in the RED-2 system is at least approximately correct.

The order of considering the findings

Sherlock Holmes says:

I have already explained to you that what is out of the common is usually a guide rather than a hindrance.[8]

and

Singularity is almost invariably a clue.[9]

and

The more outré and grotesque an incident is the more carefully it deserves to be examined, and the very point which appears to complicate a case is, when duly considered and scientifically handled, the one which is most likely to elucidate it.[10]

We compared the original RED-2 strategy, which attempted to explain the most important data (strongest reaction) first, with what we called the "Sherlock Holmes strategy," which focuses attention on the most surprising, most unusual unexplained finding. First we calculated the frequency of various reactions. The master panels of all cases in our case library were created, and for each test condition the number of antigen-antibody reactions were summarized. Also, the number of reactions of each strength were recorded separately. Data were compiled from 42 cases overall. Then we programmed a new strategy, which focused on the most unusual finding first (i.e., the reaction that belongs to the rarest condition-strength pair). For example, if there was a reaction of strength 4+ in EnzymeIS it would be chosen first because such a reaction is rare; if not, then the next rarest would be chosen, and so forth.

The cases were rerun with the new strategy (except for 5 cases that never ran because of unresolved software problems). All the steps in each assembly phase (forming the initial composite, finding the essentials, and building the alternatives) were counted and added, and the results obtained with the two strategies compared. The Sherlock Holmes strategy was more efficient in 16 and less efficient in 17 cases, and the two strategies tied in 4 cases. The Sherlock Holmes strategy evidently did not provide any improvement in computational efficiency; the average number of computational steps was essentially the same for both strategies. Consequently, we conclude that the order in which individual findings are considered is probably not important to the overall computational efficiency of the RED-2 hypothesis assembly mechanism.

An explanation of this negative result might be that unusual reactions were just as ambiguous (had just as many plausible explainers) as the more common ones. Alternatively, our estimate of rarity may have been inaccurate. A suggestion for a revised experiment is to get an estimate from experts on the frequency of particular antibodies reacting in particular test conditions, and then to use that estimate, rather than the frequencies in our limited library of cases, as a measure of rarity. Also, protocols have shown that experts consider patterns of reaction, so it might be more rewarding to look for unusual patterns of reactions than for unusual single reactions.

Hypothesis interactions

Hypothesis interactions can be considered to be of two general types, each with its own kind of significance for the problem solving:

1. *explanatory interactions* (e.g., overlapping in what the hypotheses can account for)
2. *interactions of mutual support or incompatibility* (e.g., resulting from causal or logical relations)

For example, two disease hypotheses might offer to explain the same findings without being especially compatible or incompatible causally, logically, or definitionally. On the other hand, hypotheses might be mutually exclusive (e.g., because they represent definitionally distinct subtypes of the same disease) or mutually supportive (e.g., because they are causally associated). In general the elements of a diagnostic differential need to be *exhaustive* of the possibilities so that at least one must be correct, but they need not be mutually exclusive. If they are exhaustive, then evidence against one of them is transformed into evidence in favor of the others.

Following are six specific types of possible hypothesis interactions:

1. *A* and *B* are mutually compatible and represent explanatory alternatives where their explanatory capabilities overlap.
2. Hypothesis *A* is a subhypothesis of *B* (i.e., a more detailed refinement).

If hypotheses have type-subtype relationships, which normally occurs if they are generated by a hierarchical classifier, a hypothesis assembler can preferentially pursue the goal of explanatory completeness and secondarily pursue the goal of refining the constituent hypotheses down to the level of most detail. This extension to the RED-2 mechanism was explored later (see chapter 4).

3. *A* and *B* are mutually incompatible.

The strategy used in RED-2 is to maintain the consistency of the growing hypothesis as the assembly proceeds. If a finding is encountered whose only available maximally plausible explainers are incompatible with something already present in the growing hypothesis, then one of these newly encountered hypotheses is included in the growing hypothesis and any parts inconsistent with the new one are removed from the composite in the way that we described earlier. The basic idea is that the finding must be explained, even if doing so forces a serious revision of the growing hypothesis. This seems to be a rather weak way of handling incompatibles, however, and better strategies were devised later, as will be seen.

4. *A* and *B* cooperate additively where they overlap in what they can account for.

If such interactions occur, this knowledge needs to be incorporated into the methods for computing what a composite hypothesis can explain. All of the RED systems have done this.

5. Using *A* as part of an explanation suggests also using *B*.

To handle this type of hypothesis interaction, as for example if there is available knowledge of a statistical association, we can give extra plausibility credit to the suggested hypothesis if the hypothesis making the suggestion is already part of the growing composite. This feature was incorporated into RED-2 as part of the strategy for handling ties in plausibility during assembly. A path for the hypothesis to grow preferentially along lines of statistical association provides a rudimentary ability for it to grow along causal lines as well.

6. *A*, if it is accepted, raises explanatory questions of its own that can be resolved by appeal to *B*.

An example of this last type occurs when we hypothesize the presence of a certain pathophysiological state to explain certain symptoms, and then hypothesize some more remote cause to account for the pathophysiological state. The stomachache is explained by the presence of the ulcers, and the ulcers are explained by the anxiety disorder. At the same time that a newly added hypothesis succeeds in explaining some of the findings, it might introduce a "loose end." To handle this by mildly extending the RED-2 mechanism, the newly added hypothesis can be posted as a kind of higher-level finding which needs to be explained in its turn by the growing assembly. This provides a way in which the growing hypothesis can move from hypotheses close to the findings of the case, and towards more and more remote causes of those findings. Nothing like this was actually incorporated into the RED-2 mechanism, but, as we will see, the capability was incorporated into later "layered abduction" machines.

The RED-1 strategy handles interactions of types 1 and 4. The RED-2 strategy additionally handles interactions of types 3 and 5. The generation-3 strategy (chapter 4) also handles interactions of types 2, and the layered abduction machines also handle interactions of types 6 (chapter 10). As we will see, the generations of abductive machines, starting with the first two

RED systems, developed increasingly sophisticated strategies for exploiting these relationships between hypotheses.

Notes

1 Jack W. Smith, John R. Josephson, and Charles Evans designed RED-1; Jack W. Smith, John R. Josephson and Michael C. Tanner designed RED-2.

2 Case OSU 9 is used for illustration throughout this chapter. It is documented more fully in (Tanner, Josephson, and Smith, 1991). OSU 9 represents a single workup on one particular patient on one particular occasion.

3 The information from a panel consists of approximately 50 reactions (counting non-reactions) with each reaction or nonreaction described by one of 15 symbols encoding type or degree of reaction. Thus there are approximately 15^{50} possible panels and the number of possible inputs for any version of RED is astronomically large.

4 Charles Evans programmed the RED-1 antibody classification structure and Mike Tanner programmed the RED-2 classification structure using CSRL. CSRL was developed by Tom Bylander and designed by Tom Bylander and Sanjay Mittal (Bylander, Mittal, & Chandrasekaran, 1983) (Bylander & Mittal, 1986).

5 Charles Evans designed and programmed the inferencing data base for RED-1. Mike Tanner designed and programmed the inferencing data base for RED-2.

6 Charles Evans programmed RED-1, except for the Overview mechanism, which John Josephson programmed. They were programmed using the ELISP dialect of Rutgers/UCI-LISP and run on a Decsystem-2060 computer under the TOPS-20 operating system.

7 John Josephson programmed the RED-2 Overview mechanism, and Mike Tanner programmed the rest, in part by using CSRL.

8 From "A Study in Scarlet" by Sir Arthur Conan Doyle.

9 From "The Boscombe Valley Mystery" by Sir Arthur Conan Doyle.

10 From "The Hound of the Baskervilles" by Sir Arthur Conan Doyle.

4   Generalizing the control strategy – machine 3

The PEIRCE tool

In the first generation of work on generic tasks the invocation of a generic-task problem solver was pre-programmed, hard-wired during system programming. In RED-2 we wanted to test many variations of the algorithm empirically, but a significant amount of work was required to reprogram the system each time a change was desired. Also, the RED-2 hypothesis-assembly module seemed too "algorithmic," too much like a rule follower and not enough like "fluid intelligence." So we decided to analyze the system in terms of the goals and subgoals of abductive problem solving and to identify the different methods that were used to achieve the various goals. This analysis allowed us to reorganize the program in a way that made adding new methods and modifying the goal structure easy, so that we could better experiment with new strategies for abduction. For multiple methods to be available to achieve problem-solving goals, method selection would occur at run time based on the state of the problem and the availability of needed forms of knowledge. These efforts resulted in a programming tool called "PEIRCE"[1] for building systems that perform abductive assembly and criticism in this more flexible manner.

Systems built with PEIRCE are examples of third generation abduction machines (where RED-1 is taken as the first generation and RED-2 as the second). PEIRCE allows for specifying strategies for dynamically integrating various hypothesis-improvement tactics, or operators, during the course of problem solving. The idea was to capture domain-independent aspects of abductive assembly and criticism and embed them in the tool, leaving domain-specific aspects to be programmed when building particular knowledge-based systems. Thus PEIRCE was designed to be *domain independent but task specific.*

√The PEIRCE Tool is by William F. Punch III, Michael C. Tanner, John R. Josephson, Jack W. Smith, B. Chandrasekaran, and Olivier Fischer. Reimplementing RED in PEIRCE is by William F. Punch III, Michael C. Tanner, John R. Josephson, Jack W. Smith, and Olivier Fischer. Abduction in SOAR is by Todd R. Johnson and Jack W. Smith. It is adapted from A Framework for Opportunistic Abductive Strategies which appeared in the *Proceedings of the Thirteenth Annual Conference of the Cognitive Science Society*, 1991, copyright Cognitive Science Society Incorporated, used by permission. Generic Tasks Revisited is by B. Chandrasekaran.

94

We reimplemented RED using PEIRCE, both to debug the tool and to enable experiments with other abductive-assembly strategies for red-cell antibody identification. PEIRCE was also used to build a liver-disease diagnosis system called PATHEX/LIVER and to build TIPS (Task Integrated Problem Solver), another medical diagnosis system. TIPS, especially, exploits PEIRCE's ability to dynamically integrate different problem-solving methods. In this chapter we describe PEIRCE, the reimplementation of RED, and a reimplementation of PEIRCE in SOAR, which is a software system that realizes an architecture for general intelligence developed by Laird, Rosenbloom and Newell (Laird, Rosenbloom, & Newell, 1986). This reimplementation of PEIRCE is called ABD-SOAR. In chapter 5 we describe TIPS and PATHEX/LIVER.

Abductive assembly: Generic goals and subgoals

The goal of generating the best explanatory hypothesis can be accomplished by achieving three subgoals:

1. generation of a set of plausible hypotheses
2. construction of a compound explanation for all the findings
3. criticism and improvement of the compound explanation

How each subgoal is achieved presumably varies depending on the knowledge and computational resources available and on the desired characteristics of the solution (for example how certain it must be).

As we saw in chapter 3, in RED-2 the subgoal of constructing an explanation for all the findings was, in effect, achieved by achieving a series of subgoals of finding explanations for a sufficient number of individual findings. The goal of criticizing and improving the compound explanation was itself achieved by way of the subgoals of criticism for parsimony and criticism for essentialness. RED-2 pursued these goals and subgoals in a fixed and rigid order, but a careful analysis of the dependencies shows that there is some latitude in the order in which goals are pursued. For example a cautious strategy might be followed whereby each time a new hypothesis is introduced into the composite, all those already in the composite are immediately checked to make sure that they have not become explanatorily superfluous. This contrasts with the strategy in RED-2 where the parsimony criticism did not take place until after a complete tentative composite was formed.

As we said, abductive goals can be achieved by achieving certain subgoals. A *method* is a particular way of achieving a goal, and generates specific subgoals to be pursued. Thus, as we have seen, a method for achieving the goal of creating an abductive conclusion might be to pursue the subgoals of generating plausible elementary hypotheses, assembling a complete explanation, and criticizing the explanation. Each of these subgoals will have its own method or methods. A method for assembling a complete explanation might repeatedly pursue the subgoal of extending the explanatory coverage of the working hypothesis. A method for extending explanatory coverage might pursue the subgoal of trying to explain, all at once, a whole pattern of findings; another method for the same goal might pursue the alternative subgoal of attempting to explain a single finding. Thus a problem-solving goal leads to a method for pursuing it, and that method leads to some set of subgoals, and so on, and so on, recursively. Eventually the pursuit of goals by pursuit of subgoals must bottom out in operations that can be performed directly, that is, with no further subgoal generation.

Knowledge requirements. Several distinct types of knowledge are needed for abductive-assembly knowledge-based systems, corresponding roughly to the forms needed to support the subtask decomposition just described. The PEIRCE tool provides software support for representing each of the following types of knowledge:

1. *Plausibility-assignment knowledge.* Domain knowledge is needed to assign a plausibility rating for each hypothesis. This knowledge is of two kinds:
   a. knowledge that is independent of the particular case data (prior probabilities, to use probability language); for example, knowledge of whether an antibody is rare or common
   b. knowledge that is sensitive to the case data (local-match prima facie posterior probabilities); for example, knowledge of various specific patterns of data and their significance for setting confidence values
2. Accounts-for knowledge. Domain knowledge is needed to determine what each hypothesis can explain. Under some circumstances this can take the form of a list of findings that each hypothesis can account for if those findings are present. For example, we know in advance that a flu can account for body aches, fever, nasal congestion, and so forth, but a single patient might have only some of these symptoms. In RED, determining what a hypothesis accounts for is a fairly complicated business. An antibody hypothesis might only partially account for an observed reaction under the particular test conditions, and an individual hypothesis cannot account for reactions of widely differing strengths under closely similar test conditions.
3. *Finding-importance knowledge.* It is useful to have knowledge to draw the focus of attention either to a single finding or to a particular pattern of findings. Then again, perhaps this is not so useful. In the Sherlock Holmes experiment described in chapter 3, we found no significant improvement in performance from what seemed, in advance, to be a more clever way of focusing attention.
4. *Hypothesis-hypothesis interaction knowledge.* Some types of hypothesis interaction were described in chapter 3. A recurring theme of this book is ways to bring knowledge of hypothesis interactions to bear to aid the progress of problem solving.
5. *Strategy knowledge.* The abductive-assembly strategy can rely on a fixed control regime, or a more opportunistic one. If opportunistic control is to be used, knowledge must be available at run time to assist in deciding what to do next. The set strategy in RED-2 is that of assembly, criticism, and reassembly around the essential core. In contrast, PEIRCE supports the encoding of systems that

choose at run time among a number of methods for pursuing problem-solving goals, including the invocation of hypothesis-improving operations of: (attempting to) extend explanatory coverage, refine the working hypothesis, resolve an inconsistency, criticize for parsimony (and improve the hypothesis appropriately), and criticize for essentialness (and improve). The tool user (builder of a particular knowledge-based system) is provided with the means to encode knowledge that controls when these methods and operations are invoked.

The control mechanism of PEIRCE

One main consideration in the design of PEIRCE was to provide a programmable control mechanism that would enable a knowledge engineer to determine how and when to invoke a problem-solving method. The control mechanism should provide some way to evaluate at run time, according to preprogrammed standards, each method's appropriateness for invocation, and then to select one method to invoke. To accomplish this, PEIRCE was designed to make control decisions by using a sponsor-selector mechanism borrowed from David C. Brown's DSPL (Design Specialists and Plans Language) (Brown, 1984). Figure 4.1 shows a schematic sponsor-selector structure. It consists of three kinds of parts: a *selector*, some number of *sponsors,* and an *invocable method* associated with each sponsor. Available methods are grouped under the selector, where each sponsor provides appropriateness ratings for invoking its associated method. At any choice point, that is, at any point in the problem-solving flow at which another method can be invoked, all the sponsors are invoked to rate the appropriateness of their associated methods. Then the selector chooses the next method to execute based on the sponsor supplied ratings and possibly other information about the problem state.

Since the main goal in a PEIRCE system is to generate a best explanation for the data, control is first given to a software entity called an "abducer." An abducer is a specialist in explaining a particular class of data; the PEIRCE tool supports the construction of specialized abducers. The main abducer of a PEIRCE-built system specializes in explaining all the data (that needs explaining) for a case in the particular domain for which the system has been built. To fulfill its responsibility, the main abducer may call on the services of one or more specialized subabducers, as illustrated schematically in Figure 4.2. Each abducer is a sponsor-selector structure specifically set up for its particular class of explanation-finding problems or subproblems. Figure 4.3 shows the structure of a typical abducer. Subabducers may be called upon while a method is being executed, especially the method for extending explanatory coverage.

Sponsors. Each sponsor contains knowledge for judging when its associated method is appropriate. The sponsor uses this knowledge to yield a symbolic

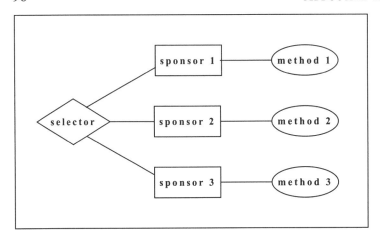

Figure 4.1. The structure of a sponsor-selector system for making control decisions.

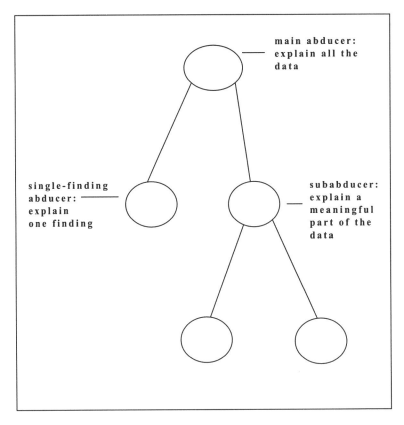

Figure 4.2. PEIRCE: Abducer hierarchy.

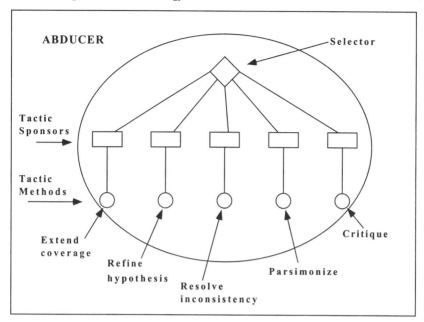

Figure 4.3. PEIRCE: Abducer control.

value that indicates how appropriate the method is under the circumstances. The information-processing task of a sponsor can be thought of as hypothesis matching, one of the generic tasks described in chapter 2, although in PEIRCE a sponsor evaluates the appropriateness of a certain hypothetical course of action, rather than the plausibility of a classificatory or explanatory hypothesis as in CSRL.

A sponsor's knowledge, put in by a knowledge engineer as part of building a knowledge-based system, is represented in a decision table similar to the knowledge groups of CSRL, the tool used to build hierarchical classification systems. (Knowledge groups were described in Chapter 3.) A sponsor's decision table maps problem-solving states to appropriateness values by representing patterns of responses to queries about the problem state and by associating each pattern with an appropriateness value.

Figure 4.4 illustrates a sponsor's decision table. (The column headings have been put into English for purposes of exposition.) Each column, except the last, is headed with a query about the system's problem-solving state. Each row represents a pattern of responses to the queries, followed by an appropriateness value that applies if the pattern occurs. The appropriateness value can come from any fixed, discrete, ordered range of symbolic values; in this example it comes from a scale that ranges from -3 (for highly inap-

Does the working hypothesis have exactly one part?	Is the working hypothesis completely refined?	Appropriateness value
T	F	3
F	F	1
?	T	- 3

Figure 4.4. Decision table for a refine-hypothesis sponsor.

propriate) to +3 (for highly appropriate). If a row *matches*, that is, if each element of the row is true for the query with which its column is headed, then the last element of the row becomes the symbolic value returned by the sponsor. The rows are evaluated in order, top to bottom, until one row matches. This representation allows the knowledge engineer to specify the order in which patterns are checked. If no patterns match and all were examined, a default value is returned, usually 0 if a seven-step -3 to +3 scale is used, as in the example.

In Figure 4.4 there are two queries: Query 1, represented by column 1, is, "Does the working hypothesis have exactly one part?" and query 2 is, "Is the working hypothesis completely refined?" Row 1 represents the following rule: If the working hypothesis has a single part, represented by the T, or True, answer to query 1, and if the working hypothesis is not completely refined, represented by the F, or False, answer to query 2, then return a 3, meaning that refining the working hypothesis now is highly appropriate. The middle row, which is tested only if the first pattern does not match, says, in effect, that if the working hypothesis has more than one part and if this hypothesis is not completely refined, then it is mildly appropriate to refine it now. The question mark (?) in the last row is a wild card or "don't care" symbol, which will always match. Thus, the last row says that, whether or not the working hypothesis has a single part, if the working hypothesis is already completely refined, then refining it further is highly inappropriate.

Selectors. Each set of sponsors is grouped under a selector. The selector does two things:

1. It organizes the set of methods that are available at the particular recurring decision point.

2.   It selects which method to invoke next based on the appropriateness ratings of the sponsors and other knowledge.

If a selector is activated, only the methods associated with it are available for invocation on each selection cycle. Other selectors may be activated as a result of some method being invoked, but only one selector at a time is responsible for deciding what to do.

A selector's main criterion is the appropriateness measures returned from its sponsors, but often this information is not sufficient; for example, there may be a tie for the best method to invoke. The knowledge engineer should not have to program each sponsor so that only one is appropriate under each set of circumstances. Good software modularity requires that each sponsor should be coded with little consideration of other sponsors and that broader considerations of proper selection are left to the selector. Thus, PEIRCE was designed so that method selection can occur in three ways:

a.   The selection can occur simply on the basis of appropriateness ratings. If there is exactly one highly rated method, that method is invoked. If there is no such clear winner and no other selection knowledge is available, a random choice will be made among the best candidates.

b.   If there is a tie for highest rated method, tie-breaking knowledge in the form of an ordered priority list, supplied by the knowledge engineer, can be used to break the tie. If more than one method is rated as maximally appropriate, the one that occurs first in the priority list is chosen.

c.   For special situations it is also possible to override the normal choice mechanism by specifying pattern-match knowledge similar to that found in the sponsors. If the pattern matches, the choice indicated in the matching row is used.

Methods can be added to an existing PEIRCE-built system by simply including their associated sponsors in the sponsor-selector system and updating the selection knowledge. Thus a PEIRCE-built system is one in which control strategies can be easily changed (e.g., by changing the order in a method-priority list) and in which it is easy to add new methods.

Reimplementing RED in PEIRCE

We implemented three systems in PEIRCE: a new version of RED, which we can call RED-3; PATHEX/LIVER for liver disease diagnosis, and TIPS. PATHEX/LIVER and TIPS are described in chapter 5. In this section we focus on RED-3. In the new implementation we wanted to break the RED-2 hypothesis assembler into its natural parts and allow the system to use these parts in a mixed order, as appropriate, to solve abductive assembly-problems. Initially, however, the sponsor-selector knowledge was encoded to resemble the RED-2 algorithm.

We hoped that our work would result in an environment in which we could easily test some of the variations that we envisioned in the RED hypothesis-assembly strategy. We proposed to examine three specific RED variations:

1. *Delaying hard decisions*. Postponing for as long as possible choosing which hypothesis to integrate into the compound explanation when the choice was not obvious.
2. *Explaining special or multiple findings*. Providing for abducers that specialize in explaining certain known patterns or clusters of domain findings. This would allow for a more knowledge-controlled divide-and-conquer strategy, rather than always attempting to explain one finding at a time.
3. *Refinement control*. Enabling the abductive assembler to provoke the hierarchical classifier to refine some hypotheses, based on explanatory needs.

These three variations are described next.

Delaying hard decisions

The process of abductive assembly can reach a choice point we call a *hard decision*. Let us suppose that a single finding, *f*, is the focus of attention and that the hypotheses available to explain *f* are *A*, *B*, and *C*. The abducer's job is to choose one of these hypotheses to explain *f*, but the only criterion of choice is the plausibility ratings of the hypotheses. (Often other grounds for choice are available, but for simplicity we will assume not in the present example.) Suppose that all three hypotheses have the same plausibility value of 3. Since there is no real basis for choice, the assembler must make a hard decision.

At this point, the RED-2 system would simply make a random choice, because in context it did not seem to matter what was chosen, and downstream criticism with potential repair was scheduled to occur anyway. However, in the PEIRCE implementation we added another tactic: delaying a hard decision. As easy decisions are made, we hoped that the hard decisions would be resolved serendipitously as their associated findings are covered by more easily decided upon hypotheses. If any hard decisions remain after all the easy decisions are made, the system attempts to make the choice on some grounds, perhaps by choosing the better of nearly equal hypotheses. If no grounds can be found, the system reverts to random choice to make these decisions. This strategy is somewhat similar to the strategy of "least commitment" found in some earlier systems (e.g., Mittal & Frayman, 1987; Stefik, 1981). It is even more closely related to the idea of "island driving" (Hayes-Roth and Lesser, 1977) first described in the HEARSAY-II system, in which islands of high confidence are found and form a basis for exploring the rest of the hypothesis space.

This tactic can be generalized to include several levels of decision difficulty, so that an explanation will be accepted only if it meets the prevailing standards of certainty (e.g., surpasses all rivals by at least a given interval) and these standards can be relaxed in stages to gain more explanatory coverage.

The PEIRCE implementation of RED (RED-3) was rerun on a number of cases for which RED-2 was previously evaluated. One problem that we encountered was providing a reasonable measure of performance to show clearly the difference between RED-3 and RED-2. Their abilities to get the "correct" answer is not a good measure because both systems either get the same answer or, where their answers differ, our experts deemed the answers to be close enough. We needed to measure *how* the two systems arrived at their answers.

We discovered that the major difference between the two assembly strategies was the contents of their initial hypotheses. This difference can be directly attributed to RED-3's postponement of some hard decisions. Moreover, RED-3 also discovered the essentialness of some hypotheses in the process of assembly, which resulted in resolving some of the outstanding hard decisions. The initial explanations were consequently much closer to the final explanations that both strategies provided. The delaying-hard-decisions feature of PEIRCE made the search process more efficient.[2]

Explaining special or multiple findings

Another issue to be explored was attempting to explain multiple findings at the same time, as opposed to always attempting to explain one finding at a time. We observed our domain experts recognizing findings as related, grouping them as a unit, and trying to explain all these findings at once. In one family of examples that we observed in the RED domain, the expert recognized a set of reactions as indicating a general Rh antibody pattern and explained it using specialized knowledge of Rh reactions.

Pathognomonic symptoms. The idea of pathognomonic symptoms is known to all clinicians.

> **Definition**   A symptom *S* is said to be pathognomonic if there exists at least one disease *D* whose existence can be automatically inferred from the presence of *S*.

In the presence of pathognomonic symptoms, a clinician can quickly focus attention on the correct disease. An example of such a symptom is Kayser-Fleischer rings, which are pathognomonic for Wilson's disease. Pathognomonic symptoms not only increase the speed of diagnosis, but also direct attention to an initial high-confidence hypothesis from which to build a complete diagnosis. The problem with the concept of a pathognomonic symptom is that it is too restrictive; pathognomonic symptoms are rare, and, so, rarely useful for reasoning.

Constrictors. Pathognomonic symptoms being of limited use, the concept of *constrictor* was first defined for the Caduceus system (Pople, 1977) as a useful extension to the idea of pathognomony.

Definition   A symptom S is said to be a constrictor if there exists at least one class of diseases D whose presence can be automatically inferred from the existence of S.

Constrictors can be used to focus the diagnostic process in the same fashion as pathognomonic findings. Though not so powerful as to enable focusing on a particular disease, constrictors are more common than pathognomonic symptoms and thus are more generally useful. An example of a constrictor is jaundice, which indicates liver disease. Caduceus begins its diagnostic process by looking for constrictors. The constrictors it finds help to focus the diagnostic process on a limited number of hypotheses.

The ability to use knowledge of constrictors, or of special meaningful patterns of findings, can be achieved in PEIRCE by allowing for special extra methods to be sponsored for the extend-explanatory-coverage goal, which arises as a result of selecting the extend-explanatory-coverage tactic. Each such method is designed to try to explain certain findings, or finding patterns, on the basis of special knowledge regarding how to recognize and attempt to explain those findings or patterns. The default would be to proceed using general methods, one finding at a time, but for each domain a new set of sponsors can be introduced to explain special cases.

Refinement control

In RED-3 we hoped to provide more control over the hypothesis-refinement process in the hierarchical classifier by guiding it according to explanatory need. By this we mean that the decision to refine a classification node (i.e., examine its subnodes) considers, not only the ability of the node to establish (i.e., set high plausibility), but also whether the node represents a hypothesis that is needed to explain any of the findings. Thus the hierarchical classifier and the abductive assembler interleave their operations. The hierarchical classifier provides a list of candidate hypotheses (and their associated plausibility ratings) to the abductive assembler, but these hypotheses have only a certain level of specificity (i.e., they were explored down to a certain level in the hierarchy). The abductive assembler then creates an explanation of the findings by using this candidate list. The assembler can then request a refinement of one of the hypotheses used in its compound explanation. The classifier refines this node and returns a list of candidate subnodes (more specific hypotheses) to replace the original node. The assembler removes the original hypothesis and attempts to reexplain the findings that it explained, using the refined hypothesis. This interaction continues until the explanation is specific enough, or the hierarchy is examined to its tip nodes.

The usefulness of PEIRCE

We want to emphasize the utility of PEIRCE as a tool for experimenting with the various methods of abductive assembly. It is fairly simple to change the conditions under which a method is invoked in the overall assembly process by modifying the knowledge of when and to what degree the method is appropriate. Such changes are local in that they affect only the invocation of one method at one recurring decision point. Adding a new method is equally simple, because it needs only to be included in the sponsor-selector tree with some knowledge of when it is appropriate, and what priority it should have.

Abduction in SOAR

Introduction. Any single algorithm for abduction requires specific kinds of knowledge and ignores other kinds of knowledge. Hence, a knowledge-based system that uses a single abductive method is restricted to using the knowledge required by that method. This restriction makes the system brittle because the single fixed method can respond appropriately only in a limited range of situations and can make use of only a subset of the potentially relevant knowledge. To remedy this problem we have endeavored to develop a framework from which abductive strategies can be opportunistically constructed at run time to reflect the problem being solved and the knowledge available to solve the problem. In this section we present this framework and describe ABD-SOAR, an implementation of the framework. We show how ABD-SOAR can be made to behave like the abductive strategy used in RED-2, and we describe the differences between ABD-SOAR and PEIRCE.

This work on ABD-SOAR contributes to our understanding of both knowledge-based systems and abduction. First, it illustrates how to increase the problem-solving capabilities of knowledge-based systems by using mechanisms that permit the use of all relevant knowledge. ABD-SOAR requires little domain knowledge to begin solving a problem but can easily make use of additional knowledge to solve the problem better or faster. Second, the framework can be used to provide a flexible abductive problem-solving capability for knowledge-based systems. Third, ABD-SOAR gives SOAR (Laird, Rosenbloom, & Newell, 1986; Newell, 1990; Rosenbloom, Laird, & Newell, 1987) an abductive capability so that many systems written in SOAR can begin to solve abduction problems. Fourth, the framework provides a simple and general mechanism for abduction that is capable of generating the behavior of various fixed methods. Fifth, ABD-SOAR can be used to experiment with different abductive strategies, including variations of existing strategies and combinations of different kinds of strategies.

SOAR has been proposed as an architecture for general intelligence. In

SOAR, all problem solving is viewed as searching for a goal state in a problem space. Viewing all problem-solving activity as search in a problem space is called the *problem-space computational model* (PSCM) (Newell, Yost, Laird, Rosenbloom, & Altmann, 1991). A problem space is defined by an initial state and a set of operators that apply to states to produce new states. The behavior of a problem-space system depends on three kinds of knowledge: *Operator-proposal knowledge* indicates the operators that can be applied to the current state of problem solving. *Operator-selection knowledge* selects from the list of applicable operators a single operator to apply to the current state. Finally, *operator-implementation knowledge* applies a selected operator to the current state to produce a new state. If any of this knowledge is incomplete, SOAR automatically sets up a subgoal to search for additional knowledge. The subgoal is treated like any other problem in that it must be achieved by searching through a problem space. The process of enumerating and selecting operators at each step of problem solving, together with automatic creation of subgoals to overcome incomplete knowledge, makes SOAR an especially appropriate framework for exploring opportunistic problem solving. Chandrasekaran (1988) says this about SOAR:

> My view is that from the perspective of modeling cognitive behavior, a GT [generic-task]-level analysis provides two closely related ideas which give additional content to phenomena at the SOAR architecture level. On the one hand, the GT theory provides a vocabulary of goals that a SOAR-like system may have. On the other hand, this vocabulary of goals also provides a means of indexing and organizing knowledge in long-term memory such that, when SOAR is pursuing a problem solving goal, appropriate chunks of knowledge and control behavior are placed in short term memory for SOAR to behave like a GT problem solver. In this sense a SOAR-like architecture, based as it is on goal achievement and universal subgoaling, provides an attractive substratum on which to implement future GT systems. In turn, the SOAR-level architecture can give graceful behavior under conditions that do not match the highly compiled nature of GT type problem solving. (pp. 208-209)

Specifying problem-solving methods

Before we describe the framework for abduction, we must first explain how we will specify it. We address this in the context of the general problem of specifying problem-solving methods.

A problem-solving method consists of a set of operators with preconditions and knowledge that indicates the order in which to apply the operators. The standard way to specify a problem-solving method is by writing an algorithm that lists each operator in the order in which the operators are to be done, along with conditionals and possibly loops. To implement the method a procedural programming language can be used to encode the algorithm. The operators are implemented directly either using built-in commands of the language or by calling subprocedures. In a procedural description of a method, the order of the operators must be completely specified. In other words, the procedure must encode enough knowledge so that the next operator can always be determined. Furthermore, a procedural language makes it difficult to encode operators that generate control knowledge.

Since we desire an opportunistic system, we need to be able to specify a set of operators without necessarily specifying a complete ordering of those operators. An opportunistic system works by enumerating possible operators to apply to the immediate situation and then selecting one of those operators based on the current goal and situation. Furthermore, a flexible system must be able to generate or use additional control knowledge. Thus, if a system must decide among several operators, it must be possible for the system to engage in complex problem solving to determine which operator is best.

In the PSCM, knowledge about when operators are applicable to a state can be specified independently of knowledge about which operator to select. Operator-selection knowledge, called *search-control knowledge*, is expressed in terms of preferences for or against applicable operators. For example, we can encode knowledge of the form "If operators A and B are applicable and X is true of the state, then B is better than A ." If at any time during the problem-solving process the search-control knowledge is insufficient to indicate which operator to select, a subgoal is set up to generate additional knowledge so that a single operator can be selected. This subgoal is achieved by searching another problem space. Operators can be implemented either by directly available knowledge or by using an operator-specific problem space.

Problem spaces cannot be adequately described unless the knowledge content of their states is specified. In the ABD-SOAR work we use *annotated models* (Newell, 1990) to describe and implement problem-space states. A model consists of objects with properties and relations, along with the assumption that every object in the model must represent an object in the referent (this is called the *correspondence principle*). An annotated model allows the correspondence principle to be modified by annotating an object. For instance, if an object is annotated with *not* , this means the object is not in the referent. Examples of other annotations are *some, many, uncertain*, and so on. Annotations can be task independent, such as *not*, or task specific, such as *explain* (an annotation used in ABD-SOAR).

The framework

The general abductive framework[3] can be described by using a single problem space with seven operators: *cover, resolve-redundancy, resolve-inconsistency, determine-certainty, determine-accounts-for, mark-redundancies,* and *mark-inconsistencies*. A problem space is described by specifying its goal, the knowledge content of its states, the initial state, operators, and search-control knowledge. First we describe the problem spaces, then we describe the minimal knowledge required to use the framework.

ABDUCTIVE INFERENCE

State description. A problem-space state for this abductive framework contains: knowledge of all the data to be explained, explanations and an indication of the data that they explain, knowledge about incomplete or redundant objects, information about whether an explanation is the only possible way to explain a datum, and knowledge about whether the implications of a newly added object have been processed. In addition, any other information necessary for solving the problem can be kept in the state.

Initial-state schema. The initial state need contain only the data to be explained. Additional information can be provided.

Desired-state schema. The desired state must meet six conditions:

1. The composite explanation should be *complete*. An explanation is complete when all the data that require an explanation are explained.
2. The hypotheses in the composite explanation should be at the desired level of detail for the problem being solved. For example, in diagnosis a disease hypothesis must be at an appropriate level of detail so that a therapy can be recommended.
3. No part of the model should be redundant (explanatorily superfluous).
4. No part of the model should be inconsistent.
5. All parts of the model should be certain. That is, each part of the model should be of high plausibility in the context of the model.
6. All parts of the model should be processed. That is, the logical implications of the object and its effect on the rest of the model should have been considered.

Operators. There are seven operators in the abductive space:

1. *Cover* is proposed for each datum that is not yet explained by a hypothesis (the explanation is not yet complete). Its goal is to add to the model one or more explanations of the datum.
2. *Resolve-redundancy* is proposed whenever there are redundant objects in the model. Its goal is to make the model irredundant (parsimonious).
3. *Resolve-inconsistency* is proposed whenever there are inconsistent objects in the model. Its goal is to make the model consistent.
4. *Determine-certainty* is proposed for each uncertain object in the model. The operator is successfully applied when the object is deemed to be certain or the object is deemed to be not present in the model. Determine-certainty uses a three-value confidence scale: an object is either in the model (if it is certain), not in the model, or uncertain. Confidence ranges with more values can be attached to objects in the model, but they must eventually be translated into the three-value range expected by *determine-certainty*.

Whenever an object is modified or added to the model, the implications of adding the object must be determined. The amount of processing depends on the object and the domain. The framework defines three operators for processing new objects: determine-accounts-for, mark-redundancies, and mark-inconsistencies:

5. *Determine-accounts-for* is proposed for each new hypothesis. Its goal is to determine the data for which the hypothesis can account.
6. *Mark-redundancies* is proposed for each new object. Its goal is to indicate which objects in the model are redundant with the newly added object. Hypotheses that offer to explain an identical set of data are considered redundant unless other knowledge indicates that they are not.
7. *Mark-inconsistencies* is proposed for each new object. Its goal is to indicate which objects are logically inconsistent with (or contradict) the newly added object.

Search-control knowledge. The following preferences apply to the seven operators just listed:

1. Determine-accounts-for is better than all other operators.
2. Resolve-redundancy, resolve-inconsistency, and determine-certainty are indifferent to one another. Note that an order can still be imposed on these operators by preferring one to another.
3. Mark-redundancies and mark-inconsistencies are equal to each other and better than all other operators except determine-accounts-for.

This is the minimum search-control knowledge needed to ensure correct operation of the abductive mechanism. However, this search control specifies only a partial ordering of the operators. Any control decisions that can be based on domain-dependent knowledge have been left unspecified. This allows the designer of the system to add appropriate search control for the task being done. For example, there is no knowledge about what to do when several cover operators tie because this decision can be based on domain-dependent knowledge.

A minimum of six additional kinds of knowledge are required to use the framework:

1. knowledge mapping each possible datum to potential explanations (to implement *cover*);
2. knowledge mapping an explanation to all the data that it can explain (to implement *determine-accounts-for*)
3. knowledge to determine the certainty of the explanations (to implement *determine-certainty*)
4. knowledge about the consistency of the model (to implement *mark-inconsistencies*)
5. knowledge about redundant objects (to implement *mark-redundancies*)
6. additional search-control knowledge to sequence the operators

Processing. As a result of the operators and the search-control knowledge, the basic method is to pick a datum to cover, add one or more explanations for this datum, determine what each new explanation explains, and then pick another (unexplained) datum to explain. This continues until all data are explained. If at any time the model becomes inconsistent, redundant, or uncertain, an operator is proposed to resolve the problem. Then a decision must be made about whether to fix the problem or to continue covering all the data.

Implementing the framework: ABD-SOAR

ABD-SOAR is a SOAR-based implementation of the abductive framework. SOAR is used because it directly supports the PSCM; however, the framework does not absolutely require SOAR – other architectures that support PSCM-like functionality can also be used. ABD-SOAR supplies all of the knowledge specified in the framework: knowledge to propose the abductive operators and detect their successful application and the minimal search-control knowledge specified in the framework. This knowledge is encoded as a set of SOAR productions (rules) that can apply to any problem space. This means that the complete body of abductive knowledge can be brought to bear during any problem-solving activity. ABD-SOAR also provides default implementation knowledge for *cover, resolve-redundancy*, and *resolve-inconsistency* and a default method for generating additional search-control knowledge.

The default knowledge for operator implementation is encoded in three problem spaces with names identical to the operators that they implement: *cover, resolve-redundancy,* and *resolve-inconsistency. Cover* generates possible explanations and then applies knowledge to select one of the candidates. The candidates are generated in response to an *explain* operator that must be implemented using domain-specific knowledge. To avoid loops, explanations that were previously removed from the model should not be added. *Resolve-redundancy* removes each redundant object until the explanation is "irredundant," that is, has no explanatorily superfluous parts. If multiple irredundant explanations are possible, all are found and the best one is used. This makes use of lookahead and the evaluation function we will describe. Any explanation that is an *absolute essential* (i.e., the only possible explanation for some piece of data) will not be removed. Also, it is possible to resolve a redundancy by explicitly indicating that particular redundant objects are not a problem. For example, two diseases might be present that cause (and therefore explain) fever – a situation that should not be considered redundant. *Resolve-inconsistency* removes each inconsistent object until the model is consistent. As in the case of *resolve-redundancy*, if multiple consistent models are possible, then each is evaluated and the best model is selected. Any explanation that is an absolute essential will not be removed.

Resolve-redundancy and *resolve-inconsistency* use lookahead to determine what to do. These operators work by removing objects from the model until the inconsistency or redundancy is resolved. However, in many cases, there might be many possible ways to resolve the problem (by removing different combinations of objects from the model). Consequently, ABD-SOAR must evaluate each possibility and choose the best one. Lookahead can also be used to generate knowledge about what to do when the system designer does not or cannot supply that knowledge. Lookahead can be used to decide what to cover first, what to remove from inconsistent composites, and what to add to explain a finding. The use of lookahead to rate composites is an example of generalized impasse handling. However, lookahead is quite computationally expensive, so it is desirable to add additional knowledge whenever possible.

The default method for generating additional search-control knowledge is to use lookahead and an evaluation function to determine which operator to select when multiple operators are applicable. This is implemented in two problem spaces: *find-best* and *evaluate-state*. *Find-best* evaluates each operator and selects the operator with the best evaluation. To evaluate an operator, *find-best* applies the operator to a copy of the original state and then continues to do problem solving from that state until a state is found that can be evaluated by using *evaluate-state*. The default evaluation function for *evaluate-state* is a sum of the number of data to be explained, the number of explanations, the number of inconsistent objects, the number of data explained by inconsistent explanations, the number of redundant objects, and the number of uncertain objects. The model with the lowest evaluation is chosen as the best alternative.

ABD-SOAR uses irredundant covers (no explanatorily superfluous parts) as the parsimony criterion; however, when the default evaluation function is used, the system also uses minimal cardinality to choose among competing composite explanations. The belief criterion (by default) is that the method attempts to pick the best explanation for a finding being covered. In the absence of plausibility ratings, the evaluation function is used to rate competing explanations for a finding, and the one with the best evaluation is selected.

To use ABD-SOAR, the system designer must provide knowledge to implement *explain* and *determine-accounts-for*. When necessary, knowledge must also be provided for *mark-inconsistencies, mark-redundancies,* and *determine-certainty*. Given only this knowledge, and the built-in defaults, abductive problems can be solved.

Optionally, the designer can choose to add more search-control knowledge and/or knowledge to override any of the default knowledge. Adding knowledge beyond the minimum requirements can greatly increase the efficiency of the abductive system. ABD-SOAR is completely open to the addition of new knowledge. Additional operators can be added to any space. New ways of implementing existing operators can be added. Search-control knowledge can be added so that lookahead can be avoided. Furthermore, the additions can be made general so that they work for all tasks, or specific so that they only work for a single task or problem. Every addition of knowledge will alter the problem-solving behavior. In this framework the available knowledge shapes the strategy, unlike the traditional approach where strategies must be designed to use prespecified kinds of knowledge.

The default strategy was used to solve a red-cell antibody case (see Figure 4.5). The correct answer for this case is anti-K and anti-Fy[a]. 1,083 decision

Red Cells

1	2	3	4
(r_1) 1+	(r_2) 3+	(r_4) 1+	(r_5) 1+
0	(r_3) 1+	0	0

Anti-K explains r_2 and r_3 (i.e., the 3+ and 1+ on red cell 2).
Anti-Fy[a] explains r_1, r_4, and r_5 (i.e., the 1+ on red cells 1, 3, and 4).
Anti-C explains r_1 and r_4 (i.e., the 1+ on red cells 1 and 3).
Anti-N explains r_4 (i.e., the 1+ on red cell 3).
0 reactions do not need to be explained.

Figure 4.5. Red-cell antibody identification case.

cycles were required to solve the problem. A decision cycle corresponds to the selection of a goal, a problem space, a state, or an operator. However, the addition of some simple search-control knowledge can greatly decrease the number of decision cycles needed to solve the problem, as shown.

RED-like abduction. RED-2 uses two heuristics to help guide the search: (1) The system prefers to cover stronger reactions before weaker reactions. If reactions are equal, then one is selected at random to cover. (2) Whenever multiple antibodies can explain the same reaction, the antibodies are ordered according to plausibility, and the one with the highest plausibility is used. If multiple antibodies have the same plausibility, then one is selected at random (this is a somewhat simplified description). This knowledge can be added to ABD-SOAR by rating antibodies for plausibility and by adding three search-control rules:

ID1   If r_1 is stronger than r_2 then *cover r_1* is better than *cover r_2*.
ID2   If r_1 is equal to r_2 then *cover r_1* is indifferent to *cover r_2*.
ID3   If a_1 has a higher plausibility than a_2 for explaining a reaction then a_1 is a better explanation than a_2.

Search-control knowledge to make equally plausible antibodies indifferent is not added. This illustrates how additional search-control knowledge can be mixed with default knowledge. In this case, if the best candidates are equally plausible, then the system will attempt to differentiate among them by using lookahead. If lookahead does not distinguish among them, then one will be selected at random.

As a result of this additional knowledge, the system solves the case in 23 decision cycles (versus 1,038 for the default run on this case). First the system decides, because of ID1, to cover the 3+ on red-cell 2. It covers with anti-K, the only antibody that explains the 3+. Next, because of ID2 the system randomly selects the 1+ reaction on red-cell 1 to explain. This reaction can be explained by either anti-Fy^a or anti-C, but anti-Fy^a is more plausible, so, because of ID3, anti-Fy^a is selected.

This example illustrates how small changes to search-control knowledge can radically alter the behavior of the system. The system in this example exhibits behavior very much like that of RED-2, without having RED-2's strategy explicitly encoded. Furthermore, whenever the search control is inappropriate, the system can fall back on the default knowledge to make progress.

Comparison to PEIRCE

ABD-SOAR can be thought of as a reimplementation of PEIRCE in SOAR to see whether such an implementation would give added flexibility to PEIRCE. Because of the generality of its goal-subgoal hierarchy and its control mechanism, PEIRCE can be used to encode many different strategies for abduction. For example, it was used to recode RED-2's strategy and several variations of that strategy. However, problems with the control mechanism and the goal-subgoal decomposition ultimately restrict flexibility by limiting the knowledge that a PEIRCE-based system can use.

First, there is no way to generate additional search-control knowledge in PEIRCE at run time. There is also no way to add new goals or methods at run time. This is not a problem in ABD-SOAR because any subgoal or impasse can be resolved using the complete processing power of the PSCM. Thus, search-control knowledge, evaluation knowledge, or operators for a problem space can be generated just as any other kind of knowledge in ABD-SOAR can.

Second, the control mechanism in PEIRCE cannot detect problem-solving impasses that result from a lack of knowledge. In ABD-SOAR, the architecture automatically detects and creates a goal for these kinds of impasses. Finally, the goal-subgoal structure in ABD-SOAR is much finer-grained than the one used in PEIRCE. This means that the abductive strategy can be controlled at a finer level of detail in ABD-SOAR.

Generic tasks revisited

As discussed in chapter 2, generic tasks were originally thought of as specialists, agents that were the primitive constituents from which more complex tasks were composed. However, as we said when we discussed PEIRCE, hard-wired modules made the systems lack flexibility. Also, as discussed in chapter 2, the idea of generic tasks brings several problems to mind: What constitutes a generic task? and How do we distinguish between generic tasks and other sorts of methods? These sorts of issues led us to develop the approach to generic tasks seen in this chapter and in chapter 5.

Instead of thinking of problem solving, such as diagnosis and design, as complex tasks that can be decomposed into elementary generic-task specialists, in these systems we think of them as complex activities involving a number of subtasks and a number of alternative methods potentially available for each subtask.

Methods

A method can be described in terms of the operators that it uses, the objects upon which it operates, and any additional knowledge about how to organize operator application to satisfy the goal.[4] At the knowledge level, the method is characterized by the knowledge that the agent needs in order to set up and apply the method. Different methods for the same task might call for different types of knowledge. Let us consider a simple example. To multiply two multidigit numbers, the logarithmic method consists of the following series of operations: Extract the logarithm of each input number, add the two logarithms, and extract the antilogarithm of the sum. Their arguments, as well as the results, are the objects of this method. Note that one does not typically include (at this level of description of the logarithmic method) specifications about how to extract the logarithm or the antilogarithm or how to do the addition. If the computational model does not provide these capabilities as primitives, the performance of these operations can be set up as subtasks of the method. Thus, given a method, the application of any of the operators can be set up as a subtask.

Some of the objects that a method needs can be generic to a class of problems in a domain. As an example, consider hierarchical classification using a malfunction hierarchy as a method for diagnosis. Establish-hypothesis and refine-hypothesis operations are applied to the hypotheses in the hierarchy. These objects are useful for solving many instances of the diagnostic problem in the domain. If malfunction hypotheses are not directly available, the generation of such hypotheses can be set up as subtasks. One method for generating such objects is compilation from so-called deep, or causal, knowledge. There is no finite set of mutually distinct methods for a task because there can be numerous variants on a method. Nevertheless, the term *method* is a useful shorthand to refer to a set of related ways to organize a computation.

A task analysis should provide a framework within which various approaches to the task at hand can be understood. Each method can be treated in terms of all the features that an information-processing analysis calls for:

the types of knowledge and information needed and the inference processes that use these forms of knowledge.

Choosing methods

How can methods be chosen for the various tasks? Following are some criteria:

1. *Properties of the solution.* Some methods produce answers that are numerically precise; others produce only qualitative answers. Some of them produce optimal solutions; others produce satisficing ones.[5]
2. *Properties of the solution process.* Is the computation pragmatically feasible? How much time does it take? How much memory does it require?
3. *Availability of knowledge required for the method to be applied.* A method for design verification might, for example, require that we have available a description of the behavior of a device as a system of differential equations; if this information is not directly available, and if it cannot be generated by additional problem solving, the method cannot be used.

Each method in a task structure can be evaluated for appropriateness in a given situation by asking questions that reflect these criteria. A delineation of the methods and their properties helps us move away from abstract arguments about ideal methods for performing a task. Although some of this evaluation can take place at problem-solving time, much of it can be done when the knowledge system is designed; this evaluation can be used to guide a knowledge-system designer in the choice of methods to implement.

Choosing methods at run time

Because of the multiplicity of possible methods and subtasks for a task, a task-specific architecture for a particular task, such as diagnosis or design, is not likely to be complete: Although diagnosis and design are generic activities, there is no single generic method for either of them. Thus, instead of building monolithic task-specific architectures for such complex tasks, as we attempted to do originally, a more useful architectural approach is one that can invoke different methods for different subtasks in a flexible way.

Following the ideas in the research on task-specific architectures, we can, however, support specific methods by means of special-purpose shells that can help encode knowledge and control problem solving for those methods. This approach is an immediate extension of the generic-task methodology as described in Chandrasekaran (1986). These methods can then be combined in a domain-specific manner; that is, methods for subtasks can be selected in advance and included as part of the application system, or methods can be recursively chosen at run time for the tasks based on the various criteria we discussed. For the latter approach, a task-independent architecture is needed capable of evaluating different methods, choosing one, executing it, setting up subgoals as they arise from the chosen method, and repeating the process. SOAR (Newell, 1990); BB1 (Hayes-Roth, 1985); sponsor-selector hierarchies, as in DSPL (Brown & Chandrasekaran, 1989) and PEIRCE, are good candidates for such an architecture. This approach combines the advantages of task-specific architectures and the flexibility of run-time choice of methods. The DSPL++ work of Herman (1992) aims to demonstrate precisely this combination of advantages.

Using method-specific knowledge and strategy representations within a general architecture that helps select methods and set up subgoals is a good first step in adding flexibility to the advantages of task-specific architectures. It can also have limitations, however. For many real-world problems, switching among methods can result in control that is too coarse-grained. A method description might call for a specific sequence of how the operators are to be applied. Numerous variants of the method, with complex sequences of the various operators, can be appropriate in different domains. It would be impractical to support all these variants by method-specific architectures or shells. It is much better in the long run to let the task-method-subtask analysis guide us in identifying the needed task-specific knowledge and to let a flexible general architecture determine the actual sequence of operator application by using additional domain-specific knowledge. The subtasks can then be flexibly combined in response to problem-solving needs, achieving a much finer-grained control behavior. This sort of control is evident in the ABD-SOAR system just discussed.

Notes

1 PEIRCE was named after Charles Sanders Peirce, the originator of the term "abduction" for a form of inference that makes use of explanatory relationships. PEIRCE was designed by John R. Josephson, Michael C. Tanner and William F. Punch III, and implemented by Punch in LOOPS (from Xerox Corporation), an object-oriented programming system in InterLisp-D (also a Xerox product).

2 Investigated in experiments conducted by Olivier Fischer (unpublished).

3 For a detailed description of the framework and several examples, see Johnson (1991).

4 The terms "task" and "goal" are used interchangeably here.

5 The term "satisficing" is due to Herbert Simon. See (Simon, 1969).

5   More kinds of knowledge: Two diagnostic systems

TIPS (Task Integrated Problem Solver) and PATHEX/LIVER were built using the PEIRCE tool. Both are examples of third-generation abduction machines. PEIRCE is not specialized for diagnoses and might be used as a shell
for any abductive-assembly system. TIPS and PATHEX/LIVER, however,
are diagnostic systems. They are complicated systems that are similar in
organization and capabilities. Despite their similarities, in the following descriptions we emphasize TIPS's ability to dynamically integrate multiple
problem-solving methods and PATHEX/LIVER's proposed ability to combine structure-function models – for causal reasoning – with compiled diagnostic knowledge. First we describe TIPS, and then PATHEX/LIVER.

TIPS

TIPS[1] is a preliminary framework that implements the idea (described in chapter 4) of making alternative problem-solving methods available for a task. Method
invocation depends on the problem state and the capabilities of the method, not
on a preset sequence of invocations. TIPS presents a general mechanism for the
dynamic integration of multiple methods in diagnosis.

One can describe diagnosis not only in terms of the overall goal (say,
explaining symptoms in terms of malfunctions), but also in terms of the rich
structure of subgoals that arise as part of diagnostic reasoning and in terms
of the methods used to achieve those goals. We call such a description a
task-structure analysis. A diagnostic system explicitly realized in these terms
has a number of advantages:

a.   Such a system has multiple approaches available for solving a problem.
      Thus the failure of one method does not mean failure for the whole prob-
      lem solver.
b.   Such a system can potentially use more kinds of knowledge.
c.   Such a system can potentially solve a broader range of diagnostic prob-
      lems.

The TIPS approach to creating dynamically integrated problem solvers is

---

[1] TIPS is by William F. Punch III and B. Chandrasekaran. PATHEX/LIVER: Structure-
Function Models for Causal Reasoning is by Jack W. Smith, B. Chandrasekaran, and Tom
Bylander.

to provide only enough mechanism to allow for monitoring goal achievement and for keeping track of methods that can achieve the various goals. How a method works is left to the designer as long as it conforms to a set of rules for keeping track of goal achievement. This extensibility allows a knowledge engineer to take advantage of tried-and-true software (such as existing generic-task problem solvers) without converting it to another format. It also allows for a diversity of methods and representations for different kinds of problem solving.

The TIPS architecture

Control is represented in TIPS using the sponsor-selector mechanism first used in DSPL (Brown & Chandrasekaran, 1986). A knowledge-based system in this framework consists of a hierarchy of specialists, in which each specialist consists of three parts: a selector, some sponsors, and an invocable method associated with each sponsor. This mechanism is contributed by PEIRCE, the tool described in chapter 4. At any choice point (i.e., a point in the flow of problem solving at which another method could be invoked) the control decision is made by invoking all the sponsors to rate their associated methods, and then the selector chooses the next method to invoke based on the sponsor ratings and other information. This architecture of selectors and sponsors and their associated methods is the same as in PEIRCE.

Control programming in the TIPS architecture, as in PEIRCE, has two parts:

1. Decision knowledge about a method's appropriateness is coded in its sponsor so that it is sensitive to the current problem state and the history of method invocation (e.g., success/failure of recent invocations of the method).
2. Decision knowledge that directly concerns the choice of method to invoke (based on sponsor ratings and other information) is coded in the selector.

Several specialists, each consisting of a selector and a family of sponsors and methods, coexist within a system. One specialist may call on another by way of a chosen method.

A specialist determines completion by *return* or *fail* sponsors. These sponsors report when the particular specialist successfully finishes its work (return) or when it fails to accomplish the task for which it was activated (fail). The return and fail sponsors are programmed by the knowledge engineer, just as any sponsor.

The structure of TIPS's top-level specialist for diagnosis is shown in Figure 5.1. Each method is realized by a software module capable of carrying out the method. Modules are often specialists themselves, each with its own selector and family of sponsors and methods.

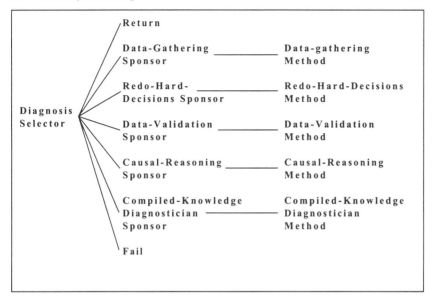

Figure 5.1. TIPS for diagnosis, top-level control.

A medical diagnosis system in TIPS

A medical diagnosis system was developed in TIPS to demonstrate its usefulness. The system deals with a broad range of liver and blood diseases and their various interactions. The following briefly summarizes the five main modules used in the system, their roles, and the knowledge of when they are appropriate (see Punch [1989] for more details).

1. *Compiled-knowledge diagnostician.* This module is responsible for creating diagnostic explanations by using a hierarchical-classification plus abductive-assembly strategy similar to that of RED-2 (see chapter 3). This module has two submodules, one for hierarchical classification and one for abductive assembly. The hierarchical classifier efficiently searches a hierarchy of disease and disease-process categories and determines the plausibility and explanatory coverage of candidates in the given situation. These candidates are used as raw material by the abductive assembler to form (hopefully) a composite explanation that is plausible, consistent, and covers all the findings.

This module is appropriate to invoke in the following circumstances: as the first module to invoke in a case (to create an initial diagnosis), if more data has just been gathered, if a data value was shown to be invalid and has just been altered by a validation method, or if causal reasoning has suggested a new hypothesis to consider for use in the composite explanation.

2. *Data-gathering module.* This module gathers further evidence that can help to establish or rule out pertinent diagnostic hypotheses. The data needed are determined by hypothesis-matching knowledge that is associated with nodes in the classification hierarchy.

This module is appropriate when the hierarchical classifier cannot explore all the way to tip-level hypotheses because of lack of data or when one of the candidate hypotheses in a hard decision has an unanswered query in the specialist that generated the hypothesis. Hard decisions (described in chapter 4) represent conditions in which a finding is ambiguous – that is, where alternative explanations are of nearly equal value. Gathering further evidence can help to resolve the ambiguity by helping to discriminate among the alternative explanations.

3. *Data-validation module.* This module checks the validity of data that were brought into question during the running of the compiled-knowledge diagnostician. This strategy for data validation is described in detail elsewhere (see Chandrasekaran & Punch, 1987). The idea is to use expectations derived from hypotheses already confidently formed by the diagnostic process. If these expectations are not met (e.g., Liver Disease expects some abnormality in liver enzyme values, and the enzyme values were reported as normal), then there is a potential data problem. Suspected data items are marked and further investigated by specifically compiled test procedures that validate their values. Even without validation knowledge, confidence in these data items can be withdrawn, and hypotheses dependent on them for their plausibility values can be rescored.

This module is appropriate if, during diagnosis, a high-confidence explanation is accepted whose data expectations are not met.

4. *Redo-hard-decisions module.* This module revisits hard-decision points in the compiled-knowledge diagnostician module. If the system is forced to make a hard decision (in the worst case by making a random choice), it records the system state at that point so that the system (or the user) can return later and explore other possible solution paths.

This module is appropriate when a hard decision has arisen during the abductive-assembly process and a forced choice was made.

5. *Causal-reasoning module.* The idea behind this module is that a composite explanation is made more plausible if its parts form a causally coherent whole – that is, if causal connections can be found among its parts. This module attempts to determine the expected consequences of suggested connections among the parts of an explanation generated by the compiled-knowl-

edge diagnostician. Associated with each diagnostic hypothesis is knowledge about how the malfunction that it represents modifies normal conditions. These changes are broadly categorized as functional changes (anemia causes loss of oxygenation function), connectivity changes (blocked common bile duct causes backing up of bile), and structural changes (swelling of pancreas can push on the liver).[2] The module has methods for exploring the causal consequences of each type of change.

The causal-reasoning module is appropriate when a possible causal connection has been noted among hypotheses of the current explanation.

An example case. Consider the following case as a concrete example of the kinds of decisions that arise during medical diagnosis (Harvey & Bordley, 1972, pp. 294–298). A 52-year-old Italian laborer presented with the following symptoms:

1. A series of "palpitations" and associated chest pains and sweating. No overt signs of heart trouble.
2. Blood test indications of anemia (low hematocrit, low red blood count, and low hemoglobin).
3. Increased liver size, increased bilirubin of the indirect (nonconjugated) type, and slight jaundice, which indicates a possible liver disease.

The diagnostician has a number of choices in reasoning at this stage:

1. Make the best diagnosis based on the available data, to wit, an unclassified type of liver disease and an anemia, probably thalassemia minor, based on the serological data and the patient's heritage. (Thalassemia minor is a common anemia of people with a Mediterranean heritage.)
2. Ask for more data that can help further the diagnosis. Given the present state of the diagnostic reasoning process, what data will give the most leverage in getting a more complete, more detailed, or more confident diagnosis? In this case, one could ask for more data about the liver disease, such as a biopsy of the organ or further blood studies to elucidate the kind of anemia.
3. Question data that do not fit with the present best diagnosis and validate them if necessary. In the subsequent work on this case, the physician ordered X rays to confirm the existence of bleeding esophageal varices (bleeding from enlarged veins in the throat). Although the X rays were negative, other evidence was sufficient for confirmation (vomiting of blood, stoppage of bleeding with a Sengstaken-Blakemore tube).
4. Use the present diagnosis as a starting point for considering possible causal interactions among the affected organs that would explain the signs and symptoms of the case. In so doing, one may discover a relationship that indicates a specific disease and data that confirm or refute this disease. This creation of a causal story can be a powerful tool in reducing the set of diagnostic hypotheses that need to be examined in more detail. In this case a possible relationship exists between the specific type of anemia, which causes an excess of iron in the blood, and the liver, which is responsible for maintaining iron equilibrium. This relationship suggests considering diseases of the liver that result from overexposure to iron.

What follows is a brief example of the run of the diagnostic system on this case. Many details have been omitted, but the trace is presented to provide an idea of the types of problem solving that occur in the system. Note that, depending on the initial data, the system may solve the problem in a completely different way.

Step 1. Given the data-base values and the findings to explain, the compiled-knowledge diagnostician, which always runs first, formed an initial diagnosis of {Thalassemia Minor, Hepatomegaly}.

Step 2. The generated explanation was rated using two criteria to determine if it was good enough. The criteria in this case were that the explanation should explain all the findings and that it should consist of hypotheses that are most detailed (i.e., come from the tip level of the classification hierarchy). The explanation was considered to be not good enough (the hypothesis elements explained all the findings but were not all at the tip level of the hierarchy), so the top-level sponsor-selector system was invoked.

Step 3. The methods deemed appropriate this time were data gathering and causal reasoning, both of which were rated +3 on a scale from +3 (completely appropriate) to -3 (completely inappropriate). Data gathering was appropriate because the hierarchy was not explored to tip level. Causal reasoning was appropriate because a possible functional relationship was noted between Thalassemia Minor and Hepatomegaly. Thalassemia Minor produces iron and the normal liver consumes iron. (Hepatomegaly is an enlarged liver.) The causal-reasoning module was selected according to the tie-breaking knowledge of the sponsor's method-priority list, since causal reasoning was set to have a higher priority than gathering data

Step 4. The causal-reasoning module focused on the possible functional relationships of iron, based on the Excess-Produce-Iron function of Thalassemia Minor and the Consume-Iron function of Liver. Note that consuming iron is a normal function of the liver and that there was no evidence of liver impairment.

Step 5. Given the proposed iron interaction, a search was made for a causal model of the iron metabolism of the liver. It was found in the Liver specialist associated with Iron-Metabolism. The liver's iron metabolism function was simulated using the initial conditions of excess iron, derived from Excess-Produce-Iron of Thalassemia Minor. It also searched for a Consume-Iron effect on Thalassemia Minor but found none.

Step 6. The simulation led to the state Iron-Deposits-In-Liver-Cells, which the inferencing database noted as abnormal (the data base stores normal ranges for all data). The causal-reasoning module searched to see if Iron-Deposits-In-Liver-Cells is associated with any known disease. It did this by searching an association list of states-to-malfunctions stored in the Liver specialist. An association was discovered between Iron-Deposits-In-Liver-Cells and the disease Hemochromatosis.

Step 7. The causal-reasoning module invoked the node of the hierarchical classifier associated with the disease Hemochromatosis to determine if there was enough evidence to establish it. The node established and so was proposed by Hemochromatosis to replace Hepatomegaly as a hypothesis for the abductive assembler, because the latter is a subtype of the former and the abductive assembler was trying to create the most detailed explanation possible. The causal-reasoning module then returned control to the top-level specialist.

Step 8. The compound explanation had not yet been changed, so the diagnostic explanation was still not good enough. The compiled-knowledge diagnostician and data-gathering modules were the only ones judged to be appropriate and both were rated at +3. The compiled-knowledge diagnostician was appropriate because the causal-reasoning module had suggested Hemochromatosis as a hypothesis for use in the composite explanation. Data gathering was appropriate because the hierarchy was still not explored to tip level. Because the compiled-knowledge diagnostician was set to have higher priority, it was invoked next.

Step 9. The compiled-knowledge diagnostician created a new explanation with the elements {Thalassemia Minor, Hemochromatosis}. This explanation was complete and detailed enough, so diagnosis was finished.

PATHEX/LIVER: Structure–function models for causal reasoning

The tools and techniques we are developing in the PATHEX project apply to the generic problem solving underlying diagnostic reasoning. As such they should have significance for knowledge-based systems in other medical domains. Of primary significance is the exploration of concepts and techniques for integrating compiled-knowledge reasoning based on symptom-disease associations with "deep reasoning," based on structure-function models within the framework of an abductive-reasoning architecture for the diagnostic process.

In large medical domains such as liver disease it is not practical to encode, in compiled-knowledge form, considerations regarding every factor bearing on a decision. A traditional problem in this regard is the difficulty of encoding considerations of co-occurring, possibly interacting disorders and the variations of presentation of a given disorder. Not only is it very labor intensive to encode this, but it is usually impossible to avoid encoding implicit unwarranted assumptions and inconsistencies into the compiled knowledge. This is true because of the complexities of programming such a system and because there is a strong tendency during the knowledge-engineering process to extract from experts oversimplified versions of the knowledge that they use in making decisions.

Systems that incorporate structure-function models have the potential for overcoming some of these difficulties because such models provide a means to explicitly represent relations and assumptions underlying compiled knowledge. Structure-function models can prove useful in this regard even if they capture only some of the justification underlying a piece of compiled knowledge.

However, a common problem with structure-function models is that they are inefficient in searching for plausible hypotheses and in determining the explanatory relationships between data items and the hypotheses that might account for the data items. If one uses structure-function models as the sole basis for diagnostic reasoning, one gains perspicuity of representation and a potential for increasing the accuracy of the knowledge base, at the cost of significantly greater computational complexity. Compiled knowledge, on the other hand, can be used efficiently in diagnostic reasoning to search for potential hypotheses, to generate diagnostic suggestions, and to determine explanatory relationships.

We contend that it is possible to build a hybrid system, a middle ground, where one can preserve the problem-solving efficiencies of compiled knowledge, when compiled knowledge is adequate to solve the case at hand, and, when compiled knowledge alone is not adequate, selectively supplement it with deeper reasoning. The proposed hybrid system PATHEX/LIVER-2 will still use compiled diagnostic knowledge in simple cases as the major means for generating plausible hypotheses, for excluding unlikely hypotheses, and for determining explanatory relationships. However, structure-function models will supplement the compiled knowledge in the system for unusual or complex situations that the compiled knowledge cannot handle.

In the following sections we present progress we have made in our investigations concerning an abductive architecture for diagnosis based on compiled knowledge, and the progress we have made in understanding structure-function models in medicine and of how to integrate such models into our abductive architecture.

Diagnosis as abduction – compiled knowledge

The idea that diagnostic reasoning is a special case of abductive problem solving is by now well accepted. The PATHEX/LIVER project takes the view that liver diagnosis based on laboratory and morphological information involves assembly of explanatory hypotheses. The overall complexity of abductive reasoning can be minimized if the overall process can be decomposed into a process that first generates plausible hypotheses, and another process that critiques and assembles these plausible hypotheses into a composite explanatory hypothesis.

Our architecture that uses compiled knowledge for performing abduction has consisted of three main cooperating modules (see Figure 5.2). These modules perform the same generic tasks that were described in detail in previous chapters (especially chapter 2). The first module is an inferencing data base that uses the IDABLE language, which has primitives for expressing data attributes, relationships, and inference procedures. (IDABLE is described in chapter 2.) The second module is a subhypothesis-selection module, which uses the generic tasks of hierarchical classification and hypothesis matching. Hierarchical classification uses the CSRL language (described in chapter 2) for representing the hierarchies of knowledge and uses the establish-refine control regime for hypothesis refinement. Hypothesis match-

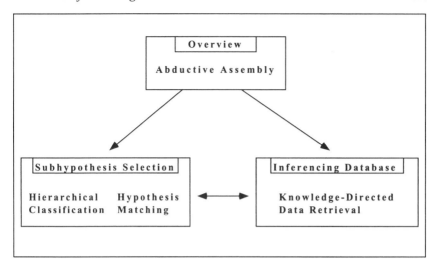

Figure 5.2. Architecture for abduction using compiled knowledge.

ing uses the HYPER language (chapter 2) to represent the knowledge for mapping patterns of data to confidence values.

The third module is an Overview module based on the PEIRCE language (see chapter 4) which performs hypothesis assembly and criticism. In the mechanism used in the Overview module for PATHEX/LIVER-1 abductive assembly alternates between assembly and criticism.[3] Assembly is performed by a means-ends problem solver that is driven by the goal of explaining all the significant findings using hypotheses that are maximally specific. At each step of assembly, the most significant datum yet to be explained is used to select the most plausible subhypothesis that offers to explain it. After the initial assembly the critic removes superfluous parts and determines which parts are essential (i.e., explains some datum that no other plausible hypothesis can explain). Assembly is repeated, starting with the essential subhypotheses. Finally, the critic again removes any superfluous parts. This is essentially the RED-2 strategy for abductive assembly (see chapter 3), although it is augmented by PEIRCE's tactic of delaying hard decisions and PEIRCE's ability to influence hypothesis refinement (see chapter 4).

Abductive assembly depends heavily on knowing which data a composite hypothesis can explain in the particular case. In RED-2, this was relatively easy because it was possible to determine what a composite hypothesis explained by "adding up" what each subhypothesis explained (see chapter 3). In PATHEX/LIVER-1, as an interim solution to the problem, we directly attached a description of the data that each subhypothesis offers to explain. This description is provided by compiled knowledge associated with each potential subhypothesis. However, for better diagnostic performance in the liver disease domain more flexibility is needed to determine how disorders interact causally. We intend to use a type of structure-function model to provide this ability in the proposed PATHEX/LIVER-2 system.

Use of functional knowledge for diagnosis

In this section we summarize what we call "functional knowledge structures" and some ways in which diagnostic reasoning can use them. The functional knowledge represented corresponds to a person's understanding of certain aspects of how something works. The representation for this knowledge organizes the knowledge of how the device's functions result from causal processes that arise from the structure of the device and the functions of its components. The representation contains specific pointers to chunks of generic domain knowledge and assumptions about alternative processes that the device uses to achieve its functions. This knowledge can be used in several ways in diagnostic systems. A functional model of the normally operating body can be used, or the disease process can be modeled as a different mechanism or as a variant of the normal model. A malfunction model can be used to reason about how a disease process works. The basic ideas for this representation were proposed in Sembugamoorthy & Chandrasekaran (1986). A more recent description appears in Keuneke (1991). The following subsection addresses the representational primitives that we believe are required. They are realized in a language called the *Functional Representation Language (FR)*. The next section illustrates how this representation can be used in diagnosis.

Our functional representation explicitly depicts complex devices as collections of subsystems with limited interactions. We may understand complex devices by a hierarchical decomposition of the system into system function, subsystem function, subsubsystem function, and so forth. Such decomposition of complex devices into subsystems makes the intellectual task of understanding them feasible. We do not typically understand a complex device only at one level, nor can it be supposed that we understand a subcomponent's function by considering how it will interact with everything else in the device.

To achieve the needed decomposition our representation provides ways to:

1. represent the system's structure.
2. name the system's functions.
3. specify the kinds of causal processes that accomplish the functions.
4. specify the conditions under which the functions are achieved.
5. represent causal processes.
6. point to various first-principle laws of the domain that explain the steps in causal-process descriptions.[4]

We illustrate the representation of function and causal processes with a simple example.

Representation of structure. We need to be able to list components and the structural relations that hold among the components. We also need to be able to express something about abstractions of components, namely, what the functions of the components are. For medical diagnosis, at the top level of this kind of representation is the overall decomposition of the human body into its constituent systems, beginning with the overall functions of the body – metabolism, mobility, perception, and so forth – and associated with them, some of the major subsystems – vascular, nervous, and so on.

Representation of function. A typical function of the vascular system is to lower the blood pressure of the body when the blood pressure is abnormally high. This information is represented in FR in a function description such as that in the upper part of Figure 5.3, with the statement *Function*: lower-blood-pressure-of-body. *ToMake* is a primitive of the FR language that takes as an argument the state of the system that will be achieved if the function is successfully accomplished. In this case it says,

> *ToMake*: decreased-blood-pressure
> *If*: blood-pressure-abnormally-high,
> *By*: lower-blood-pressure-process.

Thus, at the highest level of functional description all that is encoded is that this system has a function, that the goal of this function is to reach a certain end state given certain beginning states, and that the process (i.e., the way it is done) has a name by which its detailed description can be retrieved.

Representation of causal processes. A causal process description is shown in the lower part of Figure 5.3. In the *If* statement, blood-pressure-abnormally-high names a (partially described) state of the system. If this state occurs, using the function generate-high-BP-signal of the component sympathetic-nervous-system, the state called high-blood-pressure-signal-generated is reached. From this state, the final state – blood-pressure-reduced – is reached by using the function lower-blood-pressure of the component vascular-system. Notice that the state transitions are explained by referring to components upon whose functions these transitions depend. For example, in this case the state changed from blood-pressure-abnormally-high to high-blood-pressure-signal-generated because of the function generate-high-BP-signal of the component sympathetic-nervous-system. So, at an abstract level, only this has been represented: the statement that a certain function exists, the function's defining properties, and the fact that this function is made possible by certain causal processes (described as annotated state sequences).

Notice that if there is sufficient understanding for one's purposes at this level of detail, the representation is adequate and uncluttered by further causal detail. However, if it is desirable to know in more detail how a process or a transition takes place, this can be pursued by examining the representations

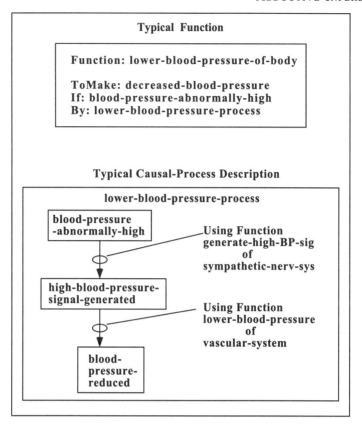

Figure 5.3. Functional representation.

of the functions of subsystems that participate in the causal process (e.g., in this case, generate-high-BP-signal).

Our representation currently provides for three ways to explain state transitions. One way, illustrated in the lower half of Figure 5.3, is by referring to a particular function of a particular component or subsystem that is taken to be responsible for the state transition. This way is represented by annotating the state transition in the causal-process description using the *Using Function* primitive of the FR language. *Using Function* attaches the function description to the state transition. The function description for the component may itself use the *By* primitive to attach a causal-process description, which may again use the *Using Function* primitive to attach a description of a lower level function, and so on. Thus, the FR language provides a kind of dual representation whereby functions are explained by the causal processes by which they are achieved, and causal processes are explained by the functions of components that are responsible for the state transitions that make up a causal process. In this way the FR represents the *roles* of the various components and subsystems by representing the functions that they perform as participants in significant causal processes.

A second way to explain a state transition is to give details by describing a sequence of intermediate states. This explanation is represented by annotating the state transition with the *By* primitive of the FR language. The *By* primitive attaches a causal-process description to the state transition. In this way a step in a causal process is explained by describing a subprocess that is responsible for the step.

A third way to explain a state transition is by reference to a general principle or a scientific law that accounts for the change. For example, a reduction in blood pressure may result from a reduction in blood volume (from rapid loss of blood, say), but a full understanding of this state transition requires understanding that a reduction of liquid volume generally results in loss of pressure in an elastic container. The *As Per* primitive attaches general-knowledge principles to state transitions. One way to represent general knowledge, especially scientific laws, is in the form of equations that relate parameters of antecedent states to parameters of subsequent states. This form of representation in FR was used in the Transgene project at Ohio State (Darden, Moberg, Thadani, & Josephson, 1992) and extensively by Jon Sticklen and his group at Michigan State University (Sticklen, Kamel, & Bond, 1991a, b).

Sometimes the states in a causal process do not form a neat linear sequence, and some work has been done using more general directed-graph representations in FR, but for simplicity we have stayed with linear representations in this exposition. In general, understanding a causal process may involve more than knowing the states and steps in the process; it may also require the ability to make certain inferences, for example, in abstracting a process of cyclic state transitions to attach the concept of oscillation. Again, some work has been done in this regard, but it is preliminary, and for simplicity we have not described it here.

Use of functional representation in diagnosis. How can functional representations be used within an abductive architecture for diagnosis? Our basic idea is that forms of compiled knowledge can be generated, or augmented, or explained, or justified, by invoking structure-function models of the subsystems or the pathophysiological states with which the compiled knowledge is associated.

Our research demonstrates several ways in which functional models can be used to produce pieces of compiled knowledge for use in diagnosis. Sembugamoorthy and Chandrasekaran (1986) showed how a hierarchical-classification structure of malfunctions useful for diagnosing a device can be built by using compilation processes on a functional representation of the device. Sticklen (1987), in the MDX2 system, used a functional representation of the complement system (part of the immune system), in conjunction with a type of qualitative simulation, to predict the states and their values that would result from particular initial states of the system (see chapter 8). Sticklen (1987) used the output of this simulation to compile potentially useful pieces of hypothesis-matching knowledge for disorders that affect the complement system. Although compiled knowledge generated in this manner is not equivalent to clinical heuristic knowledge derived from experience, it can nevertheless be used to supplement such experiential knowledge, to causally explain it, to justify it, or to check its consistency under appropriate circumstances.

Matt DeJongh explored the use of FR in the RED domain for representing the causal processes that relate data to potential explanations (DeJongh, 1991). He was able to use FR representations of the processes involved in antibody-antigen reactions to formulate explanatory hypotheses (at run time) by deriving them from the causal-process representations.

Use of structural knowledge for diagnosis: Consolidation

In this section, we briefly describe a second deep-reasoning method that we are developing and applying to medical situations. It is important to distinguish between two senses of the word *behavior*. (See Bylander & Chandrasekaran, 1985.) One sense is to describe the order of events that occur in a causal process (e.g., to describe the actual sequence of events leading to increased bile in the bile duct due to biliary obstruction). We call this sense *actual behavior*. The other sense is to describe the general characteristics of a component or a subsystem, independent of its interactions with other components or subsystems (e.g., the hepatocyte conjugates bilirubin with glucuronide to form direct bilirubin). We call the second sense *potential behavior*. The problem of simulation is to determine actual behavior from potential behavior – to determine the actual sequence of events. The problem of *consolidation* is to determine the potential behavior of a system or a subsystem from a description of its parts.

Both structure and behavior are represented for consolidation. The structural description is composed of:

1. *Components.* These form the topology of the device. Veins, arteries, heart chambers, and valves are examples of components.
2. *Substances.* The term "substance" refers to any kind of "stuff" that can be thought of as moving from one place to another. Besides physical stuff, such as liquids, the term is also intended to refer to nonmaterial stuffs that are commonsensically thought of as substances, such as heat, light, and information. Blood and nerve signals are biological examples of such substances.
3. *Connections between components.* A connection implies that certain kinds of substances can pass between the components. The left ventricle, for example, is connected to the aortic valve, and blood can pass between them.
4. *Containment of substances.* Both components and substances can contain substances. For example, arteries contain blood, and blood contains oxygen.

Behavior is represented according to the basic types of behavior that the consolidation research has identified. Some of these are:

1. *Allow.* A substance is permitted to move from one place to another. A vein has an *allow*-blood behavior. A nerve has an *allow*-nerve-signal behavior.
2. *Expel.* This is an attempt to move a substance from/to one place to/from anywhere. The chambers of the heart have *expel*-blood behaviors.
3. *Pump.* This is an attempt to move a substance through some path or in some direction. The difference between expel and pump behaviors is that pump behaviors have direction. The heart has a *pump*-blood behavior.
4. *Move.* A substance moves from one place to another. The cardiovascular system has a *move*-blood behavior. Move behaviors are implicitly constrained by the amount and the capacity of the source and sink containers.

The attributes of a behavior may depend on the occurrence of other behaviors. For example, the amount of the heart's *pump*-blood behavior depends on signals from the nervous system (i.e., on *move*-nerve-signal behaviors).

Behavioral relationships between a system and its elements. By consolidation, the behavioral description of a system is inferred from the behavior and the structure of its components and substances. This description is inferred primarily by using *causal patterns.* Causal patterns can be used to hypothesize behaviors based on structural combinations of other behaviors. Some of these causal patterns are:

1. *Serial/parallel allow.* An allow behavior can be caused by two serial or two parallel allow behaviors. For example, if one blood vessel (which has an allow-blood behavior) is connected to another blood vessel, the combination of the blood vessels also has an allow-blood behavior.
2. *Propagate expel.* A pump behavior can be caused by an allow behavior and an expel behavior that is located at an endpoint of the allow. For example, the expel-blood behavior of the left ventricle combines with the allow-blood behavior of the aortic valve to give rise to a pump-blood behavior over the combination of chamber and valve.

Consolidation can be used to generate predictions from structural descriptions of either normal or pathological systems. These predictions can be used to support diagnostic reasoning by helping to determine the data that a simple or a composite hypothesis can explain and by generating data expectations for hypotheses that can be used for hypothesis scoring and for detecting mistaken data values.

Integrating functional representation and consolidation within an abductive architecture

To integrate structure-function reasoning methods within an abductive architecture one must entertain a broad picture of the types of knowledge involved. Figure 5.4 summarizes this view of diagnostic knowledge. Both processes and knowledge structures are shown, with pieces of diagnostic and

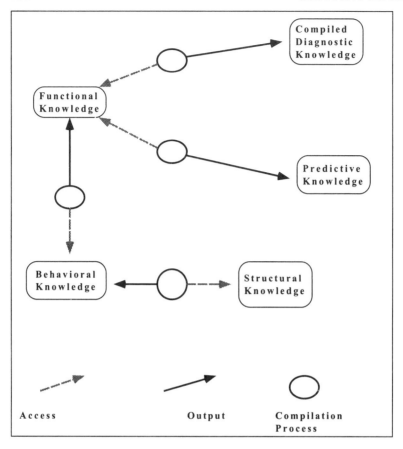

Figure 5.4. Some types of knowledge useful for diagnosis and compilation processes that derive one type from another.

predictive knowledge shown as being generated from structure-function models. The component of Figure 5.4 labeled Compiled Diagnostic Knowledge refers to the knowledge required to support the abductive architecture shown in Figure 5.2.

Figure 5.4 represents the claim that a form of functional knowledge exists that explicitly encodes how various functions of a device arise from causal processes occurring within the structure of the device. Furthermore, we suggest that there are compilation processes that can use this representation to produce forms of knowledge directly useful in diagnosis. This kind of compilation is not the only way to obtain diagnostic knowledge, but it is one way to produce some of this knowledge.

We hypothesize that the links between deep and surface types of knowledge allow physicians to understand how alterations in a body system's structure and the functions of its components lead to malfunctions and their manifestations. These links can also be used to justify their more heuristic knowledge. Given an unfamiliar diagnostic situation for which they do not have explicitly compiled experiential knowledge, physicians are still often able to use this type of deep understanding to produce plausible diagnostic hypotheses.

Figure 5.4 also represents the claim that there are compilation processes that transform knowledge describing structure, to knowledge describing behavior. So far in the artificial intelligence literature these processes have mainly been based on qualitative simulation. We have described consolidation another deep-reasoning method to accomplish this task (Bylander, 1986; Bylander & Chandrasekaran, 1985). Consolidation was inspired in part by our analysis of protocols of expert diagnosticians.

Using functional and causal knowledge for hypothesis interactions. During assembly of composite diagnostic hypotheses there is a need to take into account the various interactions among the hypotheses, both to choose correctly what subhypotheses to add to a growing composite, and to compute what the composite can account for. The need to represent these interactions and appropriately effect hypothesis assembly is discussed in this section.

Subhypotheses may interact in such a way that the presence of one may add or detract from the plausibility or accounts-for attributes of another in a number of ways. These interactions include the following:

1. Subhypotheses may simply be mutually exclusive.
2. Statistical correlations may exist between subhypotheses.
3. One subhypothesis may need another as part of its explanatory structure.
4. There may be functional, causal, and/or structural relationships among subhypotheses.

In PATHEX/LIVER-2 we hypothesize that structure-function models will be of great help in the last two cases.

RED-2 and PATHEX/LIVER-1 use a similar assembly strategy. Both can use the first two types of interactions (e.g., knowing that chronic hepatitis and acute hepatitis are mutually exclusive) to promote or demote certain subhypotheses during assembly. However, their accounts-for determinations and the assembly mechanisms must be enriched to take into account the additional types of interactions.

In RED-2 and PATHEX/LIVER-1, each subhypothesis presents what it can account for without consideration of other subhypotheses that are present. In both systems this information is generated by extracting from the known data for a case the portion that can be accounted for by a particular hypothesis; we call this process *filtering*. Currently, in PATHEX/LIVER-1 filtering relies on an explicit listing of the data in the database that can be accounted for by each hypothesis. Explicit domain knowledge of the effect of interactions of hypotheses (causally based or otherwise) needs to be incorporated so that the explanatory coverage of composite hypotheses can be determined. RED-2 and PATHEX/LIVER-1 can handle interactions of this type that are limited to additivity of manifestations. These interactions are easily accommodated in the assembly procedure that computes the data that composites can explain. However, neither of these systems can accommodate features that, instead of being additive, have opposite effects on some observable parameter. Nor is anything handled regarding functional relations among hypotheses, or hypotheses that have more complex causal structures relating the parts. PATHEX/LIVER-1 did not capture the way in which deeper causal knowledge of the domain can be mobilized to find new subhypotheses, or can be used to derive what can be explained by a composite hypothesis, or can be used to connect the parts of a composite. For liver diagnosis and other medical domains the abductive process needs to be enriched to take advantage of all these possibilities.

Furthermore, in RED-2 and PATHEX/LIVER-1, we did not provide for adjusting what a hypothesis can account for during hypothesis assembly. Each hypothesis matcher runs at most once, generating a hypothesis with a confidence value and a description of what the hypothesis can account for. Certain errors occurred because this accounts-for description was never readjusted (see the section of chapter 3 on RED-2 performance). In these cases, to explain a small residual of data left after subtracting what the leading contenders could collectively account for, the system included additional hypotheses of lower plausibility. The system had selected correct hypotheses but had incorrectly determined what they accounted for. The assembler could have avoided such errors by incorporating additional knowledge, which would have encouraged leading hypotheses to account for additional residual data. Sticklen, Chandrasekaran, & Josephson (1985) describe a method for adjusting these accounts-for descriptions.

Further extension to assembly and criticism. In addition to the extensions for improving the accounts-for behavior of hypotheses, several other extensions to assembly can be envisioned. In future PATHEX/LIVER hypothesis assemblers, a form of recursive assembly is needed, with multiple levels of organization represented in the assembled hypotheses. Hypotheses will be assembled from parts that are themselves assemblies. (PEIRCE provides for this. See chapter 4.)

Finally, the PATHEX/LIVER-1 assembly module does not encode enough domain pragmatics related to the importance or utility of alternative decisions, or the perceived significance of findings. Should we downgrade the subhypothesis cancer-of-the-stomach in a medical system because it did not account for one finding that common-cold did? Should we detract from subhypotheses not accounting for the patient's slightly red left cheek? The knowledge underlying such considerations needs to be taken into account more fully during the assembly process.

We anticipate that PATHEX/LIVER-2 will demonstrate the usefulness of a new set of concepts and techniques in improving the ability of medical knowledge-based systems to perform diagnostic reasoning by integrating structure-function models with compiled diagnostic knowledge. This will be a powerful adjunct to current knowledge-engineering techniques. In addition, we anticipate that the enhancements and additions to existing high-level knowledge-engineering tools will offer a more flexible, extensible, and modularized knowledge-engineering environment that will prove useful in many other diagnostic domains.

Notes

1 William F. Punch III designed and built TIPS as part of his doctoral dissertation work under B. Chandrasekaran and Jack Smith (Punch, 1989). John Svirbely, MD, and Jack Smith, MD, provided domain expertise.

2 [Note that {function | connection-topology | spatial-arrangements} is a domain-independent trichotomy of diagnostically useful types of knowledge for almost any device. It applies in electrical and mechanical as well as biological domains. Malfunction in a power supply may reduce voltage available to other components and cause secondary loss of function. A break in electrical connection can occur in any electrical device and has consequences that can be predicted if connectivity is known. Overheating of an electrical component may damage spatially proximate components. – J. J.]

3 Jack Smith, William Punch, Todd Johnson and Kathy Johnson designed PATHEX/LIVER-1. It was implemented by William Punch (abductive assemblers), Kathy Johnson (inferencing database, using IDABLE software written by Jon Sticklen), and Todd Johnson (CSRL re-implementation and HYPER tool for hypothesis matching). John Svirbely, MD, Jack Smith, MD, Carl Speicher, MD, Joel Lucas, MD, and John Fromkes, MD provided domain expertise.

4 For clarity we use the phrase *causal-process description* to replace what was called a *behavior* in the original representations.

6   Better task analysis, better strategy - machine 4

Abduction machines – summary of progress

All six generations of abduction machines described in this book are attempts to answer the question of how to organize knowledge and control processing to make abductive problem solving computationally feasible. How can an intelligent agent form good composite explanatory hypotheses without getting lost in the large number of potentially applicable concepts and the numerical vastness of their combinations? What general strategies can be used? Furthermore, it is not enough simply to form the best explanation, which already appears to be difficult, but an agent needs to be reasonably sure that the explanation chosen is significantly better than alternative explanations, even though generating all possible explanations so that they can be compared is usually not feasible.

Thus it seems that we are in deep trouble. Logic demands that an explanation be compared with alternatives before it can be confidently accepted, but bounded computational resources make it impossible to generate all of the alternatives. So it seems, tragically, that knowledge is impossible! Yet we are saved after all by a clever trick; and that trick is *implicit* comparison. A hypothesis is compared with alternatives without explicitly generating them all. One way to do this, as we have seen, is by comparing parts of hypotheses. By comparing hypothesis-part h_1 with hypothesis-part h_2, all composite hypotheses containing h_1 are implicitly compared with all composites containing h_2. Another way to implicitly compare hypotheses is to rely on a hypothesis generator that generates hypotheses in approximate order of most plausible first. If the plausibility ordering can be more or less trusted, then the agent simply has to explore a few more hypotheses beyond the first generated to find the best alternatives. Perhaps human memory processes work in this way and remind us of more plausible hypothesis-generating ideas before less plausible ones – at least approximately and most of the time.

√ Summary of Progress and Task Analysis of Abductive Hypothesis Formation are by John R. Josephson. Concurrent Assembly is by Ashok K. Goel, John R. Josephson, and P. Sadayappan. Efficiency of the Essentials-first Strategy is by Olivier Fischer, Ashok K. Goel, John Svirbely, and Jack W. Smith.

Machine 1

First-generation machines, such as RED-1, use the hypothesis-assembly strategy of beginning with the most plausible hypothesis and continuing to conjoin less and less plausible hypotheses until all the data are explained. Then, to ensure parsimony, the first-generation strategy is to work from least to most plausible part of the working hypothesis, removing any parts that are explanatorily superfluous. Then a form of criticism occurs that determines, for each part in the working hypothesis, whether it is essential – that is, whether it explains some datum that can be explained in no other way (known to the system). If h_1 is essential, then any composite hypothesis without h_1 will necessarily leave something unexplained. The strategy for determining essentialness is to construct the largest composite hypothesis, not including the part in question, and to check for an unexplained remainder. Essential parts of the final composite hypothesis are marked as especially confident.

This is the overall strategy of RED-1. It is domain-independent, not in being applicable in every domain, but in having a specification that makes no use of domain-specific terms. Instead the specification is confined to the domain-independent (but abduction-specific) vocabulary of hypotheses, their plausibilities, what they explain, and so forth. Systems such as RED-1 that use this strategy can be considered to be instances of the Machine 1 abstract abduction machine.

Machine 2

Second-generation abduction machines, such as RED-2, use the hypothesis-assembly strategy of focusing attention on an unexplained datum and conjoining to the working hypothesis a hypothesis that best explains that datum (typically the most plausible explainer). Then the unexplained remainder is computed, and a new focus of attention is chosen. This process continues until all the data are explained, or until no further progress can be made. In effect, the assembly strategy is to decompose the larger abduction problem, that of explaining all the data, into a series of smaller and easier abduction subproblems of explaining a series of particular data items. The smaller problems are easier to solve primarily because they usually have smaller differentials than the larger problem does, that is, there are fewer relevant alternative explainers. Second generation machines also have a way to handle incompatible hypotheses: The consistency of the growing hypothesis is maintained, even if doing so requires removing parts of the hypothesis to accommodate a new one.

Second-generation machines use the same strategy for ensuring parsimony as first-generation machines do, but they have a more elaborate strategy for determining essentialness. Some hypotheses are discovered to be essential during assembly of an initial composite (if it is noticed that a finding has only one plausible explainer), but for each part of the initial composite whose essentialness has not been determined, an attempt is made to construct a complete, consistent alternative hypothesis that does not use the part in question. If this cannot be done, the hypothesis is essential. If essential hypotheses are found, the set of essentials is used as a starting point to assemble a new composite hypothesis. Parsimony is checked again if necessary.

Overall this is the second-generation strategy. This one too is domain independent. Machines that use this strategy can be considered to be instances of abstract Machine 2. Machines of generations one and two were described in detail in chapter 3 as descriptions of RED-1 and RED-2.

Machine 3

Machine 3 (e.g., PEIRCE) has a more advanced strategy that combines improved overall flexibility and opportunism in problem solving with some new abilities. The flexibility and opportunism come from choosing at run time from among several ways of improving the working hypothesis. Most of these hypothesis-improvement tactics are already parts of the second-generation strategy, but in Machine 3 they are separated out and available in mixed order rather than always in the same fixed sequence.

Machine 3 has three main new abilities: control of hypothesis refinement, special response to special data or patterns of data, and delaying hard decisions. These three abilities, and the opportunism, are described in Chapter 4. Machine 3 also accepts "plug-in modules" that give it additional abilities to reason with explicit causal, functional, and/or structural knowledge. These extensions are described in chapter 5.

Control of hypothesis refinement enables a strategy of first assembling a general hypothesis and then pursuing greater specificity. A diagnostician might decide that the patient has some form of liver disease and also some form of anemia, and decide to pursue a more detailed explanation by considering possible subtypes. Special response to special data or patterns of data enables a reasoner to take advantage of evoking knowledge that associates specific findings or finding patterns with hypotheses or families of hypotheses especially worth considering. Delaying hard decisions – postponing choosing an explainer for an ambiguous finding – has advantages for computational efficiency and for correctness. The efficiency advantages come from not making decisions during hypothesis assembly that are arbitrary or risky, and thus avoiding the need for subsequent retraction during the process of criticism. The correctness advantage arises because a mistaken earlier decision may adversely affect later decisions during assembly, and criticism may not be able to detect and correct a mistaken choice. (The correctness advantage has not been directly tested empirically.)

Table 6.1. Six generations of abduction machines

Abduction machine No.	Main innovations	Main Implementations	Described in chapter
1	Plausibility guided greedy assembly. Criticism for parsimony and essentialness.	RED-1	3
2	Decompose big abduction problems into little abduction problems. Handle incompatible hypotheses.	RED-2	3
3	Opportunistic control. Delaying hard decisions. Control of hypo-thesis refinement. Special responses to special data or patterns.	PEIRCE, RED-3, TIPS, PATHEX/LIVER	4,5
4	Essentials-first strategy. Partial explanations; nonspeculation. Concurrent assembly.	RED-domain experiments. Concurrent none.	6
5	Incompatibility interactions used for disambiguation.	PEIRCE-IGTT, CV, Peyer Case, RED-domain experiments.	9
6	Layered abduction. Management of top-down information flow.	3-Level, ArtRec.	10

Machines 4, 5, and 6

Although some subtasks of forming a composite explanation are inherently sequential, others are not. Our work on Machine 4 was stimulated by the idea of trying to design for concurrent processing, and thereby force an analysis of the subtask dependencies. The result, however, was a new task analysis and a new abductive-assembly strategy, both of which make sense independently of concurrent processing. In Machine 4, subtasks that do not depend on one another are performed concurrently, and composite explanations are formed by starting with a kernel of essential hypotheses and working outward to less and less confident ones. Fourth-generation machines are described in this chapter, whereas fifth-generation machines are described in chapter 9 and sixth-generation machines are described in chapter 10.

Table 6.1 shows the main innovations associated with each of the six machines. The capabilities of the machines are summarized in the appendix entitled Truth Seekers in the section entitled Abduction Machines.

Task analysis of explanatory hypothesis formation

The task (goal) of forming a composite explanation for a given body of data can be achieved by way of two main subtasks (subgoals): generating elementary hypotheses, and forming a composite hypothesis using the elementary ones. One method for the larger task is to generate some initially promising elementary hypotheses, then to compose, returning for more elementary hypotheses as needed (perhaps generating more refined hypotheses, as is possible in Machine 3). In this method the two subtasks are pursued in a back-and-forth manner. A somewhat simpler method, and the only one available in Machines 1 and 2, is first to generate all plausible elementary hypotheses (those that cannot be ruled out) and then to compose. The two subtasks are pursued serially. For simplicity in this section we suppose the simpler serial method, although with suitable elaborations almost everything said here also applies to the back-and-forth method.

Figure 6.1 shows a task analysis of abductive hypothesis formation. It is intentionally left somewhat vague by leaving out criticism, and by ignoring the somewhat different character of the subtasks depending on which methods are used. Note that this describes only one family of ways to accomplish the task; it may be especially apt, but it is not necessarily unique. Generating an elementary hypothesis can usefully be considered to consist of two subtasks: evocation (stimulating consideration of a particular hypothesis-forming concept) and instantiation (particularizing the concept to the case at hand).

Evocation

One method for evocation is to search systematically for applicable con-

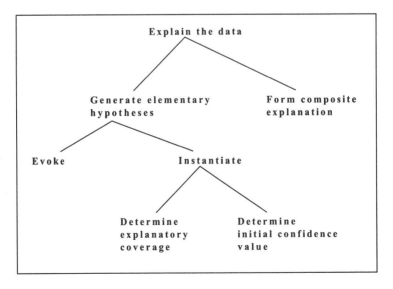

Figure 6.1. Task analysis of abductive hypothesis formation.

cepts in a top-down fashion through a concept hierarchy organized by generality. Refinements of inapplicable general concepts are not considered. This is evocation by hierarchical classification, as is done in RED-1, RED-2, and in most of the diagnostic systems we built. Note that there are usually no dependencies in judging the applicability of the refinements of a concept, so these judgments can be done in parallel. There is a natural degree of coarse-grained parallelism in hierarchical-classification problem solving.

A second method for evocation is to stimulate consideration by cueing, that is, by taking advantage of knowledge stored in the form of associations between particular data concepts (e.g., high blood pressure) and particular hypothesis-forming concepts likely to be relevant (e.g., eating too much salt). One advantage to evocation by cueing is that it is very computationally efficient; one disadvantage is that it is not exhaustive, so applicable concepts may be missed and it is difficult to be sure that they have not. Note that cueing can be done in parallel. A similar method for evocation is contextual priming, where the association with the hypothesis-forming concept comes from elements of a situation other than the data to be explained. Priming is described in more detail in chapter 10.

A third method for evocation is to use an explicit causal representation to work backward from effect to possible causes. Matt DeJongh (1991) explored this possibility in the RED domain.

Yet another method for evocation is to generate a new explanatory concept by forming an analogy.[1] This is a subtle and interesting topic, and we will be able to explore it only briefly and suggestively here. What happens is that the present situation reminds the agent of a previous one, and causal knowledge is then transferred and adapted. (See, for example, Schank, 1986.) This form of reasoning appears to rest on the quasi-logical principle that: *What happens once, can happen again.* The present situation and the previous episode are members of the same class (perhaps an ad hoc category set up by their similarity). The occurrence of the previous episode is an existence proof that things of that kind actually do happen. So they may be happening again in the present situation. The causal hypothesis adapted from the previous episode is then prima facie plausible because it is already known that such things do happen. It seems that this pattern of reasoning requires making a distinction between a mere logical possibility and the "real possibility" that something known to have occurred is occurring again. Indeed we can see analogy used everywhere to argue for plausibility, once we have eyes to see it.[2] The existence of hypothesization by analogy raises the intriguing possibility that we have been misled by the limitations of traditional logic into thinking that most general knowledge consists of universally quantified general propositions, where instead, most general knowledge is knowledge of possibilities.

Instantiation

Once evoked, a concept needs to be instantiated, or attached to the data for the current case. It is not enough, to use a perceptual example, for the frog concept to be activated in my brain; it also needs to be attached as a hypothesis to account for the croaking sound that I just heard. Besides determining what a hypothesis can account for it is also useful to have a prima facie estimate of its likelihood – an initial plausibility, a confidence estimate that can be used as a guide in comparing the hypothesis with rivals. Typically we set up our systems first to try ruling out a hypothesis based on its failure to meet certain prestored necessary conditions. If rule-out fails, explanatory coverage is determined; then a confidence estimate is made, sometimes based in part on whether the explanatory coverage is extensive, or whether the hypothesis will help explain anything at all. Clearly, the processes of determining explanatory coverage and of determining initial confidences are, in general, entangled, and we have not gone far in systematically sorting them out. Note that in general the instantiation of separate concepts can proceed in parallel, but that the set-confidence and determine-coverage subtasks of instantiating a concept are codependent and cannot be pursued separately .

Concurrent assembly

This section describes Machine 4.

The essentials-first strategy

We first describe a strategy for the abductive-assembly task (forming a composite explanation from elementary ones), assuming that there are no interactions among the elementary hypotheses except that of being explanatory alternatives whose coverages overlap. Then we briefly describe how this strategy can be extended to accommodate some types of interactions. Finally, we describe a concurrent mechanism for realizing the strategy in its unextended form.

The abductive-assembly task takes as input a set of data D, the findings, and a set of elementary hypotheses H, where each hypothesis $h \in H$ can explain some portion of D, and each $h \in H$ has an associated prima facie confidence value. The abductive-assembly task gives as output a composite explanation C $\subseteq$ H that "best" explains D. In the new strategy the formation of a composite explanation starts from islands of high confidence and grows by including hypotheses of lesser and lesser confidence, where this confidence is measured, not by the prima facie confidence values as in Machine 1, but by local abductive criteria of how well a hypothesis compares with explanatory rivals.

Machine 4 sets up three subtasks of the abductive-assembly task according to the relative certainty with which the available elementary hypotheses can be included in the composite explanation: (1) identifying and including

Essential hypotheses, (2) identifying and including *Clear-Best* hypotheses, and (3) identifying and including *Weak-Best* hypotheses. These subtasks are performed sequentially.

In the first subtask, the Essential hypotheses are identified for inclusion in the composite explanation, where an elementary hypothesis is Essential if it is the only available explanation for some finding in D. The collective explanatory coverage of the set of Essential hypotheses is then determined. If a portion of D remains unexplained, the second subtask is executed.

In the second subtask, the Clear-Best hypotheses are identified for inclusion, where an elementary hypothesis is a *Clear-Best* if it is not an Essential and if its prima facie confidence value is high both on some absolute scale and relative to its explanatory alternatives for some unexplained finding. That is, a Clear-Best must exceed some high threshold T_1 of confidence and must be at least T_2 better than alternative explanations for some finding that is not explained by an Essential. The expanded explanatory coverage of the set of Essential and Clear-Best hypotheses is then determined. If some of the data are still unexplained, the third subtask is executed.

In the third subtask, Weak-Best hypotheses are identified, where a *Weak-Best* is neither an Essential nor a Clear-Best but is the best explanation for some unexplained finding. The expanded explanatory coverage of the set of Essential, Clear-Best, and Weak-Best hypotheses is then determined.

The explanatory coverage of this composite explanation may not explain all the findings; some findings may be ambiguous, having no best explanations, and some may be unexplainable, having no elementary hypotheses offering to explain them. If there are ambiguous findings, but no unexplainable findings, and if complete explanatory coverage is important, then arbitrary choices can be made among the top-rated hypotheses for the remaining unexplained findings. Usually, however, gathering more data is preferable to making arbitrary choices. The Essential and Clear-Best hypotheses collectively represent the most confident portion of the best explanation, whereas the Weak-Best hypotheses are informed guesses, and arbitrarily chosen hypotheses are more risky informed guesses ("informed" because they are chosen only from the top-rated hypotheses for explaining some finding).

Discussion of the strategy. Like the earlier generations of abduction machines described in this book, Machine 4 forms a single explanation instead of enumerating all possible consistent explanations as is done in some models for abduction (e.g., de Kleer & Williams, 1987; Levesque, 1989; Reiter, 1987). In general, forming a single composite hypothesis is likely to be much more feasible than finding all possible composite hypotheses.

Earlier generations of our abduction machines first generate an initial composite explanation and then test for Essential hypotheses included in this explanation. In contrast, Machine 4 first finds the Essential hypotheses, then uses them as high-confidence starting places for building a composite. Machine 1 simply marks the Essentials as high-confidence parts of the com-posite conclusion. Machine 2 rebuilds the composite hypotheses around the kernel consisting of the Essentials, in effect using the initial composite merely as a trap with which to catch all the Essentials. Machine 2 already shows an awareness that starting from the high-confidence hypotheses might lead to a more accurate outcome.

Machine 4's essentials-first strategy serves some of the same purposes as Machine 3's strategy of delaying hard decisions does. It potentially avoids the need to retract earlier hypothesis selections, and by building the com-posite hypothesis in order of more confident parts first, it should contribute to more accurate conclusions. Easy decisions correspond to Clear-Best hy-potheses, and hard decisions correspond to Weak-Best and arbitrarily cho-sen hypotheses. Clearly, however, more grades of abductive confidence could be distinguished besides the two of easy decision and hard-decision, or the four of Essential, Clear-Best, Weak-Best, and Arbitrary. If we consider an Essential hypothesis to be one whose best rival is very implausible (rather than nonexistent), then abductive confidence can be considered an inverse of the plausibility of the nearest rival, with perhaps a downward adjustment for a hypothesis whose independent plausibility is already low. As many abductive confidence grades can be distinguished as there are grades of plau-sibility for potential rivals. Yet, we can expect that there will be diminishing returns from making finer and finer confidence distinctions, and increasing computational expense.

Since the composite explanation grows from islands of relative certainty, the essentials-first strategy provides a mechanism for controlling the overall uncertainty of an explanation. Since it is apparent when the confidence in including further elementary hypotheses in the composite explanation be-comes low, it is possible to stop increasing the size of the composite hypoth-esis at that stage, and perhaps to perform tests to gather more data. This point is discussed at greater length in connection with Machine 5 (chapter 9); suffice it to say that there appears to be a basic trade-off between ex-planatory coverage and confidence. In general we can cover more of the data at a greater risk of being wrong. The essentials-first strategy provides for a smooth increase in coverage along with a smooth increase in the risk of error, so the process can be stopped at any point dictated by the pragmatics of the particular task and situation.

In retrospect it appears that the delaying-hard-decisions strategy repre-sents a conceptual entanglement of the confidence with which problem-solv-ing decisions can be made, and the sequential-processing need to examine the findings one at a time. Making the conceptual leap to parallel processing led to a better understanding of which pieces of strategy are responsive to the information-processing demands (and opportunities) that arise from the abductive-assembly task, and which are responses to assumptions about the underlying computational architecture, in this case, the assumption that there is a single sequential processor.

The essentials-first strategy, by building up hypotheses in a surer, more methodical way than predecessor strategies, should typically result in fewer explanatorily superfluous parts being present in a final hypothesis. Essentials are never explanatorily superfluous, and a parsimony check can safely ignore them. A Clear-Best hypothesis can turn out to be superfluous if the finding on the basis of which it is judged a Clear-Best is explained by some lesser value hypothesis, which might be a Clear-Best or a Weak-Best in its own right for some other finding. Nevertheless, it is possible to set the Clear-Best acceptance thresholds described earlier as T_1 and T_2 in such a way that parsimony between Clear-Bests is automatically ensured.

Hypothesis interactions. The essentials-first strategy can be easily extended to accommodate several types of interactions between the elementary hypotheses. We describe briefly here how this can be done, giving only the main points.

The section in chapter 3 entitled Hypothesis Interactions describes five types of interactions besides the basic one of being explanatory alternatives: additive explanatory overlap (as occurs in all the RED systems), subtype (one hypothesis is a more detailed refinement of the other), suggestiveness (where a known statistical association suggests including one hypothesis if the other is included), where a hypothesis itself needs to be explained, and mutual incompatibility. In chapter 5 several types of causal interactions were described. Chapter 7 describes cancellation interactions, where one element of a composite hypothesis blocks the explanatory coverage that another element of the composite would otherwise have. Cancellation interactions are particularly problematic, quite probably for any abductive strategy. We postpone discussion of how to handle them, at least until after the difficulties become clearer in the next chapter.

Additive explanatory overlap. The only special difficulty with additive interactions is that it may be worth some extra computational work to detect more Essentials, Clear-Bests and Weak-Bests. For example, if h_1 and h_2 both offer to help explain some finding f, but h_1 can completely explain it while h_2 cannot, and if nothing else offers to help explain f, then h_1 is Essential but h_2 is not. Thus, there is extra inferential leverage in reasoning about local explanatory power in evaluating alternative explanations for a particular finding, instead of comparing according to confidence scores alone. The single-finding abducers of PIERCE (chapter 4) were designed especially for the sort of local abductive reasoning required.

Subtype. Machine 3 (as represented by PEIRCE) can choose to consider refinements of parts of the working hypothesis as one option during problem solving. This ability can be imparted quite easily to the essentials-first strategy by giving priority to refining the surest unrefined parts of the working hypothesis.

Suggestiveness. As hypotheses are included in the working hypothesis, known links of statistical association are used to update the confidence scores of hypotheses outside the working hypotheses. This amounts to revising the prima facie confidence estimates for these hypotheses for the new reasoning context set up by assuming (on good evidence) that certain other hypotheses are true. Downward as well as upward confidence revising is done, which may change the status of the local differentials associated with the remaining unexplained findings (e.g., by changing which hypothesis is the best explainer or by bringing out a new Clear-Best).

Where a hypothesis itself needs to be explained. As long as such a hypothesis is part of the working composite, it must also appear as data to be explained, and so it sets up its own differential and small abduction problem. This type of interaction is examined in much more detail in the chapter on layered abduction (chapter 10).

Causal interactions. The general principle of how to handle causal interactions is to base reasoning progress on the most confident conclusions arrived at by the reasoning process so far. Beyond that, almost everything about reasoning strategies remains to be worked out.

Mutual incompatibility. If mutually incompatible Essentials appear during hypothesis assembly, this is a signal that something is very wrong, and normal processing should be suspended in favor of special handling. The occurrence of mutually incompatible Essentials represents a kind of maximum-strength cognitive dissonance. Similarly, mutually incompatible Clear-Best or Weak-Best hypotheses represent cognitive dissonance, although of weaker sorts, and also call for special handling, primarily that of downgrading confidence in those hypotheses. Besides this kind of critical cross-checking, knowledge of hypothesis incompatibilities can also play a very constructive role in the main course of hypothesis assembly. A brief illustrative example is given at the end of this chapter; however, we postpone a detailed discussion of incompatibility handling until chapter 9 (Machine 5) so that we do not deviate too far from the chronological order of discovery.

Actually, the division between the strategies of Machines 4 and 5 is a somewhat arbitrary mark along the path of progress. The problem with telling the whole story of this book in a completely linear fashion is that several loosely communicating processors were doing the research, so progress had multiple paths.

Concurrent realization of the essentials-first strategy: Framework

To take advantage of concurrency, we can associate a computational process with each elementary hypothesis that offers to explain a portion of the data set, and also associate a process with each datum to be explained. The hypothesis and data processes work cooperatively to form a composite explanation. These processes may communicate with each other either through a shared data structure (Goel, Josephson, & Sadayappan, 1987) or by passing messages. We describe here a message-passing mechanism.

The earlier generations of abduction machines described in this book were completely sequential. The essentials-first strategy also contains significant elements of sequentiality, mainly the sequence of the subtasks that find Essentials, Clear-Bests, and Weak-Bests. However there are also significant opportunities for concurrent processing.

Two important perspectives are relevant during the formation of a composite explanation. From the perspective of each datum to be explained, a typical question might be, "Which available hypothesis can best explain me?" This question can be asked for each datum in parallel with the others. The second perspective is that of each available hypothesis, and a typical question might be, "Which portions of the data can I be used to explain?" This question can also be asked for each hypothesis in parallel with the others.

It is useful to assign a process to each datum and to each hypothesis. Each data process represents the perspective of its corresponding datum, and each hypothesis process represents the perspective of its corresponding hypothesis. The data processes use identical algorithms and can execute in parallel, and similarly the hypothesis processes.

The data and hypothesis processes cooperatively synthesize a best composite explanation for the given data set D by using hypotheses from the set of available hypotheses H. Each process has access only to its own local memory. Communication between the processes occurs by message passing. To synchronize the data and the hypothesis processes, we adopt the framework of Hoare's Communicating Sequential Processes (CSP) (Hoare, 1978). In CSP, communication between processes occurs when one process names another as the destination, and the second process names the first as the source. Synchronization is achieved by delaying the execution of an input or output command until the other process is ready with the corresponding output or input.

The response of a process to a message depends on which message it receives. For example, if a process corresponding to datum $d_1 \in D$ determines that some $h_1 \in H$ is essential for explaining d_1, then it sends an *Essenticl !* message to the hypothesis process representing h_1. On receiving this message, the hypothesis process sends an *Explained !* message to all the processes corresponding to the $d_i \in D$ that h_1 can explain. Besides these meaningful messages, the processes may also send and receive *Null* messages to help in coordinating activities.

Control of processing alternates between the data processes and the hypothesis processes. In each cycle of processing, when the data processes are executing, the hypothesis processes are idle; when the data processes finish executing, they communicate their results to the hypothesis processes, then the hypothesis processes can begin executing. Similarly, when the hypothesis processes are executing, the data processes are idle, and when they finish, they communicate their results to the data processes, which can then begin executing. A composite explanation is generated in three such cycles, corresponding to accumulating Essential, Clear-Best, and Weak-Best hypotheses. Then the composite is tested for parsimony, also in a multiple-process cooperative manner.

We describe the concurrent mechanism here only for the generation of composite explanations. Parsimony testing can also be done in a similar manner; see Goel et al. (1987) for details.

Concurrent realization of the essentials-first strategy: Details

A hypothesis process initially has information about the hypothesis h that it represents: the initial confidence value c(h), and the explanatory coverage e(h) of the hypothesis.

In the first cycle of processing, the Essential hypotheses are identified. Processing begins when the hypothesis process corresponding to each hypothesis h sends an *Essential ?* message to processes corresponding to data in e(h) and sends Null messages to the other data processes. Then, from the perspective of each data process, one of three things can have happened:

1. The data process received no *Essential ?* messages. In this case its corresponding datum is *Unexplainable*, and the process does nothing further.
2. The data process received exactly one *Essential ?* message. In this case the hypothesis corresponding to the hypothesis process from which the data process received the message is the only available explanation of its datum, and so it sends an *Essential !* message to that process.
3. The data process received more than one *Essential ?* message. In this case it sends a *Null* message to the processes from which it had received the *Essential ?* messages.

In the second cycle of processing, the Clear-Best hypotheses are identified. At the end of the first cycle, from the perspective of each hypothesis h, one of two things can have happened:

1. Its hypothesis process received at least one *Essential !* message. Then the hypothesis process sends an *Explained !* message to processes representing the data in e(h).
2. The hypothesis process received only *Null* messages. Then it sends *Clear-Best ?* messages, along with the confidence value c(h), to processes corresponding to the data items in e(h).

At this point a data process d has received messages from the processes corresponding to the hypotheses that can explain d. From the perspective of d, one of three things can have happened:

1. d's process received at least one *Explained !* message. In this case it does nothing.
2. d's process received only *Clear-Best ?* messages, and there is some h among the hypotheses that can explain *d* such that c(h) is above the threshold T_1, and c(h) is better than any other hypothesis offering to explain d by an amount of at least T_2. In this case d's process sends a *Clear-Best !* message to the process representing hypothesis h, and sends *Null* messages to processes corresponding to the other hypotheses that can explain d.
3. d's process received only *Clear-Best?* messages, and no hypothesis satisfies the standards for being a Clear-Best explanation for d. In this case d's process sends *Null* messages to processes corresponding to hypotheses that can explain d.

At this point hypothesis processes have received messages from data processes corresponding to data that their hypotheses are offering to explain. In the third cycle of processing, the *Weak-Best* hypotheses are identified. At the end of the second cycle, from the perspective of hypothesis h, one of two things can have happened:

1. h's process received at least one *Clear-Best!* message. Then h's process sends an *Explained !* message to processes corresponding to data in e(h).
2. h's process received only *Null* messages. Then h's process sends *Weak-Best ?* messages to processes corresponding to data in e(h).

At this point, from the perspective of a datum d, one of two things can have happened:

1. d's process received at least one *Explained !* message. Then the process does nothing.
2. d's process received only *Weak-Best ?* messages. Then d's process selects the h with the highest confidence value among the hypotheses that can explain d. (If two or more hypotheses tie with highest confidence, then an attempt can be made to break the tie according to some measure of total explanatory power for the hypotheses; the hypothesis with the greatest total explanatory power will be chosen. If the tie cannot be broken, then either a hypothesis is not chosen, or, if the pragmatics of the problem dictate setting things up in this way, an arbitrary choice can be made among the highest ranking hypotheses. Because lower ranking hypotheses are not candidates for such choices, these are informed choices, though very risky.) If a Weak-Best hypothesis can be chosen, d's process sends a *Weak-Best !* message to the process corresponding to the selected hypothesis and *Null* messages to processes corresponding to the other hypotheses offering to explain d.

At the end of the third cycle a composite hypothesis consisting of the Essential, Clear-Best, and Weak-Best hypotheses has been generated. Unexplainable data have been identified, and also ambiguous data that can be explained only by making high-risk guesses.

Extensions to the essentials-first strategy to handle hypothesis interactions are discussed in the previous section, Hypothesis Interactions. No special difficulties appear to arise from trying to take advantage of concurrency, although this should be tested in a working concurrent implementation for a real domain (which at this point has not been done).

Architectural implications. There are five interesting aspects to this design for concurrent hypothesis formation, viewed from the prospect of realizing it on a distributed-memory, message-passing, parallel computer architecture. First, the parallelism among the data processes is fine-grained, as is the parallelism among the hypothesis processes. However there is no concurrency between the data processes and the hypothesis processes; they never execute at the same time. Alternative designs that break down this strict sequentiality can be devised. For example, as soon as a hypothesis finds out from some finding that it is a Clear-Best, it could immediately start informing the findings in its explanatory coverage that they are explained, without waiting to hear from the remaining findings. Nevertheless, in the main, the nonconcurrency between the data-centered processes and those that are hypothesis-centered appears to be determined by dependencies in the hypothesis-formation task rather than by failure to design cleverly enough. Second, at any given time during the processing, the data and hypothesis processes are either idle or executing the same instruction on different data. Third, the processing is communication intensive. For instance, in the first cycle during the generation of a composite explanation, each hypothesis process communicates with every data process. Fourth, for real-world problems, the number of data and hypothesis processes is likely to be very large. Even for relatively small abduction systems, the number of data and hypothesis processes can be in the hundreds. Finally, the fine-grained characteristics of the concurrent design suggest that neural networks might be efficient for abductive-assembly problems (see Goel, 1989; Goel, Ramanujan, & Sadayappan, 1988; Peng & Reggia, 1990; Thagard, 1989).

It appears that among existing computers, the Connection Machine (Hillis, 1986) may be the most suitable for realizing the design that we just presented. The Connection Machine is a distributed-memory, message-passing, parallel computer, thus it is a good match to the processing demands of the design. It enables the same instruction to be executed over different data, which suits the control of processing called for by the design. Its architecture helps keep the communication costs within acceptable limits, which is a major concern. It supports massive, fine-grained parallelism among a large number of small, semi-autonomous processes such as is called for by the design.

Summary of Machine 4

We have described Machine 4 for forming composite explanations. This machine uses an essentials-first strategy, which sets up three subtasks according to the confidence (judged by local abductive criteria) with which elementary hypotheses are included in the composite explanation. In the first subtask, the Essential hypotheses are identified. In the second subtask, the Clear-Best hypotheses are identified, where a hypothesis is Clear-Best if its prima facie confidence value is high both on some absolute scale and relative to its explanatory alternatives for some finding. In the third subtask, Weak-Best hypotheses are identified, where a Weak-Best is simply the best explanation for some finding. First the Essentials, then the Clear-Bests, then the Weak-Best hypotheses are included in the growing composite hypothesis. This way the formation of a composite explanation grows from islands of relative certainty, the composite becoming overall less and less certain as its explanatory coverage increases. These three subtasks represent a coarse discretization of a process that could be more gradual.

After an initial composite hypothesis is built in this way, it may be tested for parsimony, and improved accordingly, before the processing is concluded.

Machine 4 uses a concurrent mechanism for the abductive-assembly task. It associates a computational process with each elementary hypothesis and with each datum to be explained. The processes communicate with each other by sending messages. The response of a process to a message depends on which message it receives. The control of processing alternates between the hypothesis and the data processes. Process synchronization results from processes waiting for responses to messages that they send.

Machine 4 offers several advantages over earlier generations of abduction machines. The main advantage lies in the computational efficiency of the essentials-first strategy, which should also improve accuracy. Additionally, concurrent processing provides for faster processing, if processors are plentiful. Machine 4 also offers advantages for management of overall uncertainty, as has been described.

No working concurrent implementation of Machine 4 has been done, although the usefulness of the essentials-first strategy has been experimentally tested. This is described in the next section.

Efficiency of the essentials-first strategy

The previous section presented a computational mechanism for concurrent formation of composite explanatory hypotheses. A central idea in this mechanism is first to identify the Essential hypotheses and include them in the composite explanation and then to identify other, nonEssential hypotheses for inclusion. In this section, we investigate some computational advantages of the essentials-first strategy for abductive assembly. We do this by comparing two assembly methods, one that does not use the essentials-first strategy and one that uses it.

Method 1 – without the essentials-first strategy – has the following steps:

1. The most plausible elementary hypothesis that can explain the most salient datum is selected for inclusion in the composite hypothesis. (An ordering of the saliency of data elements is assumed to be available as part of the domain knowledge.) In case of a plausibility tie, the hypothesis can be selected arbitrarily.
2. The data items that the current composite explanation can explain are removed from the set of data to be explained.
3. This cycle is repeated, starting with the next most salient datum to be explained until as much of the data set is explained as possible.

This method is a simplified version of the one used by the RED-2 system for forming initial composite explanations. (It ignores incompatibility handling and the subtleties of selecting among hypotheses that are tied for plausibility.)

Method 2 – using the essentials-first strategy – has the following steps:

1. The Essential hypotheses are selected for inclusion in the composite explanation.
2. The data items that the current composite explanation can explain are removed from the set of data to be explained.
3. The most salient datum is selected from the remaining data items.
4. The most plausible elementary hypothesis that explains this datum is selected for integration with the current composite hypothesis.
5. The data items that the current composite explanation can explain are removed from the set of data to be explained.
6. Steps 3 to 5 are repeated until as much of the data set is explained as possible.

Advantages for parsimony and efficiency

We give two examples illustrating the essentials-first strategy and its impact on the efficiency of synthesizing parsimonious composite explanations.

We characterize the parsimony of a composite explanation as the absence of explanatory redundancy. Thus a composite hypothesis H is parsimonious if no proper subset of H can explain as much of D as H itself does. This notion of parsimony is illustrated by the following hypothetical example (see Figure 6.2). Let us suppose that D consists of two elements, d_1 and d_2, where the saliency of d_1 is higher than that of d_2. Let us also suppose that the classification task results in the retrieval of two elementary hypotheses, h_1 and h_2, from memory, where h_1 can account for d_1, and h_2 can account for d_1 and d_2. Then, by Method 1, hypothesis h_1 is first included in the composite explanation to account for d_1, and later h_2 is added to account for d_2. Thus, the final composite explanation consists of h_1 and h_2. Clearly, h_1 is explanatorily redundant; a parsimonious explanation would not include it.

Determining the Essential hypotheses at the onset of explanation synthesis can aid in forming more parsimonious explanations. In the present ex-

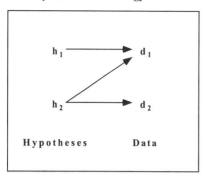

Figure 6.2. Parsimony.

ample, h_2 is an Essential hypothesis because only it explains d_2. By Method 2, h_2, and only h_2, is selected for inclusion in the composite explanation since h_2 explains both d_1 and d_2. This explanation is parsimonious.

Determining the Essential hypotheses at the onset of explanation synthesis can also increase computational efficiency. This is illustrated by the hypothetical example shown in Figure 6.3. In this example, D contains three elements, d_1, d_2, and d_3, in decreasing order of saliency. The set of available elementary hypotheses contains three elements, h_1, h_2, and h_3, in decreasing order of plausibility. The explanatory relationships are that h_1 can account for d_1, h_2 for d_1 and d_2, and h_3 for d_2 and d_3.

In this example, Method 1 requires three cycles, which result in the selection of h_1, h_2, and h_3 in that order. In contrast, Method 2 requires only two cycles for this example. Since h_3 is the only hypothesis that can account for d_3, it is an Essential hypothesis. Consequently, in the first cycle h_3 is selected for inclusion in the composite explanation. Because h_3 can explain d_3 and d_2, only d_1 is unexplained. In the second cycle, h_1 is added to the composite explanation to account for d_1.

Experiments

In this section, we report on two sets of experiments that investigated the essentials-first strategy for its computational and psychological validity. The first set of experiments evaluated the strategy on a library of 42 test cases in the RED domain. The second set of experiments involved the collection and analysis of verbal protocols of a human expert synthesizing explanations in the RED domain.

We constructed a modified version of RED-2 that uses the essentials-first strategy as described in Method 2. We ran the original and the modified RED-2 systems on all 42 cases in the test library. These cases were taken from textbooks and other course material used to train blood-bank techni-

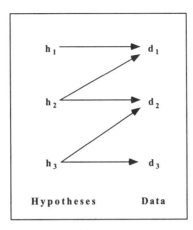

Figure 6.3. Efficiency.

cians (Smith, Josephson, Tanner, Svirbely, and Strohm [1986] describe some of these cases).

Of the 42 cases, 17 included at least one Essential hypothesis. Of these 17 cases, in 9 cases Method 2 resulted in more parsimonious explanations than Method 1 did. Also, the explanations reached in these nine cases were identical to the answers provided in the teaching material. The remaining 8 cases fell into two categories: Three cases had solutions containing only one antibody, hence there was no need to synthesize a composite explanation. In each of the remaining 5 cases the hypothesis selected to explain the most significant reaction by Method 1 was an Essential hypothesis. Thus, for these cases Method 1 found the same answers as Method 2 did, with equal efficiency. In summary, about two fifths of all cases contained Essential hypotheses, and, in approximately half these cases, using the essentials-first strategy increased the parsimony of the answer.

A second set of experiments used oral protocols that were collected at multiple sessions with an expert in the RED domain. Twenty-three cases for which the RED system had located one or more Essential hypotheses were submitted to the domain expert. The expert analyzed the 23 cases and assembled a complete explanation for each. His verbal reports were recorded.

The reports were then analyzed carefully. First, we determined the order in which the expert selected hypotheses for inclusion in the composite explanation. Next, we compared the order in which the expert selected elementary hypotheses with the order in which the RED system, using the essentials-first strategy, selected them. We expected that if the domain expert also used this kind of strategy, there would be a strong similarity between the selection orders that the domain expert and the RED system used. Whereas, if the domain expert used another method that did not make the

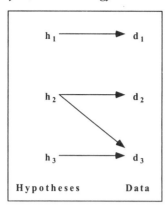

Figure 6.4. Incompatibility interaction.

Essential/nonEssential distinction, there would be a considerable divergence between the two selection orders.

In 14 of the 23 cases the domain expert selected the Essential hypotheses before selecting other hypotheses. In the remaining 9 cases, the domain expert did not select the Essential hypotheses before other hypotheses. The selection of Essential hypotheses before other hypotheses in 14 out of 23, or 61% of the cases, was much higher than what we expect from chance. This suggests that the Essential/nonEssential distinction plays a role in human abductive problem solving.

Incompatibility handling

We suggest that, besides enabling more efficient synthesis of more parsimonious explanations, the essentials-first strategy is useful for reducing uncertainty in explanation synthesis and for handling certain types of interactions, such as incompatibility interactions, more efficiently and effectively (see chapter 9). The usefulness of the essentials-first strategy for handling incompatibility interactions can be illustrated by the following example. Let D contain three elements, d_1, d_2, and d_3. Let the set of elementary hypotheses contain three elements, h_1, h_2, and h_3, where h_1 can account for d_1, h_2 can account for d_2 and d_3, and h_3 can account for d_3, as shown in Figure 6.4. Also, let h_1 and h_3 be incompatible, which implies that h_1 and h_3 cannot both be included in the same composite explanation.

In this example Method 1, which does not use the essentials-first strategy, may include h_3 in the first cycle to account for d_3. In the next cycle, when trying to explain d_1, Method 1 may select h_1, because it is the only explanation for d_1. However, h_1 and h_3 are incompatible. Therefore, Method 1 must backtrack, retract the choice of h_3, replace it with h_2, and then add h_1, yielding $\{h_1, h_2\}$ as the composite explanation.

In contrast, Method 2, using the essentials-first strategy, first selects h_1 because it is an Essential hypothesis. In the next cycle, it selects h_2 because h_1 and h_3 are incompatible. Thus, the essentials-first strategy can help reduce backtracking by taking advantage of incompatibility interactions.

Notes

1 Since making a copy is such a basic operation on information, we can reasonably conjecture that it is computationally inexpensive for humans to make copies of fragments of episodic and semantic memory. (Certainly it is inexpensive for a digital computer to make copies of representations.) If so, an analogy can be formed by a process of copy-and-modify.

2 A classical example is Descartes' plausibility argument for a evil deceiver based on an analogy with God (Descartes, 1641). We also note that the traditional Argument from Design for the existence of God is clearly an abduction. Moreover, it relies on an analogy with human designers for its initial plausibility.

7   The computational complexity of abduction

The problem of abduction can be characterized as finding the best explanation of a set of data. In this chapter we focus on one type of abduction in which the best explanation is the most plausible combination of hypotheses that explains all the data. We then present several computational complexity results demonstrating that this type of abduction is intractable (NP-hard) in general. In particular, choosing between incompatible hypotheses, reasoning about cancellation effects among hypotheses, and satisfying the maximum plausibility requirement are major factors leading to intractability. We also identify a tractable, but restricted, class of abduction problems.

Introduction

What kinds of abduction problems can be solved efficiently? To answer this question, we must formalize the problem and then consider its computational complexity. However, it is not possible to prescribe a specific complexity threshold for all abduction problems. If the problem is "small," then exponential time might be fast enough. If the problem is sufficiently large, then even $O(n^2)$ might be too slow. However, for the purposes of analysis, the traditional threshold of intractability, NP-hard, provides a rough measure of what problems are impractical (Garey & Johnson, 1979). Clearly, NP-hard problems will not scale up to larger, more complex domains.

Our approach is the following. First, we formally characterize abduction as a problem of finding the most plausible composite hypothesis that explains all the data. Then we consider several classes of problems of this type, the classes being differentiated by additional constraints on how hy-

√ This chapter is by Tom Bylander, Dean Allemang, Michael C. Tanner, and John R. Josephson. Tom Bylander is responsible for most of the mathematical results. The chapter is substantially the same as a paper by the same name that appeared originally in *Artificial Intelligence* vol. 49, 1991, except that here we omit the proofs. It appears with permission of Elsevier Science Publishers B. V. The full paper also appears in *Knowledge Representation* edited by R. J. Brachman, H. J. Lavesque, and R. Reiter published by MIT Press in 1992.

potheses interact. We demonstrate that the time complexity of each class is polynomial (tractable) or NP-hard (intractable), relative to the complexity of computing the plausibility of hypotheses and the data explained by hypotheses.

Our results show that this type of abduction faces several obstacles. Choosing between incompatible hypotheses, reasoning about cancellation effects among hypotheses, and satisfying the maximum plausibility requirement are major factors making abduction intractable in general.

Some restricted classes of abduction problems are tractable. One kind of class is when some constraint guarantees a polynomial search space, e.g., the single-fault assumption (more generally, a limit on the size of composite hypotheses), or if all but a small number of hypotheses can be ruled out.[1] This kind of class trivializes complexity analysis because exhaustive search over the possible composite hypotheses becomes a tractable strategy.

However, we have discovered one class of abduction problems in which hypothesis assembly can find the best explanation without exhaustive search. Informally, the constraints that define this class are: no incompatibility relationships, no cancellation interactions, the plausibilities of the individual hypotheses are all different from each other, and one explanation is qualitatively better than any other explanation. Unfortunately, it is intractable to determine whether the last condition holds. We consider one abduction system (RED-2) in which hypothesis assembly was applied, so as to examine the ramifications of these constraints in a real world situation.

The remainder of this chapter is organized as follows. First, we provide a brief historical background to abduction. Then, we define our model of abduction problems and show how it applies to other theories of abduction. Next, we describe our complexity results (proofs of which are given in Bylander, Allemang, Tanner, and Josephson, 1991). Finally, we consider the relationship of these results to RED-2.

Background

C. S. Peirce, who first described abductive inference, provided two intuitive characterizations: given an observation d and the knowledge that h causes d, it is an abduction to hypothesize that h occurred; and given a proposition q and the knowledge $p \rightarrow q$, it is an abduction to conclude p (Fann, 1970). In either case, an abduction is uncertain because something else might be the actual cause of d, or because the reasoning pattern is the classical fallacy of "affirming the consequent" and is formally invalid. Additional difficulties can exist because h might not always cause d, or because p might imply q only by default. In any case, we shall say that h "explains" d and p "explains" q, and we shall refer to h and p as "hypotheses" and d and q as "data."

Pople (1973) pointed out the importance of abduction to AI, and he with

Miller and Myers implemented one of the earliest abduction systems, IN-TERNIST-I, which performed medical diagnosis in the domain of internal medicine (Miller, Pople, & Myers, 1982; Pople, 1977). This program contained an explicit list of diseases and symptoms, explicit causal links between the diseases and the symptoms, and probabilistic information associated with the links. INTERNIST-I used a form of hill climbing – once a disease outscored its competitors by a certain threshold, it was permanently selected as part of the final diagnosis. Hypothesis assembly (e.g., Machine 2 in chapter 3) is a generalization of this technique. Below, we describe a restricted class of problems for which hypothesis assembly can efficiently find the best explanation.

Based on similar explicit representations, Pearl (1987) and Peng & Reggia (1990) find the most probable composite hypothesis that explains all the data, a task that is known to be intractable in general (Cooper, 1990). Later we describe additional constraints under which this task remains intractable.

In contrast to maintaining explicit links between hypotheses and data, Davis & Hamscher's (1988) model-based diagnosis, determines at run time what data need to be explained and what hypotheses can explain the data. Much of this work, such as de Kleer & Williams (1987) and Reiter (1987), place an emphasis on generating all "minimal" composite hypotheses that explain all the data. However, there can be an exponential number of such hypotheses. Recent research has investigated how to focus the reasoning on the most relevant composite hypotheses (de Kleer & Williams, 1989; Dvorak & Kuipers, 1989; Struss & Dressler, 1989). However, we have shown that it is intractable in general to find a composite hypothesis that explains all the data, and that even if it is easy to find explanations, generating all the relevant composite hypotheses is still intractable.

Whatever the technique or formulation, certain fundamentals of the abduction task do not change. In particular, our analysis shows how computational complexity arises from constraints on the explanatory relationship from hypotheses to data and on plausibility ordering among hypotheses. These constraints do not depend on the style of the representation or reasoning method (causal vs. logical, probabilistic vs. default, explicit vs. model-based, ATMS or not, etc.). In other words, certain kinds of abduction problems are hard no matter what representation or reasoning method is chosen.

Notation, definitions, and assumptions

We use the following notational conventions and definitions. d stands for a datum, e.g., a symptom. D stands for a set of data. h stands for an individual hypothesis, e.g., a hypothesized disease. H stands for a set of individual hypotheses. H can be treated as a composite hypothesis, i.e., each $h \in H$ is hypothesized to be present, and each $h \notin H$ is hypothesized to be absent or irrelevant.

Model of abduction

An **abduction problem** is a tuple $\langle D_{all}, H_{all}, e, pl \rangle$, where:

D_{all} is a finite set of all the data to be explained,
H_{all} is a finite set of all the individual hypotheses,
e is a map from subsets of H_{all} to subsets of D_{all}
   (H explains $e(H)$), and
pl is a map from subsets of H_{all} to a partially ordered set
   (H has plausibility $pl(H)$).

For the purpose of this definition and the results that follow, it does not matter whether $pl(H)$ is a probability, a measure of belief, a fuzzy value, a degree of fit, or a symbolic likelihood. The only requirement is that the range of pl is partially ordered.

H is *complete* if $e(H) = D_{all}$. That is, H explains all the data.

H is *parsimonious* if $\nexists H' \subset H (e(H) \subseteq e(H'))$. That is, no proper subset of H explains all the data that H does.

H is an *explanation* if it is complete and parsimonious. That is, H explains all the data and has no explanatorily superfluous elements. Note that an explanation exists if and only if a complete composite hypothesis exists.[2]

H is a best explanation if it is an explanation, and if there is no explanation H' such that $pl(H') > pl(H)$. That is, no other explanation is more plausible than H. It is just "*a* best" because pl might not impose a total ordering over composite hypotheses (e.g., because of probability intervals or qualitative likelihoods). Consequently, several composite hypotheses might satisfy this definition.

Relation to Other Work

These definitions are intended to formalize the notion of best explanation described in Josephson, Chandrasekaran, Smith, & Tanner (1987). However, our definitions are not limited to that paper. We consider in detail here how Reiter's theory of diagnosis (Reiter, 1987) and Pearl's theory of belief revision (Pearl, 1987) can be mapped to our model of abduction.

Reiter's theory of diagnosis. Reiter defines a diagnosis problem as a tuple $\langle$SD, COMPONENTS, OBS$\rangle$, in which SD and OBS are finite sets of first-order sentences comprising the system description and observations, respectively; COMPONENTS is a finite set of constants; and AB is a distinguished unary predicate, interpreted as abnormal. A diagnosis is defined to be a minimal set $\Delta \subseteq$ COMPONENTS such that:

$$\text{SD} \cup \text{OBS} \cup \{\text{AB}(c) \mid c \in \Delta\} \cup \{\neg \text{AB}(c) \mid c \in \text{COMPONENTS}\backslash\Delta\}[3]$$

is consistent. "Minimal set" means that no subset of D satisfies the same condition.

Each subset of COMPONENTS can be treated as a composite hypothesis, i.e., a conjecture that certain components are abnormal, and that all other components are normal. A diagnosis problem can then be mapped into an abduction problem as follows:

H_{all} = COMPONENTS
D_{all} = OBS
$e(H)$ = a maximal set $D \subseteq D_{all}$ such that[4]
    SD $\cup D \cup \{\text{AB}(h) \mid h \in H\} \cup \{\neg\text{AB}(h) \mid h \in H_{all} \setminus H\}$
    is consistent.

A solution for the diagnosis problem then corresponds to an explanation for the abduction problem, and vice versa. Reiter does not define any criteria for ranking diagnoses, so there is nothing to map to *pl*.

Pearl's theory of belief revision. A Bayesian belief network (Pearl, 1986) is a directed acyclic graph whose nodes W are propositional variables. The probabilistic dependencies between the variables are described by specifying $P(x \mid s)$ for each value assignment x to a variable $X \in W$ and each value assignment s to X's parents S.[5] The intention is that "the arcs signify the existence of direct causal influences between the linked propositions, and the strengths of these influences are quantified by the conditional probabilities of each variable given the state of its parents" (Pearl, 1987, p. 175).

For a particular belief revision problem (Pearl, 1987), some subset V of the variables W are initialized with specific values. Let v be the value assignment to V. The solution to the problem is the most probable value assignment w^* to all the variables W, i.e., $P(w^* \mid v)$ is greater than or equal to $P(w \mid v)$ for any other value assignment w to the variables W. w^* is called the *most probable explanation* (MPE).

v can be mapped to the set of data to be explained, i.e., a value assignment x to a variable $X \in V$ is a datum. v can be explained by appropriate value assignments to the other variables $W \setminus V$. Treating value assignments of *true* as individual hypotheses, a belief revision problem can be mapped to an abduction problem as follows:

D_{all} = v
H_{all} = $W \setminus V$
$e(H)$ = a maximal set $D \subseteq D_{all}$ such that
    $P(H = true \wedge H_{all} \setminus H = false \mid D) > 0$
$pl(H)$ = $P(H = true \wedge H_{all} \setminus H = false \mid e(H))$

The MPE corresponds to a complete composite hypothesis. If the MPE is also parsimonious, then it corresponds to the best explanation.[6] However, the MPE might assign *true* to more variables than necessary for explanatory purposes. In the context of other value assignments, $X = true$ might be more likely than $X = false$ even if $X = true$ is superfluous under the above mapping (Peng & Reggia, 1987).

This lack of correspondence between the MPE and the best explanation can be rectified by creating, for each $X \in W \setminus V$, a dummy variable X' and a dummy value assignment that can be "caused" only if $X \neq X'$. With this modification, the MPE corresponds to the best explanation.

Another way of rectifying the situation is to simply ignore the parsimony constraint. With this in mind, we use the mapping just given.

Other theories of abduction. These reductions from problems in Reiter's and Pearl's theories to abduction problems provide strong evidence that our model of abduction is general enough to accommodate any theory of abduction (e.g., de Kleer & Williams, 1987; Levesque, 1989; Peng & Reggia, 1987; Poole, 1989). This is because our model leaves e and pl virtually unconstrained. We exploit this freedom in this chapter by defining and analyzing natural constraints on e and pl without considering the representations – logical, causal, or probabilistic – underlying the computation of e and pl. To make the analysis complete, we also show how some of these constraints can be reduced to problems in Reiter's and Pearl's theories.

Tractability assumptions

In our complexity analysis, we assume that e and pl are tractable. We also assume that e and pl can be represented reasonably, in particular, that the size of their internal representations is polynomial in $|D_{all}| + |H_{all}|$.

Clearly, the tractability of these functions is central to abduction, since it is difficult to find plausible hypotheses explaining the data if it is difficult to compute e and pl. This should not be taken to imply that the tractability of these functions can be taken for granted. For example, it can be intractable to determine explanatory coverage of a composite hypothesis (Reiter, 1987) and to calculate the probability that an individual hypothesis is present, ignoring other hypotheses (Cooper, 1990). We make these assumptions to simplify our analysis of abduction problems. To reflect the complexity of these functions in our tractability results, we denote the time complexity of e and pl with respect to the size of an abduction problem as C_e and C_{pl}, respectively, e.g., nC_e indicates n calls to e.

For convenience, we assume the existence and the tractability of a function that determines which individual hypotheses can contribute to explaining a datum. Although it is not a true inverse, we refer to this function as e^{-1}, formally defined as:

$$e^{-1}(d) = \{h \mid \exists H \subset H_{all}(d \notin e(H) \wedge d \in e (H \cup \{h\}))\}$$

Note that $h \in e^{-1}(d)$ does not imply that $d \in e(h)$.

The key factors, then, that we consider in the complexity of finding a best explanation are properties of e and pl that allow or prevent tractable computation given that e, e^{-1}, and pl can be computed "easily." That is, given a particular class of abduction problems, how much of the space of composite hypotheses must be explicitly searched to find a best explanation? As demonstrated in what follows, intractability is the usual result in classes of problems that involve significant interaction among the elements of composite hypotheses.

Simplifications

We should note that these definitions and assumptions simplify several aspects of abduction. For example, we define composite hypotheses as simple combinations of individual hypotheses. In reality, the relationships among the parts of an abductive answer and the data being explained can be much more complex, both logically and causally.

Another simplification is that *domains* are not defined. One way to do this would be to specify what data are possible (D_{poss}) and general functions for computing explanatory coverage and plausibilities based on the data (e_{gen} and pl_{gen}). Then for a specific abduction problem, the following constraints would hold: $D_{all} \subseteq D_{poss}$, $e(H) = e_{gen}(H, D_{all})$, and $pl(H) = pl_{gen}(H, D_{all})$ (cf. Allemang, Tanner, Bylander, & Josephson, 1987).

The definitions of abduction problems or domains do not mention the data that do not have to be explained, even though they could be important for determining e and pl. For example, the age of a patient does not have to be explained, but can influence the plausibility of a disease. We assume here that e and pl implicitly take into account data that do not have to be explained, e.g., in the definition of domains just mentioned, these data can be an additional argument to e_{gen} and pl_{gen}.

Despite these simplifications, our analysis provides powerful insights concerning the computational complexity of abduction.

An example

Let us use the following example to facilitate our discussion:

$$H_{all} = \{h_1, h_2, h_3, h_4, h_5\}$$
$$D_{all} = \{d_1, d_2, d_3, d_4\}$$

$e(h_1) = \{d_1\}$	$pl(h_1) = $ superior
$e(h_2) = \{d_1, d_2\}$	$pl(h_2) = $ excellent
$e(h_3) = \{d_2, d_3\}$	$pl(h_3) = $ good
$e(h_4) = \{d_2, d_4\}$	$pl(h_4) = $ fair
$e(h_5) = \{d_3, d_4\}$	$pl(h_5) = $ poor

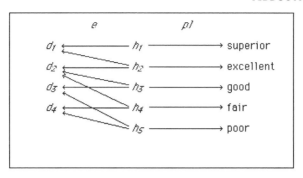

Figure 7.1. Example of an abduction problem.

Figure 7.1 is a pictorial representation of the example. The values of *pl* should simply be interpreted as indicating relative order of plausibility. If *e(H)* is the union of *e(h)* for *h* ∈ *H*, then {*h₂*, *h₃*, *h₅*} is complete, but not parsimonious since *h₃* is superfluous. {*h₂*, *h₃*} is parsimonious, but not complete since it does not explain *d₄*. Based on the plausibility ordering criterion defined in the later section on the complexity of plausibility, {*h₁*, *h₃*, *h₄*} and {*h₂*, *h₅*} would be considered the best explanations.

Using these definitions, assumptions, and example, we first discuss how properties of *e* affect the tractability of finding best explanations, and then consider properties of *pl*.

Complexity of finding explanations

Independent abduction problems

In the simplest problems, an individual hypothesis explains a specific set of data regardless of what other individual hypotheses are being considered. This constraint is assumed by INTERNIST-I (Miller et al., 1982); Reggia's set covering algorithm (Reggia, Nau, & Wang, 1983); Peng & Reggia's parsimonious covering theory (Peng & Reggia, 1987), Pearl's belief revision theory if interactions are restricted to noisy-OR (an effect can occur only if one or more of its causes are present) (Pearl, 1987); and Eshelman's cover-and-differentiate method (Eshelman, 1988). The use of conflict sets (de Kleer & Williams, 1987; Reiter, 1987) also appears to make this assumption – each conflict set corresponds to a datum to be explained, and the elements of the conflict set correspond to the hypotheses that can independently explain the datum.

Formally, an abduction problem is *independent* if:

$$\forall H \subseteq H_{all} \; \left(e(H) = \cup_{h \in H} e(h) \right).$$

That is, a composite hypothesis explains a datum if and only if one of its elements explains the datum. This constraint makes explanatory coverage equivalent to set covering (Reggia, 1983). Assuming independence, the explanations in our example (refer to Figure 7.1) are: $\{h_1, h_3, h_4\}$, $\{h_1, h_3, h_5\}$, $\{h_1, h_4, h_5\}$, $\{h_2, h_3, h_4\}$, and $\{h_2, h_5\}$. One way to find a best explanation would be to generate all explanations and then sort them by plausibility. However, it is well known that there can be an exponential number of explanations. It is not surprising then that determining the number of explanations is hard.

Theorem 7.1. For the class of independent abduction problems, it is #P-complete to determine the number of explanations.

That is, determining the number of explanations for an independent abduction problem is just as hard as determining the number of solutions to an NP-complete problem.[7]

The definition of best explanation, however, does not require that all explanations be explicitly enumerated. For example, if h is the most plausible individual hypothesis, h explains D_{all}, and $H \subset H'$ implies $pl(H) > pl(H')$, then h can be declared to be the best explanation without further search. In general, the task of finding a best explanation can be divided into two subtasks: (1) find one explanation, and (2) repeatedly find better explanations until a best one is found. In the remainder of this section, then, we consider the complexity of generating one or more explanations. The following section discusses the complexity of finding other explanations.

For independent abduction problems, it is tractable to find an explanation. Let $n = |D_{all}| + |H_{all}|$.

Theorem 7.2 For the class of independent abduction problems, there is an $O(nC_e + n^2)$ algorithm for finding an explanation, if one exists.

Algorithm 7.1 performs this task within this order of complexity. A detailed explanation of this algorithm is given in (Bylander, Allemang, Tanner, & Josephson, 1991), but we note several aspects of its operation here.

It is easy to check whether an explanation exists. If $\cup_{h \in H_{all}} e(h) \neq D_{all}$, then a union over any subset of H_{all} will not equal D_{all} either.

The loop makes one pass through the individual hypotheses. It examines each individual hypothesis in turn and removes it if no explanatory coverage is lost. Only one pass is necessary because if the result W had a superfluous element h, then h would have been superfluous for any superset of W, and thus, would have been removed by the body of the loop.

If the e^{-1} function is available (see the previous section on tractability as-

ALGORITHM 7.1. Finding an explanation in independent and monotonic abduction problems

W stands for the working composite hypothesis.
Nil is returned if no explanation exists.

Determine whether an explanation exists.
If $e(H_{all}) \neq D_{all}$ then
   Return nil

Find an explanation.
$W \leftarrow H_{all}$
For each $h \in H_{all}$
   If $e\ (W \setminus \{h\}) = D_{all}$ then
      $W \leftarrow W \setminus \{h\}$
Return W

---

sumptions for the definition of e^{-1}), then the working hypothesis W, instead of being initialized to H_{all}, can be initialized to include only one element from $e^{-1}(d)$ for each $d \in D_{all}$. This modification has an advantage if e^{-1} is easy to compute and the working hypothesis remains "small."

Monotonic abduction problems

We now consider a more general kind of problem, in which a composite hypothesis can explain additional data that are not explained by any of its elements. For example, suppose the two inputs to an AND-gate are supposed to be 0, and so the output is supposed to be 0, but the observed output of the AND-gate is 1. If the inputs are produced by components A and B, then hypothesizing a single fault in A or B is insufficient to account for the datum, but faults in both A and B are sufficient.

This sort of interaction can also occur if two individual hypotheses have an additive interaction. For example, each of the two hypotheses can explain a small value of some measurement, but together can explain a larger measurement. In this latter case, if h only partially explains d, then $d \notin e(h)$. Note though that if adding h to a composite hypothesis can result in completely explaining d, then $h \in e^{-1}(d)$.

Formally, an abduction problem is *monotonic* (Allemang et al., 1987) if:

$$\forall H, H' \subseteq H_{all}\ (H \subseteq H' \rightarrow e(H) \subseteq e(H'))$$

That is, a composite hypothesis does not "lose" any data explained by any of its subsets and might explain additional data. All independent abduction problems are monotonic, but a monotonic abduction problem is not necessarily independent. If, in Figure 7.1, $\{h_2, h_3\}$ also explained d_4, then $\{h_2, h_3\}$ would also be an explanation and $\{h_2, h_3, h_4\}$ would not be. Monotonic abduction problems from the literature include our hypothesis-assembly strategies described so far (see Allemang et al., 1987) and Pearl's belief revision theory if interactions are restricted to noisy-OR and noisy-AND (Pearl, 1987).

Because the class of monotonic abduction problems includes the independent class, it is also hard to determine the number of explanations. In addition, we have shown that it is hard to enumerate a polynomial number of explanations.

> **Theorem 7.3.** For the class of monotonic abduction problems, given a set of explanations, it is NP-complete to determine whether an additional explanation exists.

We have proved this result by a reduction from the class of independent incompatibility abduction problems, which is described in the next section. The idea of the reduction is that the addition of an individual hypothesis to a composite hypothesis can explain the rest of the data, make nearly all the elements of the composite hypothesis superfluous, and result in a previously generated explanation. It turns out to be difficult to generate an additional explanation while avoiding this kind of interaction. Whether a similar result holds for independent abduction problems is an open question.

Although the class of monotonic problems is a superset of the class of independent problems, it is just as efficient to find an explanation. Again, let $n = |D_{all}| + |H_{all}|$.

> **Theorem 7.4.** For the class of monotonic abduction problems, there is an $O(nC_e + n^2)$ algorithm for finding an explanation, if one exists.

Algorithm 7.1 performs this task within this order of complexity. Because of the monotonicity constraint, H_{all} must explain as much or more data than any other composite hypothesis. The loop in Algorithm 7.1 works for the same reasons as for independent abduction problems. Also, it is possible to use e^{-1} to initialize W, though one must be careful because more than one element from $e^{-1}(d)$ might be needed to explain d.

Incompatibility abduction problems

Implicit in the formal model so far is the assumption that any collection of individual hypotheses is possible. However, most domains have restrictions that invalidate this assumption. For example, a faulty digital switch cannot simultaneously be stuck-at-1 and stuck-at-0. More generally, the negation of a hypothesis can also be considered a hypothesis.

This kind of problem is neither independent nor monotonic because any composite hypothesis that contains a pair of mutually exclusive hypotheses cannot be an acceptable hypothesis, while a subset that excludes at least one hypothesis from each pair is acceptable. We call this kind of problem an *incompatibility abduction problem*.

Formally, an incompatibility abduction problem is a tuple $\langle D_{all}, H_{all}, e, pl, I \rangle$, where D_{all}, H_{all}, e, and pl are the same as before and I is a set of two-element subsets of H_{all} indicating pairs of hypotheses that are incompatible with each other.[8] For an incompatibility problem:

$$\forall H \subseteq H_{all} \left((\exists i \in I \, (i \subseteq H)) \rightarrow e(H) = \varnothing \right).$$

By this formal trick, a composite hypothesis containing incompatible hypotheses explains nothing, preventing such a composite from being complete (except for trivial cases) or a best explanation.

An *independent incompatibility abduction problem* satisfies the formula:

$$\forall H \subseteq H_{all} \left((\nexists i \in I \, (i \subseteq H)) \rightarrow e(H) = \cup_{h \in H} e(h) \right).$$

That is, except for incompatibilities, the problem is independent. In Figure 7.1, if $I = \{ \{h_1, h_2\}, \{h_2, h_3\}, \{h_3, h_4\}, \{h_4, h_5\} \}$, then only $\{h_1, h_3, h_5\}$ and $\{h_2, h_5\}$ would be explanations.

Incompatibility abduction problems are more complex than monotonic or independent abduction problems:

> **Theorem 7.5.** For the class of independent incompatibility abduction problems, it is NP-complete to determine whether an explanation exists.

We have proven this result by reduction from 3SAT (Garey & Johnson, 1979), which is satisfiability of Boolean expressions in conjunctive normal form, with no more than three literals in any conjunct. Informally, the reduction works as follows. Each 3SAT literal and its negation corresponds to an incompatible pair of hypotheses. Each conjunct of the Boolean expression corresponds to a datum to be explained. Satisfying a conjunct corresponds to a hypothesis explaining a datum. Clearly then, a complete composite hypothesis exists if and only if the Boolean expression is satisfiable. Furthermore, a complete composite hypothesis exists if and only if an explanation exists. Our proof shows that only $O \, (|H_{all}|)$ incompatible pairs are needed to give rise to intractability.

The underlying difficulty is that the choice between a pair of incompatible hypotheses cannot be made locally, but is dependent on the choices from all other incompatible pairs. It is interesting to note that the parsimony constraint plays no role in this result. Just finding a complete composite hypothesis is hard in incompatibility abduction problems.

It follows that:

> **Corollary 7.6.** For the class of independent incompatibility abduction problems, it is NP-hard to find a best explanation.

The class of incompatibility abduction problems can be reduced to both Reiter's theory of diagnosis (Reiter, 1987) and Pearl's theory of belief revision (Pearl, 1987).

> **Theorem 7.7.** For the class of diagnosis problems, relative to the complexity of determining whether a composite hypothesis is consistent with SD ∪ OBS, it is NP-complete to determine whether a diagnosis exists.

For this theorem, a composite hypothesis is a conjecture that certain components are abnormal, and that all other components are normal.

It is easy to translate the explanatory interactions of an independent incompatibility abduction problem into first-order sentences. For example, $e^{-1}(d) = H$ can be translated to MANIFEST$(d) \rightarrow \bigvee_{h \in H}$ AB(h). $\{h, h'\} \in I$ can be translated to AB$(h) \rightarrow \neg$ AB(h'). It is interesting that this problem is hard even if it is easy to determine the consistency of a composite hypothesis.

> **Theorem 7.8.** For the class of belief revision problems, it is NP-complete to determine whether there is a value assignment w to the variables W such that $P(w \mid v) > 0$.

This theorem directly follows from Cooper's result that it is NP-complete to determine whether $P(X = \textit{true}) > 0$ for a given variable X within a belief network (Cooper, 1990). Also, a reduction from incompatibility abduction problems can be done as follows. Map each $h \in H_{all}$ to a "hypothesis" variable. Map each $d \in D_{all}$ to a "data" variable that can be true only if one or more of the hypothesis variables corresponding to $e^{-1}(d)$ are true (e.g., noisy-OR interaction). Map each incompatible pair into a data variable that can be true only if at most one, but not both, of the two corresponding hypothesis variables is true (e.g., NAND). Initializing all the data variables to *true* sets up the problem.

Cancellation abduction problems

Another interaction not allowed in independent or monotonic abduction problems is cancellation, i.e., when one element of a composite hypothesis "cancels" a datum that another element would otherwise explain. Cancellation can occur when one hypothesis can have a subtractive effect on the explanatory coverage of another. This is common in medicine, e.g., in the domain of acid-base disorders, one disease might explain an increased blood pH, and another might explain a decreased pH, but together the result might be a normal pH (Patil, Szolovits, & Schwartz, 1982). Different faults in different components can result in cancellation, e.g., a stuck-at-1 input into an AND-gate might account for an output of 1, but not if the other input is stuck-at-0. Cancellation commonly occurs in the physical world. Newton's second law implies that forces can cancel each other. Cancellation in the form of feedback control is intentionally designed into devices.

Formally, we define a *cancellation abduction problem* as a tuple $\langle D_{all}$, H_{all}, e, pl, e_+, $e_-\rangle$. e_+ is a map from H_{all} to subsets of D_{all} indicating what data each hypothesis "produces." e_- is another map from H_{all} to subsets of D_{all} indicating what data each hypothesis "consumes." $d \in e(H)$ if and only if the hypotheses in H that produce d outnumber the hypotheses that consume d. That is:

$$d \in e(H) \leftrightarrow |\{h \mid h \in H \wedge d \in e_+(h)\}| > |\{h \mid h \in H \wedge d \in e_-(h)\}|$$

In Figure 7.1, if we let $e_+ = e$ for individual hypotheses and if $e_-(h_1) = \{d_3\}$, $e_-(h_4) = \{d_4\}$, and $e_-(h_3) = e_-(h_4) = e_-(h_5) = \emptyset$, then the only explanations would be $\{h_1, h_3, h_5\}$ and $\{h_2, h_4, h_5\}$.

Admittedly, this is a simplified model of cancellation effects, in the sense that it captures only one kind of cancellation interaction. Nevertheless, it is sufficient to derive intractability:

Theorem 7.9. For the class of cancellation abduction problems, it is NP-complete to determine whether an explanation exists.

We have proved this by reduction from finding explanations in incompatibility abduction problems. Informally, the idea of the reduction is based on the following. Suppose that a datum has two potential "producers" and two potential "consumers." Now any composite hypothesis that contains both consumers cannot explain the datum. In effect, the two consumers are incompatible. Our reduction ensures that each incompatible pair in the incompatibility abduction problem is appropriately mapped to such a situation in the corresponding cancellation abduction problem. Only $O(|H_{all}|)$ "cancellations" are needed for this result, where $\sum_{h \in Hall} |e_-(h)|$ gives the number of cancellations.

It follows that:

Corollary 7.10. For the class of cancellation abduction problems, it is NP-hard to find a best explanation.

Table 7.1. Computational complexity of finding explanations

	Condition to achieve		
Class of problems	Finding all explanations	Finding an explanation	Finding a best explanation
independent	NP	P	?
monotonic	NP	P	?
incompatibility	NP	NP	NP
cancellation	NP	NP	NP

P = known polynomial algorithm, NP = NP-hard

One aspect of cancellation abduction problems is more complex than incompatibility abduction problems. In an independent incompatibility abduction problem, if a complete composite hypothesis is found, then it is easy to find a parsimonious subset. However, this is not true for cancellation abduction problems.

Theorem 7.11. For the class of cancellation abduction problems, it is coNP-complete to determine whether a complete composite hypothesis is parsimonious.

That is, it is NP-complete to determine whether a complete composite hypothesis is not parsimonious. The idea of our reduction is the following. If a datum has three "producers" and two "consumers," we can ensure that the datum is explained by including all three producers in the composite hypothesis. However, there might be a more parsimonious composite hypothesis in which some of the producers are omitted, but finding such a composite hypothesis means that one or both consumers must be omitted as well, making them effectively incompatible.

Table 7.1 summarizes the results of this section. The question mark (?) indicates that we not have yet described the complexity of finding a best explanation in independent and monotonic abduction problems.

Complexity of plausibility

To analyze the complexity of finding a best explanation, we need to define how to compare the plausibilities of explanations. We consider one plausibility criterion based on comparing the plausibilities of the elements of the explanations. Other plausibility criteria are considered in Bylander, Allemang, Tanner, & Josephson (1989a), but they are less relevant to other theories of abduction.

The best-small plausibility criterion

Everything else being equal, smaller explanations are preferable to larger ones, and more plausible individual hypotheses are preferable to less plausible ones. Thus, in the absence of other information, it is reasonable to compare the plausibility of explanations based on their sizes and the relative plausibilities of their elements. When a conflict occurs, e.g., one explanation is smaller, but has less plausible elements, no ordering can be imposed without additional information.

The *best-small* plausibility criterion formally characterizes these considerations as follows:

$pl(H) > pl(H') \leftrightarrow$

$\exists m : H \rightarrow H'$ (m is 1-1 $\wedge$

$\forall h \in H$ (pl (h) $\geq pl$ ($m(h)$)) $\wedge$

$(|H| = |H'| \rightarrow \exists h \in H$ (pl (h) $> pl$ (m (h)))))).

That is, to be more plausible according to best-small, the elements of H need to be matched to the elements of H' so that the elements of H are at least as plausible as their matches in H'. If H and H' are the same size, then in addition some element in H must be more plausible than its match in H'. Note that if H is larger than H', then pl (H) $\not> pl$ (H'). In Figure 7.1, $\{h_1, h_3, h_4\}$ and $\{h_2, h_5\}$ would be the best explanations.

We have demonstrated that it is intractable to find best explanations using best-small.

Theorem 7.12. For the class of independent abduction problems using the best-small plausibility criterion, it is NP-hard to find a best explanation.

The simplest proof of this theorem involves a reduction from minimum cover (Garey & Johnson, 1979). If each individual hypothesis is given the same plausibility, then the smallest explanations (the covers with the smallest sizes) are the best explanations. A more general proof is a reduction from a special class of independent incompatibility abduction problems in which each individual hypothesis is in exactly one incompatible pair. In this reduction, each incompatible pair is mapped into two equally plausible hypotheses, at least one of which must be chosen. If the incompatibility abduction problem has any explanations, they turn out to be best explanations in the best-small problem.

We conjecture that it is possible to reduce from finding a best explanation using best-small to finding a best explanation using any "theory of belief" in which composite hypotheses that are smaller or have more plausible elements can have higher belief values. Of course, standard probability theory is an example of such a theory, as are all its main competitors. This conjecture is supported by the following theorem.

Theorem 7.13. For the class of belief revision problems restricted to OR interactions, it is NP-hard to find the MPE.

The restriction to OR interactions means that each effect can be true only if one or more of its parents are true. This restriction makes it easy to find a value assignment w such that $P(w \mid v) > 0$. Although this theorem could be demonstrated by adapting the proof for Theorem 7.12, it is useful to show that the best-small plausibility criterion has a correlate in probabilistic reasoning.

The reduction from independent abduction problems using best-small works as follows. Each $h \in H_{all}$ is mapped to a "hypothesis" variable. Each $d \in D_{all}$ is mapped to a "data" variable that is true if and only if one or more of the hypothesis variables corresponding to $e^{-1}(d)$ are true, i.e., an OR interaction. The a priori probabilities of the hypothesis variables being true must be between 0 and 0.5, and are ordered according to the plausibilities in the abduction problem. Initializing all the data variables to *true* sets up the problem. The MPE for this belief revision problem corresponds to a best explanation for the best-small problem. Because finding a best explanation is NP-hard, finding the MPE must be NP-hard even for belief networks that only contain OR interactions.

Ordered abduction problems

Our proofs of Theorem 7.12 depend on the fact that some individual hypotheses have similar plausibilities to other hypotheses. It turns out that finding a best explanation using best-small is tractable if the plausibilities of individual hypotheses are all different from each other and if their plausibilities are totally ordered.

Formally, an abduction problem is *ordered* if:

$$\forall h, h' \in H_{all} \ (h \neq h' \rightarrow (pl\ (h) < pl\ (h') \vee pl\ (h) > pl\ (h')))$$

Again, let $n = |D_{all}| + |H_{all}|$.

Theorem 7.14. For the class of ordered monotonic abduction problems using the best-small plausibility criterion, there is an $O(nC_e + nC_{pl} + n^2)$ algorithm for finding a best explanation.

Algorithm 7.2 performs this task within this order of complexity. It is the same as Algorithm 7.1 except that the loop considers the individual hypotheses from least to most plausible. The explanation that Algorithm 7.2 finds

ALGORITHM 7.2. Finding a best explanation in ordered independent and monotonic abduction problems using the best-small plausibility criterion

W stands for the working composite hypothesis.
Nil is returned if no explanation exists.

Determine whether an explanation exists.
If $e(H_{all}) \neq D_{all}$ then
    Return nil

Find a best explanation.
$W \leftarrow H_{all}$
For each $h \in H_{all}$ from least to most plausible
    If $e\ (W \setminus \{h\}) = D_{all}$ then
        $W \leftarrow W \setminus \{h\}$
Return W

---

is a best explanation because no other explanation can have more plausible individual hypotheses; the algorithm always chooses the least plausible individual hypotheses to remove. Of course, Algorithm 7.2 also finds a best explanation for ordered independent abduction problems.

As with Algorithm 7.1, it is possible to use e^{-1} advantageously. The working hypothesis W can be initialized to include the most plausible individual hypotheses from each $e^{-1}(d)$, i.e., because of monotonic interactions, sufficient hypotheses from $e^{-1}(d)$ must be chosen so that d is explained.

Algorithm 7.2 is an adaptation of the RED-2 hypothesis assembly algorithm, and is a serial version of the parallel parsimony algorithm described in Goel, Sadayappan, & Josephson, (1988). In Figure 7.1, assuming the independence constraint, this algorithm would find $\{h_1, h_3, h_4\}$, which is one of the two best explanations.

As in our example, there might be more than one explanation because best-small in general imposes a partial ordering on the plausibilities of composite hypotheses. Suppose that an ordered monotonic abduction problem has only one best explanation according to best-small. Because Algorithm 7.2 is guaranteed to find a best explanation, then it will find the one best explanation.

> **Corollary 7.15.** For the class of ordered monotonic abduction problems using the best-small plausibility criterion, if there is exactly one best explanation, then there is an $O\ (nC_e + nC_{pl} + n^2)$ algorithm for finding the best explanation.

This can be informally restated as: *In a well-behaved abduction problem,*

Table 7.2. Computational complexity of finding best explanations

Class of problems	Condition to achieve	
	Finding a best explanation	Finding more than one explanation
Ordered Independent/monotonic	P	NP
Unordered Independent/monotonic	NP	NP
Incompatibility	NP	NP
Cancellation	NP	NP

P = known polynomial algorithm, NP = NP-hard

if it is known that some explanation is clearly the best explanation, then it is tractable to find it. Unfortunately, it is difficult to determine if some explanation is clearly the best explanation.

Theorem 7.16. For the class of ordered independent abduction problems using the best-small plausibility criterion, given a best explanation, it is NP-complete to determine whether there is another best explanation.

We have proved this by a reduction from the special class of independent incompatibility abduction problems in which each individual hypothesis is in exactly one incompatible pair. Assuming n incompatible pairs, the best-small problem is set up so that one hypothesis out of each pair must be chosen, and so that extra hypotheses plus the most plausible element of each pair is a best explanation of size $n+2$. In our reduction, any other best-small best explanation in this reduction must be of size $n+1$ and include an explanation for the incompatibility problem. Thus, even for ordered independent abduction problems, it is intractable to find all the best explanations, or even enumerate some number of them.

As a consequence, it does not become tractable to find the MPE for ordered abduction problems. The proof for the previous theorem can be easily adapted so that any explanation of size $n+1$ will be more probable than any explanation of size $n+2$.

From these theorems, we can describe what kinds of mistakes will be made by Algorithm 7.2. While the explanation this algorithm finds will match up qualitatively to any other explanation, there might be other "qualitatively best" explanations, which might be judged better based on more precise plausibility information.

Table 7.2 summarizes some of these results.

Application to red-cell antibody identification

Description of the domain

The RED expert systems perform in the domain of blood bank antibody analysis (see chapter 3). One of the jobs done by a blood-bank technologist is to identify antibodies in a patient's serum that can react to antigens that might appear on red blood cells. This is typically done by combining, under different test conditions, samples of patient serum with samples of red blood cells known to express certain antigens. Some of these combinations might show reactions. The presence of certain antibodies in the patient serum accounts for certain reactions. The reactions are additive in the sense that if the presence of one antibody explains one reaction, and presence of another antibody explains another, then the presence of both antibodies explains both reactions. Moreover, if each antibody can account for a weak result in some reaction, then the presence of both can account for a stronger result in that reaction. Also, some pairs of antibodies cannot occur together. RED's task is to decide which antibodies are present, given a certain reaction pattern. RED-2 takes into account 27 of the most clinically significant antibodies.

Relationship to classes of abduction problems

We now examine how this task can be categorized within the classes of abduction problems discussed in this chapter.

Independent. The additive nature of the reactions means that for separate reactions and compatible hypotheses, the independence constraint is met. However, since independent abduction problems do not allow for parts of data to be explained, they cannot describe additivity of reaction strengths.

Monotonic. If we view a weak result for some reaction as a separate result from a strong result for the same reaction, then we can say that the phenomenon of additive reaction strengths falls into the class of monotonic abduction problems. That is, each of two antibodies alone might explain a weak reaction. Together, they would explain either a weak reaction or a strong reaction.

Incompatibility. In this domain, some antibodies are incompatible with others. Also, for each antibody, RED-2 distinguishes between two different, incompatible ways that it can react. Thus, red-cell antibody identification is clearly outside of monotonic abduction problems and within the intractable class of incompatibility abduction problems. We will discuss why this is not usually a difficulty in this domain.

Cancellation. No cancellation interactions take place in this domain.

Ordered. RED-2 rates the plausibility of the presence of an antibody on a seven-point qualitative scale. Because there are approximately 60 antibody subtypes, the same plausibility rating is given to several antibodies. Strictly speaking, this takes the problem out of ordered abduction problems, but we describe below why this is not usually a problem.

Incompatibility relationships and lack of plausibility ordering do not usually create difficulties in this domain for the following reasons. One is that most antibodies are usually ruled out before any composite hypotheses are considered, i.e., the evidence indicates that the antibodies cannot reasonably be part of any composite hypotheses. The more antibodies that are ruled out, the more likely that the remaining antibodies contain no or few incompatibilities, and resemble an ordered abduction problem.

Another reason is that the reaction testing is designed to discriminate between the antibodies. Thus, an antibody that is present usually explains some reaction more plausibly than any other antibody. An antibody that is not present is unlikely to have clear evidence in its favor and is usually superfluous in the context of equally or higher rated antibodies.

A final reason is that it is rare to have more than a few antibodies. Other antibodies that are rated lower than these antibodies are easily eliminated.

In rare cases, though, these reasons do not apply, with the result that RED-2 has difficulties with incompatible pairs or unordered hypotheses, or it selects an explanation with many antibodies where the preferred answer contains a smaller number of individually less plausible antibodies (chapter 3).

Discussion

We have discovered one restricted class of abduction problems in which it is tractable to find the best explanation. In this class, there can be no incompatibility relationships or cancellation interactions, the plausibilities of the individual hypotheses are all different from each other, and there must be exactly one best explanation according to the best-small plausibility criterion.

Unfortunately, it is intractable to determine whether there is more than one best explanation in ordered abduction problems. However, it is still tractable to find one of the best-small best explanations in ordered monotonic abduction problems. Incompatibility relationships, cancellation interactions, and similar plausibilities among individual hypotheses are factors leading to intractability.

For abduction in general, however, our results are not encouraging. We believe that few domains satisfy the independent or monotonic property, i.e., they usually have incompatibility relationships and cancellation interactions. Requiring the most plausible explanation appears to guarantee intractability for abduction. It is important to note that these difficulties result from the nature of abduction problems, and not the representations or algorithms being used to solve the problem. *These problems are hard no matter what representation or algorithm is used.*

Fortunately, there are several mitigating factors that might hold for specific domains. One factor is that incompatibility relationships and cancellation interactions might be sufficiently sparse so that it is not expensive to search for explanations. However, only $O(n)$ incompatibilities or cancellations are sufficient to lead to intractability, and the maximum plausibility requirement still remains a difficulty.

Another factor, as discussed in the introductory section of this chapter, is that some constraint might guarantee a polynomial search space, e.g., a limit on the size of hypotheses or sufficient knowledge to rule out most individual hypotheses. For example, if rule-out knowledge can reduce the number of individual hypotheses from h to log h, then the problem is tractable. It is important to note that such factors do not simply call for "more knowledge," but knowledge of the right type, e.g., *rule-out* knowledge. Additional knowledge *per se* does not reduce complexity. For example, more knowledge about incompatibilities or cancellations makes abduction harder.

The abductive reasoning of the RED-2 system works because of these factors. The size of the right answer is usually small, and rule-out knowledge is able to eliminate many hypotheses. RED-2 is able to avoid exhaustive search because the non-ruled-out hypotheses are close to an ordered monotonic abduction problem.

If there are no tractable algorithms for a class of abduction problems, then there is no choice but to do abduction heuristically (unless one is willing to wait for a very long time). This poses a challenge to researchers who attempt to deal with abductive inference: Provide a characterization that respects the classic criteria of good explanations (parsimony, coverage, consistency, and plausibility), but avoids the computational pitfalls that beset solutions attempting to optimize these criteria. We believe that this will lead to the adoption of a more naturalistic or satisficing conceptualization of abduction in which the final explanation is not guaranteed to be optimal, e.g., it might not explain some data. (This idea is developed in chapter 9.) Perhaps one mark of intelligence is being able to act despite the lack of optimal solutions.

Our results show that abduction, characterized as finding the most plausible composite hypothesis that explains all the data, is generally an intractable problem. Thus, it is futile to hope for a tractable algorithm that produces optimal answers for all kinds of abduction problems. To be solved efficiently, an abduction problem must have certain features that make it tractable, and there must be a reasoning method that takes advantage of those features. Understanding abduction, as for any portion of intelligence, requires a theory of reasoning that takes care for the practicality of computations.

Notes

1 The latter constraint is not the same as "eliminating candidates" in de Kleer & Williams (1987) or "inconsistency" in Reiter (1987). If a hypothesis is insufficient to explain all the observations, the hypothesis is not ruled out because it can still be in composite hypotheses.

2 Composite hypotheses that do not explain all the data can still be considered explanations, albeit partial. Nevertheless, because explaining all the data is a goal of the abduction problems that we are considering, for convenience, this goal is incorporated into the definition of "explanation."

3 The symbol "\" stands for set difference, i.e. A\B consists of the set of all members of A that are not members of B.

4 There might be more than one maximal subset of observations that satisfies these conditions. If so, then $e(H)$ selects some preferred subset.

5 For belief networks, we use a ***boldface italic*** lower case letter to stand for a (set of) value assignment(s) to a (set of) variable(s), which is denoted by a ***BOLDFACE ITALIC*** uppercase letter.

6 One difficulty with the more "natural" mapping $pl\,(H) = P\,(H = \textbf{\textit{true}} \,|\mathbf{v})$ is that even if the MPE is parsimonious, it might not be the best explanation.

7 Also, it is #P-complete to determine the number of complete composite hypotheses. The definition of #P-complete comes from Valiant (1979).

8 Incompatible pairs are the most natural case, e.g., one hypothesis of the pair is the negation of the other. n mutually exclusive hypotheses can be represented as $n(n-1)/2$ incompatible pairs. Incompatible triplets (any two of the three, but not all three) and so on are conceivable, but allowing these possibilities in the formal definition does not affect the complexity results.

8   Two more diagnostic systems

In chapter 7 abduction stumbled. Our powerful all-purpose inference pattern, maybe the basis for all knowledge from experience, was mathematically proved to be impossible (or anyway deeply impractical under ordinary circumstances). How can this be? Apparently we do make abductions all the time in ordinary life and science. Successfully. Explanation-seeking processes not only finish in reasonable time, they get right answers. Correct diagnosis is possible, even practical. (Or maybe skepticism is right after all, knowledge is impossible, correct diagnosis is an illusion.)

Maybe there is no deep question raised by those mathematical results. Perhaps all they are telling us is that we do not always get the right answer. Sometimes our best explanation is not the "true cause" (ways this can occur are systematically described in chapter 1). Sometimes we cannot find a best explanation in reasonable time, or we find one but do not have enough time to determine whether it is unique. Maybe knowledge is possible after all, but it is a kind of hit or miss affair. Yet if knowledge is possible, how can we succeed in making abductions without being defeated by incompatible hypotheses, cancellation effects, and too-close confidence values?

Whether or not knowledge is possible, we can build diagnostic systems able to achieve good performance in complex domains. This chapter presents two such systems and also includes a special section on how a kind of learning can be fruitfully treated as abduction. A fuller response to the complexity results is given in chapter 9. Here we get our hands dirty again with

✓ The opening paragraphs of this chapter are by John R. Josephson. Distributed Abduction in MDX2 is by Jon Sticklen and is taken from the paper of the same name that appears in *Artificial Intelligence in Scientific Computation: Towards Second Generation Systems* edited by R. Huber, C. Kulikowski, J. M Krivine, and J. M. David. It appears with permission of J. C. Baltzer AG Science Publishers. QUAWDS: Diagnostic System for Gait Analysis is by Michael Weintraub, Tom Bylander, and Sheldon Simon. It is taken from QUAWDS: A Composite Diagnostic System for Gait Analysis by Weintraub and Bylander that appeared in the proceedings of the Thirteenth Annual Symposium on Computer Applications in Medical Care, 1989. It appears here with permission of SCAMC, Inc. A similar paper authored by Weintraub, Bylander, and Simon appeared in *Computer Methods and Programs in Biomedicine*, vol. 32, no. 1, 1990. The present version appears with permission of Elsevier Science Publishers B.V. An Abductive Approach to Knowledge-Base Refinement is by Michael Weintraub and Tom Bylander.

180

actual knowledge-based systems. One reason for this chapter's presence is to show some variety in abductive-assembly strategies so that the reader will gain a broader view of the possibilities. Another is to show that interesting diagnostic systems have been built for complex real-world domains. Finally, we want to show that abduction gives some handle on learning.

Jon Sticklen's MDX2 is a medical diagnosis system in a subdomain of mixed clinical diseases. The system integrates generic-task problem solvers (described in chapter 2) for hierarchical classification, hypothesis matching, knowledge-directed data retrieval, and abductive assembly. It uses knowledge of function and structure to help make some decisions, and it can ask for further medical tests to help resolve difficult cases. It uses "concept clusters" to organize knowledge and to help control the abductive processing. QUAWDS by Michael Weintraub, Tom Bylander, and Sheldon Simon is a system for diagnosing human-gait disorders that result from diseases affecting motor control such as cerebral palsy or stroke. The potential for computational complexity problems is great in this domain due to an especially high density of interacting hypotheses. In the third section of this chapter, an abductive approach to learning (as knowledge-base refinement) is described. Mistakes made by a system can be explained by assigning blame to incorrect knowledge in the knowledge base. This was implemented for the QUAWDS system by Michael Weintraub.

Distributed abduction in MDX2

We believe that the goal of abduction is not to produce optimal answers, but rather to produce answers that satisfice (in Herbert Simon's sense, see Simon, 1969). We also believe that an adequate theory of abductive problem solving begins with a good theory of how knowledge used in the problem solving is *organized*.

MDX2 is an integrated medical diagnosis system whose domain is a subdomain of mixed clinical diseases. MDX2 begins with the overall generic-task approach to knowledge-based systems (see chapter 2). MDX2 uses a two-tiered organization of disease categories. At the top level, diseases are organized in clusters of related diseases (e.g., blood disease, cancer). At the second level (within one cluster), MDX2 follows the lead of MDX (Mittal, 1980): Each disease area is organized into a specialization hierarchy, with the most general diseases high in the hierarchy, and the most specific diseases low in the hierarchy. Each disease-cluster problem solver is a classification-based system. A high-level abductive assembler enfolds all the disease-cluster problem solvers. The abductive assembler is responsible for the final construction of an abductive answer and for directing the problem-solving focus among the various disease-area units.

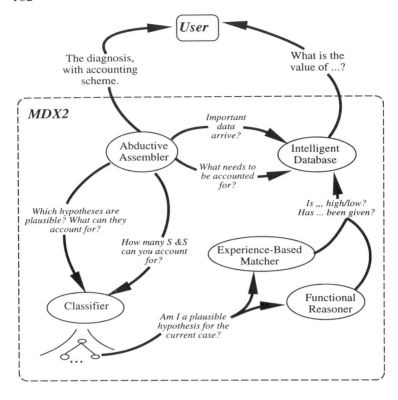

Figure 8.1. Problem-solving modules of MDX2.

Figure 8.1 shows the major types of problem-solving units in MDX2 and the major information-processing requests that the various units can make of one another. Conceptually, MDX2 consists of a compiled-level, abduction-based problem solver (the topic of this section), an intelligent database (Mittal, Chandrasekaran, & Sticklen, 1984), and a deep-level problem solver (described in Sticklen & Chandrasekaran, 1989). The fundamental abductive-control cycle in MDX2 is as follows:

Step 1. The top-level abductive assembler calls one of the disease-cluster problem solvers. The cluster selected is chosen by counting the number of patient signs and symptoms for which the cluster can account.[1] Note that the entire disease cluster is thus treated by the abductive assembler as an epistemically important object. In particular, the information required by the abductive assembler (a potential importance measure of each classifier for the current case) can be provided by the cluster based on a compiled listing of the patient observations that the categories of the cluster might explain. The cluster compares this compiled list with the observations of the current patient, then reports the number of observations that categories of the cluster may explain. The "may" is because, for any particular case, not all the categories within one cluster will be plausible.

Step 2. The selected cluster – which in MDX2 is a type of classifier – autonomously accounts for as much as possible given the constraint that it can use only the plausible diagnostic categories that it contains (i.e., the classifier produces a local abductive answer). To carry out its classification problem solving, the classifier uses other problem solvers of the system to determine how plausible a given diagnostic classification category is. When a particular classifier completes its task, it reports to the abductive assembler a listing of plausible diseases (as a simple classifier would) and an accounting of what each plausible disease can account for in the current case. The local nature of the construction of this partial accounting scheme also allows a disciplined examination of interacting diseases. Discussion of how disease interaction is handled is beyond the scope of this section but is described in Sticklen, Chandrasekaran, & Josephson (1985).

Step 3. The abductive assembler checks whether all patient signs and symptoms are accounted for. If they are, the abductive assembler first constructs a nonredundant accounting scheme for patient manifestations, returns the accounting scheme to the user, then halts. If not all patient manifestations are accounted for, the abductive assembler repeats the procedure. The final accounting algorithm that is used is similar to a portion of the RED algorithm (the portion that removes superfluous hypotheses) and is not computationally complex.

The prevalent abductive models partition the abduction problem into two subtasks, either explicitly or implicitly: Generate candidate hypotheses and construct an abductive answer from the generated hypotheses. In MDX2, the abductive problem is partitioned into three tasks: (1) Focus on appropriate clusters of hypotheses (step 1, carried out by the abductive assembler), (2) determine locally (within the individual hypothesis cluster) a partial accounting scheme of the plausible hypotheses and the observations for which they account (step 2, carried out by the hypothesis area focused on in step 1), and (3) carry out bookkeeping to determine whether all observations are accounted for and, if so, remove any superfluous hypotheses (step 3, carried out by the top-level abductive assembler).

The basic mechanism of the focusing step is for the assembler to poll the hypothesis clusters, asking for a measure of relevance for the current case. In MDX2, this measure of importance is computed in a rudimentary way: Each hypothesis area compares the current patient observations with a compiled list of the observations that its hypotheses may account for. The computed importance of a particular cluster is assigned according to the number of observations for which a cluster may account. Clearly, more sophisticated methods of determining hypothesis-cluster importance are desirable.

Discussion

An abductive answer produced by MDX2 is not ensured to be an optimal solution. MDX2 halts once all observations are accounted for. This can happen after only a few of the classification units of the system are invoked. Complete coverage of observations is a characteristic of MDX2 abduction; minimal cardinality of the final composite answer is not.

Thus, MDX2 can make mistakes. For example, suppose that the indexing to the classification units leads to invocation of classifiers in order C_1, C_2, C_3. Further, suppose that three diseases are found likely by these three classifiers; these diseases taken together account for the known patient observations. As soon as MDX2 encounters this situation, it halts and yields an answer that includes the three diseases along with the associated accounting scheme that covers all the current observations. Finally, suppose that there is a classifier C_n such that it contains a single disease that accounts for all patient observations by itself. MDX2 will miss this lower cardinality solution.

There are two responses to the awareness of this difficulty in MDX2. We could suggest that MDX2 procedures are faulty, that, in fact, all disease areas should be examined to make sure that the best abductive answer is found. However, this strategy would be computationally expensive. Alternatively, we could suggest that the indexing to the disease areas was not adequate, that the index should have led us to examine C_n first. The indexing in the MDX2 system is extremely primitive. This indexing technique has the advantage of being simple but the disadvantage of almost surely being inadequate. The point illustrated by MDX2 is not to propose a definitive indexing technique but to shift the emphasis from a search for a clever algorithm for solving a demonstrably intractable problem, to a search for the principles of memory organization and indexing that will allow us to effectively avoid the intractable problem.

QUAWDS: Diagnostic system for gait analysis

Introduction

In this section we describe QUAWDS (QUalitative Analysis of Walking DisorderS), a system for interpreting human gait. The QUAWDS system is presently restricted to pathologies resulting from diseases that affect motor control, such as cerebral palsy (CP) or stroke. CP affects the brain and manifests itself by interfering with the coordination of muscle activity. These effects – muscle tightness, spasticity, and weakness – rather than CP are the focus in pathologic gait analysis (that the patient has CP is known before the gait analysis is performed). We begin by describing the domain of human gait analysis. We then discuss the advantages and limitations of some traditional diagnostic models and describe how they have been applied to gait analysis. Next, we present a diagnostic architecture that combines "associational" and "qualitative causal" knowledge, and that takes advantage of the subtasks that each kind of knowledge can help accomplish efficiently and effectively. An abductive hypothesis assembler is used to coordinate the different modules. It produces a diagnostic solution that is *locally best* (i.e., no single change to the answer will produce a better solution). Finally, we provide an example of gait analysis.

The domain of human pathologic gait

In a normal person, the neurological system controls the muscles through coordinated commands to rotate limbs at several joints, providing body propulsion and stability for walking. A gait cycle consists of the time between a heel strike and the next heel strike of the same foot. The most significant events of the gait cycle are right heel strike (RHS), left toe-off (LTO), left heel strike (LHS), and right toe-off (RTO). These events delimit the four major phases of gait: weight acceptance (WA), single-limb stance (SLS), weight release (WR), and swing. For example, right WA is from RHS to LTO; right SLS is from LTO to LHS; right WR is from LHS to RTO; and right swing is from RTO to the next RHS. These events are illustrated in Figure 8.2.

The goal of diagnosis in this domain is to identify the improper muscle activity and the joint limitations that cause the deviations from normal that are observed in a patient's gait. The input is the information gathered at the Gait Analysis Laboratory at The Ohio State University and includes three types of data: clinical, historical, and motion. Clinical data come from the physical examination of the patient, and measure both the range of motion of the different joints and the qualitative strength of different muscle groups. Historical data include information about any past medical procedures or diagnoses. Motion data specify the time/distance parameters of walking (velocity, stride length, stance and swing times, etc.) and the angular position of the patient's leg joints (hips, knees, and ankles) in all three planes during a gait cycle. Motion data also include electromyograph (EMG) data of selected muscle groups; EMG data indicate when nervous stimulation of a muscle occurs during the gait cycle.

Gait analysis is very difficult. Many gait parameters cannot be measured directly using current technology. For example, EMG data are at best a relative measure of muscle forces (Simon, 1982). Multiple faults often occur and interact with one another. In our experience it is not unusual for a patient to have 10 or more faults. Moreover, human gait involves a number of highly interacting components and processes including mechanisms that attempt to compensate for a fault. As a result, an apparently abnormal behavior might actually serve to improve overall functioning.

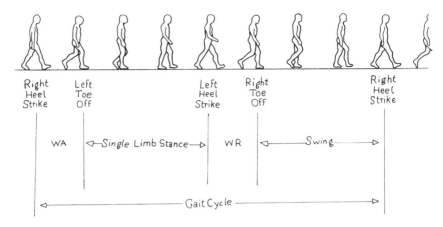

Figure 8.2. Human gait cycle.

Previous gait analysis programs

Our work on QUAWDS is motivated in part by an earlier series of gait analysis systems, Dr. Gait-1 and Dr. Gait-2 (Hirsch, Simon, Bylander, Weintraub, & Szolovits, 1989). The first system, Dr. Gait-1, was intended to diagnose gait disorders resulting from CP and operated strictly by using associational knowledge, which explicitly related patterns of observations with faults (we call this an "associational model"). Dr. Gait-1 is limited to analyzing the motions of one leg in the sagittal plane (from the side). This program matches the observed leg motions to a set of precompiled motion patterns, then matches these patterns and EMG information to hypothesize faults. Basing the diagnostic problem solving solely on associational models was also the approach taken by two other gait analysis systems, one developed by Tracy, Montague, Gabriel, and Kent (1979) and the other by Dzierzanowski (1984). These systems differ from Dr. Gait-1 primarily by their application to different, albeit simpler, subdomains of gait analysis (Hirsch, 1987).

The advantage of an associational model is that diagnostic conclusions can be derived from the case data with few or no intermediate steps. The problem with this approach is that a combinatorial number of associational rules is needed to cover all possible situations in a complex domain. For example, in Dr. Gait-1 every new situation required the addition of a new rule. The result was a large and unwieldy rule base. Because of this problem, associational models are often incomplete and make simplifying assumptions (e.g., that faults can be diagnosed independently of one another).

Furthermore, the only type of explanation that an associational model can produce is a run-time trace of the system's execution. Physiological explanations of conclusions cannot be generated because associational models do not explicitly represent relationships among components. Even though associational models are inadequate for complex domains such as gait analysis, they are still useful for certain diagnostic subtasks (e.g., determining the plausibility of faults and discriminating between them).

One way to overcome the problems of associational models is to use a device model that can determine interactions in the device and formulate physiological explanations (Davis & Hamscher, 1988). The key to doing this in gait analysis is to use some understanding about how gait is caused, namely, that the joints' motions are caused by a combination of torques resulting from muscles, body weight, and momentum. This idea is implemented in Dr. Gait-2 by qualitatively representing a device model of gait (we call this a "qualitative model"). Like Dr. Gait-1, this system is limited to considering faults resulting from CP and to analyzing the motions of one leg in the sagittal plane. Like Dr. Gait-1, this system begins by identifying the motions that need to be explained, but then uses its qualitative model of gait to generate and select hypotheses. The qualitative model represents a joint's motion during a phase as a qualitative sum of all the torques acting on it. For each abnormal motion deviation, Dr. Gait-2 hypothesizes all faults that are physically reasonable and uses heuristic knowledge about CP to choose the best hypothesis (or hypotheses) that explain the data.

Unfortunately, there are several difficulties in doing diagnosis on the basis of qualitative models. First, quantitative models with sufficient predictive and explanatory power must be available before an accurate qualitative model can be constructed. In gait analysis, developing quantitative models of gait is an open research problem (Hemami, 1985). Second, qualitative models introduce several sources of ambiguity (Kuipers, 1986, Struss, 1987). As a rule, qualitative simulation does not predict a single sequence of states but produces several alternative state sequences. Additional information is required to distinguish among them (de Kleer & Brown, 1983). Last, the computational complexity of such a model is a concern. That is, even if a powerful qualitative model can be constructed, the problem of searching a large hypothesis space remains. If n different malfunctions can occur, there are 2^n possible sets of malfunctions. A large hypothesis space is not just an abstract possibility; in pathologic gait, multiple faults are typical.

The composite architecture of QUAWDS

In gait analysis there is no direct path from a qualitative model to an efficient associational model; instead, such a model must be knowledge engineered and restricted to specific subtasks. Diagnostic associations acquired

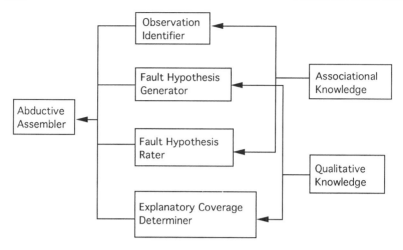

Figure 8.3. The architecture of QUAWDS.

from human experts (or other sources) are still needed to help guide the search through the hypothesis space. The diagnostic architecture of QUAWDS takes advantage of the information available from both types of models to perform diagnosis efficiently, while avoiding the potential combinatorics. Figure 8.3 shows the high-level functions and components of the architecture. The associational component identifies which observations need to be explained and determines the relative plausibilities of potential fault hypotheses; the qualitative component generates the set of fault hypotheses offering to account for an observation and determines the explanatory coverage of single- or multiple-fault hypotheses, taking hypothesis interactions into account. A third component, a hypothesis assembler, coordinates these subtasks and constructs a composite diagnosis.

Hypothesis assembly. Diagnosis by hypothesis assembly uses the observations that need to be explained (the findings) to drive the processing. An assembly strategy should consider several criteria (discussed in previous chapters) in building a composite hypothesis: (1) The assembler should work towards explanatory completeness (explaining all the findings) but (2) should also maintain parsimony by avoiding hypotheses that add little to the explanatory power, and (3) the assembler should prefer more plausible hypotheses to less plausible ones and avoid selecting hypotheses that have low plausibility.

The two basic phases of assembly are constructing a composite hypothesis and making it parsimonious. The goal of the construction phase is to include the most desirable fault hypotheses that add significant explanatory coverage. The desirability of a hypothesis is determined by three factors:

essentialness, confidence, and coverage. The importance associated with each factor is domain dependent, as is what constitutes an important finding. The goal of the parsimony phase is to remove superfluous hypotheses from the working composite hypothesis. The least plausible hypotheses in the working composite are considered first for removal.

This approach requires other problem-solving methods that perform the following functions: identifying a finding to be explained, generating the set of faults that can potentially account for a finding, determining the rating of a fault, and determining the set of findings for which a (multiple) fault hypothesis accounts. In our architecture these functions are performed by the qualitative and the associational modules, as illustrated in Figure 8.3.

Subtasks of hypothesis assembly. Given the set of observations about a case, the first subtask is to identify which observations need to be explained and the relative importance of explaining each one. Associational knowledge is used in this task. For example, rotational motions differing by more than 10 degrees from normal need to be accounted for. The importance of a motion's deviation depends on the size and duration of the deviation.

The second subtask is to find the set of faults that potentially account for an observation or observations. In QUAWDS this set is determined by qualitative knowledge. In the diagnosis of complex, interacting systems many faults can contribute, either directly or indirectly, to an observation. In the interest of efficiency, only a few fault hypotheses that potentially account for a finding should be considered. In QUAWDS we assume that each fault directly results in some observations. Thus, for each observation, only the faults that can directly contribute to the observation are generated. The qualitative model, simply by its structure, can determine which components or processes are involved in an observation. For example, the qualitative model identifies the anterior tibialis (the muscle along the shin), gastroc/soleus (the calf muscles considered as a unit), and other factors (e.g., knee flexion/extension) as possible causes of *excessive plantarflexion* of the ankle (pointing the foot down). Both the anterior tibialis and the gastroc/soleus are considered direct causes of ankle motion, whereas other muscles affecting knee motions are considered indirect.

The third subtask involves evaluating the plausibility of a fault. In QUAWDS, a classification hierarchy and hypothesis matchers rate faults (as in RED, see Chapter 3). The different categories in the hierarchy are the faults, and for each fault hypothesis there is knowledge to evaluate its presence or absence in particular cases. Figure 8.4 shows a fragment of the classification hierarchy in QUAWDS. The plausibility rating of each fault results from matching a set of data-abstraction hypotheses against the set of observations. Figure 8.5 gives an example of the knowledge groups (for encoding hypothesis-matching knowledge) used for the fault *overactive ham-*

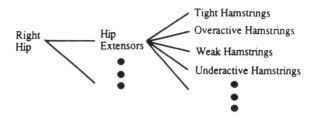

Figure 8.4. Part of the QUAWDS classification hierarchy.

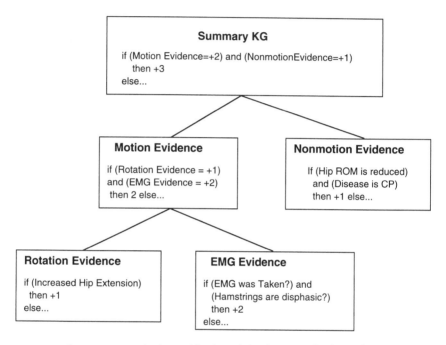

Figure 8.5. Hypothesis-matching knowledge for overactive hamstrings.

strings. As is typical in systems using associations, domain experts can provide rules associating abnormal observations with faults typically causing
them. Thus, associational knowledge can give valuable insights into which
faults should be considered. For instance, the fault *underactive anterior
tibialis* is considered to be plausible if *excessive plantarflexion* is observed
during swing.

The fourth subtask is determining which observations a single- or multiple-fault can explain. This is determined by the qualitative model; each
rotation results from a combination of the torque-producing forces – muscles,
joints, and other forces – acting on it. For example, the fault hypothesis *over-*

active gastroc/soleus accounts for *excessive plantarflexion* during SLS provided the muscle is not *weak*.

QUAWDS uses an abductive-assembly strategy based on the work described by Bylander (1991). The goal is to find the most plausible set of fault hypotheses for explaining the data. The strategy works by first adding to the working hypothesis fault hypotheses that explain part of the observations until all the observations are explained. The next phase is to remove the fault hypotheses that do not add significantly to the explanatory coverage. These two phases are repeated until no new progress is made because the same fault hypotheses are being added to, then removed from, the working hypothesis. More specifically, the abductive-assembly strategy is as follows:

For each observation, QUAWDS determines which fault hypotheses can explain the observation. From these hypotheses, QUAWDS tentatively selects the most plausible one. If this hypothesis is insufficient to explain the observation completely, the next most plausible hypothesis is also selected, and so on, until enough hypotheses are selected to explain the observation (or until there are no more candidates). If two hypotheses for explaining the observation are equally rated, and if one is selected, the other is also selected.

After repeating this process for all the observations to be explained, QUAWDS has selected a set of fault hypotheses. The removal phase then considers each of these hypotheses and removes it if it is individually superfluous with respect to the set as a whole. For example, suppose QUAWDS selects the set of hypotheses $\{h_1, h_2, h_3\}$. h_1 is removed if $\{h_2, h_3\}$ explains all the observations. Similarly, h_2 is removed if $\{h_1, h_3\}$ explains all the observations, even if h_1 is also removed. Finally, h_3 is removed if $\{h_1, h_2\}$ explains all the observations, even if both h_1 and h_2 are removed. Thus, all individually superfluous hypotheses are removed, even if they are not jointly superfluous.

The remainder after the removal phase is typically a reduced set of fault hypotheses; these hypotheses are then permanently selected. The next addition phase proceeds by considering only the observations that are not explained by this set. The addition and removal phases are repeated until the loop repeats itself – when an addition phase produces the same set of hypotheses as the previous addition phase. The result is a set of hypotheses that are definitively concluded (the permanent selections) and a set representing unresolved choices (the ones repeatedly being added and removed).

The composite hypothesis consisting of the definitively concluded set is "locally best" in the sense that each hypothesis in it is the most plausible way to explain some finding, no hypothesis is explanatorily superfluous, and adding any other most-plausible explainer will add an explanatorily superfluous hypothesis. Thus, no single change to the composite hypothesis will yield a better answer.

An example from gait analysis

To illustrate how QUAWDS works, consider the following example taken from a gait study of a 5-year-old diplegic (both legs affected) patient with CP. This patient had surgical lengthenings of the hamstring muscles on both legs because of a severely crouched gait.

The first step is to identify the set of observations that need to be explained. Each observation in this set is called a "finding." In pathologic gait analysis, findings are segments of the gait cycle in which the motion of a particular joint deviates from normal. In our example, the following set of findings need to be explained:

> The left hip's motion is decreased in WR and early swing.
> The left knee's motion is increased in the second half of SLS and in late swing.
> The left ankle's motion is increased in late SLS and WR.
> The right hip's motion is decreased in WR, swing, WA, and most of SLS.
> The right knee's motion is decreased in the first half of swing and slightly increased in late swing.
> The right ankle's motion is decreased in late swing.

A gait analysis includes data on the patient's range of motions – both those measured during the physical examination and those measured dynamically – and EMG data. The clinical examination reveals a limitation in the range of motion at the hip on both sides and a limitation in the range of ankle dorsiflexion (pointing the foot up). To keep the example simple we show only the sagittal plane motions (Figure 8.6). Dynamic range-of-motion measurements indicate a joint's observed range of motion during a gait cycle; this measurement can be different from the physical exam data because the forces exerted on a joint during gait are greater than those applied in a physical exam. EMG data (Figure 8.7) identifies muscle activity by phase over the tested muscle groups. The symbols in the table represent whether the muscle group was on, off, or unknown (DK for "Don't Know") for each muscle group and phase. From this data, disphasic (out of phase) activity is determined. In this example both knees' range of motion is significantly decreased. The physical exam also indicates some tightness of the hamstrings.

Given the set of findings, the assembler begins by asking the finding identifier to select a finding to be explained. To select a finding, the finding identifier considers the patient's medical history, the amount of deviation from normal, and the duration of the deviation. In this example the decreased motion of the right hip during nearly the entire gait cycle is selected. This choice is made because the hamstrings (which were surgically lengthened) directly affect hip motions, because of the large amount of deviation from normal motion, and because of the long duration of the deviation.

The assembler now needs to know the set of fault hypotheses that can cause this finding. Several types of faults are possible in this domain: Muscles

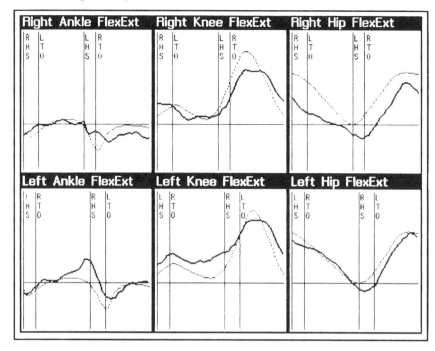

Figure 8.6. Sagittal plane motions.

can be weak, underactive, tight, or overactive, and joints can be contracted. The qualitative model determines the hypothesis set for a given finding is by tracing the finding to abnormal angular acceleration and then enumerating the possible muscle and joint faults that can cause it.

In this example, the finding is that hip flexion is abnormally decreased through most of SLS. QUAWDS first blames this motion on abnormally decreased angular accelerations that preceded or occurred during the abnormal motion. In this case QUAWDS identifies decreased angular accelerations during two intervals: from late SLS through mid-WR and during the second half of swing. The decreased angular acceleration during the second half of swing could be caused by increased torque from a hip extensor (the hamstrings or gluteus maximus) or by decreased torque from a hip flexor (the iliopsoas or rectus femoris). Physical exam data do not indicate that a tight hip extensor could cause this finding. EMG data reveal that the hamstrings are active during the second half of swing, but EMG data were not collected for the gluteus maximus. Thus, *overactive right hamstrings* and *overactive right gluteus maximus* are possible fault hypotheses. The iliopsoas is not normally on during late swing, so it cannot produce less torque than normal. However, the rectus femoris is normally active during late swing. No EMG data are available for this muscle, so the fault hypotheses *weak*

Right Side	WA	SLS1	SLS2	WR	Swing1	Swing2
Quadriceps	on	on	off	on	on	on
Hamstrings	on	on	off	off	off	on
Iliopsoas	DK	DK	DK	DK	DK	DK
Rectus	DK	DK	DK	DK	DK	DK
Gluteus Maximus	DK	DK	DK	DK	DK	DK
Gluteus Medius	DK	DK	DK	DK	DK	DK
Adductors	DK	DK	DK	DK	DK	DK
Ant. Tibialis	off	off	off	on	on	off
Gastrocnemius	on	on	on	off	off	on
Soleus	DK	DK	DK	DK	DK	DK
Peroneals	DK	DK	DK	DK	DK	DK
Post. Tibialis	DK	DK	DK	DK	DK	DK

Left Side	WA	SLS1	SLS2	WR	Swing1	Swing2
Quadriceps	on	on	off	on	on	on
Hamstrings	on	on	off	off	off	on
Iliopsoas	DK	DK	DK	DK	DK	DK
Rectus	DK	DK	DK	DK	DK	DK
Gluteus Maximus	DK	DK	DK	DK	DK	DK
Gluteus Medius	DK	DK	DK	DK	DK	DK
Adductors	DK	DK	DK	DK	DK	DK
Ant. Tibialis	off	off	off	on	on	off
Gastrocnemius	on	on	on	off	off	on
Soleus	DK	DK	DK	DK	DK	DK
Peroneals	DK	DK	DK	DK	DK	DK
Post. Tibialis	DK	DK	DK	DK	DK	DK

Figure 8.7. EMG data.

right rectus femoris and *underactive right rectus femoris* are possible. Although the equation used by the model includes the motions of other joints as forces affecting hip motion (e.g., knee motions), QUAWDS does not generate these indirect hypotheses because they will be generated when abnormal motions of that joint, if any, are considered.

For the abnormal hip motion and the case data given in this example, any of the four faults generated can explain the abnormal hip motion. Also, if the knee is less flexed during swing (or an abnormal acceleration during swing leads to less knee flexion during swing), and if some fault in the hypothesis explains the decreased knee flexion, then this fault would, in the right circumstances, also explain the abnormal hip extension. For example, if *overactive quadriceps* explains a lack of knee flexion during swing, it would also explain the hip extension, provided that the "amount" of hip extension does not exceed the "amount" of decreased knee flexion during swing.

The next step in the assembly method is to rate the plausibility of fault hypotheses by using a classification hierarchy and hypothesis matchers implemented in CSRL (Bylander & Mittal, 1986). In our example the hypothesis *overactive right hamstrings* is considered the most plausible because of: increased right hip extension during most of the gait cycle, some increased flexion of the right knee (the hamstrings also flex the knee), EMG data that indicated disphasic activity, and physical exam data that showed hip-extensor tightness. The hamstring lengthening tends to weaken the muscle, but this is contraindicated by the hip tightness indicated in the physical exam. The other hypotheses are not considered highly plausible because there is not much supporting data.

The assembler now needs to determine the explanatory coverage of the hypothesis *overactive right hamstrings*. This hypothesis is given to the qualitative model to determine what motions this hypothesis explains. The model uses a set of qualitative differential equations (de Kleer & Brown, 1984) that describe the main torque-producing forces in gait. An equation is specified for each rotational motion of interest, for each joint, during each segment of the gait cycle. Each equation specifies the muscles and indirect forces that produce torques affecting the rotation (Hirsch et al., 1989). For example, the sagittal plane motion of the hip during swing is described by:

hip flexion =   + iliopsoas + rectus femoris
              – hamstrings – gluteus maximus
              + knee flexion.

That is, the iliopsoas and rectus femoris muscles flex the hip, the hamstrings and gluteus maximus muscles extend the hip (the opposite of flexing it), and knee flexion tends to cause hip flexion. In addition, each term on the right-hand side of each equation is augmented with information describing its strength relative to the other terms.

The qualitative model determines that *overactive right hamstrings* can explain the decreased hip motion. The model also determines that the hypothesis can explain the increased knee motion in the late swing. An *overactive right gluteus maximus* is also the highest rated fault for the decreased angular acceleration during the second half of swing. The qualitative model determines that both hypotheses can explain both of the decreased angular accelerations. Overactive hamstrings explains the second decreased angular acceleration indirectly. These two hypotheses become alternative hypotheses, and the right-hip finding is removed from the set of findings yet to be explained.

The processing continues until QUAWDS determines its best explanation for each finding. To keep this example brief, we only report the results for the remaining findings. Similar to the right side, the left hip and left knee findings are explained by an overactive gluteus maximus and overactive hamstrings. The left ankle dorsiflexion in late SLS is a result of left knee flexion. The right ankle's motion in swing is the result of an overactive gastroc/soleus. The working hypothesis now contains the final diagnosis: Left and right hamstrings are overactive, left gluteus maximus and right gluteus maximus are overactive, and right gastrocnemius is overactive.

Our domain expert, Sheldon Simon, judges that two additional faults should be added to the diagnosis: *overactive right quadriceps*, to explain the decreased knee flexion in the first half of swing, and *weak left gastroc/soleus*, to explain the ankle dorsiflexion during late SLS and WR. In both cases, QUAWDS concluded that other hypotheses indirectly caused these findings. QUAWDS determined that an *overactive gluteus maximus* caused decreased hip flexion, which in turn caused decreased knee flexion, and that *overactive left hamstrings* caused increased knee flexion, which caused increased ankle dorsiflexion.[2] We are studying possible changes to QUAWDS to resolve this problem.

An abductive approach to knowledge-base refinement

Most knowledge-based systems (KBSs) cannot learn from their mistakes. A KBS can make many kinds of errors, and these often result from limited or incorrect knowledge in the KBS. Correcting these limitations is the *knowledge-base refinement problem*. To correct a knowledge base, a system must identify what caused the error ("credit assignment" [Minsky, 1963]) and then suggest repairs to implement the correction ("knowledge reformulation").

In this section, we describe an abductive framework for assigning credit (blame) for errors in a KBS. We begin by describing credit assignment in knowledge-base refinement and show how the problem is abductive. We then describe CREAM (CREdit Assignment Method), a system for assigning credit in a KBS.

Credit assignment as an abductive task

One form of the knowledge-base refinement problem is the *corrective learning task*. In this task a KBS produces an answer that does not agree with the expert's answer, which is assumed to be correct; the goal is to modify the KBS so that it produces the correct answer in future similar situations.

Credit assignment, determining which parts of a knowledge base are to blame for a mistake, is a key problem in knowledge base refinement. In the corrective-learning task, the problem is that of identifying the parts of the KBS that cause the discrepancy between the KBS's answer and the expert's answer. In general, there are many possible ways to make an error. It could result from an incorrect piece or pieces of knowledge, or the knowledge within the KBS could be incomplete.

Most systems for knowledge-base refinement rely heavily on the domain expert to identify mistakes and to provide corrections (e.g., Davis, 1979). The domain expert extends the system's knowledge, and the knowledge-acquisition task is that of trying to focus the interaction and produce useful knowledge to be included in the KBS. In some sense the domain expert plays the role of the domain theory described in explanation-based learning (EBL) (DeJong & Mooney, 1986) (Mitchell, Keller, & Kedar-Cebelli, 1986). Ideally, a system can learn autonomously if such a theory is represented within the system – provided that this theory is complete, consistent, and tractable. Unfortunately, a theory that meets these criteria is generally not possible. Thus the problem requires that some other information be given. In the corrective-learning task, the human expert provides the correct answer. One approach to solving the corrective-learning task is for the learning mechanism to generate explanations of why the correct answer is correct and why the KBS's answer is wrong. Traditional EBL requires the domain theory to have sufficient knowledge to imply the correct answer. But if the domain theory is less than ideal (incomplete, intractable, or inconsistent), the corrective-learning task is to construct plausible explanations of why the correct answer is correct and the KBS's answer is wrong, and to plausibly determine the best explanation from those generated.

There are often a number of alternative ways for a KBS to produce an error. Each possibility can be thought of as an alternative way of explaining the system's deviation from the preferred answer (Tanner, 1989). If more than one error candidate is applicable, the credit-assignment system must decide among them and select the best candidate for explaining the deviation. As inference to the best explanation, the credit-assignment problem is abductive in nature.

The credit-assignment problem can be decomposed into two subproblems. First, *error candidate generation* identifies the set of possible errors that could have caused the observed mistake. Second, *error candidate selection* chooses which error candidate or candidates to blame.

CREAM

CREAM is a system that uses an abductive method to assign credit in a knowledge base. It begins by reviewing a trace of the KBS's execution of the case to propose a set of error candidates (hypotheses). (The following subsection describes how a set of error candidates are defined for a KBS and how they are generated for a case.) CREAM uses a system called ICE (Identify Candidate Errors) to identify the error candidates. Next CREAM selects the best set of error candidates for explaining the mistake by generating and critiquing domain explanations. Not only is domain knowledge necessary for this step, but knowledge as to what constitutes an adequate explanation and criteria for selecting among the explanations must also be defined. A system called CONE (CONstrained Explainer) is used to generate appropriately detailed domain explanations of both normal and abnormal behaviors using a model of the domain represented in FR (described in chapter 5) augmented by qualitative differential equations (described for QUAWDS in

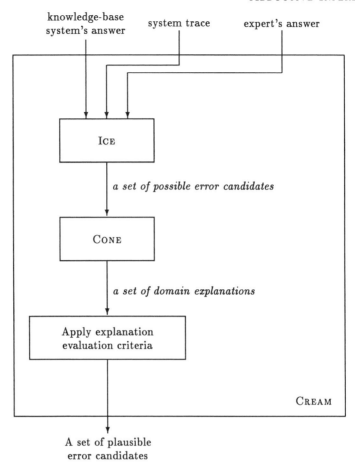

Figure 8.8. The architecture of CREAM.

the previous section). CREAM then compares these explanations using several criteria until one explanation is rated better than the others or until it is determined that one best explanation cannot be identified. The architecture of CREAM is shown in Figure 8.8. The details of the system are described in Weintraub (1991).

Identifying candidate errors. A key to generating possible error candidates for a system's mistake is to consider the tasks and methods that the system uses. The kind of description of the KBS affects the credit-assignment search directly. There are many ways to describe a KBS. One way is by specifying the inputs and outputs of the system. The system is then modeled as a function that maps the inputs to the outputs.

    In general, a KBS can be described as a set of functions and subfunctions that map a set of inputs to a set of outputs. Because many tasks are complex, smart design encourages the decomposition of the task into smaller subtasks. Thus a function for a complex task should be defined in terms of simpler functions. Let us illustrate this with hypothesis assembly, a method used in several abductive diagnostic systems, including RED and QUAWDS. Consider the following functions, where O is the set of observations for a case, D_{all} is the data to be explained, d is a datum in D_{all}, H_{all} is the set of all fault hypotheses, h is a fault hypothesis in H_{all}, R is a set of ordered confidence values, and r is a confidence value in R. The finding generator fg can then be described as a function:

$$fg(O) = D_{all} .$$

The hypothesis generator can be described as:

$$hg(d) = H$$

where $d \in D_{all}$ is a datum to be explained and $H \subseteq H_{all}$ is a set of fault hypotheses. The hypothesis rater can be described as:

$$hr(h) = r$$

where $h \in H_{all}$ is a fault hypothesis and $r \in R$ is a confidence rating. Finally, the coverage generator can be described as:

$$cg(H) = D$$

where $H \subseteq H_{all}$ is a set of fault hypotheses, and $D \subseteq D_{all}$ is a subset of the data to be explained. (The range of function cg is the explanatory coverage of the hypothesis.)

Hypothesis assembly is a function from the observations to the set of the most plausible fault hypotheses satisfying the constraints of completeness (explaining all the data) and parsimony (no hypothesis can be removed without explanatory loss). Hypothesis assembly can be described as a function mapping observations to fault hypotheses:

$$ha(O) = H$$

where H contains the most plausible fault hypotheses satisfying

$cg(H) = fg(O)$ and $\forall H' \subseteq H, H' \neq H$ (cg (H') $\subseteq cg$ (H) and cg (H') $\neq cg(H)$).

This sort of functional description is useful for describing the decomposition of tasks because the domain and range of values for each task are clearly specified. Clearly, the modularity of the task organization is an important factor in determining how well credit can be assigned.

This approach is especially applicable to generic tasks. Each generic task is characterized by a method for performing a class of tasks; that is, each generic task specifies the type of input, the type of output, the method relating the two, and the subtasks required by the method. One generic task can be used to achieve a subtask of another generic task.

Using the functional description to generate error candidates. In a perfect KBS, the output is always correct. Unfortunately, often a perfect method does not exist. Commonly, the method implementing a task can produce a result that is different from the correct output. This difference can occur for many reasons. Some methods are incomplete or inconsistent, or space and time constraints prohibit a complete computation, resulting in an approximation.

The problem of generating error candidates requires an analysis of each task and method used within a problem-solving system to define the types of errors that each task and method can make and the conditions under which each type can occur. In the corrective-learning task, as in most learning tasks, an error occurs when the problem-solving system's answer does not match the correct answer. Consider diagnostic systems such as RED and QUAWDS. Basically, a diagnostic KBS's answer can differ from the correct answer under three different conditions. Let A_s denote the KBS's answer and A_e denote the expert's answer. Because the answers are sets of fault hypotheses, the possible differences between the two answers are the following:

1. The KBS's answer is a proper subset of the correct answer, i.e., $A_s \subset A_e$. The KBS is too generous with what some hypothesis can explain, or it could not explain some finding.
2. The correct answer is a proper subset of the KBS's answer, i.e., $A_e \subset A_s$. The KBS is too cautious with what some hypothesis can explain, or the KBS mistakenly identified some finding as needing explanation.
3. The KBS chose a different answer than the expert's to explain a particular finding: namely, $A_e \neq A_s$ but $A_s \not\subset A_e$ and $A_e \not\subset A_s$. Some subtask of hypothesis assembly is in error.

Identifying which of these three differences is applicable in a case is accomplished by identifying which situation occurred. The differences that match generate error candidates.

For example, suppose a diagnostic KBS chose the fault hypothesis h_s as its answer for explaining an observation o; but the expert selected the fault hypothesis h_e. The third error situation matches – identifying that an error condition exists because the two answers are different. An explanation of why the two answers differ is needed for credit assignment.

A simple method called ICE is used to determine the reason for the difference between A_s and A_e. ICE uses information about the method used for the

KBS and the results of the method's execution (the execution trace) in deriving its answer for the present case. The basic intuition behind ICE is that at some point the system preferred its answer to the expert's, and the goal of the credit-assignment system is to identify this point. ICE searches the execution trace to find each step of the method that possibly precludes A_e. Suppose that the KBS used the method of hypothesis assembly. This method is achieved through the computations of several subtasks. Error candidates generated by ICE are refined by applying ICE to the methods used for each of the subtasks. For each task and subtask, ICE applies the error-candidate generation rules that are defined for the task to identify the set of possible error candidates.

The next step in the credit-assignment method is to select the best set of error candidates for this observed mistake. Suppose for this example that the error candidate selection method chooses the error candidate that hypothesis h_s was overrated. Then CREAM calls ICE to examine the hypothesis rating method that was used for h_s and to identify a set of error candidates. This process recursively considers a set of error candidates until no more candidates can be generated; that is, until the subtasks bottom-out and there are no more subtasks to consider. The result of this search is a set of specific points in the system's architecture where the system's knowledge is hypothesized to be incorrect.

The generality of this error-candidate generation method is independent of the particular methods used in a system. The methods used in a KBS such as QUAWDS are based on generic-task theory, but the success of this part of credit assignment is dependent only on an explicit description of the tasks and methods used within a system.

Notes

1 An initial data gathering step is carried out prior to initial classifier selection. The disease area is selected based on the observations made available during that step.
2 In Weintraub and Bylander (1989), QUAWDS did include *weak left gastrocnemius/soleus* in the final answer of the diagnosis for this case, but for the wrong reasons. At the time, QUAWDS did not infer that *overactive left hamstrings* explains knee flexion throughout SLS, which then is considered to explain the ankle dorsiflexion. Our domain expert agrees that *overactive left hamstrings* is a factor affecting the abnormal ankle dorsiflexion but judges that this fault does not cause all of the abnormality. Similarly, *overactive right gluteus maximus* is a factor that decreases knee flexion, but our domain expert judges that the fault does not explain all of the decrease.

9   Better task definition, better strategy – machine 5

Tractable abduction

Abduction can be described as "inference to the best explanation," which includes the generation, criticism, and possible acceptance of explanatory hypotheses. What makes one explanatory hypothesis better than another are such considerations as explanatory power, plausibility, parsimony, and internal consistency. In general a hypothesis should be accepted only if it surpasses other explanations for the same data by a distinct margin and only if a thorough search was conducted for other plausible explanations.

Abduction seems to be an especially appropriate and insightful way to describe the evidence-combining characteristics of a variety of cognitive and perceptual processes, such as diagnosis, scientific theory formation, comprehension of written and spoken language, visual object recognition, and inferring intentions from behavior. Thus abductive inference appears to be ubiquitous in cognition. Moreover, humans can often interpret images, understand sentences, form causal theories of everyday events, and so on, apparently making complex abductive inferences in fractions of a second.

Yet the abstract task of inferring the best explanation for a given set of data, as the task was characterized in chapter 7, has been proved to be computationally intractable under ordinary circumstances. Clearly there is a basic tension among the intractability of the abduction task, the ubiquity of abductive processes, and the rapidity with which humans seem to make abductive inferences. An adequate model of abduction must explain how cognitive agents can make complex abductive inferences routinely and rapidly.

In this section we describe two related ideas for understanding how abduction can be done efficiently: (1) a better characterization of the information-processing task of abductive assembly and (2) a better way to handle incompatibility relationships between plausible elementary hypotheses. The new characterization of the abductive-assembly task is "explaining as much as possible," or, somewhat more precisely, "maximizing explanatory cover-

√ Tractical Abduction is by John R. Josephson and Ashok K. Goel. Software: PEIRCE-IGTT is by Richard Fox and John R. Josephson. Experiment: Uncertainty and Correctness is by Michael C. Tanner and John R. Josephson.

202

age consistent with maintaining a high standard of confidence." This task is computationally tractable, in contrast to "finding the best explanation for all of the data," which is generally computationally intractable (at least as it was characterized in chapter 7). The tractability of the task under the new description is demonstrated by giving an efficient strategy for accomplishing it. Using this strategy a confident explanation is synthesized by starting from islands of relative certainty and then expanding the explanation opportunistically. This strategy does well at controlling the computational costs of accommodating interactions among explanatory hypotheses, especially incompatibility interactions. Until now incompatibility relationships have seemed to be a main source of intractability by potentially forcing a combinatorially explosive search to find a complete and consistent explanation. In contrast, the new strategy demonstrates how incompatibility relationships can be used to distinct advantage in expanding partial explanations to more complete ones.

What makes abduction computationally expensive?

Typically an abductive conclusion is a multipart composite hypothesis, with the explanatory parts playing different roles in explaining different portions of the data. For example, the meaning of a sentence must be a composite hypothesis, formed "on the fly" as the sentence is interpreted, including components that function to explain the word order, choice of vocabulary, intonation, and so on. Thus abductive conclusions must typically be composed, rather than simply retrieved, or selected, or recognized. Yet it is not a computationally efficient general strategy to consider all possible combinations of elementary hypotheses, comparing the composite hypotheses with one another to determine which is the best explanation. A practical general strategy cannot require explicitly generating all combinations, since the number of them is an exponential function of the number of elementary hypotheses available, and it rapidly becomes an impractical computation unless almost all elementary hypotheses can be ruled out in advance.

If the elementary hypotheses are well separated in confidence scores, then, in the absence of hypothesis incompatibilities or cancellation effects, these confidence scores can be a good guide to generating a best composite hypothesis (e.g., see Theorem 7.14). However, finding even one consistent composite hypothesis that explains all the data is in general computationally intractable (see Corollary 7.6) and thus appears to be practical only under restricted circumstances. Moreover, simply finding a consistent and complete explanation for a set of data is usually not enough, since before an explanation is accepted there should be some assurance that the explanation is significantly better than alternatives.

In chapter 7 the sources of computational intractability were found to be

incompatibility relationships, cancellation interactions, and similar plausibility values among elementary hypotheses. The mathematical results reported there depend on a definition of "explanation" in which only complete
explanations are considered, explanations that explain all the data. Partial
explanations are not considered, and a "best" explanation is defined in this
framework only in comparison with other complete explanations. In effect
this assumes that a complete explanation is always better than a partial one,
even if the complete explanation includes low-confidence elementary hypotheses. If the goal of explanatory completeness is to be pursued as the
highest priority, similar plausibilities for elementary hypotheses will force a
low-confidence choice among nearly equal explanatory alternatives.

Redefining the task

The characterization of abduction as "inference to the best explanation" seems
substantially correct, and able to capture something recognizable about the
evidential force of a very common pattern of inference. It is apparently a
mistake, however, to characterize cognitive agents as performing the abstract information-processing task of "finding the best complete explanation for a given set of data." One reason is that this task is computationally
intractable in general. An alternative is to suppose that the goal of complete
explanation is abandoned, at least temporarily, whenever "a significant
amount of trouble" is encountered. As cognitive agents we settle for partial
explanations. Sometimes we sensibly favor other goals, such as high confidence, over the goal of explaining everything. If high confidence is valued
over completeness, what gets explained in the end may be only a subset of
what was originally to be explained, but a subset for which a *distinctly* best
explanation can be found.

   Viewed this way, the abductive task performed by cognitive agents should
be characterized as something like, "finding an explanation for that portion
of the data that can confidently be explained" or "maximizing explanatory
coverage consistent with maintaining high confidence" or "explaining as
much as can be practically and confidently explained."

   To be more precise, let us describe the abductive assembly task for given
data in the following way:

   Let H be a set of explanatory hypotheses available in a given domain.

   Let D be a set of (potential) data in that domain.

   Let e be a mapping from subsets of H into subsets of D. For $H_x \subseteq H$, $e\,(H_x)$
      specifies the subset of D that is explained by H_x.

   Suppose that each element of H has a confidence score, specific to the case;
      these scores may be described as probabilities or in some other confidence
      vocabulary.

Then the abductive-assembly task is to find an $H_e \subseteq H$ and a $D_e \subseteq D_o$ such that:

(i) $D_e \subseteq e (H_e) (H_e$ explains $D_e)$.

(ii) H_e is consistent.

(iii) H_e is a parsimonious explanation for D_e (i.e., no proper subset of H_e can explain all of D_e).

(iv) H_e is "acceptable," i.e., the confidence score of every element of H_e is above some preset threshold of acceptability.

(v) H_e is significantly better than alternative explanations for D_e. A sufficient condition for H_e to be significantly better than H_f (both consistent explanations for D_e) is that every element of H_e is significantly better than any element of H_f for explaining some finding; more precisely, H_e is significantly better than $H_f \neq H_e$ if for every $h \in H_e$ there exists $d \in e(h) \cap D_e$ such that, if $h' \in H_f, h' \neq h, d \in e(h')$, then the confidence score of h is significantly greater than the confidence score of h'. We say that the confidence score of one element of H is significantly greater than the confidence score of another if it is greater by at least the amount of some preset threshold.

So far this characterization captures the idea that the abductive task is that of producing a confident explanation for some portion of the data (D_e). In addition it is desirable that D_e be maximal, i.e., that as much as possible be explained; ideally, D_e would be equal to D_o. Yet it may not be practical or possible to explain all the data confidently; explaining everything might require the use of more computational resources than are available, or might require accepting a hypothesis that is not significantly better than alternative explanations and thus not entitled to a sufficiently high degree of confidence. Thus we add one more condition:

(vi) Consistent with (i)–(v), D_e should be maximal; that is, the composite hypothesis should explain as much as possible.

(In general the meaning of "possible" depends on the constraints that must be obeyed, and that define the boundaries of "impossible" and "possible." Here we require only that the explanation meet the preset standards of confidence occurring in conditions (iv) and (v). Other constraints could be imposed [e.g., that processing must take place within available computational resources]. For simplicity and ease of analysis, however, we assume here only the confidence constraints.)

Characterized in this way, the abductive-assembly task is computationally tractable. This is shown by the efficient algorithm for it we will describe after a brief digression.

Digression on abduction as optimization. Abductive processing can be thought of in several ways as a problem of optimization. Most obviously, the "best" explanation is presumably the optimal one according to whatever standards are used to judge the quality of explanations. So one sort of abductive optimization problem is that of finding the best explanation.

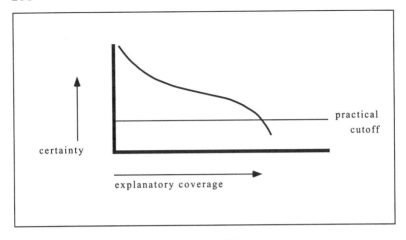

Figure 9.1   More coverage, less confidence.

Another optimization problem, just described in detail, is that of maximizing explanatory coverage consistent with maintaining confidence above some preset threshold. This is illustrated in Figure 9.1.

A third problem, illustrated by the RED systems, is that of maximizing the quality of the estimate of confidence for each of the elementary hypotheses. For the antibody-identification task of the RED systems, judgments are needed of the presence and absence of the clinically important red-cell antibodies. These judgments are made by explaining test reactions, but the main goal is not so much explaining reactions as confirming and ruling out antibody hypotheses. Since often a single suite of tests is insufficient to completely determine the confirmation/rule-out status for all the important antibodies, the next best thing is to determine confidence values as reasonably as can be done on the available evidence (and to decide which further tests to order).

Yet another optimization problem is that of minimizing error. Of course if error minimization were the only consideration in accepting explanations, the safest strategy would be not to accept any abductive conclusion, and to leave everything unexplained. A complete skeptic, for fear of making mistakes, would not accept any explanations, and thus would not understand anything (to the extent that understanding something requires accepting an explanation of it).

A related problem is that of minimizing the *cost* of error. Generally we care about explaining some things more than others, both for purely epistemic reasons (such as the difference it makes to the larger explanatory context; whether, for example, understanding this word is really critical for understanding the sentence) and also for pragmatic reasons (e.g., whether what

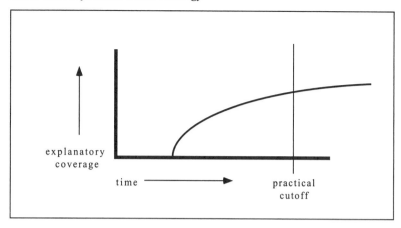

Figure 9.2. More time, more coverage.

we are trying to explain is why the nuclear reactor is rapidly getting hotter and hotter). Thus we typically want to maximize explanatory coverage while minimizing specific kinds of error costs.

Along with maximizing explanatory coverage and minimizing the cost of error, we often want to minimize the amount of time spent trying to explain. In real life the practical need to act often imposes cutoffs on our processing time. Thus we can pose the problem of maximizing explanatory coverage in a given amount of processing time. Evolution's job is to design abductive mechanisms that not only arrive at time-critical conclusions quickly, but also make good use of more processing time if it is available. Better yet are mechanisms that combine abilities to rapidly come to time-critical conclusions, to fruitfully spend more available time, and to learn from experience to perform better. Spending processing time to gain explanatory coverage is illustrated in Figure 9.2.

Finally, we would like to design or discover the optimal computational strategy for doing abductive processing. We do not claim to have done this.

We now propose to treat the generic abduction problem as that of explaining as much as possible while maintaining (fixed) standards of confidence that are given pragmatically. This is an idealization, of course, and leaves out many considerations such as processing time and cost of error. However, some simplification is necessary to facilitate analysis, and this idealization seems to improve on the previous one given in Chapter 7, at least in avoiding the paradox of abduction being simultaneously ubiquitous and computationally intractable. The previous and new characterizations of the abductive task are summarized in Figure 9.3.

Old Definition

Input: data to be explained

Output: the "best explanation" for the data
(most plausible, consistent, parsimonious,
composite hypothesis that explains all the
data)

Summary: maximize plausibility.

New Definition

Input: data to be explained

Output: the "best explanation" for the data
(the consistent, parsimonious, confident
composite hypothesis that explains the most
data)

Summary: maximize explanatory coverage.

Figure 9.3. Recharacterizing the abductive task.

Processing strategy

Suppose that we are given a set of data to be explained and a set of elementary hypotheses able to explain various portions of the data. Suppose that associated with each elementary hypothesis is a description of its explanatory coverage and an initial confidence score. This confidence score might arise as a result of matching the stored hypotheses with pre-established patterns of evidence features, or in some other way. Suppose, too, that we are given information about the interactions of elementary hypotheses; for this discussion we limit the interaction types to hypothesis-pair incompatibilities and "independent" explanatory interactions (in the sense of Chapter 7), although several other types of interactions can be handled by relatively simple extensions to the strategy described here.

We describe an abductive process that climbs a hill of increasing explanatory power, while preserving confidence, and quitting as soon as "significant difficulty" is encountered. We explicitly treat the kind of difficulty where explaining any more would require decreasing confidence below a given threshold, but the basic strategy we describe can be readily extended to other kinds of difficulty, such as exhaustion of computational resources. Similar to Machine 4's essentials-first strategy, described in chapter 6, we describe a strategy that pursues the abduction task as a sequence of subtasks, as follows:

1. *Find Essential hypotheses.* First, the Essential elementary hypotheses are identified, where, as before, a hypothesis is considered Essential if it is indispensable for explaining some datum.[1] Once all the (immediately detectable) Essential hypotheses have been identified, they are incorporated into the set of *Believed* hypotheses, and the elementary hypotheses that are incompatible with any of them are removed from the set of available hypotheses. Note that new Essential hypotheses may then be discovered as their explanatory competitors are eliminated for being inconsistent with the Believed hypotheses. Any new Essential hypotheses are also included into the set of Believed hypotheses, and again, hypotheses incompatible with any of them are removed from the set of available hypotheses. This cycle is repeated until no new Essential hypotheses can be discovered. The collective explanatory coverage of the Believed hypotheses is then determined.

2. *Find Clear-Best hypotheses.* If some portion of the data remains unexplained, then Clear-Best hypotheses are identified, where a hypothesis is a Clear-Best if its confidence score is above some given threshold, and if this confidence is significantly higher (more than a given pre-established amount) than that of alternative hypotheses available for explaining some unexplained datum.[2] Once the (immediately detectable) Clear-Best hypotheses have all been identified, they are incorporated into the set of Believed hypotheses, and elementary hypotheses incompatible with any of them are lowered significantly in confidence value (or, in a variant of this strategy, eliminated completely). As before, new Clear-Best hypotheses may appear as their explanatory competitors are down-rated for being inconsistent with Believed hypotheses. These new Clear-Best hypotheses are also included in the Believed hypotheses, and elementary hypotheses that are incompatible with any of them have their confidence values significantly lowered. This cycle is repeated until no new Clear-Best hypotheses can be discovered. The expanded explanatory coverage of the Believed hypotheses is then determined.

3. *Find Weak-Best hypotheses.* If some portion of the data is still unexplained, then, optionally, Weak-Best hypotheses are identified, where a Weak-Best hypothesis is the best explanation for some unexplained datum based on its confidence score, but either because its score is low, or because its score does not significantly exceed that of alternative explainers, it was not identified as a Clear-Best hypothesis. If two Weak-Best hypotheses are in-

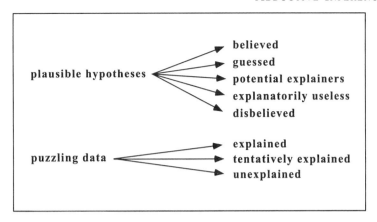

Figure 9.4. Machine 5 hypothesis assembly: Input - Output.

compatible, then neither is incorporated into the set of Believed hypotheses. This optional subtask is a kind of intelligent guessing, which is available following the processing which derives high-confidence conclusions. This subtask goes beyond what is needed to satisfy the requirements of the abduction task, as described previously in this chapter; those requirements are already satisfied after the Believed set is expanded to include the Clear-Best hypotheses.

The Essential and Clear-Best hypotheses collectively represent the confident portion of the best explanation, whereas the Weak-Best hypotheses should be viewed as tentative guesses or intelligent speculation. The normal output of the process is a confident explanation for a portion of the data, and (optionally) a tentative explanation for another portion of the data (the Weak-Bests), and an unexplained portion of the data with an unresolved set of potential explainers. The initially plausible hypotheses have been rescored, and the set of hypotheses has been partitioned into disjoint subsets of: Believed, Disbelieved (incompatible with Believed), Guessed (the Weak-Bests), Potentially Explanatorily Useful (offering to explain part of the unexplained remainder), and Explanatorily Useless. Meanwhile the initial set of data to be explained has been partitioned into disjoint subsets of: Explained, Tentatively Explained, and Unexplained. This partitioning is illustrated in Figure 9.4.

After inclusion of the Clear-Best hypotheses, the set of Believed hypotheses meets the conditions specified in the characterization of the abductive-assembly task given earlier. The set of Believed hypotheses is consistent at each stage in processing (or at least is consistent as far as available knowledge can determine).

The Believed set is guaranteed to be parsimonious if the thresholds for acceptability and for Clear-Best hypotheses are set so that all the explanatory alternatives to a Clear-Best explanation for a particular datum are below the threshold of acceptability. (If thresholds are not set in this way, further processing will be required to ensure parsimony.)

By requiring that Essential and Clear-Best hypotheses must be above the threshold for acceptability to be included in the Believed set (or by relaxing the condition and permitting Essentials to be below the threshold), the set of Believed hypotheses will be acceptable as required.

The set of Believed hypotheses will also satisfy the condition that the explanation is significantly better than alternative explanations for the same data, since it will meet the sufficient condition that every element of the Believed set will be significantly better than any element of the proposed alternative for explaining some finding. (Any element of the Believed set will be an Essential or a Clear-Best hypothesis.)

Finally, the Believed hypotheses constitute a composite hypothesis that explains as much of the data as is possible to explain with consistency and high confidence. To explain more, a hypothesis would have to be included that lacks the strong abductive justification required of an Essential hypothesis (being the only plausible way to explain something) or a Clear-Best hypothesis (being a significantly better explanation for something). Thus explanatory coverage of the composite hypothesis can be extended only by accepting reduced overall confidence levels. Coverage can be extended smoothly, if needed, by including some of the Weak-Best hypotheses.

Discussion of the strategy. As we have just described the process, the synthesis of the explanation starts from islands of relative certainty, then grows opportunistically. It uses Machine 4's essentials-first strategy, but now extends the strategy to make good use of incompatibility interactions. This new strategy for handling incompatibility interactions is Machine 5's contribution. We sometimes call this the *essentials-first leveraging-incompatibilities strategy.*

In depending on distinguishing Clear-Best hypotheses, Machine 5 is quite different from the hypothesis-assembly strategy of QUAWDS, described in chapter 8, even though, like QUAWDS, it is willing to settle for partial explanations. To clarify the difference let us consider a case with one finding to be explained, and two hypotheses offering to explain it. If these hypotheses are close in confidence values, then QUAWDS would choose the one with the larger confidence value, whereas Machine 5 would decline to choose, since a confident choice cannot be made. Machine 5 would make the choice if guessing were enabled, but then it would be marked as a low-confidence conclusion.

In many domains, such as medicine, Essential hypotheses are probably rare. The basic Machine 5 strategy is to find the highest mountains of confidence that can be found, and to leverage the hypothesis formation from that point, until there is trouble (e.g., no further progress can be made at that level of confidence). The highest mountains are the Essentials. If there are no Essentials, then the strategy calls for moving to the next highest mountains, the Clear-Best hypotheses. A hypothesis is really only "Essential" relative to a limit of implausibility for the best alternative explanation. If such hypotheses as Unknown-Disease, Data-is-Noise, Complete-Deception, or Intervention-by-Space-Aliens are considered to be plausible, then no hypothesis will be Essential, although there may still be Clear-Bests. The introduction of low-likelihood alternative hypotheses turns Essentials into high-confidence Clear-Bests without fundamentally altering anything.

The strategy as we have described it represents a discretization of a more basic strategy into the three distinct stages of accepting Essentials (and working out the consequences), Clear-Bests (working out the consequences), and Weak-Best hypotheses. The stages can be separated more finely by providing several levels of thresholds by which one elementary hypothesis can surpass rivals for explaining some finding. An Essential becomes one that far surpasses any rival, a Very Clear-Best might surpass rivals by a large margin (but less than an Essential), a Clear-Best hypothesis might surpass rivals by a somewhat lesser margin, and so on. Thus a smoother descent to lower and lower confidence levels occurs as the growing composite hypothesis gains more and more explanatory coverage. (See Figure 9.1 again.) A virtue of this approach is that it shows the way to a descent from what might be called "strongly justified explanatory conclusions," through less strongly justified conclusions, through "intelligent speculation," all the way to "pure guessing," and it provides meanings for all these terms.

Performing tests for data gathering is a natural extension of this strategy. Tests are performed to resolve ambiguities (a datum is ambiguous if multiple hypotheses offer to explain it but none stands out as Essential or Clear-Best). Such a test should be designed to discriminate among the best potential explainers.

In the idealized strategy we describe it is assumed that all plausible elementary hypotheses are generated before assembly processing. More realistically, we might suppose a hypothesis generator with a dependable tendency to supply hypotheses in rough order of plausibility, higher plausibility hypotheses first. Under these circumstances a good strategy for the hypothesis assembler, especially if time is critical, is to assemble on the basis of an initially generated set of hypotheses, provoking the generator for more hypotheses if some deficiency in the initial set is encountered (e.g., there is an unexplainable finding or the best explanation for something appears to be poor for some reason). If elementary hypotheses are generated in approximate order of plausibility, then hypotheses accepted on the basis of essentialness or clear-best-ness are probably correct and can tentatively be trusted. If the cost of error is high, and more processing time is available, then further hypotheses can be generated.

The strategy can also be easily and naturally extended to accommodate interactions of additive explanatory coverage, statistical or causal association, and logical implication (see the discussion in chapter 6 about extensions to the essentials-first strategy). It can also be extended to a layered-interpretation model of abductive processing where Believed hypotheses at one level of interpretation become data to be explained at the next level. (This model is described in chapter 10.) As described in chapter 6, the strategy can make use of concurrent processing, and this concurrency can be realized on a neural architecture (Goel, 1989; Goel, Ramanujan, & Sadayappan, 1988).

A weakness of all the abduction machines

A problem endemic to all six of our abduction machines is that they do not value parsimony quite enough. One type of parsimony is achieved when a composite hypothesis has no explanatorily superfluous parts; our machines all properly respect this type. However, another type of parsimony is that of favoring smaller composites over larger ones, which should be done sometimes, even at the expense of accepting hypothesis parts with somewhat lower plausibility values. Presented with the alternatives, all of our machines would accept a 79-part hypothesis to explain a body of data rather than a 1-part hypothesis with a slightly lower plausibility value than any of the 79. Machines 1 and 2 would always behave this way, whereas later machines would do so only if the decision were made at the hard-decisions or weak-best stage. It is reasonable that larger and larger hypotheses, insofar as they represent the addition of statistically independent suppositions, rapidly become less and less plausible (the probabilities multiply, and the probability of a composite rapidly approaches 0).

Fortunately, the parsimony problem is easily fixed. Unfortunately, there are several ways to fix it, and we do not know a principled way to decide among them. Fortunately, it should rarely occur. Unfortunately, the situations in which it does occur are a subset of those where there is not enough evidence for much confidence, but where there is a need to come to a conclusion anyway without gathering further evidence, presumably because of a need to act without delay. To be practical, abduction machines should be designed to perform reasonably well in these situations.

These are some of the alternatives that would fix the counterintuitive behavior:

1. Give extra credit in the local confidence value for explanatory power. (But how much and why?)
2. Have findings vote for all the plausible hypotheses that can account for them, then increase the scores of all the hypotheses that receive many votes (and then decrease the scores of those that are incompatible with them).

3. Note the existence of hypotheses with broad explanatory power, and consider them during a criticism stage if they were not used.
4. Give extra credit during assembly time to hypotheses that can explain a significant portion of the unexplained remainder.

A common theme in these proposed repairs is the diagnosis that the basic fault is that of undervaluing explanatory power. But it is also possible that underpenalizing big hypotheses is somehow directly the problem. Overall, what now seems best is to give extra confidence to hypotheses that can explain a high proportion of the unexplained remainder after the confident decision stage is passed. But what is the right measure?

Tractable abduction: Summary

The apparent ubiquity of abductive inferences, and the rapidity with which humans seem to make them, together with the computational intractability of the general task of finding best explanations as they were characterized in chapter 7, presents a conundrum. Yet perhaps humans do not "solve" the general task, but instead only find best explanations under favorable conditions, or only find good-enough explanations often enough to survive and reproduce. Perhaps there is a true abductive-assembly function, but people are not able to reliably compute it; instead, they solve many abductive-assembly *cases* by computing the abductive-assembly function when the computation is not too difficult.

Nevertheless, the mathematical results described in chapter 7 point to certain computational difficulties in forming composite best explanations. Abductive assembly is difficult when there are incompatible elementary hypotheses with close confidence values. We pointed out that the difficulty can be overcome if one of an incompatible pair is essential or if one is distinctly better than the alternatives for explaining some finding. If this happens, it amounts to an abductive confidence boost for the one hypothesis, or at least a way to choose among hypotheses on explanatory grounds. If there is no such way to choose, then the data are genuinely ambiguous, and it is genuinely difficult to determine with any confidence how to explain the data. Under these circumstances it is generally best not to try, but instead to set aside incompatible pairs, and settle for an incomplete explanation. The alternative is to make forced choices between incompatibles, with the potentially explosive computational costs of backtracking, and with a best composite, even if it can be found, that is not much better than other explanations.

If there are no incompatible pairs with closely similar confidences and explanatory powers, then abductive assembly will generally be easy (unless confidences and explanatory powers pull in opposite directions). Thus, incompatible hypotheses that are difficult to distinguish are a major cause of the complexity of abductive assembly. Not trying to distinguish them is the cure; incomplete explanation is the cost.

This leads to recharacterizing the abductive task as that of explaining as much as possible (with high-enough confidence). We pointed out that this new characterization better reflects the typical situation of real cognitive agents, and that it is more tractable computationally. We also described in some detail a strategy for abductive assembly under the new description, a strategy that shows how knowledge of incompatibilities between elementary hypotheses can be used to help expand partial explanations to more complete ones.

In the next section we describe PEIRCE-IGTT, a software tool for building abductive problem-solving agents that use a version of this Machine 5 strategy. In the final section of this chapter we describe experiments that test the power of the strategy, and that show, not only that the strategy works well, but also, more generally, that there is indeed a significant amount of inferential leverage in the explanatory relationships.

Software: PEIRCE-IGTT

In this section, we describe a shell for building abductive problem-solving agents that use the Machine-5 strategy. This shell is called PEIRCE-IGTT to distinguish it from a similar tool named PEIRCE constructed by Bill Punch (chapter 4).[3] The "IGTT" extension marks that this PEIRCE is a piece of the Integrated Generic-Task Toolset.[4] The IGT Toolset recognizes all the generic goals: "to recognize" (hypothesis matching), to classify, to explain, and so on (see chapter 2). Each generic goal is realized as a type of specialist with a built-in ability to pursue a goal of that type. The toolset provides for the construction of classification specialists, recognition specialists, and so on. The toolset also includes a full-featured CSRL, a hierarchical classification tool. Classification specialists built using CSRL-IGTT can call upon hypothesis matchers (in this system called "recognition agents") to set confidence values. The toolset also includes a rudimentary database tool to support the knowledge-directed information-retrieval task. If a system needs some case-specific information, then it accesses that information by way of a database specialist. For synthesizing explanatory hypotheses, PEIRCE-IGTT provides a kind of specialist, called an "abducer," which is an agent into which a version of the Machine-5 strategy is embedded by default. PEIRCE-IGTT can link these abducers into communities of abducers that pass off explanatory subproblems to subabducers, similar to the PEIRCE tool described in chapter 4.

One or more of the classical generic-task (GT) methods are associated with each generic goal, and these are provided as default methods. However if supplied methods are somehow inappropriate because of unavailable knowledge, or because of particular unusual demands of the domain, the toolset user can access Common Lisp or the Common Lisp Object System (CLOS) to program an alternative method. Thus the IGTT tools are designed to allow easy escape to Lisp so that the built-in strategies can be used, but their use is not mandatory. The toolset was designed to be programmer-friendly, more so than the original GT tools and the original PEIRCE.

Unlike the GT theory described in chapter 4, where the development was towards increased flexibility at run time, PEIRCE-IGTT is not optimized for flexibility. Yet, unlike the classical GT's described in chapter 2, the new toolset supports the idea that there is more than one way of achieving a generic goal, though there is often a best method, which is supplied as the default. So the new PEIRCE tool is positioned as conceptually intermediate between the opportunistic run-time control of the original PEIRCE and the fixed strategies of the classical GTs. It recognizes the need, in principle, for flexibility, but it takes the stance that, for each generic goal, there is a canonical method which is preferable, if it applies, because it is generally the most efficient.

How it works

The PEIRCE-IGTT default algorithm presupposes that there is a means of generating or obtaining the findings for the case and a means of generating hypotheses to explain the findings. The generated hypotheses must have initial confidence values, and they must have associations with the findings that each can explain.

The steps of the algorithm are:

1. Generate or obtain findings to be explained and generate hypotheses (with their confidence values and coverages).
2. Initialize the composite with any hypotheses predetermined to be in the composite (set up by the tool user who has decided to always include certain hypotheses or by the system user interactively while he or she explores alternative hypotheses).
3. When this algorithm is used in a layered-abduction machine, expand expectations from higher levels (if a higher level abductive conclusion has implications[5] either positively or negatively for hypotheses at the current level). The expectations will cause the confidence values of the hypotheses in question to be adjusted. (Layered abduction machines are described in chapter 10.)
4. Propagate the effects of hypotheses initially accepted into the composite. This may rule out other hypotheses that are incompatible with those in the composite, or it may alter confidence values of other hypotheses that are implied by hypotheses in the composite.
5. Loop on the following, either until all findings are accounted for or until no more progress is made in extending the explanatory coverage.
   a. Find all Confirmed hypotheses and include them in the composite. A Confirmed hypothesis is (here) one that receives the highest possible confidence score (this is an optional feature that can be turned off by the system builder if top-scoring hypotheses should not be automatically included in the composite).
      If Confirmed hypotheses are found, then propagate the effects of the latest inclusions and go back to the loop beginning, else continue.

    b. Find all Essential hypotheses and include them in the composite.
      If Essential hypotheses are found, then propagate the effects of including them in the composite, and go back to the loop beginning, else continue.

    c. Find all Clear-Best hypotheses. To be a Clear-Best, a hypothesis must have a score higher than a given threshold and must surpass all other explanations for some finding by another given threshold. (Thresholds are established by the tool user at the time the system is built; they can be easily modified during or between cases; the tool provides defaults if no thresholds are specified.)
      If Clear-Best hypotheses are found, then propagate the effects of including them in the composite, and go back to the loop beginning, else continue.

    d. Find and include all the Weak-Bests. Here we may relax the criteria set for the Clear-Bests. This step is optional.
      If Weak-Best hypotheses are included in the composite, then propagate the effects and go back to the loop beginning, else continue.
      End loop.

   6. (Optional extended-guessing step) If there are still some unaccounted findings, attempt to guess among the remaining hypotheses that have not been ruled out. Guessing is accomplished by letting each unexplained finding vote for the highest rated hypotheses offering to explain it. This voting allows hypotheses to stand out from alternatives according to their power to help explain the unexplained remainder, if in no other way.
      If any guessed hypotheses are included, then propagate the effects and go back to the loop beginning, else end.

At this point, either all findings have been accounted for, or there are no more hypotheses available to explain findings, or the only remaining hypotheses are too close in plausibility and explanatory power to decide between them.

The default algorithm given to PEIRCE-IGTT abducers propagates the effects of including a hypothesis into the working composite, in part, by removing hypotheses that are incompatible with it from the set of available hypotheses. This is a variant of the strategy (described in the section of this chapter entitled Tractable Abduction) that adjusted the confidence scores of incompatible hypotheses depending on the confidence status of an included hypothesis, and that completely eliminated the incompatible hypotheses only if the included hypothesis was an essential. This difference has implications for the proper treatment of hypotheses included at each stage. In PEIRCE-IGTT, each pass through the loop leads to conclusions whose proper confidence is relative to the previous passes. A hypothesis judged to be Essential because a competing hypothesis was ruled out as a result of its being incompatible with a Clear-Best, is only an Essential hypothesis *relative* to Clear-Bests. An Essential from the first pass through the loop is more confidently an Essential than an Essential that is relative to Clear-Bests is. Similarly, any newly included hypothesis that is relative to guessing (that is, a hypothesis is included as a result of the effects of the inclusion of a guessed hypothesis) must be regarded as less confident than any hypotheses included before guessing began. Thus, each pass through the loop portion of the algorithm further limits the confidence in any hypothesis newly included into the composite. Hypotheses may be Confirmed, Essential, Clear-Best, Weak-Best, Guessed, Disbelieved (because of incompatibility), or Ruled-Out (because of a low confidence rating), and these judgments may be relative to Confirmeds, Essentials, Clear-Best, Weak-Best, or Guessed hypotheses.

PEIRCE-IGTT can handle hypothesis-coverage interactions of the sort where hypotheses contribute to the answer either independently (where each hypothesis explains some of the findings but does not interact with how other hypotheses explain other findings, except in being alternatives) or in an additive fashion (where hypotheses may combine their explanatory power towards individual findings), but it cannot handle cancellation interactions (where hypotheses may counteract what other hypotheses can explain). PEIRCE-IGTT's default method for handling incompatibility interactions is to eliminate from further consideration hypotheses incompatible with those included in the composite. It also handles interactions whereby hypotheses have varying degrees of "sympathy" or "antipathy" for each other, either symmetrically or asymmetrically. This is done while propagating the effects of including a hypothesis in the composite, by appropriately readjusting the confidence values of related hypotheses.

A series of small and medium-sized knowledge-based systems have been constructed using PEIRCE-IGTT in domains including acoustic speech recognition, speech recognition from articulation, legal reasoning, and scientific theory evaluation. The diversity of domains demonstrates the domain independence of the abductive-assembly strategy.

An example of PEIRCE-IGTT in action

We illustrate PEIRCE-IGTT with an example based on a legal case involving California Highway police officer Craig Peyer, who was tried for the murder of Cara Knott on December 27, 1986. Peyer had pulled Knott over on the night of her death. During the trial, 22 women, all young and attractive like the victim, testified that Peyer had pulled them over. Furthermore, they testified that Peyer talked with them longer than was necessary for just a ticket and that they were all pulled over near the stretch of road where Knott's body was found. The trial in San Diego ended on February 27, 1988, in a hung jury.

Our description of the evidence presented to the jury comes from Paul Thagard's characterization of the case (Thagard, 1989), which was based on newspaper accounts. To begin with, we simply encoded Thagard's characterization into a PEIRCE-IGTT abducer.

Thagard encoded the problem into his ECHO system by treating each hypothesis and finding as a node in a neural network, with links connecting each hypothesis node to nodes corresponding to explained findings. Incompatible hypotheses were connected by inhibitory links. Thagard assigned each hypothesis the same initial confidence value, so we treated them similarly, giving each an initial confidence value of LIKELY. LIKELY is a symbolic confidence value in the 9-valued confidence set, one of several confidence vocabularies available to users of the Integrated Generic Task Toolset. From highest to lowest, these nine values are: CONFIRMED, VERY-LIKELY, LIKELY, SOMEWHAT-LIKELY, NEUTRAL, SOMEWHAT-UNLIKELY, UNLIKELY, VERY-UNLIKELY, RULED-OUT. This nine-valued vocabulary was used throughout the example. (For problems in which confidence values can be treated formally as probabilities, and where numerical values are available, the tool user can specify a built-in confidence set that uses numerical values on the [0,1] interval. Other special confidence sets are available too.)

Thagard also provided information about hypothesis incompatibilities, which we encoded. The hypotheses can be considered as belonging to two categories: those reflecting innocence, and those reflecting guilt. Guilt and innocence hypotheses offer to explain various findings. Certain guilt and innocence hypotheses were given as incompatible. For instance, the hypothesis "Peyer killed Knott" was given as incompatible with "Someone other than Peyer killed Knott," but either hypothesis can explain the finding that Knott was killed. The explanatory and incompatibility relationships helped our system to sort out the initially equally plausible alternatives, as we will describe.

What follows is Thagard's detailed description of the case. Findings are listed as E1, E2, ... ; guilt-related hypotheses as G1, G2, ... ; and innocence-related hypotheses as I1, I2, ...

E1: Knott's body and car were found on a frontage road near Interstate-15. This can be explained by I1 or G1.

E2: 22 young women reported being talked to at length by Peyer after being stopped near where Knott's body was found. This can be explained by G6.

E3: Calderwood said that he saw a patrol car pull over a Volkswagen like Knott's near Interstate-15. This can be explained by G4.

E4: Calderwood came forward only at the trial. This can be explained by G5 or I2.

E5: Calderwood changed his story several times. This can be explained by I2.

E6: 6 fibers found on Knott's body matched Peyer's uniform. This can be explained by G3 or I3.

E7: Ogilvie said Peyer quizzed her about the case and acted strangely. G1 or I4 can account for this.

E8: Dotson said Ogilvie is a liar. This can be explained by I4a.

E9: Anderson and Schwartz saw scratches on Peyer's face the night of the killing. This can be explained by G2 or I5.

E10: Martin said she saw Peyer pull Knott's Volkswagen over. This can be explained by G1 or I6.

E11: Martin came forward only just before the trial. I6 can explain this.

E12: Anderson said that she saw Peyer wipe off his nightstick in his trunk. This can be explained by G7 or I7.

E13: Anderson did not say anything about the nightstick when she was first inter-rogated. This can be explained by G8 or I7.

E14: Bloodstains found on Knott's clothes matched Peyer's blood. This can be ex-plained by G1 or (I1 and E15).

E15: 12,800 other San Diegans had blood matching that on Knott's clothes. This is treated as a fact needing no explanation.

E16: A shabby hitchhiker was lunging at cars near the Interstate-15 entrance. This can be explained by I1.[6]

E17: Peyer had a spotless record with the California Highway Patrol. This can be explained by I8.

The hypotheses pertaining to Peyer's guilt:

G1: Peyer killed Knott.

G2: Knott scratched Peyer's face.

G3: Fibers from Peyer's uniform were transferred to Knott.

G4: Peyer pulled Knott over.

G5: Calderwood was reluctant to come forward because he wanted to protect his family from publicity.

G6: Peyer liked to pull over young women.

G7: Peyer had a bloody nightstick.

G8: Anderson was having personal problems when she was first interrogated.

The hypotheses pertaining to Peyer's innocence:

I1: Someone other than Peyer killed Knott.

I2: Calderwood made his story up.

I3: The 6 fibers floated around in the police evidence room.

I4: Ogilvie lied. This can be explained by I4a.

I4a: Ogilvie is a liar.

I5: Peyer's scratches came from a fence.

I6: Martin lied.

I7: Anderson was mistaken about the nightstick.

I8: Peyer is a good man.

Incompatibilities:

> G1 is incompatible with I1, and also with I8.
> G2 is incompatible with I5
> G3 is incompatible with I3
> G5 is incompatible with I2
> G7 is incompatible with I7

The PEIRCE-IGTT abducer began by looking for essentials since there were no mandatory or CONFIRMED hypotheses in this case. It found that E2, E3, E5, E8, E11, E16, and E17 each had only one potential explainer, and so G6, G4, I2, I4a, I6, I1 and I8 were included in the working compos-ite. Thus, the first round of processing resulted in judgments that:

> Peyer liked to pull over young women (G6). This explains why 22 young women reported being talked to at length by Peyer after being stopped

near where Knott's body was found (E2).

Peyer pulled Knott over (G4), which explains why Calderwood said that he saw a patrol car pull over a Volkswagen like Knott's near Interstate-15 (E3).

Calderwood made his story up (I2), which explains why Calderwood came forward only at the trial (E4), and why Calderwood changed his story several times (E5).

Ogilvie is a liar (I4a), which explains why Dotson said that Ogilvie lied (E8).

Martin lied (I6), which explains why Martin said that she saw Peyer pull Knott's Volkswagen over (E10), and why Martin came forward only just before the trial (E11).

Someone other than Peyer killed Knott (I1), which explains why Knott's body and car were found on a frontage road near Interstate-15 (E1). It also explains why a shabby hitchhiker was lunging at cars near the Interstate-15 entrance (E16), and (with the assumed fact that 12,800 other San Diegans had blood matching that on Knott's clothes) (E15), it explains why bloodstains found on Knott's clothes matched Peyer's blood (E14).

Peyer is a good man (I8), which explains why Peyer had a spotless record with the California Highway Patrol (E17).

The abducer then propagated the effects of including the essential hypotheses into the composite. G5 was rejected for being incompatible with I2, and G1 was rejected for being incompatible with I1 and I8. That is, the abducer *rejected* the proposition that:

Calderwood was reluctant to come forward because he wanted to protect his family from publicity (G5).

The abducer did so because G5 is incompatible with the proposition that Calderwood made his story up (I2), which had already been accepted. The abducer also *rejected* the proposition that:

Peyer killed Knott (G1).

It did so because G1 is incompatible with the proposition that someone other than Peyer killed Knott (I1).

By rejecting the proposition that Peyer killed Knott, the abducer found the defendant innocent. (In principle this is a tentative judgment, since it might be retracted if the abducer subsequently ran into trouble, e.g., a contradiction). What happened was that I1 was accepted because it is the only way (given to the system) to explain E16, and G1 was then rejected for being incompatible with I1.

G1 having been eliminated, I4 became essential as the only remaining way to explain E7. So next the abducer accepted:

Ogilvie lied (I4), which explains why Ogilvie said that Peyer quizzed her about the case and acted strangely (E7).

At that point the only unexplained findings were E6, E9, E12, E13, and E15. No hypotheses offered to explain E15, but it had been encoded as a fact not needing explanation. Each of the others had two equally confident potential explainers. Because guessing was turned off, the abducer stopped. If

guessing had been turned on, I7 would have been accepted because it offered to explain both E12 and E13, while nothing else offered to explain
more than one of the unexplained findings. If I7 had been accepted, G7
would have been rejected for being incompatible with it.

The real trial ended in a hung jury. If the jurors had analyzed the case in
this way, it should have been relatively straightforward to determine Peyer's
innocence. On this analysis the case hinges on the actions of the shabby
hitchhiker, which can be explained only by supposing that someone other
than Peyer killed Knott. This seems to point to a mistake in analyzing the
case. The conclusion crucially depends on the awkward piece of analysis
that holds that I1 explains E16; that is, that 'Someone other than Peyer killed
Knott' explains 'A shabby hitchhiker was lunging at cars near the Interstate-
15 entrance.' It seems better to describe the behavior of the shabby hitchhiker as adding plausibility to the hypothesis that someone other than Peyer
killed Knott, rather than as being explained by it.

So we reencoded the case with the relationship between the hitchhiker's
behavior (E16) and the hypothesis that someone else was guilty (I1) as a soft
implication (i.e., as an evidence-giving of unspecified type) rather than as
an explanatory relationship. We similarly replaced a few other awkward-
seeming explanatory relationships with soft implications. Altogether we encoded soft implications from E15, E16, and E17 to I1, and from I4a to I4.
With this new encoding, the system propagated the soft implications from
E15, E16, and E17 to I1, raising the confidence of I1, and thus making it a
better explanation for E1 than the guilt hypothesis G1. Thus the system found
Peyer to be innocent anyway, but not so confidently. (It was no longer an
ESSENTIAL, but instead just a BEST or a CLEAR-BEST, depending on the
strengths associated with the soft implications.)

We first picked this case because Thagard had already described it precisely and it was easy to implement. We needed something to help debug the
PEIRCE-IGTT tool, and this case also provided an opportunity for comparison with ECHO. One point of comparison is that PEIRCE-IGTT can trace
its reasoning process, and this reasoning process makes sense at every step.
In contrast ECHO works by repeated cycles of propagating activations, and
even if each spread of activation can be explained as a reasoning step that
makes sense, ECHO took 78 cycles to settle, so its reasoning was much less
direct. PEIRCE formed its conclusions quickly, and, in effect, produced an
argument for innocence given the evidence. (In contrast ECHO leaned toward guilt, although it resisted complete rejection of the innocence hypothesis.)

It might be suggested that ECHO engages in a complex weighing of evidence in its attempt to maximize explanatory coherence, whereas PEIRCE
makes too much of a small number of findings.[7] We submit that PEIRCE's
behavior for the case was entirely reasonable. It considered all the evidence.

It could have found the case to be ambiguous and, like the jury, refused to come to a conclusion; but it did not. Instead it produced a conclusion, with a clear chain of reasoning leading to it.

This example demonstrates that the fifth-generation abductive-assembly strategy can generate chains of reasoning, and arrive at conclusions, even if all the hypotheses are given identical initial confidence values. The strategy makes good use of confidence differences if they are available, but it does not absolutely require them. It is able to solve a problem categorically, based on explanatory relationships and incompatibilities alone, or with the assistance of additional hypothesis interactions such as soft implications.

The Peyer example also illustrates how explanatory relationships can work synergistically with incompatibility relationships to reduce residual ambiguity. This is the phenomenon of *uncovered essentials*. What happens is that eliminating a hypothesis, based on incompatibility with some proposition already accepted, eliminates a potential explainer for some finding, thereby allowing a rival explainer to stand out as superior. (This happens similarly for uncovered clear-bests and bests, where confidence is reduced, instead of the hypothesis being eliminated.) Thus, at a point in the processing where a finding is ambiguous (it has alternative explainers with no confident way to decide between them), the ambiguity may be broken or reduced by eliminating or downgrading of one of the rival explainers. Here I1 was accepted because it was the only possible explanation for E16, which led to the elimination of G1, after which I4 became the only remaining way to explain E7. Moreover, the process of acceptance, leading to ambiguity reduction, followed by further acceptance and further ambiguity reduction, can potentially continue for many cycles, leading to a kind of spreading wave of ambiguity reduction as islands of high confidence are extended to cover data newly made unambiguous. We call this process *spreading disambiguation*.

Note that the Machine-5 abductive-assembly strategy described in this chapter goes beyond merely being efficient, beyond just reasonable-sounding ways of weighing evidence, beyond the ability to use multiple kinds of hypothesis interactions, even beyond opportunism and flexibility in taking advantage of the kinds of evidence that happen to be available. Its run-time behavior is downright clever. Next, we describe experiments that show that it works well too.

Experiment: Uncertainty and correctness

In the first section of this chapter we characterized the abductive task as that of forming an explanation that is internally consistent, parsimonious, significantly better than alternative explanations, and that explains as much of the data as possible. This was contrasted with the view of abduction as finding the best complete explanation for given data. Second, we described a computational strategy for forming confident explanations. The formation process is organized so that the explanation starts from islands of relative certainty, then grows opportunistically. This strategy helps control the computational cost of accommodating interactions among explanatory hypotheses, especially incompatibility interactions. In the past, incompatibility relationships seemed a main source of intractability by potentially forcing a combinatorially explosive search to synthesize a complete, consistent explanation. In contrast, the Machine-5 strategy shows how incompatibility relationships can be used to distinct advantage in expanding partial explanations to more complete ones. We also described a software tool, PEIRCE-IGTT, for building abductive-assembly systems that use a variant of the Machine-5 strategy.

Next, we describe an experiment designed to test the hypothesis that explicitly represented explanatory relationships can be used to significantly reduce uncertainty and to increase correctness of judgment for abductive processing. The experiment used a specific knowledge base, which existed prior to this particular use. Three types of knowledge were represented: routine-recognition knowledge (i.e., precompiled knowledge for pattern-based hypothesis scoring), hypothesis-incompatibility knowledge (that two hypotheses cannot both be true at the same time), and knowledge of explanatory relationships between hypotheses and data items. The performance of four distinct abduction machines was compared; each machine used a different combination of knowledge types and a different reasoning strategy.

Experimental design

The experiment was based on the RED-2 system described in chapter 3. RED-2 has two main components: a hierarchical classifier and an abductive assembler. The classifier rates the plausibility of each antibody hypothesis. In the modified versions of the program used for the experiment, the hypotheses are not hierarchically organized, and the classifier simply matches the prototypical pattern of data for each hypothesis to the data given in a case in order to determine a confidence score. This component will be called the "Matcher." The explanatory hypotheses will be called "antibodies" because each hypothesizes the presence of a particular antibody in the patient's serum, and each offers to explain certain test reactions (sometimes only partially explaining a reaction). The role of the abductive assembler, or "Assembler," is to form a composite hypothesis that is consistent, explains as much of the data as possible, and meets some other conditions (such as parsimony and high plausibility).

We ran 42 antibody-identification problems, here called "cases," using four distinct machines, and measured their performance. The four machines are: (1) a matcher-only machine, (2) a matcher machine with extra process-

Table 9.1. Certainty vocabulary

C	(Confirmed)
VP	(Very Plausible)
P	(Plausible)
U	(Unknown)
I	(Implausible)
VI	(Very Implausible)
RO	(Ruled Out)

ing to handle incompatible hypotheses, (3) a matcher machine with a (Machine 4) abductive hypothesis assembler, and (4) a matcher with a (Machine 4) abductive assembler with a special strategy for handling incompatible hypotheses (i.e., a Machine 5). The overall reasoning strategies embodied in these machines can be viewed as four distinct domain-independent strategies for abduction. For each machine we measured uncertainty and correctness over the same library of cases.

For each case, each machine decided on a degree of certainty regarding the truth or falsity of each antibody hypothesis. Table 9.1 shows the vocabulary for the degrees of certainty.

The four machines that were tested were variations of the same basic machine with certain features enabled or disabled. In this section we describe each machine in detail.

Matcher

The Matcher produced a confidence rating for each antibody on an ascending integer scale from −3 to +3. For each antibody, the Matcher did the following:

1. It checked for critical data that should be observed if the antibody is present. If it failed to find any of this data, it ruled out the antibody (assigned it −3).
2. If it failed to rule out the antibody, the Matcher then checked the patient's history. Once a person develops an antibody, they always have it. So, if the patient's history contained a record of the antibody's previous presence, the Matcher returned a definitive positive rating for the antibody (+3). Otherwise, the corresponding antigen was on the patient's own red blood cells, the Matcher ruled out the antibody (-3) because people do not normally develop antibodies to their own antigens. (Sometimes they do, but rarely; RED-2 was designed only to handle cases in which these autoantibodies were already ruled out.)
3. If no tests were conducted in which the antibody's presence would appear (i.e., the antibody was untested), the Matcher rated it at a middle value, 0 on the Matcher's scale. This prevented the matcher from making a commitment when it had no grounds.
4. If steps 1 through 3 failed to produce a value, the Matcher rated the antibody according to how closely the observed data matched the pattern of data expected for when the antibody is present. This produced values from −2 to +2.

Table 9.2. Assignment of certainty
values to matcher scores

Matcher	Certainty
+3	C
+2	VP
+1	P
0	U
-1	I
-2	VI
-3	RO

These values were further modified (raised or lowered) according to the antibody's frequency of occurrence (common antibodies rate higher than rare ones, other things being equal).

Table 9.2 shows how certainty values were assigned to the Matcher's confidence ratings.

Matcher with incompatible hypotheses handling

As part of its knowledge base RED-2 has a collection of pairs of incompatible hypotheses (only one member of each pair can be present). Some antibodies belong to more than one pair; that is, they are incompatible with several other antibodies. Many belong to none of the pairs, meaning that they are compatible with all other antibodies. The Matcher-with-Incompatibles used this information in a postprocessor, after the Matcher and before the final setting of certainty values. The postprocessor did the following:

1. If several incompatible antibodies were rated positively, then all their ratings were changed to 0, i.e., positive confidence in a hypothesis was shaken by positive confidence in incompatible hypotheses.
2. If an antibody was rated strongly positive (+2 or +3), and all antibodies incompatible with it were rated negatively, then the ratings of the incompatible ones were bumped one level lower. Strong positive confidence in a hypothesis became further evidence against an incompatible hypothesis that already had low confidence.

Note that there is no inconsistency in having several incompatible hypotheses rated negatively. The result of postprocessing was a set of antibodies rated on the Matcher's −3 to +3 scale, which were then assigned certainty values as shown in Table 9.2.

Matcher with assembler

The Matcher-with-Assembler used the original Matcher (without the postprocessor to handle incompatible hypotheses) to initially rate the antibody hypotheses. Then it entered the assembly algorithm:

1. *Essentials.* Search through the antibodies for those that are Essential (i.e., those that are the only way of explaining some finding). Put the essential antibodies into the working composite hypothesis. Note that an essential is the best explanation for some finding (because it is the only explanation for that finding) and thus represents a local abductive conclusion of high confidence.

2. *Clear-Bests.* Search through the remaining antibodies for those that were rated by the Matcher at least two steps higher (e.g., P vs. I) than their nearest competitors for explaining some finding. Include the Clear- Best antibodies in the working hypothesis. These antibodies are considered "Clear-Bests" because, based on the Matcher's ratings, each is clearly the best way to explain some finding. Note that a Clear-Best represents a local abductive conclusion entitled to high confidence, but not as high as that of an essential.

3. *Bests.* (These are similar to those called "Weak-Bests" in PEIRCE-IGTT.) Search through the remaining antibodies for those that were rated by the Matcher one step higher than their nearest competitors for explaining some finding, and that had some other consideration to recommend them (e.g., that they explained more in total). Include them in the working hypothesis. These antibodies are considered merely "best" explainers because each is not much better than alternative explanations.

Building up a working hypothesis in this way – essentials, then clear-bests, then bests – constitutes a strategy of starting from the most confident partial conclusions available, and then advancing through stages of less and less (but still reasonably high) confidence.

Between steps, the assembler recomputed the set of findings that remained to be explained and tested to see if the working hypothesis was a complete explanation. If it had a complete explanation at any point, it stopped. Note that the working hypothesis was not necessarily a complete explanation at the end of the process. We will return to this point later. After constructing a working hypothesis in this manner, the Assembler conducted a parsimony check to remove from the working hypothesis those antibodies that did not contribute to its explanatory coverage. This was done by first examining any Bests in order of least plausible to most plausible (as rated by the Matcher). For each antibody, the Assembler tested to see if the working hypothesis explained as much without the antibody as it did with it. If so, the antibody could be removed from the working hypothesis without loss of explanatory coverage. When the Bests had been checked, the Assembler repeated the procedure for Clear-Bests. There was no need to check the Essentials; it follows from the definition of Essential that they must all be included. The parsimony check ensured that the working hypothesis contained no proper subsets explaining as much as the whole working hypothesis. At the end of this procedure the working hypothesis was considered the best explanation of the given test data.

The Assembler produced its final ratings of the antibody hypotheses based on the best explanation and the Matcher's ratings. The Assembler's final rating categories and the assignment of certainty values is shown in Table 9.3. Essen-

Table 9.3. Assignment of certainty values
to assembler ratings

Assembler	Certainty
Confirmed	C
Clear Best	VP
Best	P
Undetected	U
Unresolved	U
Likely Absent	I
Ruled Out -2	VI
Ruled Out -3	RO

tial antibodies were called "Confirmed." "Undetected" means that the antibody was not tested. An antibody was considered "Unresolved" if it was in
the best explanation but was rated low by the Matcher, or not in the best
explanation but was rated high by the Matcher, reflecting evidence pulling
in opposite directions. Antibodies classified "Likely Absent" were not in the
best explanation, not ruled out, and not highly rated by the Matcher. "Ruled
Out –2" and "Ruled Out –3" mean that the antibody was rated –2 or –3 by
the matcher, and was not in the best explanation.

In cases where the Assembler did not produce a complete explanation, the
final rating method was modified somewhat to reflect a lowered confidence
in the result. The best explanation might fail to be a complete explanation
for one of two reasons:

1. There was a finding that no antibody could explain.
2. For each unexplained finding there was at least a near tie between possible
   explainers; that is, there were insufficient grounds for discriminating between
   them with a significant degree of confidence.

In Case 1, something was obviously wrong, a significant anomaly occurred and the system's knowledge must be incomplete or incorrect. Additional hypotheses, or more generous explaining by existing ones, might have
changed everything. So all non-ruled-out hypotheses should be reclassified
as Unresolved. The ruled-out hypotheses could be left alone because the
additional information that might make a complete explanation possible
would be unlikely to affect them. (This is a domain-specific piece of strategy, reflecting high confidence in the rule-out knowledge in this domain, a
confidence which was later empirically justified [see Table 9.7]. In domains
where rule-out knowledge is not so dependable, an unexplained finding could
be the result of a hypothesis improperly ruled out, so it would be more correct to change the classification of ruled-out hypotheses to Unresolved if
they could have helped to explain the finding.)

In Case 2, a complete explanation may have existed but it would have been hard to find or hard to determine which complete explanation was best. Under these circumstances there was no reason to change the rating of hypotheses already included in the working hypothesis, or of hypotheses classified as Ruled Out (−2 or −3). Of the rest, any that would have been classified as Likely Absent (not in the best explanation, not ruled out, not highly rated by the matcher) and offering to help explain an unexplained finding, were instead considered Unresolved. Other ratings were left unchanged.

Matcher with assembler and incompatible hypotheses handling

The Assembler-with-Incompatibles was a full-featured abduction program. It was substantially the same as the Machine 5 strategy already described and was identical to the Matcher-with-Assembler with the addition of a special procedure for handling incompatible hypotheses. This procedure did the following: Each time an antibody was added to the working hypothesis, all antibodies incompatible with it were removed from the pool of available antibodies. That is, once an antibody was thought to be present, everything incompatible with it was removed from further consideration. Antibodies could be put into the working hypothesis in any of three stages: Essentials, Clear-Bests, and Bests. If incompatible Essentials were found, the assembly process terminated with everything judged as Unresolved, since this suggested a serious problem in the data or the system's knowledge. If incompatible Clear-Bests were found, they were removed from the working hypothesis (i.e., placed back in the pool of available hypotheses) and their ratings from the Matcher were reduced by one step (e.g., from VP to P). If incompatible Bests were found, the Assembler-with-Incompatibles attempted to decide between among as follows:

1. If one antibody was clearly superior to all the others (i.e., it was rated higher by the Matcher than the others, it explained more than any of the others, etc.), then it was kept in the working hypothesis and all the others were removed.
2. If no antibody was clearly superior, all the incompatibles were removed from the working hypothesis.

After the composite best explanation was assembled, the ratings of the antibody hypotheses were further modified so that any antibody incompatible with a Confirmed antibody was moved to Ruled Out −3, incompatible with a Clear-Best went to Ruled Out −2, incompatible with a Best went to Likely Absent. In other words, positive belief in a hypothesis was converted to negative belief in all hypotheses incompatible with it in proportion to the strength of the belief. The results were assigned certainty values as shown in Table 9.3.

Results

The library of cases included correct answers for each case based on expert judgment about which antibodies were present (we will refer to these as

Table 9.4. Number of antibodies classified in each category

	Matcher	Matcher with Incompatibles	Assembler	Assembler with Incompatibles
C	0	0	23	23
VP	70	70	16	16
P	188	149	53	52
I	85	92	375	355
VI	250	250	250	242
RO	282	282	282	290
Total	875	843	999	978

"in") and which were not tested for (called "untested"). The other antibodies (i.e., the common ones that were tested for but were not in), were considered not present ("out"). We should note that we do not know the real truth about any case. Many of these cases actually occurred in a hospital blood bank. The "correct answers" were the human experts' best judgments about which antibodies were present, but they are not guaranteed to be correct. However, the experts' judgments are the best measure we have of the programs' performance.

Uncertainty. For each case, each machine produced a certainty value (C, VP, etc.) for each of the 27 common antibodies. Because identifying which antibodies were untested is a trivial task, and all machines were easily able to do it, these antibodies are ignored in our analysis. The 42 cases represent 1,012 tested antibodies, of which 83 were present and 929 were absent. Tables 9.4 through 9.10 show the results of running the four machines on the 42 cases.

Table 9.4 shows the number of antibodies that each machine classified in each category (C, VP, etc.). The Unknown (U) category is omitted from this table, which shows only where the machines were able to make some commitment (i.e., judge an antibody to be present or absent with some degree of confidence). Thus, of the 1,012 antibodies that were tested in the 42 cases, the Matcher committed itself on 875; it considered none of them to be Confirmed, 70 to be Very Plausible, and so forth. Similarly for the other machines. Some interesting points to note from this table are:

1. The matcher never confirmed anything. This was not very surprising. This is at least partly a feature of the particular domain, in which pathognomonic (directly confirming) evidence is unusual (see point 2).

2. The Assembler rated far fewer antibodies positively (Confirmed, Very Plausible, or Plausible) than the Matcher did. This may simply be a feature of the domain, which has easily available rule-out information, but supporting information is more difficult to obtain. So the Matcher can confidently rule out,

but in the absence of evidence against an antibody, the Matcher may err by rating it positively. Because missing an antibody that is actually present can have more severe consequences for the patient than asserting an antibody that is actually absent, pragmatic concerns encourage error in the direction of positive rating. The assembler, on the other hand, by taking into account explanatory relations between antibodies and data, is better able to sort things out, and moves many of the antibodies rated positively by the Matcher into the Unknown or negative categories.

3. Adding incompatibility knowledge made both the Matcher and the Assembler more cautious in general. That is, the machines tended to commit on fewer Antibodies. Incompatibility knowledge tended to increase uncertainty. This is even more obvious in Table 9.5 where the number of antibodies classified as Unknown is summarized. This increase in uncertainty might have been expected since most of the changes to the machines for handling incompatible antibodies tend to move antibodies toward uncertainty. In the Matcher the main effect was to move hypotheses from Plausible to Unknown. In the Assembler, the main effect was to move from Implausible to Unknown. Both of these turned out to be correct changes (see the discussion of Table 9.7).

4. Adding incompatibility knowledge allowed the assembler to rule out 8 more antibodies (for being incompatible with essentials). This amounted to a decrease in uncertainty for these hypotheses, contrary to the overall tendency of incompatibility knowledge to increase uncertainty.

Conclusion: Uncertainty. Knowledge of explanatory relationships (that is, using the Assembler in addition to the Matcher) had a large effect on reducing uncertainty. The Assembler made commitments on many more antibodies than the Matcher alone did (approximately 15% more). As is apparent from reading down the columns in Table 9.5, the Assembler was unable to commit on far fewer antibodies, with a reduction in the Unknown category of approximately 91% without the use of incompatibles and of approximately 80% using them. Additionally, as can be seen in Table 9.4, the Assembler made more commitments at the extremes of confidence (Confirmed and Ruled Out), doing so on approximately 8% more antibodies when not using knowledge of incompatibles, and approximately 10% more antibodies when using such knowledge. Thus the knowledge of explanatory relationships had a dramatic effect on reducing uncertainty.

Correctness. Table 9.6 shows the number of antibodies that each machine classified correctly in each category. An antibody was correctly classified if (1) it was considered "in" by the experts and the machine classified it as Confirmed, Very Plausible, or Plausible or (2) it was considered "out" by the experts and the machine classified it as Implausible, Very Implausible, or Ruled Out. Antibodies classified as Unknown were considered to be neither correct nor incorrect.

The Matchers got more positively-rated antibodies correct (those rated C, VP, or P) and fewer antibodies correct overall than the Assemblers did. These

Table 9.5. Number Classified Unknown

	Without Incompatibles	With Incompatibles
Matcher	137	169
Assembler	13	34

Table 9.6. Number of antibodies correctly classified in each category

	Matcher	Matcher with Incompatibles	Assembler	Assembler with Incompatibles
C	0	0	23	23
VP	24	24	11	11
P	40	35	20	20
I	84	90	354	338
VI	248	248	248	240
RO	282	282	282	290
Total	678	679	938	922

Table 9.7. Percentage correctly classified in each category

	Matcher	Matcher with Incompatibles	Assembler	Assembler with Incompatibles
C	—	—	100.0	100.0
VP	34.3	34.3	68.8	68.8
P	21.3	23.5	37.7	38.5
I	98.8	97.8	94.4	95.2
VI	99.2	99.2	99.2	99.2
RO	100.0	100.0	100.0	100.0
Total	77.5	80.5	93.9	94.3

results might be expected because the Matchers assign positive ratings to more antibodies and commit on fewer antibodies than the Assemblers do.

Table 9.7 summarizes the results shown in Tables 9.4 and 9.6. Since neither Matcher machine rated any antibodies as Confirmed, the percentage correct in that category is meaningless for them. Some important points to note are:

1. The machines were never wrong at the extremes of confidence (Confirmed and Ruled Out).

2. It is striking that all four machines were more often correct when they were more certain. Confidence correlated very well with correctness. This relationship was not designed into any of the machines, except in using the human experts' judgments about the kinds of data that yield more or less certain conclusions and in designing the confidence-setting rules according to what seemed to be reasonable ways of evaluating evidence. The results seem to validate both the experts' judgments and our judgments about how to evaluate evidence.

3. All machines performed better than chance. Given that 83 antibodies were present of the 1,012 antibodies that were tested, we would expect a random guess that an antibody is present to be correct only approximately 8.2% of the time. All the machines did better than that. The Matcher was correct regarding 24.8% of its positively rated antibodies; with incompatibility knowledge the Matcher improved slightly to 26.9% correct; the Assembler was correct regarding 58.7% of its positively rated antibodies; and with incompatibility knowledge it improved slightly to 59.3% correct. Thus the Assemblers were approximately twice as good by this measure as the Matchers were, but even the Matchers had three times the success rate of a random guesser. This is particularly important because generally few of the antibodies are present, so committing to a positive rating for an antibody puts any machine out on a limb. (We suspect that this is a general truth. That is, in any situation, most of the things that could be true are not. A reasoner could be pretty accurate by just saying "no" all the time. Saying "yes" is going against the odds.) Since the machines all performed significantly better than guessing, the use of knowledge apparently contributed to correct behavior in positively rating the antibodies. A similar effect occurred with the negatively rated antibodies, but it is not as striking.

4. The Very Implausible and Ruled Out categories for the Assembler were dominated by the Matcher's ratings. This might be expected from the design of the Assembler, which considers only non-ruled-out antibodies for explaining the reactions, and from the rules for assigning confidence values, which change the values assigned by the Matcher only under special circumstances. This might also be expected because the Matcher rated very many antibodies in these categories (Table 9.4) and was almost always correct in doing so (Table 9.7), so there should rarely be any reason to change the Matcher's values and rarely any opportunity to add further antibodies to these confidence categories.

5. The machines with incompatibility knowledge were slightly more accurate than those without. In particular, the Matcher improved from 21.3% to 23.5% in the Plausible category, where the main effect of incompatibility knowledge was to move antibodies to Unknown. The Assembler improved from 94.4% to 95.2% in the Implausible category, where incompatibility knowledge apparently had a similar effect.

6. The Assemblers were much more often correct on the positive side than the Matchers were.

7. The Assemblers were slightly less accurate than the Matchers were in the Implausible category. However, the Assemblers rated approximately four times as many antibodies in this category, mostly moving them from Unknown.

Conclusion: Correctness. Explanatory knowledge increased correctness. That is, using the Assembler in addition to the Matcher made a distinct difference, increasing both the number and percentage of antibodies correctly judged to be present or absent. This is summarized in Tables 9.8 and 9.9,

Table 9.8. Summary: Number correctly classified

	Without Incompatibles	With Incompatibles
Matcher	678	679
Assembler	938	922

Table 9.9 Summary: Percentage correctly classified

	Without Incompatibles	With Incompatibles
Matcher	77.5	80.5
Assembler	93.9	94.3

where the effect can readily be seen by reading down the columns. Thus, in concert with a like effect for reducing uncertainty, knowledge of explanatory relationships had a dramatic effect for increasing correctness.

Incompatibility knowledge contributed surprisingly little to correctness, as can be seen by reading across the rows in Tables 9.8 and 9.9. In retrospect it seems likely that this was a domain-specific effect, and perhaps should not have been so surprising. We have seen that the introduction of incompatibility knowledge can give rise to complications resulting in an overall increase in uncertainty (see Table 9.5). In addition Bylander has shown that finding a complete explanation in the presence of incompatible hypotheses is an NP-Complete problem (see chapter 7). One way to make it tractable is to rule out enough hypotheses so that there are no incompatible pairs among the non-ruled-out hypotheses (i.e., reduce it to the problem of finding a complete explanation when there are no incompatible hypotheses). It appears that the antibody-identification knowledge has been optimized to do this; that is, tests have been designed and knowledge has been compiled to discriminate between incompatible hypotheses, thus reducing the processing load for test interpretation and increasing the chances of arriving at a complete explanation. Since the Matchers are good at ruling out (better than 99% accuracy), and since subsequent processing only uses the hypotheses not ruled out by the Matchers, there should be few incompatible pairs among these hypotheses most of the time, so incompatibility knowledge should usually be of little further use.

Problem difficulty. Let us see how the various machines fared on difficult versus easy problems. There are several possible measures of difficulty: number of reactions to explain, commonness of the antibodies

Table 9.10. Percentage correctly classified by difficulty

No. of antibodies present	Matcher	Matcher with Incompatibles	Assembler	Assembler with Incompatibles
1	77.6	81.9	95.3	95.3
2	85.8	86.5	96.3	96.3
3	66.3	70.5	89.4	90.4
Overall	77.5	80.5	93.9	94.3

present or absent, commonness of the reactions, and so forth. But the simplest measure available is the number of antibodies present. Normally, the more antibodies present, the more difficult the problem, because the reaction patterns overlap and tend to hide one another, because more interactions must be considered, and because more steps might be needed to solve the problem. This is not universally true since it might be harder to become convinced that a single rare antibody is present than that two or three common ones are. Although it is not a perfect measure, it is a good crude measure of difficulty. Our library of test cases contained 14 one-antibody problems (i.e., cases in which exactly one antibody was present), 15 two-antibody problems, and 13 three-antibody problems.

Table 9.10 summarizes the results according to the number of antibodies – each row shows how each machine performed on cases of a certain difficulty (one-, two-, or three-antibody cases). Following are some points to note about the results:

1. The Assemblers were more accurate than the Matchers were at all levels of difficulty. Thus the increased correctness attributable to explanatory knowledge was a persistent and broadly occurring phenomenon.
2. As expected, all the machines were at their worst on the most difficult cases.
3. The effect of incompatibility knowledge for the Matcher was also persistent, serving to improve its performance at all difficulty levels, but primarily on the easiest and hardest cases. This effect probably occurred because the Matcher rated far too many antibodies positively, and incompatibility knowledge pushed antibodies from low positive ratings to Unknown. For the Assembler, incompatibility knowledge made only a slight difference in accuracy, and that just on the hardest cases. The way the Assembler's algorithm works, incompatibility knowledge is likely to have more of an effect when the answer has more parts.
4. Surprisingly, all the machines performed better on the two-antibody cases than on the one-antibody cases (i.e., they did not perform as well on the easiest cases as they did on somewhat more difficult cases). Each case tests for approximately the same number of antibodies, so a random guess on a two-antibody problem is twice as likely to produce a correct answer as a random guess on a one-antibody problem is. So machines such as the Matchers, which assign positive ratings when there is no reason not to, will be correct more

often when more antibodies are present. Indeed, the phenomenon was largest with the Matchers. However, the phenomenon also occurred with the Assemblers, although it was smaller. Furthermore, the Matchers' performance decreased on the three-antibody cases, so the random-hit hypothesis cannot explain the phenomenon completely. Perhaps it is a result of some bias in the test cases.

Because the number of antibodies in the correct answer is only a crude measure of case difficulty, and because the proportion of antibodies present to antibodies tested is higher in the multiple-antibody cases, we cannot rely strongly on the numbers in Table 9.10 to reveal the true change in accuracy of each machine with increasing case difficulty. Nevertheless, the comparative performance of the four machines clearly holds for each level of difficulty.

Implications for RED. Some facts stand out from the data presented here, and suggest possible improvements to future versions of RED.

1. The Matcher is well suited to ruling out hypotheses. In this experiment it was correct in its negative ratings more than 99% of the time. Therefore, RED should be cautious about assigning an antibody a positive rating after the Matcher assigns it a negative rating. In particular, the Assembler can ignore antibodies rated Implausible or lower by the Matcher (currently it ignores only those that are ruled out) and use them only if it cannot find a complete explanation otherwise.
2. When an antibody is not useful in forming a complete explanation, this is not good evidence against it. So it should not be lowered in confidence more than about one step.

Further study is needed to determine the effects of these proposed changes.

Conclusions

We conducted an experiment to measure the degree to which explicitly represented knowledge of explanatory relationships can contribute to reducing uncertainty and increasing correctness for abductive reasoning. Explanatory relationships were found to make a significant contribution to reducing uncertainty and to increasing correctness. In both cases the effect was dramatic.

Explicitly represented knowledge of hypothesis incompatibility was also tested. The apparent effect of using this knowledge was increased overall uncertainty, but a slightly increased rate of correct judgments. The increase was so slight, however, that it should not be considered significant.

Confidence values correlated well with correctness. All four machines were more often correct when they were more certain, and they were never wrong at the extremes of confidence. This fact provides a form of validation for the qualitative confidence vocabulary used in the experiment, and for the confidence-setting rules used in the machines. In particular, the strategy for weighing explanatory evidence should be considered to be validated in the large, although not in every detail. The confidence-setting behavior of the machines was not only *reasonable* (according to internal considerations), but also *realistic* (based on correspondence with the facts).

This experiment is in the spirit of others done on knowledge-based systems, though testing the contribution of a particular type of knowledge may be unique. It is a reasonable sort of validation to ask for any advisory system that makes judgments qualified by confidence estimates, that its confidence should correlate with its correctness, though to our knowledge this is rarely done.

Notes

1 If two Essential hypotheses are incompatible, then a serious anomaly has occurred, and normal processing is suspended. It is possible that the conflict can be resolved by generating more hypotheses or by performing tests to reconfirm the existing data, but both of these solutions are outside the scope of the present discussion.

2 Again, if two Clear-Best hypotheses are incompatible, then special handling takes over.

3 PEIRCE-IGTT was designed by John R. Josephson, Hari Narayanan, and Diana Smetters, and implemented in Common Lisp and CLOS (Common Lisp Object System) by Diana Smetters and Richard Fox.

4 The Integrated Generic-Task Toolset (IGTT) used in many of our systems benefited greatly from the sponsorship of The Defense Research Projects Agency under the Strategic Computing Program. Other significant support for its development came at various times from Xerox, IBM, DEC, and Texas Instruments corporations.

5 Implications can be *hard* or *soft*. A soft implication has a degree of strength.

6 Thagard gave a somewhat counterintuitive analysis of the explanatory relationships here and in a few other places. We first encoded the case using his analysis, ran it, and then reencoded it in a form that seemed more natural. The changes were few, and the performance was not greatly altered. This alteration is described later in this section.

7 Compare this with the popular TV detective Columbo, who often solves a difficult case by doggedly trying to find a satisfactory explanation for some seemingly insignificant fact.

10   Perception and language understanding

This chapter develops the hypothesis that perception is abduction in layers and that understanding spoken language is a special case. These rather grand hypotheses are rich with implications: philosophical, technological, and physiological.

We present here a layered-abduction computational model of perception that unifies bottom-up and top-down processing in a single logical and information-processing framework. In this model the processes of interpretation are broken down into discrete layers where at each layer a best-explanation composite hypothesis is formed of the data presented by the layer or layers below, with the help of information from above. The formation of such a hypothesis is an abductive inference process, similar to diagnosis and scientific theory formation. The model treats perception as a kind of frozen or "compiled" deliberation. It applies in particular to speech recognition and understanding, and is a model both of how people process spoken language input, and of how a machine can be organized to do it.

Perception is abduction in layers

There is a long tradition of belief in philosophy and psychology that perception relies on some form of inference (Kant, 1787; Helmholtz; Bruner, 1957; Rock, 1983; Gregory, 1987; Fodor, 1983). But this form of inference has been typically thought of as some form of deduction, or simple recognition, or feature-based classification, not as abduction. In recent times researchers have occasionally proposed that perception, or at least language understanding, involves some form of abduction or explanation-based inference (Charniak & McDermott, 1985, p. 557; Charniak, 1986; Dasigi, 1988; Josephson, 1982, pp. 87-94; Fodor, 1983, pp. 88, 104; Hobbs, Stickel, Appelt and Martin, 1993). Peirce actually says in one place, "Abductive inference shades into perceptual judgment without any sharp line of demarcation between them" (Peirce, 1902, p. 304).

Perception is Abduction in Layers, Computational Model of Abduction in Layers, Multi-sense Perception, and Knowledge from Perception are by John R. Josephson. Speech Understanding as Layered Abduction is by John R. Josephson and Terry Patten. Three Pilot Speech Recognition Systems has contributions from John R. Josephson, Richard Fox, Osamu Fujimura, Donna Erickson, and Kevin Lenzo.

Also, computational models of information processing for both vision and spoken language understanding have commonly supposed an orderly progression of layers, beginning near the retina or auditory periphery, where hypotheses are formed about "low-level" features, e.g., edges (in vision) or bursts (in speech perception), and proceeding by stages to higher level hypotheses. Models intended to be comprehensive often suppose three or more major layers, often with sublayers, and sometimes with parallel channels that separate and combine to support higher level hypotheses. For example, shading discontinuities and color contrasts may separately support hypotheses about object boundary (Marr, 1982). Recent work on primate vision appears to show the existence of separate channels for information about shading, texture, and color, not all supplying information to the same layers of interpretation (Livingstone & Hubel, 1988). Audition, phonetics, grammar, and semantics have sometimes been proposed as distinct layers of interpretation for speech understanding.

In both vision and speech understanding most of the processing of information is presumably bottom up, from information produced by the sensory organ, through intermediate representations, to the abstract cognitive categories that are used for reasoning. Yet top-down processing is presumably also significant, as higher level information imposes biases and helps with identification and disambiguation. Both vision and speech understanding can thus be thought of as layered-interpretation tasks wherein the output from one layer becomes data to be interpreted at the next. Layered-interpretation models for nonperceptual interpretive processes make sense too. For example, medical diagnosis can be thought of as an inference that typically proceeds from symptoms to pathological states to diseases to etiologies. Similar to perception, medical diagnosis is presumably mostly bottom up, but with a significant amount of top-down processing serving similar functions.

It is reasonable to expect that perceptual processes have been optimized over evolutionary time (become efficient, not necessarily optimal) and that the specific layers and their hypotheses, especially at lower levels, have been compiled into special-purpose mechanisms. Within the life span of a single organism, language learning and perceptual learning provide additional opportunities for compilation and optimization. Nevertheless, it seems that at each layer of interpretation the abstract information-processing task is the same: that of forming a coherent, composite best explanation of the data from the previous layer or layers. That is, the task is abduction, and, in particular, abduction requiring the formation of composite hypotheses.

If the information processing that occurs in the various layers and senses is functionally similar, then perhaps their mechanisms are similar too at a certain level of description. Thus we are led to hypothesize that the information-processing mechanisms that occur in vision, in hearing, in understanding spoken language, and in interpreting information from other senses (natural and robotic) are all variations, incomplete realizations, or compilations (domain-specific optimizations) of one basic computational mechanism. Thus we propose what we may call the *layered-abduction model of perception*. What is new in this model is the specific hypothesis that perception uses abductive inferences, occurring in layers, together with a specific computational model of abductive processing.

Perception as compiled deliberation

Thinking of perception as inferential is not to suppose that perception uses deliberative reasoning. The abductive inferences that we hypothesize to occur in perception are presumably very efficient, with little explicit search at run time (perception time). Moreover, some of the parts of abductive processing might not be fully realized by actual processing at run time, or they may be done very efficiently with no extraneous support processing. For example, alternative hypotheses may be prestored, and simply activated during perception, rather than generated fresh. Similarly, hypothesis interactions, such as degrees of compatibility and incompatibility, may be prestored. This kind of storing of knowledge in just the right form for efficient task-specific processing is what we mean by "compiled" cognition. It is a kind of thinking well without thinking much.

Cognition might be compiled either as "software" or as "hardware" (or in some intermediate "firmware" form). Moreover, compilation might be done by evolution, or through some sort of learning, or incrementally as needed for perception-time processing. Hardware-compiled structures are presumably not plastic, whereas learned structures can be subsequently revised (in principle anyway). Thus particular abductive mechanisms might be formed either by evolution, or by learning, or at run time.

The point of compilation for perception is to avoid computationally expensive run-time search. This can be done by compiling hypothesis fragments and evidential links, as we said. These evidential links may be implemented by currents that run along wires, by firing rates of connections between neurons, by weighted symbol associations, or in some other way; but however they are implemented, they will still really be evidential links (that is, this level of description is not dispensable).

Thus, one way in which perception may plausibly be hypothesized to be very much like deliberation is that the steps and dependencies should make sense logically (abductively). Each piece of processing should be justifiable in ways such as ". . . is apparently the only plausible interpretation for this datum," ". . . combine to make this hypothesis better than that one," ". . . was ruled out because . . .," and so on.

Another bridge to deliberative reasoning is that functionally similar kinds of impasses can occur during processing. Each such impasse creates a need to fall back on some other form of processing, and provides an opportunity to learn. One type of impasse occurs when there are no good hypotheses to account for a firmly established data item. In this case (if there is time) a deliberative strategy might be to derive a new hypothesis with the needed properties from background causal knowledge. Apparently this goes on in diagnosis in domains where there are good causal models of the system being diagnosed. Another way to handle this type of impasse is first to capture a description of the data to be accounted for, to assume that it can be accounted for by a new hypothesis-forming concept C, and to begin to build up more description of C based upon what can be inferred or reasonably conjectured from the context. This additional analysis presumably occurs not so much immediately at run time in the heat of the original problem solving, but shortly thereafter at learn time, when run-time information is still available but urgency has subsided and resources are available for more expensive processing. This learning strategy is neutral between deliberative and perceptual abduction. In a speech-recognition system we would like to build someday, we propose to capture new words in this way. First the system will detect that it has no word in the lexicon that accounts for a particular word-sized phonetic hunk, then it will capture the phonetic description, hypothesizing that it represents a new word, and it will begin to derive information about the grammatical role of the new word from the linguistic context (e.g., is it a name? a person's name?).

Even in "high cognition," abductive processing is presumably very perception-like in the main. An experienced diagnostician should rarely need to reason "from first principles," but instead will have compiled useful information and organized it for efficient access so that run-time processing is "automated," and recognition-like. On this view (from this perspective, seeing things this way) the visual metaphors that we use for intellectual insight are more than simply apt metaphors. We hypothesize *literal isomorphisms of computational architecture and information processing* between perception and deliberative abduction.[1]

Besides the reliance on some nearly serial computational resource (attention perhaps), deliberative abduction is presumably so much slower than perception because it tends to generate certain subtasks for which efficient knowledge has not been precompiled. "Who could have done this awful crime? Well, let's see . . ." (need to generate hypotheses); "Could this patient's symptoms be due to overconsumption of vitamin B_6?" (need to generate recognition patterns, i.e., hypothesis-scoring knowledge); "What is the main function of sleep?" (need to generate at least one plausible hypothesis); "Is it a genuine need for help? Or just complaining?" (need to generate a way to discriminate between alternative explanations).

A good example of compiled abduction in perception is three-dimensional vision. The data to be explained are the disparities between the images presented by the two eyes; the explanatory hypotheses are something like over-lapping planes (i.e., front-back relationships across edge boundaries).

Computational model of abduction in layers

Machine 6: Layers of Machine 5s

The layered-abduction computational model is our sixth-generation abstract abduction machine. Machine 6 is similar to Machine 5 (chapter 9) except that composite hypotheses are formed in several places at once in a coordinated manner. We call each locus of hypothesis formation an *agora* after the marketplace where the ancient Greeks gathered for dialog and debate. The idea is that an agora is a place where hypotheses of a certain type gather and contend and where, under good conditions, a consensus hypothesis emerges. In typical cases the emerging hypothesis will be a composite, coherent in itself, and with different subhypotheses accounting for different portions of the data. For example in vision the *edge agora* is the presumed location where edge hypotheses are formed and accepted; each specific edge hypothesis accounting for certain specific data from lower level agoras.

The agoras are organized in an information-flow network with a clear sense of direction defining the difference between bottom-up and top-down flow. Bottom up is from data to interpretation. The main output from an agora is "upward," the data to be interpreted by "higher" agoras. Another possible output is "downward," for example expectation might influence the consideration and evaluation of hypotheses at lower agoras. Thus the relationship between "data" and "explanation" is a relative one, and an explanation accepted at one agora becomes data to be explained at the next. Although we sometimes use the word "layer" to describe an agora or a contiguous cluster of agoras, we do not suppose that the agoras are all neatly lined up. The paths may branch and join (but no cycles are permitted).

We suppose that the information processing at each agora is decomposed into three functionally distinct types of activity: *evocation of hypotheses*, *instantiation of hypotheses*, and *composition of hypotheses*.

Evocation can occur bottom up, a hypothesis being stimulated for consideration – cued – by the data presented at a layer below. In diagnosis we would say that the presence of a certain finding suggests that certain hypotheses are appropriate to consider. More than one hypothesis may be suggested by a given datum. Evocation can also occur top down, either as the result of *priming* (an expectation from a level above) or as a consequence of data-seeking activity from above, which can arise from the need for evaluation (e.g., in diagnosis a need to evaluate a disease hypothesis might cause the hypothesis elevated-white-blood-count to be considered). Evocations can generally be performed in parallel and need not be synchronized. Besides these pointed evocations of hypotheses from below or above, if potential hypotheses are organized hierarchically according to specificity, exhaustive search can be performed efficiently for all applicable hypotheses. (See chapter 2 regarding the establish-refine strategy for hierarchical classification.)

Instantiation occurs when each stimulated hypothesis is independently scored for confidence (*evaluation*) and a determination is made of what part or aspect of the data the hypothesis can account for (*determination of explanatory scope*). Instantiation is in general top down.[2] During instantiation, data may be sought that were not part of the original stimulus for evoking a hypothesis. Each hypothesis is given a confidence value on some scale, which can be taken to be a "local-match" or prima facie likelihood, a likelihood of being true based only on consideration of the match between the hypothesis and the data, with no consideration of interactions between potentially rival or otherwise related hypotheses. Typically, many evoked hypotheses receive low scores and can be tentatively eliminated from further consideration. The data that a hypothesis accounts for may or may not be identical to the data used to score the hypothesis or the data that evoked it.

During instantiation, the hypothesis set may be expanded by including subtypes and supertypes of high-confidence hypotheses, if the space of potential hypotheses is organized hierarchically by level of specificity. Instantiation is most efficient when it is done by matching against prestored patterns of features, but slower processes of instantiation are also possible whereby the features to match are generated at run time.

The result of a wave of instantiation activity is a set of hypotheses, each with a measure of confidence, and each offering to account for a portion of the data. Within a particular wave of instantiation, hypotheses are considered independently of one another, so this can go on in parallel.

Composition occurs when the instantiated hypotheses interact with one another and (under good conditions) a coherent best interpretation emerges. At first, many hypotheses will probably have intermediate scores, representing hypotheses that can be taken neither as practically certain nor as of such low confidence as to be ignorable. So knowledge of interactions between the hypotheses is brought to bear to reduce the degree of uncertainty, increasing confidence in some of them, and decreasing confidence in others. The basic strategy is to try to solve the overall abduction problem at a given agora by solving a sufficient number of smaller and easier abductive subproblems at that agora. The strategy used is basically that of Machine 5, described in chapter 9.

The Machine 5 strategy begins the composition process by tentatively accepting the highest confidence, small abductive conclusions that can be identified and then propagating the logical consequences of that acceptance along known lines of hypothesis interaction. If the hypothesis composition process stalls after accepting the highest confidence conclusions and propagating the consequences, and some data remain ambiguous, then the process can be continued by accepting somewhat less confident conclusions, and again propagating the consequences. The process halts when all data are interpreted or when the remaining unexplained data are too ambiguous to be discriminated with sufficient confidence (see chapter 9 for a fuller description). In the layered-abduction, Machine 6 model, it is also possible that remaining ambiguities will be resolved later, either as a result of additional processing stimulated by downward-flowing expectations from layers above or by reverberations of downward processing appearing later as revisions flowing upward from below.

Regions of data are ambiguous if, for each datum, more than one viable hypothesis exists, and no distinctly best interpretation can be chosen given the current evidence. Regions of ambiguous data (or equivalently, the corresponding sets of alternative hypotheses with no distinctly best combination) can be the targets of further data gathering, guided by the need to discriminate between the leading hypotheses. In medical diagnosis we might order more tests to try to resolve the differential diagnosis problem; in active vision we might take another look in the region of the ambiguous perception; in empirical science we might design and perform a crucial experiment. Further data gathering is governed by pragmatics – whether resolving the ambiguity is important for currently active goals.

Top-down information flow

Downward-flowing information processing between layers can occur in at least four ways. One is that the data-seeking needs of hypothesis evaluation or discrimination can provoke instantiation (top-down evocation and evaluation of a hypothesis). Another is that expectations based on firmly established hypotheses at one layer can prime certain data items (i.e., evoke consideration of them and bias their scores upwards). A third way is that hypotheses that are uninterpretable as data at the higher level (no explanation can be found) can be "doubted," and reconsideration of them provoked (also reconsideration of any higher level hypotheses whose confidence depended on the questionable datum can be provoked). Finally, data pairs that are jointly uninterpretable (e.g., two words, the co-occurrence of which cannot be reconciled syntactically or semantically) can be considered to be incompatible (to some degree of strength), and reconsideration can be provoked from above. In these ways higher level interpretations can exert a strong influence on the formation of hypotheses at lower levels, and layer-layer harmony is a two-sided negotiation.

Recovering from mistakes

Abductive inferences are fallible. The mechanism described here can minimize the occurrence of certain mistakes and can recover from certain errors that do occur. We discuss two types of errors: mistakes in initial hypothesization and scoring, and mistakes in choice of initial islands of confidence.

Mistakes in initial hypothesization and scoring.

1. Hypothesis suggestions come from above as well as below, thus hypotheses that would be missed on bottom-up processing can still be considered.
2. If initially cued hypotheses are inadequate, either because some portion of the data has no proposed interpretation or because all hypotheses score poorly, exhaustive search, hierarchically organized for efficiency, can be undertaken to broaden the set of hypotheses being considered (supposing that the hypothesis space is organized hierarchically).
3. Hypothesis evaluation is augmented by encouragement and discouragement from positive and negative associations with other hypotheses in the same agora. This occurs as part of the hypothesis-composition processing common to Machine 5 and Machine 6. Thus the initial local-match confidence score is improved by contextual information.
4. Hypothesis evaluation is also augmented by encouragement and discouragement based on expectations from confident higher level hypotheses. This constitutes another kind of context-based improvement and check on the confidence score.
5. A hypothesis is accepted according to how well it surpasses explanatory alternatives. Thus, after recognition-based scoring, a significant additional uncertainty-reducing operation (based on explanatory relationships) is performed before acceptance.
6. Strength of confidence is supported by "the consilience of inductions,"[3] whereby converging lines of inference all support the same hypothesis. Thus hypothesis scoring should not be excessively sensitive to single factors, and overall system performance should be robust.
7. Acceptance, when it finally occurs, is still tentative and liable to be overthrown by relationships to the mass of other confident hypotheses or because of an unresolved anomaly.

Mistakes in choice of initial islands of confidence.

1. Actually the islands are strong. They are never based only on a hypothesis having high initial confidence; a hypothesis must also be a best explanation for some datum.
2. Inconsistencies lead to detected anomalies, which lead to special strategies that weigh alternative courses of action. Originally accepted hypotheses can collide with others and subsequently be called into question.
3. Inconsistency collisions can occur laterally or from above (violation of expectation) and they can come in degrees of strength. In effect there is broad cross-checking of accepted hypotheses.
4. An inexplicable datum can be doubted and called into question. If after reevaluation the datum remains strong despite the doubt, then the system can detect that it has encountered the limits of its knowledge, and it is positioned to learn a new hypothesis category.
5. Sometimes two parts of a compound hypothesis are inconsistent in context , that is, a consistent hypothesis cannot be formed at the next highest level. (It seems that this can account for unstable perceptual objects such as the Necker

cube.) Under these circumstances special handling takes over, similar to that for other kinds of detected inconsistencies.

Notice the level of description that we gave for Machine 6. It might be implemented as an *algorithmic computer* – an instruction follower – or as a *connectionist computer*, whose primitive processing elements work by propagating activations. We described the functional and semantic significance of various actions of the machine, and the flow of control, but we did not describe precisely how these actions are implemented on an underlying machine.

Summary of the control strategy

We may summarize the Machine 6 control strategy for hypothesis composition by saying that it employs multilevel and multiple intralevel island-driven processing. Islands of relative certainty are seeded by local abductions and propagate laterally (incompatibilities, positive associations), downward (expectations), and upward (accepted hypotheses become data to be accounted for). Processing occurs concurrently and in a distributed fashion. Higher levels provide *soft* constraints through the impact of expectations on hypothesis evocation and scoring, but this does not strictly limit the hypotheses that may be accepted at lower levels.

This control strategy is somewhat similar to that of the HEARSAY-II speech-understanding system (Erman & Lesser, 1980; Hayes-Roth & Lesser, 1977), which had a layered blackboard upon which hypotheses were suggested, tested, and composed, and where they triggered the formation of further hypotheses. One important difference is that our model replaces the general-purpose blackboard with a control structure designed specifically for layered, interpretive, inferential tasks. Although our control structure could in principle be implemented on a blackboard machine, doing so would impose an unnecessary and undesirable centralization of control. A second important difference is that HEAR-SAY-II's "islands of certainty" were based simply on the highest scoring hypotheses rather than on hypotheses whose initial scores were significantly higher than alternatives for explaining some datum (our Essentials and Clear-Bests). That is, HEARSAY-II's initial acceptance was "recognition driven," rather than "abduction seeded," thus producing initial hypotheses that were not very secure. As a result, HEARSAY-II encountered a significant computational expense from backtracking, and did not scale up well.

Speech understanding as layered abduction

Overall the speech-understanding task is that of inferring what the speaker is intending to communicate, based on the evidence of the acoustic signal (and also typically relying on information from other sources, e.g., visual evidence, information about the situation, etc.). This process of inference uses many sorts of knowledge: knowledge about the speaker, knowledge about the world, and also, importantly, knowledge of the language that is being spoken. It is not hard to see this as one big abductive inference. The speaker's intention to communicate something results, by a sort of rapid skillful planning, in purposive articulatory behavior of the speech organs, and from this behavior the intended sounds of speech result. To infer the speaker's intent, we infer back up the causal chain from effects to causes, from the raw data of the acoustic signal to its causes in the intentions of the speaker. Thus we infer from data to causal explanations of the data and make abductions.

From this perspective "speech recognition" is somewhat misnamed. Words are not so much *recognized in* sounds as they are *inferred from* them. One difference this makes is whether, in designing automatic speech recognition, we should be searching for acoustic invariants by which linguistic units can be directly recognized. It appears that there are no such simple acoustic invariants, and that something inferentially more complex than simple recognition is probably required. The acoustic manifestations of a /p/ are very different depending on whether it is word-initial or word-final and whether it follows another consonant such as /s/. However, a /p/ is always accompanied by a closing of the lips; so if there are invariants to be exploited for recognition, they are more likely to be articulatory invariants than acoustic ones.

Strata for spoken language understanding

The acoustic manifestations of spoken language are highly variable and context dependent, varying according to principles that are poorly understood. Three important interacting sources of variability are prosodic effects (stress, intonation, phrasing effects, and related phenomena), articulatory effects, and variability due to the nonlinear nature of sound production from articulation. These are probably the largest impediments to robust computer-based recognition of natural speech.

We present here a model of spoken language understanding that is intended to describe human information processing, and that is also a proposal about how humanlike speech understanding can be done by computer.[4,5] Human language-understanding abilities are rich and complicated, and any computer-based imitation of them can also be expected to be rich and complicated; also extremely large.

We hypothesize that the major layers, or *strata*, of interpretation for spoken language understanding are these six: acoustic, auditory, phonetic, phonological-prosodic, grammatical, and pragmatic (see Figure 10.1). Within each stratum multiple types of information are represented, organized either as parallel channels or as *ranks* of a constituent hierarchy. Within each rank

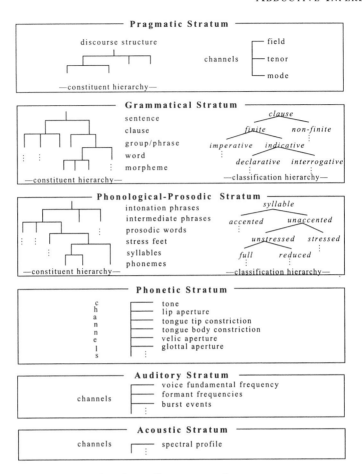

Figure 10.1. Speech understanding representations.

the units are organized into a classification hierarchy. For example, as shown
in Figure 10.1, the grammatical stratum has these ranks: sentence, clause,
phrase, word, and morpheme; clauses can be classified as finite or nonfinite
and even further subclassified. Composite hypotheses are formed at each
rank and channel by processes that are abductive inferences, both logically
and procedurally (and thus go beyond simply recognition and classification). The direction of *interpretive* inferences is from bottom towards top,
whereas the direction of inference based on *expectation* is from the top down.
Let us describe each of the six strata in more detail.

Acoustic stratum. At the bottom is the acoustic stratum of time-varying features extracted from the acoustic wave by the human auditory system. The
acoustic stratum produces representations primarily of the spectral characteristics of the input signal as a function of time.

Auditory stratum. Next is the auditory stratum, which takes its input from the acoustic stratum and derives information specifically relevant to speech perception, such as voice fundamental frequency, formant frequencies, and burst events. It is likely that information processing between the acoustic and auditory strata has the procedural characteristics of specialized signal processing rather than abductive inference, but from this stratum up, the information processing is explicitly abductive.

Phonetic stratum. Next is the phonetic stratum, which represents speech-production activity as a *gestural score* of articulatory states and events, such as lip closure, nasality, and vowel backing (Browman & Goldstein, 1989). These events are inferred from the outputs of the auditory-processing stratum. Thus our model supposes what is sometimes called the "motor theory of speech perception," namely, that some sort of representation of the processes of speech *production* participates in the processes of speech *perception*.

Phonological-prosodic stratum. At the phonological-prosodic stratum a representation is produced of constituents at various ranks of a prosodic tree that groups phonemes[6] into syllables, syllables into stress feet, and so on up to the level of intonation phrases (see Figure 10.1). The detection of larger phonological constituents such as stress feet allows a human or a computer to focus on the parts of the utterance in which salient information is likely to be concentrated. For example, once it is recognized that a given stretch of the speech signal corresponds to a stressed syllable, hypothesis evaluation involving the recognition of precise vowel quality and the like can be concentrated on this stretch, where the vowel is likely to be fully articulated.

Grammatical stratum. The outputs of the phonological-prosodic stratum are used to infer information at the grammatical stratum, which represents syntactic and semantic relationships such as word meanings and case. There are five ranks within the grammatical stratum: morpheme, word, phrase, clause, and sentence. Using Halliday's systemic grammar (Halliday, 1985; Winograd, 1983) relations can be specified between any of the ranks at the grammatical stratum and any of the ranks at the phonological-prosodic stratum.

Each category at each rank is described by a classification hierarchy. The model includes a clause hierarchy, a nominal-group hierarchy, a prepositional-phrase hierarchy, a noun hierarchy, and so on. Associated with each class in each hierarchy are realization rules that describe either interrank realization (e.g., ordering of constituents) or interstratal realization (e.g., constraining how a grammatical constituent is realized prosodically). Note that the abduction mechanism can use these realization rules in four ways: to trigger consideration of grammatical hypotheses by the presence of relevant lower level features by which they are realized, for scoring grammatical hypotheses by the presence and absence of the relevant features, for evoking or promoting lower level hypotheses in a top-down manner according to expectations from above (more on this later), and for higher level hypotheses to account for features found to occur at lower ranks or strata.

Pragmatic stratum. Last is the pragmatic stratum. The grammatical structure from the stratum below can be used to infer attributes of the pragmatic context, such as the social relationship between speaker and hearer and the role of the utterance in the discourse. Our model emphasizes compiled relationships between pragmatics and the other strata and de-emphasizes explicit reasoning about beliefs and intentions.

A *register* (Halliday, 1978) is the restricted language that is used in a particular social context. Even general clues about the register can greatly improve the ability of hearers to interpret speech input (Bruce, 1958). Register knowledge is organized by *field*, the setting and propositional content, *tenor*, the social relationship between the speaker and hearer, and *mode*, whether the language is spontaneously spoken or read aloud, and so forth.

Three pilot speech recognition systems

We have conducted three pilot studies so far to investigate the use of layered abduction for speech recognition. The Machine 6 model was used as a guide to the choice of representations, the structure of modularization, and the strategies for the control of processing. Three experimental systems were constructed: CV recognized isolated consonant-vowel monosyllables from acoustic input, 3-Level inferred words from qualitative descriptions of articulatory gestures, and ArtRec, still under development, infers words from X-ray traces of articulation. These systems have been limited in scope, able to handle only a small range of phonetic material. Nevertheless, the results so far have been encouraging, both for the workability of the layered-abduction computational model and for its applicability to speech recognition.

CV and 3-Level

CV was a first step in using abduction for speech recognition from acoustic signals.[7] The system had many interesting features, including abductive formant trackers that worked by assembling consistent hypotheses to explain spectral peaks at each time slice.[8] CV demonstrated that a multicriterial, feature-based recognizer can produce reasonable accuracy where the acoustic correlates of phonetic features are fairly well understood. Yet it appears to be difficult to determine place of articulation in any direct way from acoustic evidence, at least not with any reliability. (*Place of articulation* is where the vocal tract is constricted to produce a consonant, e.g., it is the basis for the difference between /b/, /d/, and /g/.) However, the system used a classification hierarchy for its hypotheses. So, for example, even when it was unable to distinguish between /b/ and /d/, it could nevertheless confidently identify the sound as a voiced stop consonant (which might be good enough in some contexts). Although CV used separate abducers for formant tracking and for arriving at its final output, it was not really a layered-abduction machine in the sense of the Machine 6 model.

The 3-Level system was a first attempt to use abduction to infer words from articulatory input, one of the interlayer inferences called for by the model of speech processing described earlier in this chapter.[9] It was also a first attempt to stack abducers into a multilevel machine and to try top-down processing. The system inferred phonemes from articulation and words from phonemes, thus using two levels of abductive interpretation to bridge three levels of representation.[10] The input was a (hand-coded) gestural score (Browman & Goldstein, 1989) of articulatory events laid out over time, including such events as lip closure, tongue lowering, and onset of voicing. Taking the articulatory events as data to be explained, the system evoked phoneme hypotheses and then rated these hypotheses according to prestored knowledge of associations (positive and negative) of phonemes with articulatory events. It then assembled a best explanation (using the PEIRCE-IGTT version of the abductive-assembly strategy described in chapter 9). (The entire system was built using the IGT toolset.) The best explanation accepted at the phoneme agora became data to be explained at the word agora, where a similar process of hypothesis evocation, scoring, and composition occurred. The output was a word or set of words that explained the input gestures.[11]

With accurate inputs, the system had no difficulty finding the correct phonemes and then the correct words. Layered abduction worked. With "dirty" inputs (perturbations introduced by hand), performance degraded as expected. When knowledge of incompatibles and implications was added, performance on dirty inputs improved significantly. Thus the mechanisms for using these forms of knowledge also functioned as expected.

Finally, a form of top-down discrimination was encoded. Sometimes more than one equally rated word hypothesis offered to account for approximately the same stretch of phonemes. In one example, "beet," "boot," and "bat" were the only alternatives, and they were equally rated. This sort of situation triggered a reevaluation of the unknown phoneme by which they differed, in this case the middle vowel. In this example the matter had been left unresolved at the phoneme agora because the two rivals /I/ and /er/ could not be distinguished (the tongue was high, but how far back was indefinite). "Beet" wanted the vowel /I/, "boot" wanted /uw/, and "bat" wanted /æ/. Intersecting the possibilities from above and below, /I/ was the only remaining possibility, so /I/ was chosen at the phoneme agora, causing the word "beet" to win. (The processing strategy was actually encoded as top-down expectation-based encouragement for the remaining possibilities from above, which made /I/ the winner.) Thus a definite improvement was demonstrated for this form of top-down processing.

3-Level was able to find word boundaries by trading off alternative word-level explanations for the occurrence of phonemes. The choice between word-boundary locations is a byproduct of the choice between alternative composite word-level hypotheses. This is especially interesting because, with current technology, computer-based interpretation of continuous speech lags far behind computer-based recognition of isolated words precisely because word boundaries are not well marked acoustically (in English at least). Our abductive machinery even (properly) allows a phoneme to belong to two different words at the same time; so, for example, the middle /s/ in "six stones" can be explained as belonging to both words (just as in RED a reaction may be explained by the presence of two different antibodies).

ArtRec: Word recognition from articulation

The initial setup. ArtRec is a more sophisticated multilayered abductive system, using actual measurements of articulatory activity as input instead of the hand-coded gestural scores used by 3-Level.[12] The measurements were acquired from the Wisconsin X-ray Microbeam facility (Fujimura, Ishida, & Kiritani 1973). Data from the microbeam consists of traces of the positions of small gold pellets glued to various articulators and tracked as a person speaks. Typical locations for the pellets are the tongue tip, tongue blade, tongue dorsum, lower lip, and mandible incisor; however, the number and exact location of the pellets vary from speaker to speaker. Pellet-position data were smoothed by a low-pass filter before input to ArtRec. Note that there was no acoustic input and that the pellets provide no information about voicing or nasality.

The data used for the initial series of experiments consisted of 14-word utterances of the form "Is it nine five five Pine Street? No, it's nine five NINE Pine Street," in which "five" and "nine" occurred in various combinations, and negative and positive answers were given. (A positive answer was "Yes, it's nine five five Pine Street.") In negative answers, the speaker emphasized the corrected word (the final "NINE" in the negative sentence just described). Each utterance was approximately 5 seconds in length and was composed entirely of words from a 9-word lexicon consisting of "is," "it," "five," "nine," "Pine," "Street," "it's," "no" and "yes."

How ArtRec works. The task of ArtRec is to infer the words, and to determine which word, if any, is being emphasized. A three-layered abduction system is used, consisting of three layers of representation with two abductive transitions between them. Each abductive transition uses the basic strategy of evocation, instantiation, and composition of hypotheses.

The first findings to be explained are the motions of the pellets, represented by their extremes, and evident as peaks and valleys in the horizontal and vertical components of the pellet motions (viewed from the side of the head). The available explanatory hypotheses are qualitative vocal tract gestures, including apical (alveolar) closure, labial closure, labiodental closure, dorsal closure, tongue-forward, tongue retroflection, tongue lowering, tongue blade retraction, tongue high and front, mandible low, tongue dorsal forward, and palatal-glide tongue motion. Motion extremes that surpass preset thresholds cue gestures that might explain them. Gestures are then scored by comparison with ideal forms of the gestures and based on the presence and absence of other relevant pellet-motion features. An eventual attempt is made to explain all peaks and valleys no matter how extreme (whether they pass a threshold or not), but certain hypotheses are plausible only if the events of interest have surpassed a threshold. (Apical closure, for example, requires that the tongue tip is raised far enough to reach the alveolar ridge.) Usually, many more gesture hypotheses are cued than are needed to explain a particular peak or valley.

The gesture hypotheses receive initial plausibility scores based on pellet-motion features chosen by human examination of the pellet data. We identified necessary, impossible, and other positively and negatively associated features. A gesture receives a high confidence score if all the necessary features and none of the impossible features are present; it receives a lower score if necessary features are missing or if impossible features occur. Then, other associated features are checked, and small additional alterations to the confidence score may be made.

After initial plausibility scoring, the system determines what each gesture hypothesis can explain. The cueing of a gesture hypothesis is based on the pellet motions necessarily associated with the gesture, but typically other motions can be accounted for as well. For example, apical closure requires that the tongue tip be raised, but apical closure can also explain other motions such as the tongue blade being raised.

Besides articulatory-gesture hypotheses, *noise* hypotheses are generated and can be used to explain portions of the data. The articulatory data are inherently noisy because of the need to minimize X-ray exposures of the subjects. In addition, some motions of the articulators are unintentional or in other ways are not a result of linguistic control. These nonlinguistic phenomena are treated simply as noise (i.e., apparent pellet motions not best explained as gestures). Noise hypotheses are treated as explanatory hypotheses, much like any others. A noise hypothesis has a modest initial plausibility (which depends on various factors), and will be accepted if, in context, it is the best explanation for some datum.

After evocation and scoring of noise and gesture hypotheses, the first abducer is run. This abducer generates a composite hypothesis consisting of gesture and noise hypotheses and constituting a best explanation for the pellet motions. Typically 75 to 100 gesture hypotheses and 25 to 50 noise hypotheses are generated. The abducer prunes this down to only 25 to 50, which together constitute the best gesture-level explanation for the pellet data in the 5-second utterance. This hypothesis then becomes data to be explained at the word level.

A word is hypothesized to be centered at each point where the mouth is maximally open. This is detected as a point where the mandible (jaw) reaches a local low point. This simple method works largely because all the words in our initial lexicon are monosyllables, and it cannot be expected to work for polysyllabic words (though it may be a good way to cue consonant-vowel-consonant syllables in a future system).

For each hypothesized word location, all the gestures nearby are clustered and are used to cue word hypotheses. The word hypotheses are then scored based on the presence, absence, and temporal ordering of gestures of interest in that cluster. For example, the word "nine" expects two alveolar closures surrounding a tongue-blade lowering gesture. If these are found, the "nine" hypothesis is scored as highly plausible, unless unexpected or impossible gestures are found nearby. The word "nine" would not expect labial closure; in fact it is impossible to pronounce the word "nine" with one's lips closed. The presence of unexpected gestures lowers the plausibility score to one degree or another.

The next step is to determine the gestures that each word hypothesis can explain. As usual, word hypotheses can account for more gestures than just those that are used to score the hypotheses.

Word hypotheses that overlap too much in time are set to be incompatible because two words cannot be uttered simultaneously. Incompatibility relationships are subsequently used to reduce ambiguity, according to the abductive-assembly strategy that was described in chapter 9.

Besides word hypotheses, this level, too, has noise hypotheses, which may be used to explain gestures not explained by any word. Even if a gesture is correctly accepted at the lower level as part of the best explanation, there is no guarantee that the gesture is actually part of a word. Such gestures may be well formed but unintentional, or they may be byproducts of motions associated with preceding or succeeding gestures, or they may be manifestations of a speaker who is nervous, who is tired, who is excited, or who speaks idiosyncratically. ArtRec covers for all these possibilities by judiciously using explicit noise hypotheses to account for data items that have, in context, no better alternative explanations. Noise hypotheses are introduced automatically as possible explanations for gestures that were not given high plausibility scores. They are also introduced if all the word hypotheses score poorly. Noise hypotheses are set to be incompatible with word hypotheses that are attempting to explain the same gestures.

Using the word and noise hypotheses, the second abducer forms a best explanation of the gestures accepted by the previous abducer. The abductive-assembly strategy at both levels is the strategy described in chapter 9. In particular, the abducers accept Confirmed, Essential, Clear-Best, and Weak-Best hypotheses, but they do not go any further in attempting to resolve ties between equally plausible hypotheses (e.g., by voting).

After forming a composite word-level hypothesis, mandible motion is used to determine which word (if any) was emphasized in the utterance. The emphasized word is one in which the mandible movement is exaggerated (i.e., significantly larger than the mandible movement of other words surrounding it).

Experimental results. Before describing the results we want to point out that the lexicon is very small, but tricky, because there are many close articulatory similarities among the words. For example, "five," "nine," and "pine" are very difficult to distinguish because there are no acoustic inputs to indicate voicing, nasality, or the acoustic bursts indicative of stop consonants. This lexicon was chosen because we wanted to explore the phenomenon of corrective emphasis.

Five sets of speaker data were initially acquired from the Wisconsin Microbeam facility. Each of the five English speakers uttered 80 different question-answer pairs, using all the combinations of "five" and "nine," and using affirmative and negative assertion patterns, as described earlier in the subsection entitled The Initial Setup.

After creating the initial ArtRec system using the integrated generic task toolset and PEIRCE-IGTT (described in chapter 9), we tested it on 20 utterances from a single speaker. This testing required examining the pellet data and tuning the recognition (hypothesis-scoring) knowledge to the specifics of the individual speaker. Speakers differ not only in the dimensions of their articulatory apparatuses, but also in the number and exact placements of the gold pellets. After the system was run on the 20 utterances, the mistakes were analyzed, and a process of retuning began. After some time the system achieved approximately 90% accuracy on the 20 utterances. The next step was to run the system on all the utterances of that speaker (60 more). This required further tuning and testing, but eventually all 80 cases were run. Results were again in the 90% range.

The next step was to use the system on the data from a different speaker. Frustratingly, this required making further modifications to the system. As a consequence, the system was redesigned so that almost all speaker differences could be handled by setting a small number of parameters, primarily threshold values for recognizing gestures from pellet positions. Tuning these parameters to each new speaker is an iterative process of examining the new pellet data, setting parameters, testing, and adjusting again until satisfactory results are obtained. This was done for each new speaker. Finally, the system had been tuned for all five speaker sets, and all the data were run through the system. Results were encouraging although not entirely satisfying. Consequently, the system was redesigned to work as described earlier in the subsection entitled How ArtRec Works. Let us briefly examine the differences between the initial system (the one just described tuned for all five speaker sets) and the redesigned system.

First, the initial system had a single abduction layer. The same three levels of representations were used – pellet motions, articulatory gestures, and words – but the transition from motions to gestures was simply recognition-based and did not use abductive assembly. That is, gesture hypotheses were generated and scored, but all hypotheses that were not ruled out (lowest score) were passed upward to be explained at the word agora by an explicitly abductive process. The result was that many more gesture hypotheses were generated than were needed to explain the data, and many more than were actually true. The single abducer then attempted to explain all these gestures with word hypotheses. Because of the lack of explicit explanatory relationships at the motions-to-gestures transition, and because there was no attempt to explain the motions, no noise hypotheses were generated. The redesigned system added a lower level abducer for explaining motion events using articulatory-gesture hypotheses, and noise hypotheses were made available.

Second, the initial system used mandible closings to locate word boundaries. This overly constrained where a word hypothesis might find its associated gestures, because gestures outside the word boundaries were not considered part of the word. Because the mandible closings were not closely synchronized with the beginnings and endings of words, this was a source of many errors. The redesigned system instead used mandible openings to locate word centers.

After the system was redesigned, the data for the five speakers were run again . The accuracy noticeably improved. These newer results are presented in Table 10.1.

Table 10.1 lists the five speakers. For each speaker it shows the total number of utterances, the total number of words that ArtRec found in all of the speaker's utterances, the number of words for which the system committed to a word identity, the number of these words that were correctly identified, the percentage of the words located that were correctly identified, and the percentage of the committed-to words that were correctly identified. An utterance consisted of the entire question-answer pair (e.g., "Is it five five nine Pine Street? No, it's NINE five nine Pine Street.") and lasted approximately 5 seconds. We had 80 utterances for each speaker, but some of these were not usable because they contained pellet-tracking errors or other forms of significantly bad data. Even for usable utterances, often words at the end were not captured in the pellet data. Consequently, the average number of words per usable utterance was approximately 11 of the 14.

Table 10.1. ArtRec performance

Speaker	Utterances	Words located	Words decided	Words correct	Located % correct	Decided % correct
5p	77	708	650	610	86.2	93.8
6pp	80	919	733	695	75.6	94.8
7p	76	820	720	689	84.0	95.7
11pp	80	848	792	762	90.0	96.2
12ppp	71	785	740	703	89.6	95.0
Total	384	4,080	3,635	3,459	84.8	95.2

The use of mandible-opening maximums was a good hypothesizer of word locations (actually syllable locations). The numbers in the Words Located column in Table 10.1, with few exceptions, reflect all the complete words recorded in the data.

ArtRec's overall accuracy was good, even allowing for the small vocabulary, considering that no acoustic information was used, that only 4 or 5 locations within the mouth were tracked, and that no information was used about nasality, voicing, duration, or context. Surprisingly, ArtRec was no more accurate at identifying emphasized words than nonemphasized words. However, it was good at identifying which word in an utterance was the emphasized one.

The system attempted to find an emphasized word only under two conditions: the word "no" had to have been found somewhere in the utterance, and the system had to be willing to commit itself to the identities of the final three numbers. That is, if the best that the system could determine was, "No it's five ??? ??? Pine Street," no emphasis determination was made. ArtRec's performance in finding the emphasized words is given in Table 10.2.

Next steps

Speech recognition from articulation is more to us than simply a real-world domain to use for experimentation with layered abduction. We intend to use it as a step towards computer-based understanding of naturally spoken language. Articulatory effects, and prosodic phenomena such as emphasis, appear to be at the core of the technical impediments to computer-based recognition of natural speech.

One of the deep, main disadvantages of the currently popular statistical approaches to speech recognition is that a prototypical linguistic unit is exaggerated, whereas a typical unit is reduced. Systems trained on the typical will tend to fail on the prototypical, so statistical systems tend to fail if something is fully pronounced. Humans, in contrast, seem to learn on the basis of prototypes and then recognize using (we believe) best-explanation inference based on redundant information present in scattered evidence. Thus,

Table 10.2. ArtRec emphasis determination

Speaker	Emphasized words	Emphasis correct	Emphasis % correct
5p	54	39	72
6pp	44	29	66
7p	31	31	100
11pp	38	35	92
12ppp	35	32	91
Total	202	166	82.2

if an utterance is near to the prototype, it is especially easy to recognize because the one explanation stands out as best. Humans can rely on the intelligence of the hearer to fill in missing detail, when it matters, which allows rapid speech and is why it is usually not important to pronounce close to the prototypes. Emphasis conveys, "let there be no mistake about identification," which is done by pronouncing close to the prototype (also more slowly and more loudly).

Osamu Fujimura recently proposed a new model of articulatory organization (the Converter/Distributor, or C/D, model), which is intended to replace traditional segment-concatenation and coarticulation models (Fujimura, 1992). The C/D model asserts systematic and computable relationships between prosodic control, fullness of articulatory gestures (reduction, completeness, degree of exaggeration), and timing of articulatory gestures. The model includes new concepts of syllable and boundary strength that have good prospects of unifying disparate prosodic phenomena. ArtRec has been influenced by the developing C/D model, and we expect ArtRec's successors to be even more strongly influenced by the C/D model as the model matures. We also anticipate that ArtRec and its successors will assist the development of the C/D model by testing it and helping to fill in the details.

We plan next to enlarge ArtRec's lexicon of words and articulatory gesture types to include approximately 50 words and most of the gestures characteristic of English. Some words will be polysyllabic, so we will introduce a layer for syllables between the layers for gestures and words. This will require introducing another abducer for the additional layer-layer transition, and will make three abductive transitions in all. We plan to add a syntactic layer soon as well. The present ArtRec system does not use top-down processing, and we plan to make some use of it before long.

Multisense perception

Combining information from different senses is functionally no different than combining information from different channels within a single sense.

The different senses are simply different channels to central, higher "senses." Separate channels within the visual system deliver up the data useful at a certain level to form hypotheses about the locations of 3-d objects; similarly, both sight and hearing can deliver up the data useful for forming hypotheses about object identity. Think of distinctive bird calls, for example, or a lecturer whose identity is uncertain.

One special problem for multisense integration is the problem of identifying a "that" delivered up by one sense, with a "that" delivered up by another. Is it one entity or two? Is the same object being seen in the infrared as that being seen in the ultraviolet? Which person is the one that is speaking? Logically, it should be possible for information derived from one sense to help with resolving distinct objects within the other sense. There is actually some evidence that vision can help hearing to separate distinct streams of tones (Massaro, 1987, p. 83) and to hear the tone stream as two distinct auditory objects.

One useful representation for multisense object perception is that of a *hot map* consisting of overlaid spatial representations (i.e., spatial representations from the different senses brought into registry or correlated into a single spatial representation). Thus, for example, a robot might bring together separate channels of information from its visual and tactile senses to form a unified spatial representation of its immediate surroundings. Such a map should be maintained continually and updated and revised as new information arrives and is interpreted. This hot map, with its symbols on it, can be seen as the resulting composite hypothesis formed at the *agora of objects in the immediate surroundings* by a process of abductive interpretation.

We can imagine computational support for multisense robot perception in the form of pattern-based recognition knowledge, in which the compiled recognition patterns for a perceptual category rely on features from more than one sense. This is analogous to medical diagnosis in which a disease is recognized from evidence from such disparate sources as laboratory tests, images, and patient history. This sort of recognition knowledge supports an *agora of the patient's disease* in much the same manner as the robot might maintain its map of objects in its surroundings. Somewhat further ahead we can envision a robot that maintains an *agora of causal understanding* whereby it monitors a complex device and continually maintains a representation of the states and causal processes going on in it. Much further ahead we can imagine a robot scientist with an *agora of theoretical understanding* where its best theories of the world are maintained.

Knowledge from perception

In chapter 1 we argued that abductions are "knowledge producing," meaning that the conclusion of an abduction is logically justified by the force of the abductive argument, and that this justification is such that the conclusion, if true, is "knowledge" in the philosophical sense. Yet abductions are fallible, so abductive conclusions are always somewhat uncertain. Thus abductions produce knowledge without absolute certainty. We pointed out that abductions are ampliative inferences that abductions can transcend the information given in their premises. We described this by saying that successful abductions are "truth producing." Beyond these abstract points of logical and conceptual analysis, we have shown by many experiments and working systems that abductive processes actually function well to yield true conclusions. Abductive processes are good at "truth finding." Conceptual analysis also reveals that abductions can produce conclusions that are more certain than any of their premises. We called this phenomenon "emergent certainty." Experiments reported in chapter 9 show that abductions are uncertainty reducing.

If perceptions are abductions, then perceptions come with implicit abductive justifications. *Veridical perceptions are knowledge.* The "conclusion" of a perception is a best explanation and is logically justified, though it might be false anyway. Perceptions have just the same sorts of vulnerabilities as scientific theories: there may be a better explanation that was not considered, or one that was mistakenly ruled out, and so forth (see the section of chapter 1 on abductive justification). Thus, perceptual "theory formation" is logically the same as scientific theory formation, and also the theory formation of diagnosticians, crash investigators, journalists, and juries. Perceptions go beyond the given information in a way similar to scientific theories; they change the vocabulary of description and make the leap from data language to theory language. Perceptual processes are explanation-seeking and explanation-accepting processes with the same characteristics as scientific reasoning of being knowledge producing, truth producing, fallible, truth finding, and uncertainty reducing. Scientific knowledge is paradigmatic of knowledge; scientific knowledge is real knowledge if anything is. Since perceptions have the same logic, perceptions are knowledge too.

Knowledge comes from experience by abduction – in science, ordinary life, and perception.

Notes

1 That is, there is an isomorphism after factoring out the subtask processing described in the text.
2 Under certain circumstances it is good enough just to score on the basis of voting by the stimulating data from below, and then no top-down processing need occur, at least for scoring. Although this strategy is less than logically ideal, it is computationally less expensive, at least in the short run. This represents a type of compilation in which accuracy is traded for quickness.
3 An idea from William Whewell, British philosopher and historian of science, 1794-1866.
4 Ideas about the lower strata have benefited greatly from discussions with Mary Beckman, Robert Fox, Lawrence Feth, and Ashok Krishnamurthy.
5 [The best performing current technology for computer speech recognition, based on Hidden Markov Models, is covertly abductive. I suggest that it can be improved by selecting hypotheses

preferentially according to the difference among the scores of the best and its alternatives, rather than by simply selecting the highest scoring hypothesis. – J. J.]

6 For many reasons we doubt that traditionally construed phonemes are an accurate way to describe speech. They serve as a placeholder here, but we expect this to be revised.

7 CV was designed by Richard Fox, Mary Beckman, Robert Fox, and John Josephson with additional contributions of linguistic, perceptual, and signal-processing expertise provided by Ashok Krishnamurthy, Jane Rauschenberg, and Benjamin Ao. The system was implemented by Richard Fox using the IGT toolset described in chapter 9. This work benefited from support from the National Science Foundation and the Defense Advanced Project Agency under grant CBT-8703745.

8 Formants are distinctive spectral concentrations characteristic of human speech sounds.

9 3-Level was designed by Richard Fox, John Josephson, and Sunil Thadani, and implemented by Richard Fox and Sunil Thadani. Linguistic expertise was provided by Mary Beckman, Robert Fox, and Benjamin Ao.

10 As we said before, we doubt that traditionally construed phonemes are an accurate way to describe human speech. However, they are good enough for these initial experiments.

11 The outputs should be considered to be prosodic rather than lexical words; that is, they are distinctive, word-sized speaking events without grammatical associations.

12 ArtRec was designed and built by Richard Fox, with some guidance from John Josephson. Kevin Lenzo assisted with the experiments and the write-up. Osamu Fujimura and Donna Erickson provided linguistic expertise and overall encouragement and support. ArtRec was implemented in Common Lisp and the IGT toolset described in Chapter 9.

Appendix A   Truth seekers

Abduction machines

In this book, we described six generations of abduction machines. Each generation's story was told by describing an abstract machine and experiments with realizations of the machine as actual computer programs. Each realization was approximate, partial, something less than a full realization of the abstract machine. Each realization was also more than the abstract machine: an actual chunk of software, a knowledge-based expert system constructed to do a job, with an abundance of insights, domain-specific solutions, and engineering shortcuts to get the job done. The abstract machines are simplified idealizations of actual software.

An abstract abduction machine is a design for a programming language for building knowledge systems. It is also a design for a tool for constructing these systems (a partial design, since a tool also has a programming environment).

Each of the six machines has a strategy for finding and accepting best explanations. Machine 6 inherits all the abilities of the earlier machines. Suppose that we connect it to abstract machines for the subtasks of hypothesis matching, hierarchical classification, and knowledge-directed data retrieval (see chapter 2). Then we conjoin abstract machines able to derive knowledge for various subtasks from certain forms of causal and structural knowledge (see chapters 5 and 8). Then we implement the whole abductive device as a program written for a problem-solving architecture, which is an abstract device of a different sort that provides control for generalized, flexible, goal-pursuing behavior (see chapter 4). The result is an abduction machine capable of the following:

- forming hypotheses by instantiation and by composition (Machine 1)
- forming maximally plausible composite hypotheses (Machine 1)
- making composite hypotheses parsimonious by removing explanatorily superfluous parts (Machine 1)
- critically evaluating hypotheses, determining their most confident parts (Machine 1)

This appendix was written by John R. Josephson.

- making use of elementary hypotheses with varying levels of specificity organized into a taxonomic hierarchy (Machine 1 with CSRL)
- justifying its conclusions (Machine 1)
- decomposing larger explanation problems into smaller ones (Machine 2)
- handling incompatible hypotheses to ensure a consistent composite explanation (Machine 2)
- flexible, opportunistic control (Machine 3)
- assembling composite hypotheses from parts that are themselves composite hypotheses (Machine 3)
- assembling low-specificity hypotheses, then controlling their refinement (Machine 3)
- using explicitly represented causal and structural knowledge to derive hypothesis-matching knowledge, to derive explanatory relationships, and to assemble causally integrated composite hypotheses (TIPS, PATHEX/ LIVER, MDX2, QUAWDS)
- processing concurrently (Machine 4)
- minimizing backtracking by forming the most confident partial conclusions first (Machine 4)
- descending gradually from higher to lower confidence partial conclusions, all the way to intelligent guessing or even arbitrary choice if necessary (Machine 4)
- forming confident partial explanations with ambiguous data left unexplained (Machine 4)
- using incompatibility relationships to reduce ambiguity and to extend partial explanations to more complete ones (Machine 5)
- handling hard and soft incompatibility and implication relationships (Machine 5)
- coordinating multiple sites of hypothesis formation while integrating bottom-up and top-down flow of information (Machine 6)
- handling noise and novelty (described with Machine 6)
- forming a composite hypothesis that follows a causal chain from effects to causes (Machines 2 and 6)

Machine 3 shows how abduction machines can have parts that are themselves abduction machines. Machine 6 shows how abduction machines can be composed of layers of communicating abduction machines and how these layered machines can be used for perception.

Machines 1 through 3 are goal-seeking machines with the primary goal of forming a complete explanation, while maintaining consistency, maximizing plausibility, and so forth. Machine 4 is transitional, and for Machines

5 and 6 the primary goal is that of explaining as much as possible while maintaining standards of confidence. All the machines are explanation seekers.

In synthetic worlds

Suppose that an explanation-seeking abduction machine is placed in a synthetic world with certain predefined characteristics. Suppose the machine is equipped with sensors that detect certain elements of the world and deliver sensory events as findings to be explained. The abduction machine is a synthetic agent in a synthetic world. Under what conditions can it infer the characteristics of its world?

We can try to answer this question by designing and building systems, proving theorems, and performing experiments, while controlling the characteristics of the worlds. By this process we turn philosophical questions about the limits of knowledge into technical questions about the behavior of information-processing systems.

Suppose that the synthetic world is changing. Instead of "snapshot" abduction we need "moving picture" abduction and a machine capable of tracking the changing conditions and of dynamically maintaining a changing representation of its world. One way to do this is with a snapshot machine able to take pictures fast enough to make a movie. A better way is with a machine that uses its best estimate of the state of the world to generate predictions, and then detects deviations from these predictions and tries to explain them. Explanations for the deviations result in revising the estimate of the world state and appropriately revising predictions.[1]

Suppose that the synthetic world has general characteristics unknown to the abductive agent. Suppose that there are unknown causal processes, hidden mechanisms, and unknown laws. Is it more difficult to design abduction machines capable of forming general theories than to design ones that form minitheories for explaining particular cases? It should be possible to design abduction machines that hypothesize empirical generalizations to explain observed regularities (see chapter 1 on how inductive generalization is abduction) and that explain empirical generalizations by hypothesizing hidden causality.

In any reasonably complex world a seeker must prioritize the search for explanations; there is simply too much to be known. Abductive agents need *pragmatic bias*. They need goals.

Suppose that the synthetic world is populated with other agents capable of abduction and prediction and of having goals and of planning to achieve them. Suppose that an agent has the goal of understanding other agents, of inferring their intentions from overt behavior (which may include linguistic behavior). Can we design abductive agents for this world? One reasonable way to form hypotheses about other agents is by analogy to oneself. (Hypothesization from analogy is described in chapter 6 and in Appendix B.) So it seems that empathy may be an important computational strategy. We should be able to investigate empathy formally and empirically by designing empathetic agents and by experimenting with software realizations of them.

Notes

1 [Harry Pople's EAGOL system does this for power-plant diagnosis and monitoring; my information comes from spoken communication; as far as I know a description has not been published. – J. J.] Also see Leake (1992). Prediction as a separate form of inference is discussed in Chapter 1.

Appendix B   Plausibility

Throughout this book we have depended in numerous ways on the idea of plausibility. It appears as "confidence value," "symbolic plausibility value," "degree of certainty," "plausibilities of elementary hypotheses," and the like.

Just what is this idea of plausibility? Can it be made precise? Is a plausibility a kind of likelihood, a kind of probability? What are the semantics? How much plausibility should be set for a given hypothesis under given circumstances? Is an objective standard possible? Does it even matter for a theory of intelligence, or for epistemology? Unfortunately, we cannot yet give definite answers to these questions.

The plausibility talk in this book is, in the first place, naturalistic. People mention plausibility when they describe their reasoning processes and when they write discussions of results in scientific papers. Plausibility talk seems to come naturally to us and is reflected in our ordinary language. Common usage allows both categorical judgments that something is or is not plausible, and graded comparative judgments, such as that one thing is "a lot" or "a little bit" more plausible than another. Throughout the work that we describe in this book we used our best judgments of when hypotheses were plausible, of how to evaluate evidence, and of how to weigh hypotheses. We were encouraged in our judgments by other people being likewise persuaded by appeals to "because it is the only plausible explanation," and "more plausible than any other explanation for the data," and the like. We were encouraged by the systems we built acting mostly according to our expectations, and producing correct answers. Thus, plausibilities seem to be naturally occurring epistemic evaluations, which we modeled in our systems. It would be good to understand this natural phenomenon better.

MDX, our earliest diagnostic system, used physician judgments as the basis for setting confidence scores. MDX used no global formula for confidence handling, but instead a confidence-setting rule reflected the expert's judgment that a particular pattern of findings would (or should) lead to a particular symbolic confidence value such as *very likely* or *ruled out*. These confidence values were organized as a seven-step scale, and all available evidence supported the view that seven confidence grades are more than

This appendix was written by John R. Josephson

266

sufficient to represent physician reasoning during diagnosis. In most of our later systems, including the RED systems, we continued to use coarse confidence scales. We also continued to set initial confidence values and updating methods to reflect our own, and domain experts', estimates of what seemed reasonable, usually keeping in mind some English language equivalents such as "very implausible," "neutral confidence," and "highly plausible." This worked very well overall (see, for example, the experiments reported in chapter 9). But how can we understand these confidence values? Are they likelihoods? Probabilities? We discuss these alternatives next.

Plausibility and probability

The mathematical theory of probability has given humanity many insights by formalizing an already existing set of usages and intuitions about concepts of likelihood. Presumably there are residual uses of likelihood concepts that have not been well formalized in this framework, successful as it has been overall. We wonder if plausibility can be successfully and advantageously formalized, perhaps by linking to likelihoods, and thence to probabilities, and perhaps thence to some known semantics for probabilities, such as frequencies or causal propensities.

Indeed this can apparently be done, in the sense that we can give a probability interpretation to the plausibility values used in the abduction machines. The initial confidence values assigned to the elementary hypotheses can be considered to be local-match posterior probabilities. That is, the initial confidence of hypothesis H can be considered an estimate of $p(H \mid D_0)$, where D_0 is the subset of the case data that is directly and significantly relevant to the truth of H. "Directly relevant" implies determining a confidence without estimating confidence for other hypotheses at the same agora as H (see chapter 10). Thus the confidence for H is set in respect to the case-specific data – so it is a *posterior* probability – but it does not take into account possible interactions with other hypotheses of the same type; these hypotheses might be explanatory rivals, might be incompatible with H, or might interact with H in some other way. Data are consulted to set an initial confidence for H only if they help to set confidence without much subsidiary problem solving, which, besides considering hypothesis interactions, might include other kinds of problem solving such as that involved in projecting causal consequences or in elaborately determining whether preconditions are satisfied. Consequently, as we said, initial confidence values in the abduction machines can be considered local-match posterior or prima facie probabilities.

Even if the requirement of no significant amounts of subsidiary problem solving is relaxed, as we have done in many of our systems, it is still desirable to postpone most consideration of interactions with other hypotheses, leaving this consideration for a cycle of confidence updating after initial confidence is set. This strategy takes advantage of the prospects for eliminating low-likelihood elementary hypotheses immediately, thus simplifying the hypothesis space, and it makes it possible to use initial confidences scores as a guide to steering through the complexity of interactions and combinations.

After an initial confidence value is set for a hypothesis, and if that initial confidence is not so low that the hypothesis is immediately rejected, then eventually the abduction machine updates the confidence to an "all-things-considered" confidence value. This can be viewed as an estimate of posterior probability conditioned by all the data for the case. In our most mature abstract abduction machine, Machine 6 of chapter 10, many steps of updating may occur before a final value is reached. These steps would reflect the impacts of hypothesis interactions of various sorts, including the impacts of expectations from hypotheses at other agoras and the impacts of incompatible hypotheses at the same agora. Especially, the final confidence value takes account of explanatory interactions that arise for the case, such as that a hypothesis is the most plausible (highest confidence at the time) explanation for some datum.

Thus the confidence values used in our abduction machines can be considered to be probabilities, with an abduction machine providing an elaborate strategy for arriving at all-things-considered posterior probabilities.

Yet it is not clear that much, if anything, is gained by interpreting the confidences as probabilities. Coarse-scale confidence values seem to be good enough for purposes of reasoning. Coarse-scale confidence values seem to be all we can usually get from experience, considering the reference-class problem (see chapter 1). Coarse-scale confidence values are almost always sufficient to decide action. Moreover, as we argued in chapter 1, if fine-scale confidence values are needed to solve a problem, probably the problem cannot be confidently solved. Therefore, the property of mathematical probabilities that they come with a continuum of values from 0 to 1 is of no use. Worse, if we use high-precision numbers to represent plausibilities in our systems, we may mislead system builders by encouraging them to expend unnecessary resources in setting values precisely and may mislead users into overestimating the precision of confidence estimates. If one decimal digit of precision already exaggerates what is needed, the use of floating-point numbers to represent confidences in computers encourages abuse (poor software design).

Of course people can easily be trained not to take precise numbers too seriously, or the excess precision can be hidden behind a user interface, so misinterpretation and abuse are not important objections. The important question is whether the plausibilities should be considered estimates of *probabilities*, however imprecise the estimates. Perhaps probability theory provides the proper theory of rationality for confidences; perhaps human thinking is only truly intelligent to the degree to which it approximates the ideal.

Actually, three alternatives present themselves: Plausibilities *should* be considered to be probabilities, *may* consistently be interpretable as probabilities, or *cannot* reasonably be considered to be probabilities. Just now it seems most likely that plausibilities may consistently be interpreted as mathematical probabilities, but that there is no significant computational payoff from making this interpretation, and it appears to oversimplify a multi-dimensional phenomenon into a single dimension.

The abductive-confidence function

We argued that, even if initial confidence values are considered to be probabilities (identified with frequencies), there is no objective way to set them precisely because of short-term statistics and the reference-class problem (see chapter 1). Moreover, a probability interpretation does not seem to contribute much toward understanding how to update confidence values during abductive problem solving. The critical point for confidence updating is computing the abductive-confidence function, which may be defined as follows:

Suppose that there is a finding f for which there are alternative explanations H_1 through H_k. Suppose that the $\{H_i\}$ form an exhaustive set (this can always be arranged by introducing a hypothesis of OTHER). Suppose that confidence values are given for each H_i that do not take account of the fact that the $\{H_i\}$ form an exhaustive set of possible explainers for f (although they may take account of the occurrence of f). Without loss of generality we may assume that H_1 is the highest scored hypothesis, or is at least tied for that position. What should be the confidence of H_1 after taking account of the fact that the $\{H_i\}$ form an exhaustive set of potential explainers for f? The *abductive-confidence function* is the presumed mapping that takes the confidence values of the $\{H_i\}$ as input, along with any information about interactions of the $\{H_i\}$, and outputs the correct updated confidence value for the highest scoring hypothesis.

It is not satisfying to say that the abductive confidence function is different for each domain. How then can we learn to handle new domains? Anyway, it should be possible to develop a domain-independent theory of evidence evaluation, which seems to imply the existence of a domain-independent abductive-confidence function. The basic question is this: How much confidence are we entitled to have in a best explanation by warrant of the fact that it is a best explanation?

Irene Ku derived mathematical descriptions of the abductive-confidence function for certain special cases under the assumption that plausibilities are probabilities (Ku, 1991). The difficulty in providing a general mathematical characterization in probability terms is what to presume about the unknown and unspecified relationships among the $\{H_{ij}\}$; should the $\{H_i\}$ be treated as statistically independent? Mutually exclusive?

Ku also investigated the behavior of the abductive-confidence function empirically, using the RED library of 42 cases and setting initial confidence values by using hypothesis matchers previously constructed by Mike Tanner. Ignoring antibody reactions in which there was a tie for best, Ku found 395 reactions for which there was a unique best explanation (unique highest scoring antibody hypothesis). Whether the best explanation was correct, or not, was decided by consulting the record of expert judgment for each case. Ku investigated how the correctness of best explanations correlated with various conditions.

As expected, correctness correlated highly with the difference in scores between the best and second best hypotheses; the larger the difference, the greater the likelihood that the best explanation was correct. Also, for antibody reactions for which the best and second best were one or two steps of confidence apart (on the seven-step scale), correctness correlated negatively with the number of hypotheses tied for second best: The greater the number of ties for second best, the less likely that the best explanation was correct. Correctness was also sensitive to the distance between the scores of the best and third best hypotheses when the distance between best and second best was held constant. Thus correctness was sensitive to more than just the score of the best explanation and the difference between the scores of best and second best. Overall the behavior was consistent with what would be expected if the plausibility scores were acting like measures of probability.

Ku found several other interesting correlations. Viewed from a certain perspective, her findings seem to suggest that the correct abductive-confidence function ignores the score of the highest scoring hypothesis (other than noting that it is the highest) and sets the final score for this hypothesis as a function of the entire mass of alternatives; the more alternatives and the higher their scores, the less confidence there should be that the best explanation is correct. Overall it appears that the score of the best explanation is insignificant as an indicator of its likely correctness (apart from making it the best explanation), but rather correctness depends primarily on the scores of the explanatory alternatives. It is as if the best explanation must fight for acceptance, while the alternatives combine forces in an attempt to pull it down.

The need to go beyond probability

The mathematical study of probability and statistics has been applied to the analysis of scientific reasoning with great success, with many accomplishments concerning the design of experiments and for determining the appropriate confidence to have in interpreting experimental and observational results. It has seemed the most promising path to mathematical treatment of hypothesis acceptance, apart from purely deductive phenomena. However, causality is not the same as correlation, David Hume notwithstanding (see Josephson, 1982). If scientific reasoning is based on abduction, and if abduction essentially depends on explanatory relationships, and further, if explanatory relationships essentially depend on causality (discussed in chapter 1), then the mathematics of probability and statistics will not be sufficient to characterize evidence evaluation for science. Causality has not been satisfactorily axiomatized, despite more than 2,000 years of attempts, nor has it been successfully reduced to fancy kinds of co-occurrence correlations. The importance for abductive reasoning of going beyond just probabilities and of also using explicitly represented causal (or explanatory) relationships has been recognized by several researchers in artificial intelligence (Pearl, 1987; Peng & Reggia, 1990), although it has not been recognized by many others.

Dimensions of plausibility

Throughout the research described in this book we avoided making commitments to the manner in which the confidence in a composite hypothesis may depend on the confidence values of the constituents.[1] Other things being equal, of course, more confident constituents should yield a more confident composite hypothesis. But typically other things are not equal, and composite hypotheses differ in explanatory power, parsimony, internal coherence, or other characteristics, and these characteristics have no obvious common measure. It is not at all obvious that plausibility is a one-dimensional magnitude, a simple intensity.

Alternatives to probability

What are the alternatives to considering plausibilities to be probabilities? Probabilities presumably measure likelihoods, ranging on a scale (in frequency terms) from *never*, through increasing degrees of *sometimes*, to *always*. Plausibilities (for initial confidence estimates) may be case-specific estimates of *possibility* ranging from *impossible*, up through decreasing degrees of doubt, all the way to *definitely-could-be*.

In chapter 6 we pointed to the phenomenon of hypothesization by analogy, in which the present situation reminds an agent of a previous episode and causal knowledge is then brought over and adapted.[2] The present situation and the previous episode are members of the same class, which may be a new category set up by the similarity relationship. The occurrence of the previous episode is then an existence proof that things of that kind actually happen, so they may be happening again in the present situation. The new hypothesis adapted from the previous episode is then prima facie plausible because it is already known that such things happen.

Whether a hypothesis is generated from an analogy or arises in some other way, an analogy can be used to argue for plausibility. (What happened once may be happening again.) Plausibility arguments based on analogy are extremely common. (This is obvious after we know to look for them. Some examples are given in chapter 6.) Note that a plausibility argument based on analogy is an argument that a hypothesis *could be true*, that it represents a *real possibility* rather than an argument that it is likely to be true (although the plausibility argument might be part of a larger likelihood argument).

Possibilities are the kinds of things that have probabilities. Possibilities are the bearers of likelihood.

A common pattern is to generate a plausible hypothesis by forming an analogy, then to test the hypothesis for consistency with the present case. If it survives the tests, the hypothesis becomes even more plausible. Having gone from being a mere "logical possibility," to being a "real possibility" when the analogy was formed, the hypothesis advances to being a "very real possibility" by surviving rule-out tests. (Testing a hypothesis by generating causal expectations and checking to see if they occur is a little more complicated. If there are no other plausible explanations for some of the consequences, this sets up an abductive argument for the *likelihood* of the hypothesis.)

If the degree of plausibility properly depends on the closeness of an analogy, then it seems unlikely that plausibility (of this sort) can ever be quantified, since it appears unlikely that we will ever have an objective quantitative measure of degree of similarity.

Plausibility and intelligence

Perhaps the power of intelligence is relatively unrelated to the pure semantics of plausibilities. It could be that the true mathematical theory of the true semantics of plausibilities would not be feasibly computable, or if it were, that the computations would be so sensitive to initial conditions, or so numerically unstable, that there would be no gain pragmatically for making smart machines from knowing the true semantics. It could be that heuristic shortcuts are almost always necessary and that these heuristics do most of the work in accounting for intelligence and in accounting for how it is possible for knowledge to come from experience.

Notes

1 The best-small plausibility criterion described in chapter 7 represents a minimal constraint on the plausibility of composites.

2 These ideas about plausibility from analogy have benefited greatly from discussions with Lindley Darden.

Extended Bibliography

Achinstein, P. (1971). *Law and Explanation*. New York: Oxford University Press.

Ajjanagadde, V. (1991). *Abductive Reasoning in Connectionist Networks*. Technical Report, Wilhelm Schickard Institute, Tübingen, Germany.

Ajjanagadde, V. (1991). *Incorporating Background Knowledge and Structured Explananda in Abductive Reasoning*. Technical Report, Wilhelm Schickard Institute, Tübingen, Germany.

Allemang, D., Tanner, M. C., Bylander, T., & Josephson, J. R. (1987). On the Computational Complexity of Hypothesis Assembly. In *Proceedings of the Tenth International Joint Conference on Artificial Intelligence*, Milan, Italy: IJCAI.

Allen, J. F. (1984). Towards a General Theory of Time and Action. *Artificial Intelligence*, 23(2), 123–154.

American Association of Blood Banks. (1977). *Technical Manual*. Washington, DC: American Association of Blood Banks.

Aristotle. (1941). Posterior Analytics. In R. McKeon (Ed.), *The Basic Works of Aristotle* (G. R. G. Mure, Trans.). (pp. 110–186). New York: Random House.

Ayeb, B. E., Marquis, P., & Rusinowitch, M. (1990). Deductive / Abductive Diagnosis: The DA-Principles. In *Proceedings of the Ninth European Conference on Artificial Intelligence (ECAI)*, Pitman.

Ayeb, B. E., Marquis, P., & Rusinowitch, M. (in press). Preferring Diagnoses by Abduction. *IEEE Transactions on Systems, Man and Cybernetics*.

Bareiss, R. (1989). *Exemplar-Based Knowledge Acquisition: A Unified Approach to Concept Representation, Classification, and Learning*. Boston: Academic Press.

Bhaskar, R. (1981). Explanation. In W. F. Bynum, E. J. Browne, & R. Porter (Eds.), *Dictionary of the History of Science*. (pp. 140–142). Princeton University Press.

Bhatnagar, R., & Kanal, L. K. (1991). Abductive Reasoning with Causal Influences of Interactions. In *Notes from the AAAI Workshop on Domain-Independent Strategies for Abduction*, (pp. 1–8). Anaheim, California. (Josephson & Dasigi, 1991).

Bhatnagar, R., & Kanal, L. K. (1991). *Hypothesizing Causal Models for Reasoning*. Technical Report, Computer Science Department, University of Cincinnati, Cincinnati.

Black, M. (1967). Induction. In P. Edwards (Ed.), *The Encyclopedia of Philosophy*. New York: Macmillan and The Free Press.

Blois, R. (1989). *Information and Medicine: The Nature of Medical Description*. Berkeley: University of California Press.

Bonneau, A., Charpillet, F., Coste, S., Haton, J. P., Laprie, Y., & Marquis, P. (1992). A Model for Hypothetical Reasoning applied to Speech Recognition. In *Proceedings of the Tenth European Conference on Artificial Intelligence (ECAI)*, New York: Wiley.

Boole, G. (1854). *An Investigation of the Laws of Thought, on Which are Founded the Mathematical Theory of Logic and Probabilities*. N.p.

Boose, J., & Bradshaw, J. (1988). Expertise Transfer and Complex Problems: Using AQUINAS as a Knowledge-Acquisition Workbench for Knowledge-Based Systems. In J. H. Boose & B. R. Gaines (Eds.), *Knowledge Acquisition Tools for Expert Systems, Volume 2*. (pp. 39–64). New York: Academic Press.

Bromberger, S. (1966). Why-Questions. In *Mind and Cosmos: Essays in Contemporary Science and Philosophy*. Pittsburgh, PA: University of Pittsburgh Press. Reprinted in *Readings in the Philosophy of Science*, edited by Baruch A. Brody, Prentice Hall, 1970.

Browman, C. P., & Goldstein, L. (1989). Tiers in Articulatory Phonology with some Implications for Casual Speech. In J. Kingston & M. E. Beckman (Eds.), *Laboratory Phonology I: Between the Grammar and the Physics of Speech*. (pp. 341–376). Cambridge University Press.

Brown, D. C. (1984). *Expert Systems for Design Problem-Solving Using Design Refinement with Plan Selection and Redesign*. Ph.D. diss., Department of Computer and Information Science, The Ohio State University, Columbus.

Brown, D. C., & Chandrasekaran, B. (1985). Plan Selection in Design Problem-Solving. In *Proceedings of the AISB 85 Conference*, Warwick, UK: The Society for Artificial Intelligence and the Simulation of Behavior.

Brown, D. C., & Chandrasekaran, B. (1986). Knowledge and Control for a Mechanical Design Expert System. *IEEE Computer*, 19, 92–101.

Brown, D. C., & Chandrasekaran, B. (1989). *Design Problem Solving: Knowledge Structures and Control Strategies*. London & San Mateo: Pitman & Morgan Kaufmann.

Bruce, D. J. (1958). The effect of listeners' anticipations on the intelligibility of heard speech. *Language and Speech*, 1(2).

Bruner, J. S. (1957). On Perceptual Readiness. *Psychological Review*, 64(2), 123–152.

Bruner, J. S. (1973). *Beyond the Information Given*. New York: W. W. Norton.

Buchanan, B. G., & Feigenbaum, E. A. (1981). Dendral and Meta-Dendral: Their Applications Dimension. In B. L. Webber & N. J. Nilsson (Eds.), *Readings in Artificial Intelligence*. (pp. 313–322). Palo Alto: Tioga.

Buchanan, B. G., & Shortliffe, E. H. (Eds.). (1984). *Rule-Based Expert Systems: The MYCIN Experiments of the Stanford Heuristic Programming Project*. Reading, MA: Addison-Wesley.

Buchanan, B. G., Sutherland, G., & Feigenbaum, E. A. (1969). Heuristic Dendral: A program for generating explanatory hypotheses in organic chemistry. In B. Meltzer & D. Michie (Eds.), *Machine Intelligence*. (pp. 209–254). Edinburgh: Edinburgh University Press.

Bylander, T. (1985). A Critique of Qualitative Simulation from a Consolidation Viewpoint. In *Proceedings of the International Conference on Cybernetics and Society*, (pp. 589–596). IEEE Computer Society Press.

Bylander, T. (1986). *Consolidation: A Method for Reasoning about the Behavior of Devices*. Ph.D. diss., Department of Computer and Information Science, The Ohio State University, Columbus.

Bylander, T. (1987). *Using Consolidation for Reasoning About Devices*. Technical Report, The Ohio State University, Laboratory for Artificial Intelligence Research, Columbus.

Bylander, T. (1991). The Monotonic Abduction Problem: A Functional Characterization on the Edge of Tractability. In J. Allen, R. Fikes, & E. Sandewall (Eds.), *Proceedings of the Second International Conference on Principles of Knowledge Representation and Reasoning*, (pp. 70–77). Morgan Kaufmann.

Bylander, T. (1991). A Tractable Partial Solution to the Monotonic Abduction Problem. In *Notes from the AAAI Workshop on Domain-Independent Strategies for Abduction*, (pp. 9–13). Anaheim. (Josephson & Dasigi, 1991).

Bylander, T., Allemang, D., Tanner, M. C., & Josephson, J. R. (1989a). Some Results Concerning the Computational Complexity of Abduction. In R. J. Brachman, H. J. Levesque, & R. Reiter (Eds.), *Proceedings of the First International Conference on Principles of Knowledge Representation and Reasoning*, (pp. 44–54). Toronto.

Bylander, T., Allemang, D., Tanner, M. C., & Josephson, J. R. (1989). *When Efficient Assembly Performs Correct Abduction and Why Abduction is Otherwise Trivial or Intractable*. Technical Report, The Ohio State University, Laboratory for Artificial Intelligence Research, Columbus.

Bylander, T., Allemang, D., Tanner, M. C., & Josephson, J. R. (1991). The Computational Complexity of Abduction. *Artificial Intelligence*, 49, 25–60.

Bylander, T., Allemang, D., Tanner, M. C., & Josephson, J. R. (1992). The Computational Complexity of Abduction. In R. J. Brachman, H. J. Levesque, & R. Reiter (Eds.), *Knowledge*

Representation. (pp. 25–60). Cambridge, MA: MIT Press. Also appears in volume 49 of *Artificial Intelligence*.

Bylander, T., & Chandrasekaran, B. (1985). Understanding Behavior Using Consolidation. In *Proceedings of the Ninth International Joint Conference on Artificial Intelligence*, (pp. 450–454). Los Angeles.

Bylander, T., & Chandrasekaran, B. (1989). Understanding Behavior Using Consolidation. In *Proceedings of the Ninth International Joint Conference on Artificial Intelligence*, 1 (pp. 300–306). San Mateo: Morgan Kaufmann.

Bylander, T., Chandrasekaran, B., & Josephson, J. R. (1987). The Generic Task Toolset. In G. Salvendy (Ed.), *Proceedings of the Second International Conference on Human-Computer Interaction and Expert Systems*, (pp. 507–514). Amsterdam: Elsevier.

Bylander, T., Johnson, T. R., & Goel, A. K. (1991). Structured matching: A task-specific technique for making decisions. *Knowledge Acquisition*, 3(1), 1–20.

Bylander, T., & Mittal, S. (1986). CSRL: A Language for Classificatory Problem Solving and Uncertainty Handling. *AI Magazine*, 7(3), 66–77.

Bylander, T., Mittal, S., & Chandrasekaran, B. (1983). CSRL: A Language for Expert Systems for Diagnosis. In *Proceedings of the Eighth International Joint Conference on Artificial Intelligence*, (pp. 218–221). IJCAI.

Bylander, T., & Smith, J. W. (1985). Mapping Medical Knowledge into Conceptual Structures. In K. N. Karna (Ed.), *Proceedings of the Expert Systems in Government Symposium*, (pp. 503–511). IEEE Computer Society Press.

Bylander, T., Smith, J. W., & Svirbely, J. (1986). Qualitative Representation of Behavior in the Medical Domain. In R. Salamon, B. Blum, & M. Jorgenson (Eds.), *Proceedings of the Fifth Conference on Medical Informatics*, (pp. 7–11). New York: North Holland.

Bylander, T., & Weintraub, M. A. (1988). A Corrective Learning Procedure Using Different Explanatory Types. In *1988 AAAI Spring Symposium Series on Explanation-Based Learning*, Stanford University.

Cain, T. (1991). Constraining Abduction in Integrated Learning. In *Notes from the AAAI Workshop on Domain-Independent Strategies for Abduction*, (pp. 14–17). Anaheim. (Josephson & Dasigi, 1991).

Calistri, R. J. (1989). *Classifying and Detecting Plan-Based Misconceptions*. Technical Report, Brown University Department of Computer Science.

Carver, N., & Lesser, V. (1991). Blackboard-based Sensor Interpretation Using a Symbolic Model of the Sources of Uncertainty in Abductive Inference. In *Notes from the AAAI Workshop on Domain-Independent Strategies for Abduction*, (pp. 18–24). Anaheim. (Josephson & Dasigi, 1991).

Chandrasekaran, B. (1983). Towards a Taxonomy of Problem-Solving Types. *AI Magazine*, Winter/Spring, 9–17.

Chandrasekaran, B. (1986). Generic Tasks in Knowledge-Based Reasoning: High-Level Building Blocks for Expert System Design. *IEEE Expert*, 1(3), 23–30.

Chandrasekaran, B. (1987). Towards a Functional Architecture for Intelligence Based on Generic Information Processing Tasks. In *Proceedings of the Tenth International Joint Conference on Artificial Intelligence*, Morgan Kaufmann.

Chandrasekaran, B. (1988). Generic Tasks as Building Blocks for Knowledge-Based Systems: The Diagnosis and Routine Design Examples. *Knowledge Engineering Review*, 3(3), 183–210.

Chandrasekaran, B. (1989). Task Structures, Knowledge Acquisition, and Learning. *Machine Learning*, 4, 339–345.

Chandrasekaran, B. (1990). Design Problem Solving: A Task Analysis. *Artificial Intelligence Magazine*, 11(4), 59–71.

Chandrasekaran, B. (1991). Models versus Rules, Deep versus Compiled, Content versus Form: Some distinctions in knowledge systems research. *IEEE Expert*, 6(2), 75–79.

Chandrasekaran, B., Bylander, T., & Sembugamoorthy, V. (1985). Functional Representations and Behavior Composition by Consolidation: Two Aspects of Reasoning about Devices. *SIGART*, 21–24.

Chandrasekaran, B., & Goel, A. (1988). From Numbers to Symbols to Knowledge Structures: Artificial Intelligence Perspectives on the Classification Task. *IEEE Transactions on Systems, Man, and Cybernetics*, 18(3), 415–424.

Chandrasekaran, B., Gomez, F., Mittal, S., & Smith, J. W. (1979). An Approach to Medical Diagnosis Based on Conceptual Structures. In *Proceedings of the Sixth International Joint Conference on Artificial Intelligence*, (pp. 134–142). IJCAI.

Chandrasekaran, B., & Johnson, T. R. (to appear). Generic Tasks and Task Structures: History, Critique and New Direction. In J. M. David, J. P. Krivine, & R. Simmons (Eds.), *Second Generation Expert Systems*. New York: Springer-Verlag.

Chandrasekaran, B., & Josephson, J. R. (1986). Explanation, Problem Solving, and New Generation Tools: A Progress Report. In *Proceedings of the Expert Systems Workshop*, (pp. 122–126). Pacific Grove, CA: Science Applications International Corporation.

Chandrasekaran, B., Josephson, J. R., & Herman, D. (1987). The Generic Task Toolset: High Level Languages for the Construction of Planning and Problem Solving Systems. In J. Rodriguez (Ed.), *Proceedings of the Workshop on Space Telerobotics*, III (pp. 59–65). Pasadena: Jet Propulsion Laboratories and the California Institute of Technology.

Chandrasekaran, B., & Mittal, S. (1983). Conceptual Representation of Medical Knowledge for Diagnosis by Computer: MDX and Related Systems. In M. Yovits (Ed.), *Advances in Computers*. (pp. 217–293). New York: Academic Press.

Chandrasekaran, B., & Mittal, S. (1983). On Deep Versus Compiled Approaches to Diagnostic Problem-Solving. *International Journal of Man-Machine Studies*, 19(5), 425–436.

Chandrasekaran, B., & Punch, W. F., III (1987). Data Validation During Diagnosis: A Step Beyond Traditional Sensor Validation. In *Proceedings of AAAI-87 Sixth National Conference on Artificial Intelligence*, (pp. 778–782). Los Altos: Morgan Kaufmann.

Chandrasekaran, B., Smith, J. W., & Sticklen, J. (1989). 'Deep' Models and Their Relation to Diagnosis. *Artificial Intelligence in Medicine*, 1(1), 29–40.

Chandrasekaran, B., & Tanner, M. (1986). Uncertainty Handling in Expert Systems: Uniform vs. Task-Specific Formalisms. In L. N. Kamal & J. Lemmer (Eds.), *Uncertainty in Artificial Intelligence*. New York: North Holland.

Charniak, E. (1983). The Bayesian Basis of Common Sense Medical Diagnosis. In *Proceedings of the National Conference on Artificial Intelligence*, (pp. 70–73). Los Altos: Morgan Kaufmann.

Charniak, E. (1986). A Neat Theory of Marker Passing. In *Proceedings of AAAI-86*, 1 (pp. 584–588). Los Altos: Morgan Kaufmann.

Charniak, E. (1988). Motivation Analysis, Abductive Unification, and Nonmonotonic Equality. *Artificial Intelligence*, 275–295.

Charniak, E., & Goldman, R. P. (1988). A logic for semantic interpretation. In *Proceedings of the 26th Annual Meeting of the Association for Computational Linguistics*, (pp. 87–94).

Charniak, E., & Goldman, R. P. (1989). Plan recognition in stories and in life. In *The Fifth Conference on Uncertainty in Artificial Intelligence*, (pp. 54–60).

Charniak, E., & Goldman, R. P. (1989). A semantics for probabilistic quantifier-free first-order languages, with particular application to story understanding. In *Proceedings of the International Joint Conference on Artificial Intelligence*, (pp. 1074–1079).

Charniak, E., & Goldman, R. P. (1991). A Probabilistic Model of Plan Recognition. In *Proceedings of the 1991 Conference of the American Association for Artificial Intelligence*, (pp. 160–165).

Charniak, E., & Goldman, R. P. (forthcoming). A Bayesian Model of Plan Recognition. *Artificial Intelligence*.

Charniak, E., & McDermott, D. (1985). *Introduction to Artificial Intelligence*. Reading, MA: Addison-Wesley.

Charniak, E., & Santos, E. (1992). Dynamic MAP calculations for abduction. In *Proceedings of the Tenth National Conference on Artificial Intelligence*, (pp. 552–557). Menlo Park: AAAI Press/MIT Press.

Charniak, E., & Shimony, S. E. (1990). A new algorithm for finding MAP assignments to belief networks. In *Proceedings of the Conference on Uncertainty in Artificial Intelligence*.

Charniak, E., & Shimony, S. E. (1990). Probabilistic Semantics for Cost Based Abduction. In *Proceedings of the National Conference on Artificial Intelligence*, (pp. 106–111). Boston.

Clancey, W. J. (1985). Heuristic Classification. *Artificial Intelligence*, 27(3), 289–350.

Clancey, W. J. (1992). Model Construction Operators. *Artificial Intelligence*, 53, 1–115.

Clancey, W. J., & Letsinger, R. (1981). NEOMYCIN: Reconfiguring a Rule-Based Expert System for Application to Teaching. In *Proceedings of the International Joint Conference on Artificial Intelligence*, (pp. 829–836). Vancouver, British Columbia.

Clancey, W. J., & Shortliffe, E. H. (Eds.). (1984). *Readings in Medical Artificial Intelligence*. Reading, MA: Addison-Wesley.

Console, L., Dupr'e, D. T., & Torasso, P. (1991). On the Relationship between Abduction and Deduction. *Journal of Logic and Computation*, 1(5), 661–690.

Console, L., & Torasso, P. (1991). On the co-operation between abductive and temporal reasoning in medical diagnosis. *Artificial Intelligence in Medicine*, 3, 291–311.

Coombs, M. J., & Hartley, R. T. (1987). The MGR algorithm and its application to the generation of explanations for novel events. *International Journal of Man-Machine Studies*, 679–708.

Coombs, M. J., & Hartley, R. T. (1988). Explaining novel events in process control through model generative reasoning. *International Journal of Expert Systems*, 89–109.

Cooper, G. (1990). The Computational Complexity of Probabilistic Inference Using Bayesian Belief Networks. *Artificial Intelligence*, 42, 393–405.

Craik, K. (1967). *The Nature of Explanation*. London: Cambridge University Press.

Darden, L. (1990). Diagnosing and Fixing Faults in Theories. In J. Schrager & P. Langley (Eds.), *Computational Models of Scientific Discovery and Theory Formation*. (pp. 319–346). San Mateo: Morgan-Kaufmann.

Darden, L. (1991). *Theory Change in Science: Strategies from Mendelian Genetics*. New York: Oxford University Press.

Darden, L., Moberg, D., Thadani, S., & Josephson, J. (1992). *A Computational Approach to Scientific Theory Revision: The TRANSGENE Experiments*. Technical Report, The Ohio State University, Laboratory for Artificial Intelligence Research.

Darden, L., & Rada, R. (1988). Hypothesis Formation Using Part-Whole Interrelations. In D. Helman (Ed.), *Analogical Reasoning*. (pp. 341–375). Dordrecht, The Netherlands: Kluwer Academic Publishers.

Dasigi, V. (1991). Abductive Modeling in Sub-Domains of Language Processing. In *Notes from the AAAI Workshop on Domain-Independent Strategies for Abduction*, (pp. 25–31). Anaheim. (Josephson & Dasigi, 1991).

Dasigi, V. R. (1988). *Word Sense Disambiguation in Descriptive Text Interpretation: A Dual-Route Parsimonious Covering Model*. Ph.D. diss., University of Maryland, College Park.

Dasigi, V. R., & Reggia, J. A. (1988). *Parsimonious Covering as a Method for Natural Language Interfaces to Expert Systems*. Technical Report, University of Maryland, College Park.

Davis, R. (1979). Interactive Transfer of Expertise: Acquisition of New Inference Rules. *Artificial Intelligence*, 12, 121–157.

Davis, R. (1982). Applications of Meta-Level Knowledge to the Construction, Maintenance, and Use of Large Knowledge Bases. In R. Davis & D. Lenat (Eds.), *Knowledge-Based Systems in Artificial Intelligence*. (pp. 229–490). New York: McGraw-Hill.

Davis, R. (1984). Diagnostic Reasoning Based on Structure and Function. *Artificial Intelligence*, 24, 347–410.

Davis, R. (1989). Form and Content in Model-Based Reasoning. In *1989 AAAI Workshop on Model-Based Reasoning*, Detroit.

Davis, R., & Hamscher, W. (1988). Model-Based Reasoning: Troubleshooting. In H. E. Shrobe (Ed.), *Exploring Artificial Intelligence*. (pp. 297–346). San Mateo: Morgan Kaufmann.

de Kleer, J. (1986). Reasoning About Multiple Faults. *AI Magazine*, 7(3), 132–139.

de Kleer, J., & Brown, J. S. (1983). Assumptions and Ambiguities in Mechanistic Mental Models. In D. Gentner & A. Stevens (Eds.), *Mental Models*. (pp. 155–190). Hillsdale, NJ: Lawrence Erlbaum.

de Kleer, J., & Brown, J. S. (1984). A Qualitative Physics Based on Confluences. *Artificial Intelligence*, 24, 7–83.

de Kleer, J., Mackworth, A. K., & Reiter, R. (1992). Characterizing Diagnoses and Systems. *Artificial Intelligence*, 56(2–3), 197–222.

de Kleer, J., & Williams, B. C. (1987). Diagnosing Multiple Faults. *Artificial Intelligence*, 32(1), 97–130.

de Kleer, J., & Williams, B. C. (1989). Diagnosis With Behavioral Modes. In *Proceedings of the Eleventh International Joint Conference on Artificial Intelligence*, (pp. 1324–1330). Detroit.

DeJong, G., & Mooney, R. (1986). Explanation-Based Learning: An Alternative View. *Machine Learning*, 1, 145–176.

DeJongh, M. (1991). *Causal Processes in the Problem Space Computational Model: Integrating Multiple Representations of Causal Processes in Abductive Problem Solving*. Ph.D. diss., Department of Computer and Information Science, The Ohio State University, Columbus.

Descartes, R. (1641). *Meditations on First Philosophy*. (Lawrence Lafleur, Trans.). (Second revised ed.). Bobbs-Merrill, (1960).

Donaldson, M. L. (1986). *Children's Explanations: A Psycholinguistic Study*. Cambridge: Cambridge University Press.

Doyle, A. C. (1967). *The Annotated Sherlock Holmes*. Edited by W. S. Baring-Gould. New York: Clarkson N. Potter.

Doyle, A. C. (1967). The Sign of the Four. In W. S. Baring-Gould (Ed.), *The Annotated Sherlock Holmes*. (pp. 610–688). New York: Clarkson N. Potter. Originally published in 1890.

Dumouchel, P., & Lennig, M. (1987). Using Stress Information in Large Vocabulary Speech Recognition. In P. Mermelstein (Ed.), *Proceedings of the Montreal Symposium on Speech Recognition*, (pp. 73–74). Montreal.

Dvorak, D., & Kuipers, B. (1989). Model-Based Monitoring of Dynamic Systems. In *Proceedings of the Eleventh International Joint Conference on Artificial Intelligence*, (pp. 1238–1243). Detroit.

Dzierzanowski, J. (1984). *Artificial Intelligence Methods in Human Locomotor Electromyography*. Ph.D. diss., Vanderbilt University, Nashville.

Eco, U., & Sebeok, T. A. (Eds.). (1983). *The Sign of Three: Dupin, Holmes, Peirce*. Bloomington: Indiana University Press.

Eiter, T., & Gottlob, G. (1992). *The Complexity of Logic-Based Abduction*. Technical Report, Christian Doppler Lab. for Expert Systems, Vienna Univ. of Technology, Vienna.

Ennis, R. (1968). Enumerative Induction and Best Explanation. *The Journal of Philosophy*, LXV(18), 523–529.

Ericsson, K., & Simon, H. (1984). *Protocol Analysis: Verbal Reports as Data*. Cambridge, MA: MIT Press.

Erman, L. D., & Lesser, V. R. (1980). The Hearsay-II Speech Understanding System: A Tutorial. In W. Lea (Ed.), *Trends in Speech Recognition*. Englewood Cliffs, NJ: Prentice Hall. Reprinted in *Readings in Speech Recognition*, Ed. Alex Waibel and Kai-Fu Lee, Morgan Kaufmann, 1990.

Eshelman, L. (1988). MOLE: A Knowledge-Acquisition Tool for Cover-and-Differentiate Systems. In S. Marcus (Ed.), *Automating Knowledge Acquisition for Expert Systems*. (pp. 37–80). Boston: Kluwer Academic Publishers.

Fann, K. T. (1970). *Peirce's Theory of Abduction*. The Hague: Martinus Nijhoff.

Fattah, Y. E., & O'Rorke, P. (1991). Learning Multiple Fault Diagnosis. In *Proceedings of the Seventh IEEE Conference on Artificial Intelligence Applications*, (pp. 235–239). IEEE Computer Society Press.

Fattah, Y. E., & O'Rorke, P. (1992). *Explanation-Based Learning for Diagnosis*. Technical Report, Department of Information and Computer Science, University of California, Irvine. (Report No. 92–21).

Fattah, Y. E., & O'Rorke, P. (1992). Learning Approximate Diagnosis. In *Proceedings of the Eighth IEEE Conference on Artificial Intelligence Applications*, (pp. 150–156). Monterey: IEEE Computer Society Press.

Fine, A. (1984). The Natural Ontological Attitude. In J. Leplin (Ed.), *Scientific Realism*. (pp. 83–107). Berkeley and Los Angeles: University of California Press.

Fink, P. K., & Lusth, J. C. (1987). Expert Systems and Diagnostic Expertise in the Mechanical and Electrical Domains. *IEEE Transactions on Systems, Man and Cybernetics*, 17, 340–349.

Fischer, O. (1991). *Cognitively Plausible Heuristics to Tackle the Computational Complexity of Abductive Reasoning*. Ph.D. diss., Department of Computer and Information Science, The Ohio State University, Columbus.

Fischer, O., & Goel, A. (1990). Abductive Explanation: On Why the Essentials are Essential. In Ras, Zemenkova, & Emrich (Eds.), *Intelligent Systems Methodologies – V*. (pp. 354–361). Amsterdam: North Holland.

Fischer, O., & Goel, A. (1990). Explanation: The Essentials versus the non-Essentials. In J. Moore & M. Wick (Eds.), *Proceedings of the AAAI-90 Workshop on Explanation*, (pp. 142–151). Boston.

Fischer, O., Goel, A., Svirbely, J., & Smith, J. (1991). The Role of Essential Explanation in Abduction. *Artificial Intelligence in Medicine*, 3(4), 181–191.

Fischer, O., Smith, J. W., & Smith, P. (1991). MetaAbduction: A Cognitively Plausible Domain-Independent Computational Model of Abductive Reasoning. In *Notes from the AAAI Workshop on Domain-Independent Strategies for Abduction*, (pp. 32–36). Anaheim. (Josephson & Dasigi, 1991).

Fodor, J. (1983). *The Modularity of Mind*. Cambridge, MA: MIT Press.

Forbus, K. D. (1984). Qualitative Process Theory. *Artificial Intelligence*, 24, 85–168.

Forgy, C., & McDermott, J. (1977). OPS: A Domain-Independent Production System. In *Proceedings of the Fifth International Joint Conference on Artificial Intelligence*, (pp. 933–939). Pittsburgh.

Fox, R. K. (1992). *Layered Abduction for Speech Recognition from Articulation*. Ph.D. diss., Department of Computer and Information Science, The Ohio State University, Columbus.

Friedrich, G., Gottlob, G., & Nejdl, W. (1990). Hypothesis Classification, Abductive Diagnosis and Therapy. In G. Gottlob & W. Nejdl (Eds.), *Expert Systems in Engineering*. (pp. 69–78). Berlin: Springer-Verlag.

Fujimura, O. (1992). Phonology and phonetics – A syllable-based model of articulatory organization. *Journal of the Acoustical Society of Japan*, E(13), 39–48.

Fujimura, O., Ishida, Y., & Kiritani, S. (1973). Computer-Controlled Radiography for Observation of Movements of Articulatory and other Human Organs. *Comp. Biology and Med.*, 3, 371–384.

Fumerton, A. (1980). Induction and Reasoning to the Best Explanation. *Philosophy of Science*, 47, 589–600.

Garey, M., & Johnson, D. (1979). *Computers and Intractability*. New York: W. H. Freeman.

Geffner, H., & Pearl, J. (1987). An Improved Constraint-Propagation Algorithm for Diagnosis. In *Proceedings of the International Joint Conference on Artificial Intelligence*, (pp. 1105–1111). Milan.

Genesereth, M. R. (1984). The use of design descriptions in automated diagnosis. *Artificial Intelligence*, 24, 411–436.

Ginsberg, A. (1988). Theory Revision via Prior Operationalization. In *Proceedings of AAAI-88: The Seventh National Conference on Artificial Intelligence*, (pp. 590–595). San Mateo: Morgan Kaufmann.

Ginsberg, A., Weiss, S., & Politakis, P. (1985). SEEK2: A Generalized Approach to Automatic Knowledge Base Refinement. In *Ninth International Joint Conference on Artificial Intelligence*, (pp. 367–374). Los Altos: Morgan Kaufmann.

Goel, A. (1989). What is Abductive Reasoning? *Neural Network Review*, 3(4), 181–187.

Goel, A., Josephson, J. R., & Sadayappan, P. (1987). Concurrency in Abductive Reasoning. In *Proceedings of the Knowledge-Based Systems Workshop*, (pp. 86–92). St. Louis: Science Applications International Corporation.

Goel, A., Ramanujan, J., & Sadayappan, P. (1988). Towards a Neural Architecture for Abductive Reasoning. In *Proceedings of the Second IEEE International Conference on Neural Networks*, 1 (pp. 681–688). San Diego: IEEE Computer Society Press.

Goel, A., Sadayappan, P., & Josephson, J. R. (1988). Concurrent Synthesis of Composite Explanatory Hypotheses. In *Proceedings of the Seventeenth International Conference on Parallel Processing*, (pp. 156–160). The Pennsylvania State University Press.

Goldman, R. P. (1990). *A Probabilistic Approach to Language Understanding*. Ph.D. diss., Brown University.

Goldman, R. P., & Charniak, E. (1991). Dynamic construction of belief networks. In P. P. Bonissone, M. Henrion, L. N. Kanal, & J. F. Lemmer (Eds.), *Uncertainty in Artificial Intelligence, Volume 6*. (pp. 171–184). Elsevier.

Goldman, R. P., & Charniak, E. (1992). Probabilistic text understanding. *Statistics and Computing*, 2, 105–114.

Goldman, R. P., & Charniak, E. (forthcoming). A language for construction of belief networks. *IEEE Transactions on Pattern Analysis and Machine Intelligence*.

Gomez, F., & Chandrasekaran, B. (1984). Knowledge Organization and Distribution for Medical Diagnosis. In W. J. Clancey & E. H. Shortliffe (Eds.), *Readings in Medical Artificial Intelligence*. (pp. 320–338). Reading, MA: Addison-Wesley. Also appears in *IEEE Transactions on Systems, Man and Cybernetics*, SMC-11(1):34–42, January, 1981.

Goodman, N. D. (1987). Intensions, Church's thesis, and the formalization of mathematics. *The Notre Dame Journal of Formal Logic*, 28, 473–489.

Gregory, R. L. (1987). Perception as Hypotheses. In R. L. Gregory (Ed.), *The Oxford Companion to the Mind*. (pp. 608–611). New York: Oxford University Press.

Gregory, R. L. (1990). *Eye and Brain: The Psychology of Seeing*. Princeton, NJ: Princeton University Press.

Halliday, M. (1978). *Language as Social Semantic*. London: Edward Arnold.

Halliday, M. (1985). *An Introduction to Functional Grammar*. London: Edward Arnold.

Hamscher, W., Console, L., & de Kleer, J. (Eds.). (1992). *Readings in Model-Based Diagnosis*. San Mateo: Morgan Kaufmann.

Hanson, N. R. (1958). *Patterns of Discovery*. London: Cambridge University Press.

Harman, G. (1965). The Inference to the Best Explanation. *Philosophical Review*, 74, 88–95.

Harman, G. (1968). Enumerative Induction as Inference to the Best Explanation. *The Journal of Philosophy*, 65(18), 529–533.

Harman, G. (1986). *Change in View*. Cambridge, MA: MIT Press.

Harvey, A. M., & Bordley, J., III (1972). *Differential Diagnosis, the Interpretation of Clinical Evidence*. Philadelphia: W. B. Saunders.

Hayes-Roth, F. (1985). A Blackboard Architecture for Control. *Artificial Intelligence*, 26, 251–321.

Hayes-Roth, F., & Lesser, V. (1977). Focus of Attention in the HEARSAY-II System. In *Proceedings of the Fifth International Joint Conference on Artificial Intelligence*, (pp. 27–35).

Helft, N., & Konolige, K. (1991). Integrating Evidential Information with Abduction. In *Notes from the AAAI Workshop on Domain-Independent Strategies for Abduction*, (pp. 37–43). Anaheim. (Josephson & Dasigi, 1991).

Hemami, H. (1985). Modeling, Control, and Simulation of Human Movement. *Critical Reviews in Biomedical Engineering*, 13(1), 1–34.

Hempel, C. G. (1965). *Aspects of Scientific Explanation*. New York: Free Press.

Herman, D. J. (1992). *An Extensible, Task-Specific Shell for Routine Design Problem Solving*. Ph.D. diss., Department of Computer and Information Science, The Ohio State University, Columbus.

Heustis, D. W., Bove, J. R., & Busch, S. (1976). *Practical Blood Transfusion*. Little, Brown.

Hillis, W. D. (1986). *The Connection Machine*. Cambridge, MA: MIT Press.

Hirsch, D. (1987). *An Expert System for Diagnosing Gait for Cerebral Palsy Patients*. Technical Report, Laboratory for Computer Science, MIT, Cambridge, MA. (Report No. MIT/LCS/TR-388).

Hirsch, D., Simon, S. R., Bylander, T., Weintraub, M. A., & Szolovits, P. (1989). Using Causal Reasoning in Gait Analysis. *Applied Artificial Intelligence*, 3(2–3), 253–272.

Hoare, C. A. R. (1978). Communicating Sequential Processes. *Communications of the ACM*, 23(9), 666–677.

Hobbs, J. R. (1987). *Implicature and Definite Reference*. Technical Report, Center for the Study of Language and Information, Stanford University, Stanford, California.

Hobbs, J. R. (1992). Metaphor and Abduction. In A. Ortony, J. Slack, & O. Stock (Eds.), *Communication from an Artificial Intelligence Perspective: Theoretical and Applied Issues*. (pp. 35–58). Springer.

Hobbs, J. R., Appelt, D. E., Bear, J., Tyson, M., & Magerman, D. (1992). Robust Processing of Real-World Natural-Language Texts. In P. Jacobs (Ed.), *Text-Based Intelligent Systems: Current Research and Practice in Information Extraction and Retrieval*. (pp. 13–33). Hillsdale, NJ: Lawrence Erlbaum.

Hobbs, J. R., Appelt, D. E., Bear, J. S., Tyson, M., & Magerman, D. (1991). *The TACITUS System: The MUC-3 Experience*. Technical Report, SRI International.

Hobbs, J. R., & Kameyama, M. (1990). Translation by Abduction. In H. Karlgren (Ed.), *Proceedings of the Thirteenth International Conference on Computational Linguistics*, (pp. 155–161). Helsinki.

Hobbs, J. R., Stickel, M., Appelt, D., & Martin, P. (1993). Interpretation as Abduction. *Artificial Intelligence Journal*, 63(1–2), 69–142.

Holland, J. H., Holyoak, K. J., Nisbett, R. E., & Thagard, P. R. (1987). *Induction*. Cambridge, MA: MIT Press.

Hunt, J. (1989). *Towards a Generic, Qualitative-Based, Diagnostic Architecture*. Technical Report, Department of Computer Science, University College of Wales, Aberystwyth, Dyfed, U.K. (Report No. RRG-TR-145-89).

Inman, V. T., Ralston, H. J., & Todd, F. (1981). *Human Walking*. Baltimore: Williams and Wilkins.

Jackson, P. (1991). Possibilistic Prime Implicates and their Use in Abduction. In *Notes from the AAAI Workshop on Domain-Independent Strategies for Abduction*, (pp. 44–50). Anaheim. (Josephson & Dasigi, 1991).

Johnson, K., Sticklen, J., & Smith, J. W. (1988). IDABLE – Application of an Intelligent Data Base to Medical Systems. In *Proceedings of the AAAI Spring Artificial Intelligence in Medicine Symposium*, (pp. 43–44). Stanford University: AAAI.

Johnson, T., Chandrasekaran, B., & Smith, J. W. (1989). Generic Tasks and Soar. In *Working notes of the AAAI Spring Symposium on Knowledge System Development Tools and Languages*, Menlo Park: AAAI.

Johnson, T. R. (1986). HYPER: The Hypothesis Matcher Tool. In *Proceedings of the Expert Systems Workshop*, (pp. 122–126). Pacific Grove, CA: Science Applications International Corporation.

Johnson, T. R. (1991). *Generic Tasks in the Problem-Space Paradigm: Building Flexible Knowledge Systems While Using Task-Level Constraints*. Ph.D. diss., Department of Computer and Information Science, The Ohio State University, Columbus.

Johnson, T. R., & Smith, J. W. (1991). A Framework for Opportunistic Abductive Strategies. In *Proceedings of the Thirteenth Annual Conference of the Cognitive Science Society*, (pp. 760–764). Hillsdale, NJ: Lawrence Erlbaum.

Johnson, T. R., Smith, J. W., & Bylander, T. (1988). HYPER – Hypothesis Matching Using Compiled Knowledge. In *Proceedings of the Spring Symposium Series: Artificial Intelligence in Medicine*, (pp. 45–46). Stanford University.

Josephson, J. R. (1982). *Explanation and Induction*. Ph.D. diss., Department of Philosophy, The Ohio State University, Columbus.

Josephson, J. R. (1988). Reducing Uncertainty by Using Explanatory Relationships. In *Proceedings of the Space Operations Automation and Robotics 1988 Workshop*, (pp. 149–151). Dayton: NASA, The United States Air Force, and Wright State University.

Josephson, J. R. (1989). Inference to the Best Explanation is Basic. *Behavioral and Brain Sciences*, 12(3). Appears as a commentary on "Explanatory Coherence" by Paul Thagard.

Josephson, J. R. (1989). A Layered Abduction Model of Perception: Integrating Bottom-up and Top-down Processing in a Multi-Sense Agent. In *Proceedings of the NASA Conference on Space Telerobotics*, (pp. 197–206). Pasadena: JPL Publication 89–7.

Josephson, J. R. (1989). Speech Understanding Based on Layered Abduction: Working Notes for the Symposium on Spoken Language Systems. In *Proceedings of the AAAI-89 Spring Symposium Series*, Stanford University: AAAI.

Josephson, J. R. (1990). *Spoken Language Understanding as Layered Abductive Inference*. Technical Report, The Ohio State University, Laboratory for Artificial Intelligence Research, Columbus.

Josephson, J. R., Chandrasekaran, B., & Smith, J. (1984). Assembling the Best Explanation. In *Proceedings of the IEEE Workshop on Principles of Knowledge-Based Systems*, (pp. 185–190). Denver, CO: IEEE Computer Society.

Josephson, J. R., Chandrasekaran, B., Smith, J., & Tanner, M. C. (1986). Abduction by Classification and Assembly. In A. Fine & P. Machamer (Eds.), *PSA 1986*, 1 (pp. 458–470). East Lansing: Philosophy of Science Association.

Josephson, J. R., Chandrasekaran, B., Smith, J., & Tanner, M. C. (1987). A Mechanism for Forming Composite Explanatory Hypotheses. *IEEE Transactions on Systems, Man and Cybernetics, Special Issue on Causal and Strategic Aspects of Diagnostic Reasoning*, 17(3), 445–54.

Josephson, J. R., & Dasigi, V. (1991). *Notes from the AAAI Workshop on Domain-Independent Strategies for Abduction*. Available as a technical report from the Laboratory for Artificial Intelligence Research, Department of Computer and Information Science, The Ohio State University, Columbus, Ohio, 43210. Internet: lair-librarian@cis.ohio-state.edu

Josephson, J. R., Smetters, D., Fox, R., Oblinger, D., Welch, A., & Northrup, G. (1989). *The Integrated Generic Task Toolset, Fafner Release 1.0*. Technical Report, The Ohio State University, Laboratory for Artificial Intelligence Research.

Josephson, J. R., Tanner, M. C., Smith, J., Svirbely, J., & Strohm, P. (1985). Red: Integrating Generic Tasks to Identify Red-Cell Antibodies. In K. N. Karna (Ed.), *Proceedings of The Expert Systems in Government Symposium*, (pp. 524–531). IEEE Computer Society Press.

Kant, I. (1787). *Critique of Pure Reason*. (Norman Kemp Smith, Trans.). New York: St. Martins Press, (1968).

Kautz, H. A. (1987). *A Formal Theory of Plan Recognition*. Ph.D. diss., University of Rochester.

Kautz, H. A., & Allen, J. F. (1986). Generalized Plan Recognition. In *Proceedings of AAAI-86*, 1 (pp. 32–35). Los Altos: Morgan Kaufmann.

Keller, R. (1990). In Defense of Compilation. In *Second AAAI Workshop on Model-Based Reasoning*, (pp. 22–31). Boston.

Keuneke, A. M. (1989). *Understanding Devices: Causal Explanation of Diagnostic Conclusions*. Ph.D. diss., Department of Computer and Information Science, The Ohio State University, Columbus.

Keuneke, A. M. (1991). Device representation: the significance of functional knowledge. *IEEE Expert*, 6(2), 22–25.

Kitcher, P., & Salmon, W. C. (Eds.). (1989). *Scientific Explanation*. Minneapolis: University of Minnesota Press.

Konolige, K. (1992). Abduction versus Closure in Causal Theories. *Artificial Intelligence*, 53(2–3), 255–272.

Korner, S. (Ed.). (1975). *Explanation*. New Haven: Yale University Press.

Kosaka, M., & Wakita, H. (1987). Syllable Structure of English Words: Implications for Lexical Access. In P. Mermelstein (Ed.), *Proceedings of the Montreal Symposium on Speech Recognition*, (pp. 59–60). Montreal.

Koton, P. (1988). Reasoning About Evidence in Causal Explanations. In *Proceedings of AAAI-88: The Seventh National Conference on Artificial Intelligence*, (pp. 256–261). San Mateo: Morgan Kaufmann.

Ku, I. O.-C. (1991). *Theoretical and Empirical Perspectives on the Abductive Confidence Function*. Master's thesis, Department of Computer and Information Science, The Ohio State University, Columbus.

Kuhn, T. (1970). *The Structure of Scientific Revolutions*. Chicago: University of Chicago Press.

Kuipers, B. J. (1986). Qualitative Simulation. *Artificial Intelligence*, 29(3), 289–338.

Laird, J., Rosenbloom, P., & Newell, A. (1986). *Universal Subgoaling and Chunking*. Boston: Kluwer Academic Publishers.

Laudan, L. L. (1971). William Whewell on the Consilience of Inductions. *The Monist*, 55.

Leake, D. B. (1992). *Evaluating Explanations: A Content Theory*. Hillsdale, NJ: Lawrence Erlbaum.

Lesser, V. R., Fennell, L. D., Erman, L. D., & Reddy, R. D. (1975). The Hearsay-II Speech Understanding System. *IEEE Transactions on Acoustics, Speech and Signal Processing*, 23, 11–24.

Levesque, H. J. (1989). A Knowledge-Level Account of Abduction. In *Proceedings of the Eleventh International Joint Conference on Artificial Intelligence*, (pp. 1061–1067). Detroit.

Lin, D. (1991). Obvious Abduction. In *Notes from the AAAI Workshop on Domain-Independent Strategies for Abduction*, (pp. 51–58). Anaheim. (Josephson & Dasigi, 1991).

Lin, D. (1992). *Obvious Abduction*. Ph.D. diss., Department of Computing Science, University of Alberta.

Lin, D. (1993). Principle-based Parsing without Overgeneration. In *Proceedings of ACL-93*, (pp. 112–120). Columbus.

Lin, D., & Goebel, R. (1991). Integrating probabilistic, taxonomic and causal knowledge in abductive diagnosis. In *Uncertainty in Artificial Intelligence: Volume VI*, (pp. 77–87). Elsevier Science Publishers.

Lin, D., & Goebel, R. (1991). A Message Passing Algorithm for Plan Recognition. In *Proceedings of the International Joint Conference on Artificial Intelligence*, (pp. 280–285).

Lipton, P. (1991). *Inference to the Best Explanation*. London: Routledge.

Livingstone, M., & Hubel, D. (1988). Segregation of Form, Color, Movement, and Depth: Anatomy, Physiology, and Perception. *Science*, 240, 740–749.

Lycan, W. G. (1985). Epistemic Value. *Synthese*, 64, 137–164.

Lycan, W. G. (1988). *Judgement and Justification*. Cambridge: Cambridge University Press.

Mackie, J. L. (1974). *The Cement of the Universe: A Study of Causation*. Oxford, UK: Clarendon Press.

Maier, J. (Ed.). (1988). *AAAI-88 Workshop on Plan Recognition*. St. Paul: AAAI.

Marquis, P. (1991). Extending Abduction from Propositional to First-Order Logic. In *Proceedings of the First International Workshop on Fundamentals of Artificial Intelligence Research (FAIR)* , New York: Springer-Verlag.

Marquis, P. (1991). Mechanizing Skeptical Abduction and its Applications to Artificial Intelligence. In *Proceedings of the Third IEEE International Conference on Tools for Artificial Intelligence*, San Jose: IEEE Computer Society Press.

Marquis, P. (1991). Novelty Revisited. In *Proceedings of the Sixth International Symposium on Methodologies for Intelligent Systems (ISMIS)* , New York: Springer-Verlag.

Marquis, P. (1991). Towards Data Interpretation by Deduction and Abduction. In *Notes from the AAAI Workshop on Domain-Independent Strategies for Abduction*, (pp. 59–63). Anaheim. (Josephson & Dasigi, 1991).

Marquis, P. (1992). Hypothetico-Deductive Diagnoses. In *Proceedings of the International Symposium of the Society for Optical Engineering (SPIE), Applications of Artificial Intelligence: Knowledge-Based Systems*. SPIE Society Press.

Marr, D. (1979). Representing and Computing Visual Information. In P. H. Winston & R. H. Brown (Eds.), *Artificial Intelligence: An MIT Perspective*. (pp. 17–82). Cambridge, MA: MIT Press.

Marr, D. (1981). Artificial Intelligence: A Personal View. In J. Haugeland (Ed.), *Mind Design*. (pp. 129–142). Cambridge, MA: MIT Press. Also appears in *Artificial Intelligence* 9(1):47–48, 1977.

Marr, D. (1982). *Vision*. San Francisco: W. H. Freeman.

Massaro, D. W. (1987). *Speech Perception by Ear and Eye: A Paradigm for Psychological Inquiry*. Hillsdale, NJ: Lawrence Erlbaum.

McCarthy, J. (1980). Circumscription – A Form of Non-Monotonic Reasoning. *Artificial Intelligence*, 13, 27–39.

McDermott, D. (1990). A Critique of Pure Reason. In M. A. Boden (Ed.), *The Philosophy of Artificial Intelligence*. (pp. 206–230). New York: Oxford University Press.

McDermott, J. (1988). Preliminary Steps Toward a Taxonomy of Problem Solving Types. In S. Marcus (Ed.), *Automating Knowledge Acquisition for Expert Systems*. (pp. 225–256). Boston: Kluwer Academic Publishers.

Miller, R. A., Pople, H. E., Jr. , & Myers, J. D. (1982). INTERNIST-I, An Experimental Computer-Based Diagnostic Consultant for General Internal Medicine. *New England Journal of Medicine*, 307(8), 468–476.

Milne, A. A. (1926). *Winnie-the-Pooh*. E. P. Dutton and Co.

Minsky, M. (1963). Steps Towards Artificial Intelligence. In E. A. Feigenbaum & J. Feldman (Eds.), *Computers and Thought*. New York: McGraw-Hill.

Minsky, M. (1975). A Framework for Representing Knowledge. In P. H. Winston (Ed.), *The Psychology of Computer Vision*. New York: McGraw-Hill.

Mitchell, T., Keller, R., & Kedar-Cebelli, S. (1986). Explanation-Based Generalization: A unifying view. *Machine Learning*, 1, 47–80.

Mittal, S. (1980). *Design of a Distributed Medical Diagnosis and Database System*. Ph.D. diss., Department of Computer and Information Science, The Ohio State University, Columbus.

Mittal, S., & Chandrasekaran, B. (1980). Conceptual Representation of Patient Data Bases. *Journal of Medical Systems*, 4, 169–185.

Mittal, S., Chandrasekaran, B., & Sticklen, J. (1984). PATREC: A Knowledge-Directed Data Base for a Diagnostic Expert System. *IEEE Computer Special Issue*, 17, 51–58.

Mittal, S., & Frayman, F. (1987). Making Partial Choices in Constraint Reasoning Problems. In *Sixth National Conference on Artificial Intelligence*, (pp. 631–636). Los Altos: Morgan Kaufmann.

Moberg, D., Darden, L., & Josephson, J. (1992). Representing and Reasoning About a Scientific Theory. In *Proceedings of the AAAI Workshop on Communicating Scientific and Technical Knowledge*, (pp. 58–64). Stanford University.

Moberg, D., & Josephson, J. R. (1990). Implementation Note on Diagnosing and Fixing Faults in Theories. In J. Shrager & P. Lindley (Eds.), *Computational Models of Scientific Discovery and Theory Formation*. (pp. 347–353). San Mateo: Morgan Kaufmann.

Monastersky, R. (1990). The scoop on dino droppings. *Science News*, Vol. 138, No. 17, p. 270.

Newell, A. (1982). The Knowledge Level. *Artificial Intelligence*, 18, 82–106.

Newell, A. (1990). *Unified Theories of Cognition*. Cambridge, MA: Harvard University Press.

Newell, A., & Simon, H. A. (1963). GPS, A Program That Simulates Human Thought. In Feigenbaum & Feldman (Eds.), *Computers and Thought*. (pp. 279–293). New York: McGraw-Hill.

Newell, A., & Simon, H. A. (1976). Computer Science as Empirical Inquiry: Symbols and Search, The 1976 ACM Turing Lecture. *Communications of the ACM*, 19(3), 113–126. Reprinted in *Mind Design*, J. Haugeland (ed.),1981, MIT Press.

Newell, A., Yost, G., Laird, J. E., Rosenbloom, P. S., & Altmann, E. (1991). Formulating the Problem Space Computational Model. In R. F. Rashid (Ed.), *Carnegie-Mellon Computer Science: A 25-Year Commemorative Reading*, Boston: ACM-Press: Addison-Wesley.

Ng, H. T. (1992). *A General Abductive System with Application to Plan Recognition and Diagnosis*. Ph.D. diss., University of Texas.

Norvig, P. (1987). *A Unified Theory of Inference for Text Understanding*. Ph.D. diss., University of California, Berkeley.

Norvig, P., & Wilensky, R. (1990). A Critical Evaluation of Commensurable Abduction Models for Semantic Interpretation. In *Proceedings of the Thirteenth International Conference on Computational Linguistics*, Helsinki, Finland.

Nusbaum, H., & Pisoni, D. (1987). The Role of Structural Constraints in Auditory Word Recognition. In P. Mermelstein (Ed.), *Proceedings of the Montreal Symposium on Speech Recognition*, (pp. 57–58). Montreal.

O'Rorke, P. (1988). Automated Abduction and Machine Learning. In G. DeJong (Ed.), *Working Notes of the AAAI 1988 Spring Symposium on Explanation-Based Learning*, (pp. 170–174). Stanford University: AAAI.

O'Rorke, P. (1989). LT Revisited: Explanation-Based Learning and the Logic of Principia Mathematica. *Machine Learning*, 4(2), 117–159.

O'Rorke, P. (1990). Integrating Abduction and Learning. In *Working Notes of the AAAI 1990 Spring Symposium on Automated Abduction*, (pp. 30–32). Available as Technical Report 90–32, University of California, Irvine, Department of Information and Computer Science.

O'Rorke, P. (1990). Review of the AAAI-1990 Spring Symposium on Automated Abduction. *Sigart Bulletin*, 1(3), 12–13.

O'Rorke, P., & Josephson, J. (Eds.). (planned). *Computational Models for Abduction*.

O'Rorke, P., & Morris, S. (1992). Abductive Signal Interpretation for Nondestructive Evaluation. In *Applications of Artificial Intelligence X: Knowledge-Based Systems*, 1707 (pp. 68–75). SPIE – The International Society for Optical Engineering.

O'Rorke, P., Morris, S., & Schulenburg, D. (1989). Abduction and World Model Revision. In *Proceedings of the Eleventh Annual Conference of the Cognitive Science Society*, (pp. 789–796). Hillsdale, NJ: Lawrence Erlbaum.

O'Rorke, P., Morris, S., & Schulenburg, D. (1989). Theory Formation by Abduction: Initial Results of a Case Study Based on the Chemical Revolution. In *Proceedings of the Sixth International Workshop on Machine Learning*, San Mateo: Morgan Kaufmann.

O'Rorke, P., Morris, S., & Schulenburg, D. (1990). Theory Formation by Abduction: A Case Study Based on the Chemical Revolution. In J. Shrager & P. Lindley (Eds.), *Computational Models of Scientific Discovery and Theory Formation*. (pp. 197–224). San Mateo: Morgan Kaufmann.

O'Rorke, P., & Ortony, A. (1992). Abductive Explanation of Emotions. In *Proceedings of the Fourteenth Annual Conference of the Cognitive Science Society*, Hillsdale, NJ: Lawrence Erlbaum.

O'Rorke, P., & Ortony, A. (1992). *Explaining Emotions*. Technical Report, University of California, Irvine, Department of Information and Computer Science. (Report No. 92–22).

Patil, R. S. (1981). *Causal Representation of Patient Illness for Electrolyte and Acid-Base Diagnosis*. Ph.D. diss., Laboratory for Computer Science, Massachusetts Institute of Technology.

Patil, R. S., Szolovits, P., & Schwartz, W. B. (1981). Causal Understanding of Patient Illness in Medical Diagnosis. In *Proceedings of the Seventh International Joint Conference on Artificial Intelligence*, (pp. 893–899). Vancouver, B.C. IJCAI.

Patil, R. S., Szolovits, P., & Schwartz, W. B. (1982). Modeling Knowledge of the Patient in Acid-Base and Electrolyte Disorders. In P. Szolovits (Ed.), *Artificial Intelligence in Medicine*. (pp. 191–226). Boulder: Westview Press.

Patten, T. (1988). *Systemic Text Generation as Problem Solving*. New York: Cambridge University Press.

Patten, T., & Richie, G. (1987). A Formal Model of Systemic Grammar. In G. Kempen (Ed.), *Natural Language Generation*. (pp. 279–299). The Hague: Martinus Nijhoff.

Pazzani, M. (1988). Selecting the Best Explanation for Explanation-Based Learning. In *Proceedings of the AAAI Symposium on Explanation-Based Learning*, Stanford University.

Pazzani, M. J. (1990). *Creating a Memory of Causal Relationships*. Hillsdale, NJ: Lawrence Erlbaum.

Pearl, J. (1986). Fusion, Propagation, and Structuring in Belief Networks. *Artificial Intelligence*, 29(3), 241–288.

Pearl, J. (1987). Distributed Revision of Composite Beliefs. *Artificial Intelligence*, 33(2), 173–215.

Pearl, J. (1988). Evidential Reasoning Under Uncertainty. In H. Shrobe (Ed.), *Exploring Artificial Intelligence*. San Mateo: Morgan Kaufmann.

Pearl, J. (1988). *Probabilistic Reasoning in Intelligent Systems*. San Mateo: Morgan Kaufmann.

Pearl, J. (1990). Probabilistic and Qualitative Abduction. In *Proceedings of the AAAI Spring Symposium on Abduction*, (pp. 155–158). Stanford: AAAI.

Peirce, C. S. (1839–1914). *Collected Papers of Charles Sanders Peirce*. Edited by C. Hartshorne, P. Weiss, & A. Burks. Cambridge, MA: Harvard University Press, (1931–1958).

Peirce, C. S. (1902). Perceptual Judgments. In J. Buchler (Ed.), *Philosophical Writings of Peirce*. (pp. 302–305). New York: Dover (1955).

Peirce, C. S. (1903). Abduction and Induction. In J. Buchler (Ed.), *Philosophical Writings of Peirce*. (pp. 150–156). New York: Dover (1955).

Peirce, C. S. (1955). *Philosophical Writings of Peirce*. Edited by J. Buchler. New York: Dover Publications Inc.

Peng, Y. (1986). *A Formalization of Parsimonious Covering and Probabilistic Reasoning in*

286   ABDUCTIVE INFERENCE

Abductive Diagnostic Inference. Ph.D. diss., University of Maryland, College Park.
Peng, Y., & Reggia, J. A. (1986). Plausibility of Diagnostic Hypotheses: The Nature of Simplicity. In *Proceedings of the Fifth Annual National Conference on Artificial Intelligence*, (pp.
140–145). Philadelphia: Morgan Kaufmann.
Peng, Y., & Reggia, J. A. (1987). A Probabilistic Causal Model for Diagnostic Problem Solv-
ing – Part 1. *IEEE Transactions on Systems, Man, and Cybernetics*, 17(2), 147–162.
Peng, Y., & Reggia, J. A. (1987). A Probabilistic Causal Model for Diagnostic Problem Solv-
ing – Part 2. *IEEE Transactions on Systems, Man, and Cybernetics*, 17(3), 395–406.
Peng, Y., & Reggia, J. A. (1990). *Abductive Inference Models for Diagnostic Problem Solving*.
New York: Springer-Verlag.
Pennington, N., & Hastie, R. (1988). Explanation-based decision making: Effects of Memory
Structure on Judgment. *Journal of Experimental Psychology: Learning, Memory, and Cog-
nition*, 14(3), 521–533.
Peterson, I. (1990). Stellar X-ray burst brings theory shock. *Science News*, Vol. 138, No. 16, p.
246.
Piaget, J. (1969). *The Child's Conception of Physical Causality*. Totowa, NJ: Littlefield, Adams.
Piaget, J. (1974). *Understanding Causality*. New York: W. W. Norton.
Politakis, P., & Weiss, S. (1984). Using Empirical Analysis to Refine Expert System Knowledge
Bases. *Artificial Intelligence*, 22(1), 23–84.
Poole, D. (1988). A Logical Framework for Default Reasoning. *Artificial Intelligence*, 36(1),
27–47.
Poole, D. (1989). Explanation and Prediction: An Architecture for Default and Abductive Rea-
soning. *Computational Intelligence*, 5(2), 97–110.
Pople, H. (1973). On the Mechanization of Abductive Logic. In *Proceedings of the Third Inter-
national Joint Conference on Artificial Intelligence*, Stanford, CA.
Pople, H. (1977). The Formation of Composite Hypotheses in Diagnostic Problem Solving: An
Exercise in Synthetic Reasoning. In *Proceedings of the Fifth International Joint Confer-
ence on Artificial Intelligence*, (pp. 1030–1037). Pittsburgh.
Pople, H. (1982). Heuristic Methods for Imposing Structure on Ill-Structured Problems: The
Structure of Medical Diagnosis. In P. Szolovits (Ed.), *Artificial Intelligence in Medicine*.
(pp. 119–190). Boulder: Westview Press.
Pople, H. E. (1985). Evolution of an Expert System: From INTERNIST to Caduceus. *Artificial
Intelligence In Medicine*, 179–208.
Punch, W. F., III (1989). *A Diagnosis System Using a Task Integrated Problem Solver Architec-
ture (TIPS), Including Causal Reasoning*. Ph.D. diss., Department of Computer and Infor-
mation Science, The Ohio State University, Columbus.
Punch, W. F., III, Tanner, M. C., & Josephson, J. R. (1986). Design Considerations for PEIRCE,
a High-Level Language for Hypothesis Assembly. In K. N. Karna, K. Parsaye, & B. G.
Silverman (Eds.), *Proceedings of the Expert Systems in Government Symposium*, (pp. 279–
281). IEEE Computer Society Press.
Punch, W. F., III, Tanner, M. C., Josephson, J. R., & Smith, J. W. (1990). PEIRCE: A Tool for
Experimenting with Abduction. *IEEE Expert*, 5(5), 34–44.
Pylyshyn, Z. (1979). Complexity and the Study of Artificial and Human Intelligence. In J.
Haugeland (Ed.), *Mind Design*. (pp. 67–94). Cambridge, MA: MIT Press.
Pylyshyn, Z. (1984). *Computation and Cognition: Towards a Foundation for Cognitive Sci-
ence*. Cambridge, MA: MIT Press.
Ramesh, T. S. (1989). *A Knowledge-Based Framework for Process and Malfunction Diagnosis
in Chemical Plants*. Ph.D. diss., Department of Chemical Engineering, The Ohio State Uni-
versity, Columbus.
Reggia, J. A. (1985). Abductive Inference. In K. N. Karna (Ed.), *Proceedings of The Expert
Systems in Government Symposium*, (pp. 484–489). IEEE Computer Society Press.
Reggia, J. A., & Nau, D. S. (1985). A Formal Model of Diagnostic Inference. *Information Sci-
ences*, 37, 227–285.
Reggia, J. A., Nau, D. S., & Wang, P. (1983). Diagnostic Expert Systems Based on a Set Cover-

ing Model. *International Journal of Man-Machine Studies,* 19(5), 437–460.

Reggia, J. A., Perricone, B. T., Nau, D. S., & Peng, Y. (1985). Answer Justification in Diagnostic Expert Systems. *IEEE Transactions on Biomedical Engineering,* 32(4), 263–272.

Reiter, R. (1987). A Theory of Diagnosis from First Principles. *Artificial Intelligence,* 32(1), 57–95.

Rock, I. (1983). *The Logic of Perception.* Cambridge, MA: MIT Press.

Rosenbloom, P. S., Laird, J. E., & Newell, A. (1987). SOAR: An Architecture for General Intelligence. *Artificial Intelligence,* 33, 1–64.

Roth, E. M., Woods, D. D., & Pople, H. E. (1992). Cognitive simulation as a tool for cognitive task analysis. *Ergonomics,* 35(10), 1163–1198.

Rubin, A. (1975). The Role of Hypotheses in Medical Diagnosis. In *Proceedings of the International Joint Conference on Artificial Intelligence,* (pp. 856–862).

Salmon, W. C. (1967). *The Foundations of Scientific Inference.* Pittsburgh, PA: University of Pittsburgh Press.

Salmon, W. C. (1975). Theoretical Explanations. In S. Koerner (Ed.), *Explanation.* (pp. 118–184). New Haven: Yale University Press.

Salmon, W. C. (1990). *Four Decades of Scientific Explanation.* Minneapolis: University of Minnesota Press.

Santos, E., Jr. (1991). Cost-Based Abduction, Constraint Systems and Alternative Generation. In *Notes from the AAAI Workshop on Domain-Independent Strategies for Abduction,* (pp. 64–71). Anaheim. (Josephson & Dasigi, 1991).

Santos, E. (1991). On the generation of alternative explanations with implications for belief revision. In *Proceedings of the Conference on Uncertainty in Artificial Intelligence,* (pp. 339–348).

Santos, E. (Forthcoming). A linear constraint satisfaction approach to cost-based abduction. *Artificial Intelligence.*

Schank, R., & Abelson, R. (1977). *Scripts, Plans, Goals, and Understanding.* Hillsdale, NJ: Lawrence Erlbaum.

Schank, R. C. (1986). *Explanation Patterns: Understanding Mechanically and Creatively.* Hillsdale, NJ: Lawrence Erlbaum.

Schrager, J., & Langley, P. (Eds.). (1990). *Computational Models of Scientific Discovery and Theory Formation.* San Mateo: Morgan-Kaufman.

Schum, D. A. (1987). *Evidence and Inference for the Intelligence Analyst.* Lanham, MD: University Press of America.

Schwartz, L. M., & Miles, W. (1977). *Blood Bank Technology.* Baltimore: Williams and Wilkins.

Searle, J. (1980). Minds, Brains and Programs. *Behavioral and Brain Sciences,* 3, 417–457.

Sebeok, T. A., & Umiker-Sebeok, J. (1983). "You Know My Method": A Juxtaposition of Charles S. Peirce and Sherlock Holmes. In U. Eco & T. A. Sebeok (Eds.), *The Sign of Three: Dupin, Holmes, Peirce.* (pp. 11–54). Bloomington: Indiana University Press.

Selman, B., & Levesque, H. J. (1990). Abductive and Default Reasoning: A Computational Core. In *Proceedings of the Eighth National Conference on Artificial Intelligence,* (pp. 343–348). Boston: AAAI Press, Menlo Park, California.

Sembugamoorthy, V., & Chandrasekaran, B. (1986). Functional Representation of Devices and Compilation of Diagnostic Problem Solving Systems. In J. L. Kolodner & C. K. Riesbeck (Eds.), *Experience, Memory and Reasoning.* (pp. 47–73). Hillsdale, NJ: Lawrence Erlbaum.

Shimony, S. (1991). Algorithms for Irrelevance-Based Partial MAPs. In *Proceedings of the Conference on Uncertainty in Artificial Intelligence,* (pp. 370–378).

Shimony, S. (1991). Explanation, Irrelevance and Statistical Independence. In *Proceedings of the Ninth National Conference on Artificial Intelligence,* (pp. 482–487). Cambridge, MA: MIT Press.

Shimony, S., & Charniak, E. (forthcoming). Cost-based abduction and MAP explanation. *Artificial Intelligence.*

Shortliffe, E. H. (1976). *Computer-Based Medical Consultations: MYCIN.* Elsevier.

Shrager, J., & Langley, P. (Eds.). (1990). *Computational Models of Discovery and Theory Formation.* San Mateo: Morgan Kaufmann.

Simmons, R., & Davis, R. (1987). Generate, Test and Debug: Combining Associational Rules and Causal Models. In *Proceedings of the Tenth International Joint Conference on Artificial Intelligence*, (pp. 1071–78). Milan.

Simon, H. A. (1981). *The Sciences of the Artificial.* (Second Edition). Cambridge, MA: MIT Press.

Simon, S. R. (1982). Kinesiology—Its Measurement and Importance to Rehabilitation. In V. L. Nickel (Ed.), *Orthopedic Rehabilitation.* New York: Churchill Livingstone.

Smith, J., Svirbely, J. R., Evans, C. A., Strohm, P., Josephson, J. R., & Tanner, M. C. (1985). RED: A Red-Cell Antibody Identification Expert Module. *Journal of Medical Systems*, 9(3), 121–138.

Smith, J. W. (1985). *RED: A Classificatory and Abductive Expert System.* Ph.D. diss., Department of Computer and Information Science, The Ohio State University, Columbus.

Smith, J. W., Josephson, J. R., Evans, C., Strohm, P., & Noga, J. (1983). Design For a Red-Cell Antibody Identification Expert. In *Proceedings of the Second International Conference on Medical Computer Science and Computational Medicine.* IEEE Society Press.

Smith, J. W., Josephson, J. R., Tanner, M. C., Svirbely, J., & Strohm, P. (1986). *Problem Solving in Red Cell Antibody Identification: Red's Performance on 20 Cases.* Technical Report, The Ohio State University, Laboratory for Artificial Intelligence Research.

Smolensky, P. (1988). On the Proper Treatment of Connectionism. *Behavioral and Brain Sciences*, 11(1), 1–23.

Sosa, E. (Ed.). (1975). *Causation and Conditionals.* New York: Oxford University Press.

Spiegelhalter, D. J., & Lauritzen, S. L. (1989). *Sequential Updating of Conditional Probabilities on Directed Graphical Structures.* Technical Report, Institut for Electorniske Systemer, Aalborg Univrsity, Aalborg, Denmark.

Steels, L. (1990). Components of Expertise. *AI Magazine*, 11(2), 28–49.

Stefik, M. (1981). Planning with Constraints MOLGEN: Part 1. *Artificial Intelligence*, 16, 111–140.

Stickel, M. (1989). Rationale and Methods for Abductive Reasoning in Natural-Language Interpretation. In R. Studer (Ed.), *Proceedings, Natural Language and Logic, International Scientific Symposium, Hamburg, Germany, May 1989*, (pp. 233–252). Berlin: Springer-Verlag.

Stickel, M. E. (1988). A Prolog-like Inference System for Computing Minimum-Cost Abductive Explanations in Natural-Language Interpretation. In *Proceeding of the International Computer Science Conference-88*, (pp. 343–350). Hong Kong.

Sticklen, J. (1987). *MDX2: An Integrated Medical Diagnostic System.* Ph.D. diss., Department of Computer and Information Science, The Ohio State University, Columbus.

Sticklen, J. (1989). Distributed Abduction in MDX2. In C. Kulikowski, J. M. Krivine, & J. M. David (Eds.), *Artificial Intelligence in Scientific Computation: Towards Second Generation Systems.* Basel: J. C. Baltzer.

Sticklen, J., Chandrasekaran, B., & Bond, W. E. (1989). Distributed Causal Reasoning. *Knowledge Acquisition*, 1(2), 139–162.

Sticklen, J., Chandrasekaran, B., & Josephson, J. (1985). Control Issues in Classificatory Diagnosis. In *Proceedings of the Ninth International Joint Conference on Artificial Intelligence*, Los Altos: Morgan Kaufmann.

Sticklen, J., Kamel, A., & Bond, W. E. (1991). Integrating Quantitative and Qualitative Computations in a Functional Framework. *Engineering Applications of Artificial Intelligence*, 4(1), 1–10.

Sticklen, J., Kamel, A., & Bond, W. E. (1991). A Model-Based Approach for Organizing Quantitative Computations. In *Proceedings of the Second Annual Conference on AI, Simulation and Planning in High Autonomy Systems*, Orlando.

Struss, P. (1987). Problems of Interval-Based Qualitative Reasoning. In Fruechtennicht & others (Eds.), *Wissenrepraesentation und Schlussfolgerungsverfahren fuer Technische Expertsysteme.* Munich: INF 2 ARM-1–87, Seimens.

Struss, P., & Dressler, O. (1989). 'Physical Negation'— Integrating Fault Models into the General Diagnostic Engine. In *Proceedings of the Eleventh International Joint Conference on Artificial Intelligence*, (pp. 1318–1323). Detroit.

Suwa, M., & Motoda, H. (1991). Learning Abductive Strategies from an Example. In *Notes from the AAAI Workshop on Domain-Independent Strategies for Abduction*, (pp. 72–79). Anaheim. (Josephson & Dasigi, 1991).

Swartout, W. R. (1983). XPLAIN: A System for Creating and Explaining Expert Consulting Programs. *Artificial Intelligence*, 21(3), 285–325.

Szolovits, P., & Pauker, S. G. (1984). Categorical and Probabilistic Reasoning in Medical Diagnosis. *Artificial Intelligence*, 11, 115–144.

Tanner, M. C. (1989). *Explaining Knowledge Systems: Justifying Diagnostic Conclusions*. Ph.D. diss., Department of Computer and Information Science, The Ohio State University, Columbus.

Tanner, M. C., Fox, R., Josephson, J. R., & Goel, A. K. (1991). On a Strategy for Abductive Assembly. In *Notes from the AAAI Workshop on Domain-Independent Strategies for Abduction*, (pp. 80–83). Anaheim. (Josephson & Dasigi, 1991).

Tanner, M. C., Josephson, J., & Smith, J. W. (1991). *RED-2 Demonstration Case OSU-9*. Technical Report, The Ohio State University, Laboratory for Artificial Intelligence Research.

Tanner, M. C., & Josephson, J. R. (1988). *Abductive Justification*. Technical Report, The Ohio State University, Laboratory for Artificial Intelligence Research, Columbus.

Thagard, P. (1987). The best explanation: Criteria for theory choice. *Journal of Philosophy*, 75, 76–92.

Thagard, P. (1988). *Computational Philosophy of Science*. Cambridge, MA: MIT Press.

Thagard, P. (1989). Explanatory Coherence. *Behavioral and Brain Sciences*, 12(3).

Thagard, P. (1992). *Conceptual Revolutions*. Princeton: Princeton University Press.

Thagard, P. (unpublished). *Probabilistic Networks and Explanatory Coherence*. To appear in a volume edited by P. O'Rorke and J. Josephson.

Thirunarayan, K., & Dasigi, V. (1991). On the Relationship Between Abductive Reasoning and Boolean Minimization. In *Notes from the AAAI Workshop on Domain-Independent Strategies for Abduction*, (pp. 84–88). Anaheim. (Josephson & Dasigi, 1991).

Torasso, P., & Console, L. (1989). *Diagnostic Problem Solving*. New York: Van Nostrand Reinhold.

Tracy, K., Montague, E., Gabriel, R., & Kent, B. (1979). Computer-Assisted Diagnosis of Orthopedic Gait Disorders. *Physical Therapy*, 59(3), 268–277.

Truzzi, M. (1983). Sherlock Holmes: Applied Social Psychologist. In U. Eco & T. A. Sebeok (Eds.), *The Sign of Three: Dupin, Holmes, Peirce*. (pp. 55–80). Bloomington: Indiana University Press.

Tuhrim, S., Reggia, J. A., & Goodall, S. (1991). An experimental study of criteria for hypothesis plausibility. *Journal of Experimental and Theoretical Artificial Intelligence*, 3, 129–144.

Valiant, L. G. (1979). The Complexity of Enumeration and Reliability Problems. *SIAM Journal of Computing*, 8(3), 410–421.

Waibel, A. (1989). Suprasegmentals in Very Large Vocabulary Word Recognition. In E. C. Schwab & H. C. Nusbaum (Eds.), *Pattern Recognition by Humans and Machines*. (pp. 159–186). Boston: Academic Press.

Waibel, A., & Lee, K.-F. (Eds.). (1990). *Readings in Speech Recognition*. San Mateo: Morgan Kaufmann.

Wallace, W. A. (1972). *Causality and Scientific Explanation, Volume 1, Medieval and Early Classical Science*. Ann Arbor: University of Michigan Press.

Wallace, W. A. (1974). *Causality and Scientific Explanation, Volume 2, Classical and Contemporary Science*. Ann Arbor: University of Michigan Press.

Weintraub, M. A. (1991). *An Explanation-Based Approach for Assigning Credit*. Ph.D. diss., Department of Computer and Information Science, The Ohio State University, Columbus.

Weintraub, M. A. (1991). Selecting an Appropriate Explanation. In *Notes from the AAAI Workshop on Domain-Independent Strategies for Abduction*, (pp. 89–91). Anaheim. (Josephson & Dasigi, 1991).

Weintraub, M. A., & Bylander, T. (1989). QUAWDS: A Composite Diagnostic System for Gait Analysis. In L. C. Kingsland (Ed.), *Proceedings of the Thirteenth Annual Symposium on Computer Applications in Medical Care*, (pp. 145–151). Washington, D.C. IEEE Computer Society Press.

Weintraub, M. A., & Bylander, T. (1991). Generating Error Candidates for Assigning Blame in a Knowledge Base. In *Proceedings of the Eighth International Workshop on Machine Learning*, (pp. 33–37). San Mateo: Morgan Kaufmann.

Weintraub, M. A., Bylander, T., & Simon, S. R. (1990). QUAWDS: A Composite Diagnostic System for Gait Analysis. *Computer Methods and Programs in Biomedicine*, 32(1), 91–106.

Winograd, T. (1983). *Language as a Cognitive Process*. Reading, MA: Addison-Wesley.

Zadrozny, W. (1991). Perception as Abduction: Some Parallels with NLU. In *Notes from the AAAI Workshop on Domain-Independent Strategies for Abduction*, (pp. 92–97). Anaheim. (Josephson & Dasigi, 1991).

Acknowledgments

Innumerable beings improving hypotheses have brought forth the insights gathered into this book. We cannot hope to name them all. However, we thank the contributors for their engagement and enthusiasms, especially Chandra for many discussions and hard questions that pushed the development of these ideas toward understanding intelligence, dislodging premature satisfaction with mere algorithms for well-defined tasks. We give special thanks to Lindley Darden, whose persistent encouragement and many detailed comments really helped to bring this book into being. Thanks to Jim MacDonald, William Lycan, Dean Allemang, and Robert Ennis for valuable comments on chapter 1, and to Judah Pearl for arguing with John about probabilities. We also thank James Reggia for encouragement and very many helpful comments. We thank William Lycan for helpful comments on earlier drafts, and for his encouragement to both of us over many years. Thanks to Jim MacDonald for his careful reading of an earlier draft and for generous work on the index. Thanks to Paul Thagard for his useful advice on the first proposal for a book based on Red and John's dissertation. Thanks to Wendy Cooke, Radha Pyati, Chris Putnam and Elizabeth Hinkelman for encouragement, and to Elizabeth Fannin and Seth Josephson for help with the bibliography. Thanks to Sandra Thomas and Sandra Bogenschutz for office support, and to Scott Murrer for keeping the castle walls from crumbling while we were secluded in the tower. We thank Ruth Gardocki for her encouragement and emotional support over the years. Thanks to Arun Welch and Bryan Dunlop for coming to the rescue when various computers would act unpleasantly. We would also like to acknowledge the help of the late and remembered Michael J. Herring for the LaTeX to Microsoft Word translation of the complexity of abduction chapter.

Special thanks are owed to the people of the United States of America, who paid most of the bills through various grants and research contracts, and to the several organizations and institutions that provided support in one form or another, including the State of Ohio, The Ohio State University, the College of Engineering, the Center for Cognitive Science, and the

By John and Susan Josephson

291

Department of Computer and Information Science. We are grateful for substantial support from the Defense Advanced Research Projects Agency and the US Air Force by way of research contracts F30602-85-C-0010 and F49620-89-C-0110. Research on abduction in the RED domain has been supported by the National Heart, Lung and Blood Institute, NIH Grant 1 R01 HL 38776-01. At a critical time we were encouraged to continue working in the speech domain by grant IRI-8902142 from DARPA and the National Science Foundation. Support has come indirectly from the NEC Corporation by way of a gift to Osamu Fujimura in support of research on speech science. Some work has been supported by the National Library of Medicine under grant LM-04298. The Integrated Generic Task Toolset used in several of our systems benefited greatly from the sponsorship of DARPA under the Strategic Computing Program. Other significant support for toolset development came at various times from Xerox Corporation, IBM, Digital Equipment Corporation, and Texas Instruments. Development of CREAM described in chapter 8 was supported by National Institute on Disability and Rehabilitation Research grants H133E80017 and H133C90090, and partially supported by McDonnell-Douglas research contract Z 81 225 on functional reasoning.

Special software credits: Microsoft Word, DoItAll!, LaTeX, BibTex, Interlisp D, Loops, GNU Emacs, TOPS-20, Medley, MM, Apple Macintosh System 7, and CLOS.

Some parts of Chapter 1 are derived from a technical report distributed as "On the Logical Form of Abduction," some from John Josephson's Ph.D. dissertation (Josephson, 1982), some from "A Mechanism for Forming Composite Explanatory Hypotheses" (Josephson et al., 1987), some from "Inference to the Best Explanation is Basic" (Josephson, 1989), and from a technical report distributed as "Abductive Justification." The first section of chapter 2 is derived from a paper presented by Susan Josephson in June 1990 at the workshop entitled "Artificial Intelligence: Emerging Science or Dying Art Form" held at the State University of New York at Binghamton, sponsored by the Research Foundation of the State University of New York and by the American Association for Artificial Intelligence. Other parts of chapter 2 are adapted from: "Expert Systems: Matching Techniques to Tasks," which appears in *Artificial Intelligence Applications for Business*, edited by W. Reitman, Ablex Corp., publishers; "Generic Tasks in Knowledge-Based Reasoning: High-Level Building Blocks for Expert System Design" (Chandrasekaran, 1986); "Generic Tasks as Building Blocks for Knowledge-Based Systems: The Diagnosis and Routine Design Examples" (Chandrasekaran, 1988); "What Kind of Information Processing is Intelligence? A Perspective on AI Paradigms and a Proposal," in *The Foundations of Artificial Intelligence, A Sourcebook*, edited by Derek Partridge and

Yorick Wilks, Cambridge University Press, 1990; and "Towards a Functional Architecture for Intelligence Based on Generic Information Processing Tasks" (Chandrasekaran, 1987). Parts of chapter 3 are adapted from: Michael Tanner's Ph.D. dissertation (Tanner, 1989); "Red: Integrating Generic Tasks to Identify Red-Cell Antibodies" (Josephson et al., 1985); "Design for a Red-Cell Antibody Identification Expert" (Smith et al., 1983); "A Mechanism for Forming Composite Explanatory Hypotheses" (Josephson et al, 1987); "Problem Solving in Red Cell Antibody Identification: RED's Performance on 20 Cases," (Smith et al., 1986); and from a technical report distributed as "Abduction Experiment, 'Sherlock Holmes' Strategy" by Susan T. Korda, Michael Tanner, and John Josephson. Parts of chapter 4 are drawn from "Pierce: A Tool for Experimenting with Abduction" (Punch et al., 1990); parts from "A Framework for Opportunistic Abductive Strategies" (Johnson & Smith, 1991), copyright Cognitive Science Society Incorporated, used with permission. One paragraph of chapter 4 is from "Generic Tasks as Building Blocks for Knowledge-Based Systems: The Diagnosis and Routine Design Examples" (Chandrasekaran, 1988). The concluding section of chapter 4 draws from "Design Problem Solving: A Task Analysis" (Chandrasekaran, 1990). Chapter 5 draws from: "An Investigation of the Roles of Problem-Solving Methods in Diagnosis" by W.F. Punch III and B. Chandrasekaran, which appears in the *Proceedings of the Tenth International Workshop on Expert Systems and their Applications: Second Generation Expert Systems*, May 1990. Chapter 6 draws from: "Concurrent Synthesis of Composite Explanatory Hypotheses" (Goel et al., 1988); and "Concurrency in Abductive Reasoning" by Ashok Goel, John Josephson, and P. Sadayappan, which appears in the *Proceedings of the Knowledge-Based Systems Workshop*, St. Louis, published by Science Applications International Corporation. Chapter 7 is from "The Computational Complexity of Abduction," (Bylander et. al., 1991) and is reprinted with permission from Elsevier Science Publishers B. V. Chapter 8 draws from "Distributed Abduction in MDX2," (Sticklen, 1989), used with permission of J. C. Baltzer AG Science Publishers; "QUAWDS: A Composite Diagnostic System for Gait Analysis" by Weintraub and Bylander that appeared in the *Proceedings of the Thirteenth Annual Symposium on Computer Applications in Medical Care*, 1989, used here with permission of SCAMC, Inc. A similar paper by Weintraub, Bylander, and Simon appeared in *Computer Methods and Programs in Biomedicine*, vol. 32, no. 1, 1990; material is used here with permission of Elsevier Science Publishers B.V. Chapter 9 draws from technical reports distributed as: "Practical Abduction," by John Josephson and Ashok K. Goel; PEIRCE-IGTT by Richard Fox and John Josephson; and "Experimental Comparison of Strategies for Abduction: Contribution of Explicit Explanatory Relationships" by Michael C. Tanner and John Josephson. Chapter 10 draws from "A Layered Abduction Model of Perception: Integrating Bottom-up and Top-down Processing in a Multi-Sense Agent" (Josephson, 1989); from a technical report circulated as "Spoken Language Understanding as Layered Abductive Inference" by John Josephson; and from "Speech Understanding Based on Layered Abduction" (Josephson, 1989).

Index

3-D vision 241
3-Level system 250–252
A-B-O blood typing 64
ABD-SOAR 95, 105–113, 116
abducer 97, 215
abduction
  and bounded resources 214
  characterization of 5, 14, 29, 139, Figure
    6.1, 178, 207, 223
  complexity independent of model 159
  computational costs 203
  computational feasibility of 136
  conclusion 14, 16
  and deduction 12–13
  deliberate 6
  descriptive theory of 14
  evaluative theory of 14
  explanatory theory of 14
  fallibility of 16, 180
  goal of 13
  in historical scholarship 8
  includes generation and possible
    acceptance 9
  intractability, factors that cause 158
  is a distinct form of inference 3
  in language understanding 6, 8
  in learning 197
  normative theory of 14
  optimal algorithm 178
  optimal strategy 207
  as optimization 205
  in ordinary life 6, 29, 260
  pandemonious control of 150
  as part of logic 12
  as a pattern of evidential relationships 12
  as a pattern of justification 9
  in perception 6, chapter 10
  perceptual 6
  and prediction 26
  and probabilities 26–27
  process 9
  real-time 207
  as reasoning from effect to cause 29
  in science 7, 29, 260, 271

  seeded processing 246
  snapshot vs. moving-picture 264
  as a subtask of prediction 26
  success with difficult domain 192
  successful 260
  suspended 14
  task analysis 139, Figure 6.1
  task definition 9, 204–207, 215
  ubiquitous in cognition 202
abduction machines
  a problem endemic to all six 213–214
  composable 263
  Machine 1 *see Machine 1*
  Machine 2 *see Machine 2*
  Machine 3 *see Machine 3*
  Machine 4 *see Machine 4*
  Machine 5 *see Machine 5*
  Machine 6 *see Machine 6*
  six generations of 136, 139
  summary of capabilities 262–264
abduction problem 160
abductive argument, force of 259
abductive assembly 58–59
  can be computationally expensive 74
  characterizing the information-processing
    task 202
  in RED-1&2 74–75
  knowledge requirements 96–97
  by message passing 147, 148
  refinement control 104
  stages of processing 212
  three generic subgoals 95
  tractability of 205
abductive formant trackers 250
abductive hypothesis assembly *see hypothesis assembly*
abductive justification 9–12, 263
abductive-assembly function 214
abductive-confidence function 269
Abelson, R. P. 47
abstract machines 262
abstract psychology 52
abstracting from low-level descriptions 43
acceptance, degrees of 210

295